S.C.
Sci Fic

ANALOG'S LIGHTER SIDE

SEP 18 1996

San Mateo Public Library
San Mateo, CA 94402
"Questions Answered"

analog's LIGHTER SIDE

VOLUME #4

analog's LIGHTER SIDE

Edited by
Stanley Schmidt

The Dial Press
DAVIS PUBLICATIONS, INC.
380 LEXINGTON AVENUE
NEW YORK, NEW YORK 10017

FIRST PRINTING

Copyright © 1982 by Davis Publications, Inc.
All rights reserved.
Library of Congress Catalog Card Number: 80-69078
Printed in the U.S.A.

COPYRIGHT NOTICES AND ACKNOWLEDGMENTS

Grateful acknowledgment is hereby made for permission to reprint the following:

Ex Machina by Lewis Padgett; copyright © 1948 by Lewis Padgett, © renewed 1976 by Mrs. Catherine Moore Kuttner; reprinted by permission of the Harold Matson Company, Inc.

Paté de Foie Gras by Isaac Asimov; copyright 1956 by Isaac Asimov; reprinted by permission of the author.

Peek! I See You by Poul Anderson; copyright © 1968 by The Conde Nast Publications, Inc.; reprinted by permission of Scott Meredith Literary Agency, Inc.

The Exhalted by L. Sprague de Camp; copyright 1940 by L. Sprague de Camp, renewed; reprinted by permission of the author.

Gone With the Gods by Andrew Offutt; copyright © 1974 by The Conde Nast Publications, Inc.; reprinted by permission of the author.

Mail Supremacy by Hayford Peirce; copyright © 1975 by The Conde Nast Publications, Inc.; reprinted by permission of the author.

The Gentle Earth by Christopher Anvil; © 1957 by Street & Smith Publications, Inc.; reprinted by permission of Scott Meredith Literary Agency, Inc.

A !Tangled Web by Joe Haldeman; © 1981 by Davis Publications, Inc.; reprinted by permission of Kirby McCauley, Ltd.

Despoilers of the Golden Empire by David Gordon; © 1959 by Street & Smith Publications, Inc., reprinted by permission of Blackstone Literary Agency.

The Present State of Igneos Research by Gordon R. Dickson; copyright © 1974 by The Conde Nast Publications, Inc.; reprinted by permission of Kirby McCauley, Ltd.

Ye Prentice and Ye Dragon by Gordon R. Dickson; copyright © 1974 by The Conde Nast Publications, Inc.; reprinted by permission of Kirby McCauley, Ltd.

Make Mine Homogenized by Rick Raphael; © 1960 by Street & Smith Publications, Inc.; reprinted by permission of Scott Meredith Literary Agency, Inc.

Allamagoosa by Eric Frank Russell; copyright 1955 by Street & Smith Publications, Inc.; reprinted by permission of Scott Meredith Literary Agency, Inc.

Ravenshaw of WBY, Inc. by W. Macfarlane; copyright © 1970 by The Conde Nast Publications, Inc.; reprinted by permission of the author.

CONTENTS

INTRODUCTION — 9
Stanley Schmidt

EX MACHINA — 11
Lewis Padgett (April 1948)

PATÉ DE FOIE GRAS — 37
Isaac Asimov (September 1956)

PEEK! I SEE YOU — 50
Poul Anderson (February 1968)

THE EXHALTED — 74
L. Sprague de Camp (November 1940)

GONE WITH THE GODS — 92
Andrew J. Offutt (October 1974)

MAIL SUPREMACY — 113
Hayford Peirce (March 1975)

THE GENTLE EARTH — 116
Christopher Anvil (November 1957)

A !TANGLED WEB — 160
Joe Haldeman (September 1981)

DESPOILERS OF THE GOLDEN EMPIRE — 180
David Gordon (March 1959)

THE PRESENT STATE OF IGNEOS RESEARCH — 209
Gordon R. Dickson (January 1975)

MAKE MINE HOMOGENIZED — 221
Rick Raphael (April 1960)

ALLAMAGOOSA — 255
Eric Frank Russell (May 1955)

RAVENSHAW OF WBY, INC. — 266
W. Macfarlane (March 1970)

Introduction

by Stanley Schmidt

Shortly after I became editor of *Analog* (formerly *Astounding*) I finally cornered a certain author (or vice versa) and we sat down for a long-overdue get-acquainted chat. This author (who appears, by the way, in these pages, so I suppose whichever of us bought the drinks got his money's worth) is known far and wide for his wit and irrepressible good humor, but he seemed surprised to hear that I was interested in seeing humorous stories. I assured him I was, and his first sale to me was a completely outrageous (and thoroughly delightful) three-part *serial*.

I'm not sure exactly *why* this illustrious bard was so surprised to hear that I was interested in humor. Perhaps it was my inordinately dignified appearance and demeanor. (My lawyers are still investigating how my name came to be attached to a story called "A Midsummer Newt's Dream.") More likely it has to do with the long-standing reputation of *Analog* as a foremost magazine of serious science fictional speculation about the future.

But there's no reason why you can't speculate seriously and have fun at the same time—in fact, a lot of us are in this business precisely because speculation *is* so much fun. Sometimes some of us get pretty frisky about it, too. The fact is that humor has always been an important part of *Analog*. I like to have at least one truly funny story in every issue, and I'm perfectly willing to have more—when I can get them. If overt humor has been a relatively small part of our contents, in terms of pages occupied, it's not because my predecessors or I have been averse to it, but because good humor is hard to come by. Lots of people *try* to write it, but it's fiendishly difficult to do really well. To me, there is no higher art than comedy at its best. It has always seemed to me unfair that awards (in this field and most others) so seldom recognize this, and I have the utmost admiration for writers who can produce stories like those in this book.

Not all of these are rib-ticklers or thigh-slappers (though some are); the spectrum of comedy is wider than that. There are moments of broad farce, but there are also the quiet whimsy of Gordon Dickson's treatise on dragons, Isaac Asimov's scholarly discourse on the goose which laid golden eggs, and a healthy helping of satire (for which *Analog* readers seem to have a special affinity, perhaps because so many of them are personally employed by bureaucracies suspiciously resembling those in certain stories). There's even one story here which you may not realize is a joke at all until you reach the end—at which point you'll see that the whole thing is its own punch line.

But enough of this chatter. These stories don't need me to tell you why you'll enjoy them. Gallegher, Pazilliwheep, Johnny Black, Ravenshaw, and all the rest speak more than adequately for themselves, and they are ably assisted by a sampling of the art which accompanied their original appearances. And if you enjoy them as much as I think you will, I hope you'll remember that there's lots more where these came from—every month in the pages of *Analog*. ■

EX MACHINA
by Lewis Padgett

Illustration by Edd Cartier.
Copyright 1948 by Street & Smith Publications, Inc.; renewed 1975 by The Conde Nast Publications, Inc.

"I got the idea out of a bottle labeled 'DRINK ME,' " Gallegher said wanly. "I'm no technician, except when I'm drunk. I don't know the difference between an electron and an electrode, except that one's invisible. At least I do know, sometimes, but they get mixed up. My trouble is semantics."

"Your trouble is you're a lush," said the transparent robot, crossing its legs with a faint crash. Gallegher winced.

"Not at all. I get along fine when I'm drinking. It's only during my periods of sobriety that I get confused. I have a technological hangover. The aqueous humor in my eyeballs is coming out by osmosis. Does that make sense?"

"No," said the robot, whose name was Joe. "You're crying, that's all. Did you turn me on just to have an audience? I'm busy at the moment."

"Busy with what?"

"I'm analyzing pholosophy, *per se*. Hideous as you humans are, you sometimes get bright ideas. The clear, intellectual logic of pure philosophy is a revelation to me."

Gallegher said something about a hard, gemlike flame. He still wept sporadically, which reminded him of the bottle labeled "DRINK ME," which reminded him of the liquor organ beside the couch. Gallegher stiffly moved his long body across the laboratory, detouring around three bulky objects which might have been the dynamos, Monstro and Bubbles, except for the fact that there were three of them. This realization flickered only dimly through Gallegher's mind. Since one of the dynamos was looking at him, he hurriedly averted his gaze, sank down on the couch, and manipulated several buttons. When no liquor flowed through the tube into his parched mouth, he removed the mouthpiece, blinked at it hopelessly, and ordered Joe to bring beer.

The glass was brimming as he raised it to his lips. But it was empty before he drank.

"That's very strange," Gallegher said. "I feel like Tantalus."

"Somebody's drinking your beer," Joe explained. "Now do leave me alone. I've an idea I'll be able to appreciate my baroque beauty even more after I've mastered the essentials of philosophy."

"No doubt," Gallegher said. "Come away from that mirror. Who's drinking my beer? A little green man?"

"A little brown animal," Joe explained cryptically, and turned to the mirror again, leaving Gallegher to glare at him hatefully. There were times when Mr. Galloway Gallegher yearned to bind Joe securely under a steady drip of hydrochloric. Instead, he tried another beer, with equal ill luck.

In a sudden fury, Gallegher rose and procured soda water. The little brown animal had even less taste for such fluids than Gallegher himself; at any rate, the water didn't mysteriously vanish. Less thirsty but more confused than ever, Gallegher circled the third dynamo with the bright blue eyes and morosely examined the equipment littering his workbench. There were bottles filled with ambiguous liquids, obviously non-alcoholic, but the labels meant little or nothing. Gallegher's subconscious self, liberated by liquor last night, had marked them for easy reference. Since Gallegher Plus, though a top-flight technician, saw the world through thoroughly distorted lenses, the labels were not helpful. One said "RABBITS ONLY." Another inquired "WHY NOT?" A third said "CHRISTMAS NIGHT."

There was also a complicated affair of wheels, gears, tubes, sprockets, and light tubes plugged into an electric outlet.

"*Cogito, ergo sum,*" Joe murmured softly. "When there's no one around on the quad. . . No. Hm-m-m."

"What about this little brown animal?" Gallegher wanted to know. "Is it real or merely a figment?"

"What is reality?" Joe inquired, thus confusing the issue still further. "I haven't resolved that yet to my own satisfaction."

"Your satisfaction!" Gallegher said. "I wake up with a tenth-power hangover and can't get a drink. You tell me fairy stories about little brown animals stealing my liquor. Then you quote moldy philosophical concepts at me. If I pick up that crowbar over there, you'll neither be *nor* think in very short order."

Joe gave ground gracefully. "It's a small creature that moves remarkably fast. So fast it can't be seen."

"How come you see it?"

"I don't. I varish it," said Joe, who had more than the five senses normal to humans.

"Where is it now?"

"It went out a while ago."

"Well—" Gallegher sought inconclusively for words. "Something must have happened last night."

"Naturally," Joe agreed. "But you turned me off after the ugly man with the ears came in."

"I remember that. You were beating your plastic gums . . . *what* man?"

"The ugly one. You told your grandfather to take a walk, too, but you couldn't pry him loose from his bottle."

"Grandpa. Uh. Oh. Where's he?"

"Maybe he went back to Maine," Joe suggested. "He kept threatening to do that."

"He never leaves till he's drunk out the cellar," Gallegher said. He tuned in the audio system and called every room in the house. There was no response. Presently Gallegher got up and made a search. There was no trace of Grandpa.

He came back to the laboratory, trying to ignore the third dynamo with the big blue eyes, and hopelessly studied the workbench again. Joe, posturing before the mirror, said he thought he believed in the basic philosophy of intellectualism. Still, he added, since obviously Gallegher's intellect was in abeyance, it might pay to hook up the projector and find out what had happened last night.

This made sense. Some time before, realizing that Gallegher sober never remembered the adventures of Gallegher tight, he had installed a visio-audio gadget in the laboratory, cleverly adjusted to turn itself on whenever circumstances warranted it. How the thing worked Gallegher wasn't quite sure any more, except that it could run off miraculous blood-alcohol tests on its creator and start recording when the percentage was sufficiently high. At the moment the machine was shrouded in a blanket. Gallegher whipped this off, wheeled over a screen, and watched and listened to what had happened last night.

Joe stood in a corner, turned off, probably cogitating. Grandpa, a wizened little man with a brown face like a bad-tempered nutcracker, sat on a stool cuddling a bottle. Gallegher was removing the liquor-organ mouthpiece from between his lips, having just taken on enough of a load to start the recorder working.

A slim, middle-aged man with large ears and an eager expression jittered on the edge of his relaxer, watching Gallegher.

"Claptrap," Grandpa said in a squeaky voice. "When I was a kid we went out and killed grizzlies with our hands. None of these new-fangled ideas—"

"Grandpa," Gallegher said, "shut up. You're not that old. And you're a liar anyway."

"Reminds me of the time I was out in the woods and a grizzly came at me. I didn't have a gun. Well, I'll tell you. I just reached down his mouth—"

"Your bottle's empty," Gallegher said cleverly, and there was a pause while Grandpa, startled, investigated. It wasn't.

"You were highly recommended," said the eager man. "I do hope you can help me. My partner and I are about at the end of our rope."

Gallegher looked at him dazedly. "You have a partner? Who's he? For that matter, who are you?"

Dead silence fell while the eager man fought with his bafflement. Grandpa lowered his bottle and said: "It wasn't empty, but it is now. Where's another?"

The eager man blinked. "Mr. Gallegher," he said faintly. "I don't understand. We've been discussing—"

Gallegher said, "I know. I'm sorry. It's just that I'm no good on technical problems unless I'm . . . ah . . . stimulated. Then I'm a genius. But I'm awfully absent-minded. I'm sure I can solve your problem, but the fact is I've forgotten what it is. I suggest you start from the beginning. Who are you and have you given me any money yet?"

"I'm Jonas Harding," the eager man said. "I've got fifty thousand credits in my pocket, but we haven't come to any terms yet."

"Then give me the dough and we'll come to terms," Gallegher said with ill-concealed greed. "I need money."

"You certainly do," Grandpa put in, searching for a bottle. "You're so overdrawn at the bank that they lock the doors when they see you coming. I want a drink."

"Try the organ," Gallegher suggested. "Now, Mr. Harding—"

"I want a bottle. I don't trust that dohinkus of yours."

Harding, for all his eagerness, could not quite conceal a growing skepticism. "As for the credits," he said, "I think perhaps we'd better talk a little first. You were very highly recommended, but perhaps this is one of your off days."

"Not at all. Still—"

"Why should I give you the money before we come to terms?" Harding pointed out. "Especially since you've forgotten who I am and what I wanted."

Gallegher sighed and gave up. "All right. Tell me what you are and who you want. I mean—"

"I'll go back home," Grandpa threatened. "Where's a bottle?"

Harding said desperately. "Look, Mr. Gallegher, there's a limit. I come in here and that robot of yours insults me. Your grandfather insists I have a drink with him. I'm nearly poisoned—"

"I was weaned on corn likker," Grandpa muttered. "Young whippersnappers can't take it."

"Then let's get down to business," Gallegher said brightly. "I'm beginning to feel good. I'll just relax here on the couch and you can tell me everything." He relaxed and sucked idly at the organ's mouthpiece, which trickled a gin buck. Grandpa cursed.

"Now," Gallegher said, "the whole thing, from the beginning."

Harding gave a little sigh. "Well—I'm half partner in Adrenals, Incorporated. We run a service. A luxury service, keyed to this day and age. As I told you—"

"I've forgotten it all," Gallegher murmured. "You should have made a carbon copy. What is it you do? I've got a mad picture of you building tiny prefabricated houses on top of kidneys, but I know I must be wrong."

"You are," Harding said shortly. "Here's your carbon copy. We're in the adrenal-rousing business. Today man lives a quiet, safe life—"

"Ha!" Gallegher interjected bitterly.

"—what with safety controls and devices, medical advances, and the general structure of social living. Now the adrenal glands serve a vital functional purpose, necessary to the health of the normal man." Harding had apparently launched into a familiar sales talk. "Ages ago we lived in caves, and when a sabertooth burst out of the jungle, our adrenals, or suprarenals, went into instant action, flooding our systems with adrenalin. There was an immediate explosion of action, either toward fight or flight, and such periodic flooding of the blood stream gave tone to the whole system. Not to mention the psychological advantages. Man is a competitive animal. He's losing that instinct, but it can be roused by artificial stimulation of the adrenals."

"A drink?" Grandpa said hopefully, though he understood practically nothing of Harding's explanation.

Harding's face became shrewder. He leaned forward confidentially.

"Glamour," he said. "That's the answer. We offer adventure. Safe, thrilling, dramatic, exciting, glamorous adventure to the jaded modern man or woman. Not the vicarious, unsatisfactory excitement of television; the real article. Adrenals, Incorporated, will give you adventure plus, and at the same time improve your health physically and mentally. You must have seen our ads: 'Are you in a rut? Are you jaded? Take a Hunt—and return refreshed, happy, and healthy, ready to lick the world!' "

"A Hunt?"

"That's our most popular service," Harding said, relapsing into more businesslike tones. "It's not new, really. A long time ago travel bureaus were advertising thrilling tiger hunts in Mexico—"

"Ain't no tigers in Mexico," Grandpa said. "I been there. I warn you, if you don't find me a bottle, I'm going right back to Maine."

But Gallegher was concentrating on the problem. "I don't see why you need me, then. I can't supply tigers for you."

"The Mexican tiger was really a member of the cat family. Puma, I think. We've got special reservations all over the world—expensive to set up and maintain—and there we have our Hunts, with every detail carefully planned in advance. The danger must be minimized—in fact, eliminated. But there must be an illusion of danger or there's no thrill for the customer. We've tried conditioning animals so they'll stop short of hurting anyone, but . . . ah . . . that isn't too successful. We lost several customers, I'm sorry to say. This is an enormous investment, and we've got to recoup. But we've found we can't use tigers or, in fact, any of the large carnivora. It simply isn't safe. But there must be that illusion of danger! The trouble, is we're degenerating into a trapshooting club. And there's no personal danger involved in trapshooting."

Grandpa said: "Want some fun, eh? Come on up to Maine with me and I'll show you some real hunting. We still got bear back in the mountains."

Gallegher said: "I'm beginning to see. But that personal angle—I wonder! What is the definition of danger, anyhow?"

"Danger's when something's trying to git you," Grandpa pointed out.

"The unknown—the strange—is dangerous too, simply because we don't understand it. That's why ghost stories have always been popular. A roar in the dark is more frightening than a tiger in the daylight."

Harding nodded. "I see your point. But there's another factor. The game mustn't be made too easy. It's a cinch to outwit a rabbit. And, naturally, we have to supply our customers with the most modern weapons."

"Why?"

"Safety precautions. The trouble is, with those weapons and scanners and scent-analyzers, any fool can track down and kill an animal. There's no thrill involved unless the animal's a man-eating tiger, and that's a little too thrilling for our underwriters!"

"So what do you want?"

"I'm not sure," Harding said slowly. "A new animal, perhaps. One that fulfills the requirements of Adrenals, Incorporated. But I'm not sure what the answer is, or I wouldn't be asking you."

Gallegher said: "You don't make new animals out of thin air."

"Where do you get them?"

"I wonder. Other planets? Other time-sectors? Other probability-words? I got hold of some funny animals once—Lybblas—by tuning in on a future time-era on Mars, but they wouldn't have filled the bill."

"Other planets, then?"

Gallegher got up and strolled to his workbench. He began to piece together stray cogs and tubes. "I'm getting a thought. The latent factors inherent in the human brain— My latent factors are rousing to life. Let me see. Perhaps—"

Under his hands a gadget grew. Gallegher remained preoccupied. Presently he cursed, tossed the device aside, and settled back to the liquor-organ. Grandpa had already tried it, but choked on his first sip of a gin buck. He threatened to go back home and take Harding with him and show him some real hunting.

Gallegher pushed the old gentleman off the couch. "Now look, Mr. Harding," he said. "I'll have this for you tomorrow. I've got some thinking to do—"

"Drinking, you mean," Harding said, taking out a bundle of credits. "I've heard a lot about you, Mr. Gallegher. You never work except under pressure. You're got to have a deadline, or you won't do a thing. Well—do you see this? Fifty thousand credits." He glanced at his wrist watch. "I'm giving you one hour. If you don't solve my problem by then, the deal's off."

Gallegher started up from the couch as though he had been bitten. "That's ridiculous. An hour isn't time enough—"

Harding said obdurately: "I'm a methodical man. I know enough about you to realize that you're not. I can find other specialists and technicians, you know. One hour! Or I go out that door and take these fifty thousand credits with me!"

Gallegher eyed the money greedily. He took a quick drink, cursed quietly, and went back to his gadget. This time he kept working on it.

After a while a light shot up from the worktable and hit Gallegher in the eye. He staggered back, yelping.

"Are you all right?" Harding asked, jumping up.

"Sure," Gallegher growled, cutting a switch. "I think I'm getting it. That light . . . ouch. I've sunburned my eyeballs." He blinked back tears. Then he went over to the liquor-organ.

After a hearty swig, he nodded at Harding. "I'm getting on the trail of what you want. I don't know how long it'll take, though." He winced. "Grandpa. Did you change the setting on this thing?"

"I dunno. I pushed some buttons."

"I thought so. This isn't a gin buck. Wheeooo!"

"Got a wallop, has it?" Grandpa said, getting interested and coming over to try the liquor-organ again.

"Not at all," Gallegher said, walking on his knees toward the audiosonic recorder. "What's this? A spy, huh? We know how to deal with spies in this house, you dirty traitor." So saying, he rose to his feet, seized a blanket, and threw it over the projector.

At that point the screen, naturally enough, went blank.

"I cleverly outwit myself every time," Gallegher remarked, rising to switch off the projector. "I go to the trouble of building that recorder and then blindfold it just when matters get interesting. I know less than I did before, because there are more unknown factors now."

"Men can know the nature of things," Joe murmured.

"An important concept," Gallegher admitted. "The Greeks found it out quite a while ago, though. Pretty soon, if you keep on thinking hard, you'll come up with the bright discovery that two and two are four."

"Be quiet, you ugly man," Joe said. "I'm getting into abstractions now. Answer the door and leave me alone."

"The door? Why? The bell isn't singing."

"It will," Joe pointed out. "There it goes."

"Visitors at this time of the morning," Gallegher sighed. "Maybe it's Grandpa, though." He pushed a button, studied the doorplate screen, and failed to recognize the lantern-jawed, bushy-browed face. "All right," he said. "Come in. Follow the guide-line." Then he turned to the liquor-organ thirstily before remembering his current Tantalus proclivities.

The lantern-jawed man came into the room. Gallegher said: "Hurry up. I'm being followed by a little brown animal that drinks all my liquor. I've several other troubles, too, but the little brown animal's the worst. If I don't get a drink, I'll die. So tell me what you want and leave me alone to work out my problems. I don't owe you money, do I?"

"That depends," said the newcomer, with a strong Scots accent. "My name is

Murdoch Mackenzie, and I assume you're Mr. Gallegher. You look untrustworthy. Where is my partner and the fifty thousand credits he had with him?"

Gallegher pondered. "Your partner, eh? I wonder if you mean Jonas Harding?"

"That's the lad. My partner in Adrenals, Incorporated."

"I haven't seen him—"

With his usual felicity, Joe remarked, "The ugly man with the big ears. How hideous he was."

"Vurra true," Mackenzie nodded. "I note you're using the past tense, or rather that great clanking machine of yours is. Have you perhaps murdered my partner and disposed of his body with one of your scientific gadgets?"

"Now look—" Gallegher said. "What's the idea? Have I got the mark of Cain on my forehead or something? Why should you jump to a conclusion like that? You're crazy."

Mackenzie rubbed his long jaw and studied Gallegher from under his bushy gray brows. "It would be no great loss, I know," he admitted. "Jonas is little help in the business. Too methodical. But he had fifty thousand credits on his person when he came here last night. There is also the question of the body. The insurance is perfectly enormous. Between ourselves, Mr. Gallegher, I would not hold it against you if you had murdered my unfortunate partner and pocketed the fifty thousand. In fact, I would be willing to consider letting you escape with . . . say . . . ten thousand, provided you gave me the rest. But not unless you provided me with legal evidence of Jonas's death, so my underwriters would be satisfied."

"Logic," Joe said admiringly. "Beautiful logic. It's amazing that such logic should come from such an opaque horror."

"I would look far more horrible, my friend, if I had a transparent skin like you," Mackenzie said, "if the anatomy charts are accurate. But we were discussing the matter of my partner's body."

Gallegher said wildly: "This is fantastic. You're probably laying yourself open to compounding a felony or something."

"Then you admit the charge."

"Of course not! You're entirely too sure of yourself, Mr. Mackenzie. I'll bet you killed Harding yourself and you're trying to frame me for it. How do you know he's dead?"

"Now that calls for some explanation, I admit," Mackenzie said. "Jonas was a methodical man. Vurra, I have never known him to miss an appointment for any reason whatsoever. He had appointments last night, and more this morning. One with me. Moreover, he had fifty thousand credits on him when he came here to see you last night."

"How do you know he got here?"

"I brought him, in my aircab. I let him out at your door. I saw him go in."

"Well, you didn't see him go out, but he did," Gallegher said.

Mackenzie, quite unruffled, went on checking points on his body fingers.

"This morning I checked your record, Mr. Gallegher, and it is not a good one.

Unstable, to say the least. You have been mixed up in some shady deals, and you have been accused of crimes in the past. Nothing was ever proved, but you're a sly one, I suspect. The police would agree."

"They can't prove a thing. Harding's probably home in bed."

"He is not. Fifty thousand credits is a lot of money. My partner's insurance amounts to much more than that. The business will be tied up sadly if Jonas remains vanished, and there will be litigation. Litigation costs money."

"I didn't kill your partner!" Gallegher cried.

"Ah," Mackenzie smiled. "Still, if I can prove that you did, it will come to the same thing, and be reasonably profitable for me. You see your position, Mr. Gallegher. Why not admit it, tell me what you did with the body, and escape with five thousand credits."

"You said ten thousand a while ago."

"You're daft," Mackenzie said firmly. "I said nothing of the sort. At least, you canna prove that I did."

Gallegher said: "Well, suppose we have a drink and talk it over." A new idea had struck him.

"An excellent suggestion."

Gallegher found two glasses and manipulated the liquor-organ. He offered one drink to Mackenzie, but the man shook his head and reached for the other glass. "Poison, perhaps," he said cryptically. "You have an untrustworthy face."

Gallegher ignored that. He was hoping that with two drinks available, the mysterious little brown animal would show its limitations. He tried to gulp the whisky fast, but only a tantalizing drop burned on his tongue. The glass was empty. He lowered it and stared at Mackenzie.

"A cheap trick," Mackenzie said, putting his own glass down on the workbench. "I did not ask for your whisky, you know. How did you make it disappear like that?"

Furious with disappointment, Gallegher snarled: "I'm a wizard. I've sold my soul to the devil. For two cents I'd make you disappear, too."

Mackenzie shrugged. "I am not worried. If you could, you'd have done it before this. As for wizardry, I am far from skeptical, after seeing that monster squatting over there." He indicated the third dynamo that wasn't a dynamo.

"What? You mean you see it, too?"

"I see more than you think, Mr. Gallegher," Mackenzie said darkly. "In fact, I am going to the police now."

"Wait a minute. You can't gain anything by that—"

"I can gain nothing by talking to you. Since you remain obdurate, I will try the police. If they can prove that Jonas is dead, I will at least collect his insurance."

Gallegher said: "Now wait a minute. Your partner did come here. He wanted me to solve a problem for him."

"Ah. And have you solved it?"

"N-no. At least—"

"Then I can get no profit from you," Mackenzie said firmly, and turned to the door. "You will hear from me vurra soon."

He departed. Gallegher sank down miserably on the couch and brooded. Presently he lifted his eyes to stare at the third dynamo.

It was not, then, a hallucination, as he had at first suspected. Nor was it a dynamo. It was a squat, shapeless object like a truncated pyramid that had begun to melt down, and two large blue eyes were watching him. Eyes, or agates, or painted metal. He couldn't be sure. It was about three feet high and three feet in diameter at the base.

"Joe," Gallegher said, "why didn't you tell me about that thing?"

"I thought you saw it," Joe explained.

"I did, but—what is it?"

"I haven't the slightest idea."

"Where could it have come from?"

"Your subconscious alone knows what you were up to last night," Joe said. "Perhaps Grandpa and Jonas Harding know, but they're not around, apparently."

Gallegher went to the teleview and put in a call to Maine. "Grandpa may have gone back home. It isn't likely he'd have taken Harding with him, but we can't miss any bets. I'll check on that. One thing; my eyes have stopped watering. What *was* that gadget I made last night?" He passed to the workbench and studied the cryptic assemblage. "I wonder why I put a shoehorn in that circuit?"

"If you'd keep a supply of materials available here, Gallegher Plus wouldn't have to depend on makeshifts," Joe said severely.

"Uh. I could get drunk and let my subconscious take over again . . . no, I can't. Joe, I can't drink any more! I'm bound hand and foot to the water wagon!"

"I wonder if Dalton had the right idea after all?"

Gallegher snarled: "Do you have to extrude your eyes that way? I need help!"

"You won't get it from me," Joe said. "The problem's extremely simple, if you'd put your mind to it."

"Simple, is it? Then suppose you tell me the answer!"

"I want to be sure of a certain philosophical concept first."

"Take all the time you want. When I'm rotting in jail, you can spend your leisure hours pondering abstracts. *Get me a beer!* No, never mind. I couldn't drink it anyway. What does this little brown animal look like?"

"Oh, use your head," Joe said.

Gallegher growled, "I could use it for an anchor, the way it feels. You know all the answers. Why not tell me instead of babbling?"

"Men can know the nature of things," Joe said. "Today is the logical development of yesterday. Obviously you've solved the problem Adrenals, Incorporated, gave you."

"What? Oh. I see. Harding wanted a new animal or something."

"Well?"

"I've got two of 'em," Gallegher said. "That little brown invisible dipsomaniac and that blue-eyed critter sitting on the floor. Oh-*ho!* Where did I pick them up? Another dimension?"

"How should I know? You've got 'em."

"I'll say I have," Gallegher agreed. "Maybe I made a machine that scooped them off another world—and maybe Grandpa and Harding are on that world now! A sort of exchange of prisoners. I don't know. Harding wanted nondangerous beasts elusive enough to give hunters a thrill—but where's the element of danger?" He gulped. "Conceivably the pure alienage of the critters provides that illusion. Anyway, I'm shivering."

"Flooding of the bloodstream with adrenalin gives tone to the whole system," Joe said smugly.

"So I captured or got hold of those beasts somehow, apparently, to solve Harding's problem . . . mm-m." Gallegher went to stand in front of the shapeless blue-eyed creature. "Hey, you," he said.

There was no response. The mild blue eyes continued to regard nothing. Gallegher poked a finger tentatively at one of them.

Nothing at all happened. The eye was immovable and hard as glass. Gallegher tried the thing's bluish, sleek skin. It felt like metal. Repressing his mild panic, he tried to lift the beast from the floor, but failed completely. It was either enormously heavy or it had sucking-disks on its bottom.

"Eyes," Gallegher said. "No other sensory organs, apparently. That isn't what Harding wanted."

"I think it clever of the turtle," Joe suggested.

"Turtle? Oh. Like the armadillo. That's right. It's a problem, isn't it? How can you kill or capture a . . . a beast like this? Its exoderm feels plenty hard, it's immovable—that's it, Joe. Quarry doesn't have to depend on flight or fight. The turtle doesn't. And a barracuda could go nuts trying to eat a turtle. This would be perfect quarry for the lazy intellectual who wants a thrill. But what about adrenalin?"

Joe said nothing. Gallegher pondered, and presently seized upon some reagents and apparatus. He tried a diamond drill. He tried acids. He tried every way he could think of to rouse the blue-eyed beast. After an hour his furious curses were interrupted by a remark from the robot.

"Well, what about adrenalin?" Joe inquired ironically.

"Shut up!" Gallegher yelped. "That thing just sits there looking at me! Adren . . . what?"

"Anger as well as fear stimulates the suprarenals, you know. I suppose any human would become infuriated by continued passive resistance."

"That's right," said the sweating Gallegher, giving the creature a final kick. He turned to the couch. "Increase the nuisance quotient enough and you can substitute anger for fear. But what about that little brown animal? I'm not mad at it."

"Have a drink," Joe suggested

"All right, I am mad at the kleptomaniacal so-and-so! You said it moved so fast I can't see it. How can I catch it?"

Ex Machina   21

"There are undoubtedly methods."

"It's as elusive as the other critter is invulnerable. Could I immobilize it by getting it drunk?"

"Metabolism."

"Burns up its fuel too fast to get drunk? Probably. But it must need a lot of food."

"Have you looked in the kitchen lately?" Joe asked.

Visions of a depleted larder filling his mind, Gallegher rose. He paused beside the blue-eyed object.

"This one hasn't got any metabolism to speak of. But it has to eat, I suppose. Still, eat what? Air? It's possible."

The doorbell sang. Gallegher moaned, "What now?" and admitted the guest. A man with a ruddy face and a belligerent expression came in, told Gallegher he was under tentative arrest, and called in the rest of his crew, who immediately began searching the house.

"Mackenzie sent you, I suppose?" Gallegher said.

"That's right. My name's Johnson. Department of Violence, Unproved. Do you want to call counsel?"

"Yes," said Gallegher, jumping at the opportunity. He used the visor to get an attorney he knew, and began outlining his troubles. But the lawyer interrupted him.

"Sorry. I'm not taking any jobs on spec. You know my rates."

"Who said anything about spec?"

"Your last check bounced yesterday. It's cash on the line this time, or no deal."

"I . . . now wait! I've just finished a commissioned job that's paying off big. I can have the money for you—"

"When I see the color of your credits, I'll be your lawyer," the unsympathetic voice said, and the screen blanked. The detective, Johnson, tapped Gallegher on the shoulder.

"So you're overdrawn at the bank, eh? Needed money?"

"That's no secret. Besides, I'm not broke now, exactly. I finished a—"

"A job. Yeah, I heard that, too. So you're suddenly rich. How much did this job pay you? It wouldn't be fifty thousand credits, would it?"

Gallegher drew a deep breath. "I'm not saying a word," he said, and retreated to the couch, trying to ignore the Department men who were searching the lab. He needed a lawyer. He needed one bad. But he couldn't get one without money. Suppose he saw Mackenzie—

The visor put him in touch with the man. Mackenzie seemed cheerful.

"Hello," he said. "I see the police have arrived."

Gallegher said, "Listen, that job your partner gave me—I've solved your problem. I've got what you want."

"Jonas's body, you mean?" Mackenzie seemed pleased.

"No! The animals you wanted! The perfect quarry!"

"Oh. Well. Why didn't you say so sooner?"

"Get over here and call off the police!" Gallegher insisted. "I tell you, I've got your ideal Hunt animals for you!"

"I dinna ken if I can call off the bloodhounds," Mackenzie said, "but I'll be over directly. I will not pay vurra much, you understand?"

"Bah!" Gallegher snarled, and broke the connection. The visor buzzed at him. He touched the receiver, and a woman's face came in.

She said: "Mr. Gallegher, with reference to your call of inquiry regarding your grandfather, we report that investigation shows that he has not returned to our Maine sector. That is all."

She vanished. Johnson said: "What's this? Your grandfather? Where's he at?"

"I ate him," Gallegher said, twitching. "Why don't you leave me alone?"

Johnson made a note. "Your grandfather. I'll just check up a bit. Incidentally, what's that thing over there?" He pointed to the blue-eyed beast.

"I've been studying a curious case of degenerative osteomyelitis affecting a baroque cephalopod!"

"Oh, I see. Thanks. Fred, see about this guy's grandfather. What are you gaping at?"

Fred said: "That screen. It's set up for projection."

Johnson moved to the audio-sonic recorder. "Better impound it. Probably not important, but—" He touched a switch. The screen stayed blank, but Gallegher's voice said: *"We know how to deal with spies in this house, you dirty traitor."*

Johnson moved the switch again. He glanced at Gallegher, his ruddy face impassive, and in silence began to rewind the wire tape. Gallegher said: "Joe, get me a dull knife. I want to cut my throat, and I don't want to make it too easy for myself. I'm getting used to doing things the hard way."

But Joe, pondering philosophy, refused to answer.

Johnson began to run off the recording. He took out a picture and compared it with what showed on the screen.

"That's Harding, all right," he said. "Thanks for keeping this for us, Mr. Gallegher."

"Don't mention it," Gallegher said. "I'll even show the hangman how to tie the knot around my neck."

"Ha-ha. Taking notes, Fred? Right."

The reel unrolled relentlessly. But, Gallegher tried to make himself believe, there was nothing really incriminating recorded.

He was disillusioned after the screen went blank, at the point when he had thrown a blanket over the recorder last night. Johnson held up his hand for silence. The screen still showed nothing, but after a moment or two voices were clearly audible.

"You have thirty-seven minutes to go, Mr. Gallegher."

"Just stay where you are. I'll have this in a minute. Besides, I want to get my hands on your fifty thousand credits."

"But—"

"Relax. I'm getting it. In a very short time your worries will be over."

"Did I say that?" Gallegher thought wildly. "What a fool I am! Why didn't I turn off the radio when I covered up the lens?"

Grandpa's voice said: *"Trying to kill me by inches, eh, you young whippersnapper!"*

"All the old so-and-so wanted was another bottle," Gallegher moaned to himself. "But try to make those flatfeet believe that! Still—" He brightened. "Maybe I can find out what really happened to Grandpa and Harding. If I shot them off to another world, there might be some clue—"

"Watch closely now." Gallegher's voice said from last night. *"I'll explain as I proceed. Oh-oh. Wait a minute. I'm going to patent this later, so I don't want any spies. I can trust you two not to talk, but that recorder's still turned on to audio. Tomorrow, if I played it back, I'd be saying to myself, 'Gallegher, you talk too much. There's only one way to keep a secret safe.' Off it goes!"*

Someone screamed. The shriek was cut off midway. The projector stopped humming. There was utter silence.

The door opened to admit Murdoch Mackenzie. He was rubbing his hands.

"I came right down," he said briskly. "So you've solved our problem, eh, Mr. Gallegher? Perhaps we can do business then. After all, there's no real evidence that you killed Jonas—and I'll be willing to drop the charges, *if* you've got what Adrenals, Incorporated, wants."

"Pass me those handcuffs, Fred," Johnson requested.

Gallegher protested, "You can't do this to me!"

"A fallacious theorem," Joe said, "which, I note, is now being disproved by this empirical method. How illogical all you ugly people are."

The social trend always lags behind the technological one. And while technology tended, in these days, toward simplification, the social pattern was immensely complicated, since it was partly an outgrowth of historical precedent and partly a result of the scientific advance of the era. Take jurisprudence. Cockburn and Blackwood and a score of others had established certain general and specific rules—say, regarding patents—but those rules could be made thoroughly impractical by a single gadget. The Integrators could solve problems no human brain could manage, so, as a governor, it was necessary to build various controls into those semimechanical colloids. Moreover, an electronic duplicator could infringe not only on patents but on property rights, and attorneys prepared voluminous briefs on such questions as whether "rarity rights" are real property, whether a gadget made on a duplicator is a "representation" or a copy, and whether mass-duplication of chinchillas is unfair competition to a chinchilla breeder who depended on old-fashioned biological principles. All of which added up to the fact that the world, slightly punch-drunk with technology, was trying desperately to walk a straight line. Eventually the confusion would settle down.

It hadn't settled down yet.

So legal machinery was a construction far more complicated than an Integrator. Precedent warred with abstract theory as lawyer warred with lawyer. It was all perfectly clear to the technicians, but they were much too impractical to be consulted; they were apt to remark wickedly, "So my gadget unstabilizes property rights? Well—why have property rights, then?"

And you can't do that!

Not to a world that had found security, of a sort, for thousands of years in rigid precedents of social intercourse. The ancient dike of formal culture was beginning to leak in innumerable spots, and, had you noticed, you might have seen hundreds of thousands of frantic, small figures rushing from danger-spot to danger-spot, valorously plugging the leaks with their fingers, arms, or heads. Some day it would be discovered that there was no encroaching ocean beyond that dike, but that day hadn't yet come.

In a way, that was lucky for Gallegher. Public officials were chary about sticking their necks out. A simple suit for false arrest might lead to fantastic ramifications and big trouble. The hard-headed Murdoch Mackenzie took advantage of this situation to vise his own personal attorney and toss a monkey wrench in the legal wheels. The attorney spoke to Johnson.

There was no corpse. The audiosonic recording was not sufficient. Morever, there were vital questions involving *habeas corpus* and search warrants. Johnson called Headquarters Jurisprudence and the argument raged over the heads of Gallegher and the imperturbable Mackenzie. It ended with Johnson leaving, with his crew—and the increasing recording—and threatening to return as soon as a judge could issue the appropriate writs and papers. Meanwhile, he said, there would be officers on guard outside the house. With a malignant glare for Mackenzie, he stamped out.

"And now to business," said Mackenzie, rubbing his hands. "Between ourselves"—he leaned forward confidentially—"I'm just as glad to get rid of that partner of mine. Whether or no you killed him, I hope he stays vanished. Now I can run the business my way, for a change."

"It's all right about that," Gallegher said, "but what about me? I'll be in custody again as soon as Johnson can wangle it."

"But not convicted," Mackenzie pointed out. "A clever lawyer can fix you up. There was a similar case in which the defendant got off with a defense of *non esse*—his attorney went into metaphysics and proved that the murdered man had never existed. Quite specious, but so far the murderer's gone free."

Gallegher said: "I've searched the house, and Johnson's men did, too. There's simply no trace of Jonas Harding or my grandfather. And I'll tell you frankly, Mr. Mackenzie, I haven't the slightest idea what happened to them."

Mackenzie gestured airily. "We must be methodical. You mentioned you had solved a certain problem for Adrenals, Incorporated. Now, I'll admit, that interested me."

Silently Gallegher pointed to the blue-eyed dynamo. Mackenzie studied the object thoughtfully.

"Well?" he said.

"That's it. The perfect quarry."

Mackenzie walked over to the thing, rapped its hide, and looked deeply into the mild azure eyes. "How fast can it run?" he asked shrewdly.

Gallegher said: "It doesn't have to run. You see, it's invulnerable."

"Ha. Hum. Perhaps if you'd explain a wee bit more—"

But Mackenzie did not seem pleased with the explanation. "No," he said, "I don't see it. There would be no thrill to hunting a critter like that. You forget our customers demand excitement—adrenal stimulation."

"They'll get it. Anger has the same effect as rage—" Gallegher went into detail.

But Mackenzie shook his head. "Both fear and anger give you excess energy you've got to use up. You can't, against a passive quarry. You'll just cause neuroses. We try to get rid of neuroses, not create them."

Gallegher, growing desperate, suddenly remembered the little brown beast and began to discuss that. Once Mackenzie interrupted with a demand to see the creature. Gallegher slid around that one fast.

"Ha," Mackenzie said finally. "It isna canny. How can you hunt something that's invisible?"

"Oh—ultraviolet. Scent-analyzers. It's a test for ingenuity—"

"Our customers are not ingenious. They don't want to be. They want a change and a vacation from routine, hard work—or easy work, as the case may be—they want a rest. They don't want to beat their brains working out methods to catch a thing that moves faster than a pixy, nor do they want to chase a critter that's out of sight before it even gets there. You are a vurra clever man, Mr. Gallegher, but it begins to look as though Jonas's insurance is my best bet after all."

"Now wait—"

Mackenzie pursed his lips. "I'll admit the beasties *may*—I say may—have some possibilities. But what good is quarry that can't be caught? Perhaps if you'd work out a way to capture these other-worldly animals of yours, we might do business. At present, I willna buy a pig in a poke."

"I'll find a way," Gallegher promised wildly. "But I can't do it in jail."

"Ah. I am a little irritated with you, Mr. Gallegher. You tricked me into believing you had solved our problem. Which you havena done—yet. Consider the thought of jail. Your adrenalin may stimulate your brain into working out a way to trap these animals of yours. Though, even so, I can make no rash promises—"

Murdoch Mackenzie grinned at Gallegher and went out, closing the door softly behind him. Gallegher began to dine off his fingernails.

"Men can know the nature of things," Joe said, with an air of solid conviction.

At that point matters were complicated even further by the appearance, on the televisor screen, of a gray-haired man who announced that one of Gallegher's checks had just bounced. Three hundred and fifty credits, the man said, and how about it?

Gallegher looked dazedly at the identification card on the screen. "You're with United Cultures? What's that?"

The gray-haired man said silkily, "Biological and medical supplies and laboratories, Mr. Gallegher."

"What did I order from you?"

"We have a receipt for six hundred pounds of Vitaplasm, first grade. We made delivery within an hour."

"And when—"

The gray-haired man went into more detail. Finally Gallegher made a few lying promises and turned from the blanking screen. He looked wildly around the lab.

"Six hundred pounds of artificial protoplasm," he murmured. "Ordered by Gallegher Plus. He's got delusions of economic grandeur."

"It was delivered," Joe said. "You signed the receipt, the night Grandpa and Jonas Harding disappeared."

"But what could I do with the stuff? It's used for plastic surgery and for humano-prosthesis. Artificial limbs and stuff. It's cultured cellular tissue, this Vitaplasm. Did I use it to *make* some animals? That's biologically impossible. I think. How could I have molded Vitaplasm into a little brown animal that's invisible? What about the brain and the neural structure? Joe, six hundred pounds of Vitaplasm has simply disappeared. Where has it gone?"

But Joe was silent.

Hours later Gallegher was furiously busy. "The trick is," he explained to Joe, "to find out all I can about those critters. Then maybe I can tell where they came from and how I got 'em. Then perhaps I can discover where Grandpa and Harding went. Then—"

"Why not sit down and think about it?"

"That's the difference between us. You've got no instinct of self-preservation. You could sit down and think while a chain reaction took place in your toes and worked up, but not me. I'm too young to die. I keep thinking of Reading Gaol. I need a drink. I could only get high, my demon subconscious could work out the whole problem for me. Is that little brown animal around?"

"No," Joe said.

"Then maybe I can steal a drink." Gallegher exploded, after an abortive attempt that ended in utter failure: "Nobody can move *that* fast."

"Accelerated metabolism. It must have smelled the alcohol. Or perhaps it has additional senses. Even I can scarcely varish it."

"If I mixed kerosene with the whisky, maybe the dipsomaniacal little monster wouldn't like it. Still, neither would I. Ah, well. Back to the mill," Gallegher said, as he tried reagent after reagent on the blue-eyed dynamo, without any effect at all.

"Men can know the nature of things," Joe said irritatingly.

"Shut up. I wonder if I could electroplate this creature? That would immobilize it, all right. But it's immobilized already. How does it eat?"

"Logically, I'd say osmosis."

"Very likely. Osmosis of what?"

Joe clicked irritatedly. "There are dozens of ways you could solve your problem. Instrumentalism. Determinism. Vitalism. Work from *a posteriori* to *a priori*. It's perfectly obvious to me that you've solved the problem Adrenals, Incorporated, set you."

"I have?"

"Certainly."

"How?"

"Very simple. Men can know the nature of things."

"Will you stop repeating that outmoded basic and try to be useful? You're wrong, anyway. Men can know the nature of things by experiment and reason combined!"

Joe said: "Ridiculous. Philosophical incompetence. If you can't prove your point by logic, you're failed. Anybody who has to depend on experiment is beneath contempt."

"Why should I sit here arguing philosophical concepts with a robot?" Gallegher demanded of no one in particular. "How would you like me to demonstrate the fact that ideation is dependent on your having a radioatomic brain that isn't scattered all over the floor?"

"Kill me, then," Joe said. "It's your loss and the world's. Earth will be a poorer place when I die. But coercion means nothing to me. I have no instinct of self-preservation."

"Now look," Gallegher said, trying a new tack, "if you know the answer, why not tell me? Demonstrate that wonderful logic of yours. Convince me without having to depend on experiment. Use pure reason."

"Why should I want to convince you? *I'm* convinced. And I'm so beautiful and perfect that I can achieve no higher glory than to admire me."

"Narcissus," Gallegher snarled. "You're a combination of Narcissus and Nietzsche's Superman."

"Men can know the nature of things," Joe said.

The next development was a subpoena for the transparent robot. The legal machinery was beginning to move, an immensely complicated gadget that worked on a logic as apparently twisted as Joe's own. Gallegher himself, it seemed, was temporarily inviolate, through some odd interpretation of jurisprudence. But the State's principle was that the sum of the parts was equal to the whole. Joe was classified as one of the parts, the total of which equaled Gallegher. Thus the robot found itself in court, listening to a polemic with impassive scorn.

Gallegher, flanked by Murdoch Mackenzie and a corps of attorneys, was with Joe. This was an informal hearing. Gallegher didn't pay much attention; he was concentrating on finding a way to put the bite on the recalcitrant robot, who knew all the answers, but wouldn't talk. He had been studying the philosophers, with an eye toward meeting Joe on his own ground, but so far had succeeded only in acquiring a headache and an almost unendurable longing for a drink. Even out of his laboratory, though, he remained Tantalus. The invisible little brown animal followed him around and stole his liquor.

One of Mackenzie's lawyers jumped up. "I object," he said. There was a brief wrangle as to whether Joe should be classified as a witness or as Exhibit A. If the latter, the subpoena had been falsely served. The Justice pondered.

"As I see it," he declared, "the question is one of determinism versus voluntarism. If this . . . ah . . . robot has free will—"

"Ha!" Gallegher said, and was shushed by an attorney. He subsided rebelliously.

"—then it, or he, is a witness. But, on the other hand, there is the possibility that the robot, in acts of apparent choice, is the mechanical expression of heredity and past environment. For heredity read . . . ah . . . initial mechanical basics."

"Whether or not the robot is a rational being, Mr. Justice, is beside the point," the prosecutor put in.

"I do not agree. Law is based on *res*—"

Joe said: "Mr. Justice, may I speak?"

"Your ability to do so rather automatically gives you permission," the Justice said, studying the robot in a baffled way. "Go ahead."

Joe had seemingly found the connection between law, logic, and philosophy. He said happily: "I've figured it all out. A thinking robot is a rational being. I am a thinking robot—therefore I am a rational being."

"What a fool," Gallegher groaned, longing for the sane logics of electronics and chemistry. "The old Socratic syllogism. Even I could point out the flaw in that!"

"Quiet," Mackenzie whispered. "All the lawyers really depend on is tying up the case in such knots nobody can figure it out. Your robot is perhaps not such a fool as you think."

An argument started as to whether thinking robots really were rational beings. Gallegher brooded. He couldn't see the point, really. Nor did it become clear until, from the maze of contradictions, there emerged the tentative decision that Joe was a rational being. This seemed to please the prosecutor immensely.

"Mr. Justice," he announced, "we have learned that Mr. Galloway Gallegher two nights ago inactivated the robot before us now. Is this not true, Mr. Gallegher?"

But Mackenzie's hand kept Gallegher in his seat. One of the defending attorneys rose to meet the question.

"We admit nothing," he said. "However, if you wish to pose a theoretical question, we will answer it."

The query was posed theoretically.

"Then the theoretical answer is 'yes,' Mr. Prosecutor. A robot of this type can be turned on and off at will."

"Can the robot turn itself off?"

"Yes."

"But this did not occur? Mr. Gallegher inactivated the robot at the time Mr. Jonas Harding was with him in his laboratory two nights ago?"

"Theoretically, that is true. There was a temporary inactivation."

"Then," said the prosecutor, "we wish to question the robot, who has been classed as a rational being."

"The decision was tentative," a defense attorney objected.

"Accepted. Mr. Justice—"

"All right," said the Justice, who was still staring at Joe, "you may ask your questions."

"Ah . . . ah—" The prosecutor, facing the robot, hesitated.

"Call me Joe," Joe said.

"Thank you. Ah . . . is this true? Did Mr. Gallegher inactivate you at the time and place stated?"

"Yes."

"Then," the prosecutor said triumphantly, "I wish to bring a charge of assault and battery against Mr. Gallegher. Since this robot has been tentatively classed as a rational being, any activity causing him, or it, to lose consciousness or the power of mobility is *contra bonos mores,* and may be classed as mayhem."

Mackenzie's attorneys were ruffled. Gallegher said: "What does that mean?"

A lawyer whispered: "They can hold you, and hold that robot as a witness." He stood up. "Mr. Justice. Our statements were in reply to purely theoretical questions."

The prosecutor said: "But the robot's statement answered a nontheoretical question."

"The robot was not on oath."

"Easily remedied," said the prosecutor, while Gallegher saw his last hopes slipping rapidly away. He thought hard, while matters proceeded.

"Do you solemnly swear to tell the truth the whole truth and nothing but the truth so help you God?"

Gallegher leaped to his feet. "Mr. Justice. I object."

"Indeed. To what?"

"To the validity of that oath."

Mackenz'e said: "Ah-*ha!*"

The Justice was thoughtful. "Will you please elucidate, Mr. Gallegher? Why should the oath not be administered to this robot?"

"Such an oath is applicable to man only."

"And?"

"It presupposes the existence of the soul. At least it implies theism, a personal religion. Can a robot take an oath?"

The Justice eyed Joe. "It's a point, certainly. Ah . . . Joe. Do you believe in a personal deity?"

"I do."

The prosecutor beamed. "Then we can proceed."

"Wait a minute," Murdoch Mackenzie said, rising. "May I ask a question, Mr. Justice?"

"Go ahead."

Mackenzie stared at the robot. "Well, now. Will you tell me, please, what this personal deity of yours is like?"

"Certainly," Joe said. "Just like me."

After a while it degenerated into a theological argument. Gallegher left the attorneys debating the apparently vital point of how many angels could dance on the head of a pin, and went home temporarily scot-free, with Joe. Until such points as the robot's religious basics were settled, nothing could be done. All the way, in the aircab, Mackenzie insisted on pointing out the merits of Calvinism to Joe.

At the door Mackenzie made a mild threat. "I did not intend to give you so much rope, you understand. But you will work all the harder with the threat of prison hanging over your head. I don't know how long I can keep you a free man. If you can work out an answer quickly—"

"What sort of answer?"

"I am easily satisfied. Jonas's body, now—"

"Bah!" Gallegher said, and went into his laboratory and sat down morosely. He siphoned himself a drink before he remembered the little brown animal. Then he lay back, staring from the blue-eyed dynamo to Joe and back again.

Finally he said: "There's an old Chinese idea that the man who first stops arguing and starts swinging with his fists admits his intellectual defeat."

Joe said: "Naturally. Reason is sufficient; if you need experiment to prove your point, you're a lousy philosopher and logician."

Gallegher fell back on casuistry. "First step, animal. Fist-swinging. Second step, human. Pure logic. But what about the third step?"

"What third step?"

"Men can know the nature of things—but you're not a man. Your personal deity isn't an anthropomorphic one. Three steps; animal, man, and what we'll call for convenience superman, though *man* doesn't necessarily enter into it. We've always attributed godlike traits to the theoretical superbeing. Suppose, just for the sake of having a label, we call this third-stage entity Joe."

"Why not?" Joe said.

"Then the two basic concepts of logic don't apply. Men can know the nature of things, by pure reason, and also by experiment *and* reason. But such second-stage concepts are as elementary to Joe as Plato's ideas were to Aristotle." Gallegher crossed his fingers behind his back. "The question is, then, what's the third-stage operation for Joe?"

"Godlike?" the robot said.

"You've got special senses, you know. You can varish, whatever that is. Do you need ordinary logical methods? Suppose—"

"Yes," Joe said, "I can varish, all right. I can skren, too. Hm-m-m."

Gallegher abruptly rose from the couch. "What a fool I am. 'DRINK ME.' That's the answer. Joe, shut up. Go off in a corner and varish."

"I'm skrenning," Joe said.

"Then skren. I've finally got an idea. When I woke up yesterday, I was thinking about a bottle labeled 'DRINK ME.' When Alice took a drink, she changed size, didn't she? Where's that reference book? I wish I knew more about technology.

Vasoconstrictor . . . hemostatic . . . here it is—demonstrates the metabolic regulation mechanisms of the vegetative nervous system. Metabolism. I wonder now—"

Gallegher rushed to the workbench and examined the bottles. "Vitalism. Life is the basic reality, of which everything else is a form or manifestation. Now. I had a problem to solve for Adrenals, Incorporated. Jonas Harding and Grandpa were here. Harding gave me an hour to fill the bill. The problem . . . a dangerous and harmless animal. Paradox. That isn't it. Harding's clients wanted thrills and safety at the same time. I've got no lab animals on tap at the moment . . . *Joe!*"

"Well?"

"Watch." Gallegher said. He poured a drink and watched the liquid vanish before he tasted it. "Now. What happened?"

"The little brown animal drank it."

"Is that little brown animal, by any chance—Grandpa?"

"That's right," Joe said.

Gallegher blistered the robot's transparent hide with sulphurous oaths. "Why didn't you tell me? You—"

"I answered your question," the robot said smugly. "Grandpa's brown, isn't he? And he's an animal."

"But—little! I thought it was a critter about as big as a rabbit."

"The only standard of comparison is the majority of the species. That's the yardstick. Compared to the average height of humans, Grandpa is little. A little brown animal."

"So it's Grandpa, is it?" Gallegher said, returning to the workbench. "And he's simply speeded up. Accelerated metabolism. Adrenalin. Hm-m-m. Now I know what to look for, maybe—"

He fell to. But it was sundown before Gallegher emptied a small vial into a glass, siphoned whisky into it, and watched the mixture disappear.

A flickering began. Something flashed from corner to corner of the room. Gradually it became visible as a streaking brownness that resolved itself, finally, into Grandpa. He stood before Gallegher, jittering like mad as the last traces of the accelerative formula wore off.

"Hello, Grandpa," Gallegher said placatingly.

Grandpa's nutcracker face wore an expression of malevolent fury. For the first time in his life, the old gentleman was drunk. Gallegher stared in utter amazement.

"I'm going back to Maine," Grandpa cried, and fell over backwards.

"Never seen such a lot of slow pokes in my life," Grandpa said, devouring a steak. "My, I'm hungry. Next time I let you stick a needle in me I'll know better. How many months have I been like this?"

"Two days," Gallegher said, carefully mixing up a formula. "It was a metabolic accelerator, Grandpa. You just lived faster, that's all."

"All! Bah. Couldn't eat nothing. Food was solid as a rock. Only thing I could get down my gullet was liquor."

"Oh?"

"Hard chewing. Even with my store teeth. Even whisky tasted hotter. As for a steak like this, I couldn't of managed it."

"You were living faster." Gallegher glanced at the robot, who was still quietly skrenning in a corner. "Let me see. The antithesis of an accelerator is a decelerator—Grandpa, where's Jonas Harding?"

"In there," Grandpa said, pointing to the blue-eyed dynamo and thus confirming Gallegher's suspicion.

"Vitaplasm. So that was it. That's why I had a lot of Vitaplasm sent over a couple of nights ago. Hm-m-m." Gallegher examined the sleek, impermeable surface of the apparent dynamo. After a while he tried a hypodermic syringe. He couldn't penetrate the hard shell.

Instead, using a new mixture he had concocted from the bottles on his workbench, he dripped a drop of the liquid on the substance. Presently it softened. At that spot Gallegher made an injection, and was delighted to see a color-change spread out from the locus till the entire mass was pallid and plastic.

"Vitaplasm," he exulted. "Ordinary artificial protoplasm cells, that's all. No wonder it looked hard. I'd given it a decelerative treatment. An approach to molecular stasis. Anything metabolising that slowly would seem hard as iron." He wadded up great bunches of the surrogate and dumped it into a convenient vat. Something began to form around the blue eyes—the shape of a cranium, broad shoulders, a torso—

Freed from the disguising mass of Vitaplasm, Jonas Harding was revealed crouching on the floor, silent as a statue.

His heart wasn't beating. He didn't breathe. The decelerator held him in an unbreakable grip of passivity.

Not quite unbreakable. Gallegher, about to apply the hypodermic, paused and looked from Joe to Grandpa. "Now why did I do that?" he demanded.

Then he answered his own question.

"The time limit. Harding gave me an hour to solve his problem. Time's relative—especially when your metabolism is slowed down. I must have given Harding a shot of the decelerator so he wouldn't realize how much time had passed. Let's see." Gallegher applied a drop to Harding's impermeable skin and watched the spot soften and change hue. "Uh-huh. With Harding frozen like that, I could take weeks to work on the problem, and when he woke up, he'd figure only a short time had passed. But why did I use the Vitaplasm on him?"

Grandpa downed a beer. "When you're drunk, you're apt to do anything," he contended, reaching for another steak.

"True, true. But Gallegher Plus is logical. A strange, eerie kind of logic, but logic nevertheless. Let me see. I shot the decelerator into Harding, and then—there he was. Rigid and stiff. I couldn't leave him kicking around the lab, could I? If anybody came in, they'd think I had a corpse on my hands!"

"You mean he ain't dead?" Grandpa demanded.

"Of course not. Merely decelerated. I know! I camouflaged Harding's body. I sent out for Vitaplasm, molded the stuff around his body, and then applied the decelerator to the Vitaplasm. It works on living cellular substance—slows it down. And slowed down to that extent, it's impermeable and immovable!"

"You're crazy," Grandpa said.

"I'm short-sighted," Gallegher admitted. "At least, Gallegher Plus is. Imagine leaving Harding's eyes visible, so I'd be reminded the guy was under that pile when I woke up from my binge! What did I construct that recorder for, anyhow? The logic Gallegher Plus uses is far more fantastic than Joe's."

"Don't bother me," Joe said. "I'm still skrenning."

Gallegher put the hypodermic needle into the soft spot on Harding's arm. He injected the accelerator, and within a moment or two Jonas Harding stirred, blinked his blue eyes, and got up from the floor. "Ouch!" he said, rubbing his arm. "Did you stick me with something?"

"An accident," Gallegher said, watching the man warily. "Uh . . . this problem of yours—"

Harding found a chair and sat down, yawning. "Solved it?"

"You gave me an hour."

"Oh. Yes, of course." Harding looked at his watch. "It's stopped. Well, what about it?"

"Just how long a time do you think has elapsed since you came into this laboratory?"

"Half an hour?" Harding hazarded.

"Two months," Grandpa snapped.

"You're both right," Gallegher said. "I'd have another answer, but I'd be right, too."

Harding obviously thought that Gallegher was still drunk. He stayed doggedly on the subject.

"What about that specialized animal we need? You still have half an hour—"

"I don't need it," Gallegher said, a great white light dawning in his mind. "I've got your answer for you. But it isn't quite what you think it is." He relaxed on the couch and considered the liquor organ. Now he could drink again, he found he preferred to prolong the anticipation.

"I came upon no wine so wonderful as thirst," he remarked.

"Claptrap," Grandpa said.

Gallegher said: "The clients of Adrenals, Incorporated, want to hunt animals. They want a thrill, so they need dangerous animals. They have to be safe, so they can't have dangerous animals. It seems paradoxical, but it isn't. The answer doesn't lie in the animal. It's in the hunter."

Harding blinked. "Come again?"

"Tigers. Ferocious man-eating tigers. Lions. Jaguars. Water buffalo. The most vicious, carnivorous animals you can get. That's part of the answer."

"Listen—" Harding said. "Maybe you've got the wrong idea. The tigers aren't our customers. We don't supply clients to the animals, it's the other way round."

"I must make a few more tests," Gallegher said, "but the basic principle's right here in my hand. An accelerator. A latent metabolic accelerator with a strong concentration of adrenalin as the catalyst. Like this—"

He sketched a vivid verbal picture.

Armed with a rifle, the client wandered through the artificial jungle, seeking quarry. He had already paid his fee to Adrenals, Incorporated and got his intravenous shot of the latent accelerator. That substance permeated his blood stream, doing nothing as yet, waiting for the catalyst.

The tiger launched itself from the underbrush. It shot toward the client like catapulted murder, fangs bared. As the claws neared the man's back, the suprarenals shot adrenalin into the blood stream in strong concentration.

That was the catalyst. The latent accelerative factor became active.

The client speeded up—tremendously.

He stepped away from the body of the tiger, apparently frozen in midair, and did what seemed best to him before the effect of the accelerator wore off. When it did, he returned to normal—and by that time he could be in the supply station of Adrenals, Incorporated, getting another intravenous shot—unless he'd decided to bag his tiger the easy way.

It was as simple as that.

"Ten thousand credits," Gallegher said, happily counting them. "The balance due as soon as I work out the catalytic angle. Which is a cinch. Any fourth-rate chemist could do it. What intrigues me is the forthcoming interview between Harding and Murdoch Mackenzie. When they compare the time element, it's going to be funny."

"I want a drink," Grandpa said. "Where's a bottle?"

"Even in court, I think I could prove I only took an hour or less to solve the problem. It was Harding's hour, of course, but time *is* relative. Entropy — metabolish — what a legal battle *that* would be. Still, it won't happen. I know the formula for the accelerator and Harding doesn't. He'll pay the other forty thousand—and Mackenzie won't have any kicks. After all, I'm giving Adrenals, Incorporated the success factor they needed."

"Well, I'm still going back to Maine," Grandpa contended. "Least you can do is give me a bottle."

"Go out and buy one," Gallegher said, tossing the old gentleman several credits. "Buy several. I often wonder what the vintners buy—"

"Eh?"

"—one-half so precious as the stuff they sell. No, I'm not tight. But I'm going to be." Gallegher clutched the liquor-organ's mouthpiece in a loving grip and began to play alcoholic arpeggios on the keyboard. Grandpa, with a parting sneer at such newfangled contraptions, took his departure.

Silence fell over the laboratory. Bubbles and Monstro, the two dynamos, sat quiescent. Neither of them had bright blue eyes. Gallegher experimented with cocktails and felt a warm, pleasant glow seep through his soul.

Joe came out of his corner and stood before the mirror, admiring his gears.

"Finished skrenning?" Gallegher asked sardonically.

"Yes."

"Rational being, forsooth. You and your philosophy. Well, my fine robot, it turned out I didn't need your help after all. Pose away."

"How ungrateful you are," Joe said, "after I've given you the benefit of my superlogic."

"Your . . . what? You've slipped a gear. What superlogic?"

"The third-stage, of course. What we were talking about a while back. That's why I was skrenning. I hope you didn't think all your problems were solved by your feeble brain, in that opaque cranium of yours."

Gallegher sat up. "What are you talking about? Third-stage logic? You didn't—"

"I don't think I can describe it to you. It's more abstruse than the noumenon of Kant, which can't be perceived except by thought. You've got to be able to skren to understand it, but—well, it's the third stage. It's . . . let's see . . . demonstrating the nature of things by making things happen by themselves."

"Experiment?"

"No. By skrenning, I reduce all things from the material plane to the realm of pure thought, and figure out the logical concepts and solutions."

"But . . . wait. Things have been *happening!* I figured out about Grandpa and Harding and worked out the accelerator—"

"You think you did," Joe said. "I simply skrenned. Which is a purely superintellectual process. After I'd done that, things couldn't help happening. But I hope you don't think they happened by themselves!"

Gallegher said: "What's skrenning?"

"You'll never know."

"But . . . you're contending you're the First Cause . . . no, it's voluntarism . . . third-stage logic? No — " Gallegher fell back on the couch, staring. "Who do you think you are? *Deus ex machina?*"

Joe glanced down at the conglomeration of gears in his torso.

"What else?" he asked smugly. ∎

PATE DE FOIE GRAS
by Isaac Asimov

Illustration by Kelly Freas.
© 1956 by Street & Smith Publications, Inc.

I couldn't tell you my real name if I wanted to and, under the circumstances, I don't want to.

I'm not much of a writer myself, unless you count the kind of stuff that passes muster in a scientific paper, so I'm having Isaac Asimov write this up for me.

I've picked him for several reasons. First, he's a biochemist, so he understands what I tell him; some of it, anyway. Secondly, he can write; or at least he has published considerable fiction, which may not, of course, be the same thing.

But most important of all, he can get what he writes published in science-fiction magazines and he has written two articles on thiotimoline, and that is exactly what I need for reasons that will become clear as we proceed.

I was not the first person to have the honor of meeting The Goose. That belongs to a Texas cotton farmer named Ian Angus MacGregor, who owned it before it became government property. (The names, places and dates I use are deliberately synthetic. None of you will be able to trace anything through them. Don't bother trying.)

MacGregor apparently kept geese about the place because they ate weeds, but not cotton. In this way, he had automatic weeders that were self-fueling and, in addition, produced eggs, down, and, at judicious intervals, roast goose.

By summer of 1955, he had sent an even dozen of letters to the Department of Agriculture requesting information on the hatching of goose eggs. The department sent him all the booklets on hand that were anywhere near the subject, but his letters simply got more impassioned and freer in their references to his "friend," the local congressman.

My connection with this is that I am in the employ of the Department of Agriculture. I have considerable training in agricultural chemistry, plus a smattering of vertebrate physiology. (This won't help you. If you think you can pin my identity out of this, you are mistaken.)

Since I was attending a convention at San Antonio in July of 1955, my boss asked me to stop off at MacGregor's place and see what I could do to help him. We're servants of the public and besides we had finally received a letter from MacGregor's congressman.

On July 17, 1955, I met The Goose.

I met MacGregor first. He was in his fifties, a tall man with a lined face full of suspicion. I went over all the information he had been given, explained about incubators, the values of trace minerals in the diet, plus some late information on Vitamin E, the cobalamins and the use of antibiotic additives.

He shook his head. He had tried it all and still the eggs wouldn't hatch.

What could I do? I'm a Civil Service employee and not the archangel, Gabriel. I'd told him all I could and if the eggs still wouldn't hatch, they wouldn't and that was that. I asked politely if I might see his geese, just so no one could say afterward I hadn't done all I possibly could.

He said, "It's not geese, mister; it's one goose."

I said, "May I see the one goose?"

"Rather not."

"Well, then, I can't help you any further. If it's only one goose, then there's just something wrong with it. Why worry about one goose? Eat it."

I got up and reached for my hat.

He said, "Wait!" and I stood there while his lips tightened and his eyes wrinkled and he had a quiet fight with himself.

He said, "If I show you something, will you swear to keep it secret?"

He didn't seem like the type of man to rely on another's vow of secrecy, but it was as though he had reached such a pit of desperation that he had no other way out.

I said, "If it isn't anything criminal—"

"Nothing like that," he snapped.

And then I went out with him to a pen near the house, surrounded by barbed wire, with a locked gate to it, and holding one goose—The Goose.

"That's The Goose," he said. The way he said it, I could hear the capitals.

I stared at it. It looked like any other goose, heaven help me, fat, self-satisfied and short-tempered. I said, "Hm-m-m" in my best professional manner.

MacGregor said, "And here's one of its eggs. It's been in the incubator. Nothing happens." He produced it from a capacious overall pocket. There was a queer strain about his manner of holding it.

I frowned. There was something wrong with the egg. It was smaller and more spherical than normal.

MacGregor said, "Take it."

I reached out and took it. Or tried to. I gave it the amount of heft an egg like that ought to deserve and it just sat where it was. I had to try harder and then up it came.

Now I knew what was queer about the way MacGregor held it. It weighed nearly two pounds. (To be exact, when we weighed it later, we found its mass to be 852.6 grams.)

I stared at it as it lay there, pressing down the palm of my hand, and MacGregor grinned sourly. "Drop it," he said.

I just looked at him, so he took it out of my hand and dropped it himself.

It hit soggy. It didn't smash. There was no spray of white and yolk. It just lay where it fell with the bottom caved in.

I picked it up again. The white eggshell had shattered where the egg had struck. Pieces of it had flaked away and what shone through was a dull yellow in color.

My hands trembled. It was all I could do to make my fingers work, but I got some of the rest of the shell flaked away, and stared at the yellow.

I didn't have to run any analyses. My heart told me.

I was face to face with The Goose!

The Goose That Laid The Golden Eggs!

You don't believe me. I'm sure of that. You've got this tabbed as another thiotimoline article.

Good! I'm *counting* on your thinking that. I'll explain later.

Meanwhile, my first problem was to get MacGregor to give up that golden egg. I was almost hysterical about it. I was almost already to clobber him and make off with the egg by force if I had to.

I said, "I'll give you a receipt. I'll guarantee you payment. I'll do anything in reason. Look, Mr. MacGregor, they're no good to you anyway. You can't cash the gold unless you can explain how it came into your possession. Holding gold is illegal. And how do you expect to explain? If the government—"

"I don't want the government butting in," he said, stubbornly.

But I was twice as stubborn. I followed him about. I pleaded. I yelled. I threatened. It took me hours. Literally. In the end, I signed a receipt and he dogged me out to my car and stood in the road as I drove away, following me with his eyes.

He never saw that egg again. Of course, he was compensated for the value of the gold—$656.47 after taxes had been subtracted—but that was a bargain for the government.

When one considers the potential value of that egg—

The *potential* value! That's the irony of it. That's the reason for this article.

The head of my section at the Department of Agriculture is Louis P. Bronstein. (Don't bother looking him up. The "P" stands for Pittfield if you want more misdirection.)

He and I are on good terms and I felt I could explain things without being placed under immediate observation. Even so, I took no chances. I had the egg with me and when I got to the tricky part, I just laid it on the desk between us.

Finally, he touched it with his finger as though it were hot.

I said, "Pick it up."

It took him a long time, but he did, and I watched him take two tries at it as I had.

I said, "It's a yellow metal and it could be brass only it isn't because it's inert to concentrated nitric acid. I've tried that already. There's only a shell of gold because it can be bent with moderate pressure. Besides, if it were solid gold, the egg would weigh over ten pounds."

Bronstein said, "It's some sort of hoax. It *must* be."

"A hoax that uses real gold? Remember, when I first saw this thing, it was covered completely with authentic unbroken eggshell. It's been easy to check a piece of the eggshell. Calcium carbonate. That's a hard thing to gimmick. And if we look inside the egg—I didn't want to do that on my own, chief—and find real egg, then we've got it, because that would be impossible to gimmick. Surely, this is worth an official project."

"How can I approach the Secretary with—" He stared at the egg.

But he did in the end. He made phone calls and sweated out most of a day. One or two of the department brass came to look at the egg.

Project Goose was started. That was July 20, 1955.

I was the responsible investigator to begin with and remained in titular charge throughout, though matters quickly got beyond me.

We began with the one egg. Its average radius was 35 millimeters (major axis, 72 millimeters; minor axis, 68 millimeters). The gold shell was 2.45 millimeters in thickness. Studying other eggs later on, we found this value to be rather high. The average thickness turned out to be 2.1 millimeters.

Inside *was* egg. It looked like egg and it smelled like egg.

Aliquots were analyzed and the organic constituents were reasonably normal. The white was 9.7 per cent albumin. The yolk had the normal complement of vitellin, cholesterol, phospholipid and carotenoid. We lacked enough material to test for trace constituents but later on with more eggs at our disposal we did, and nothing unusual showed up as far as the contents of vitamins, co-enzymes, nucleotides, sulfhydryl groups, et cetera, et cetera were concerned.

One important gross abnormality that showed was the egg's behavior on heating. A small portion of the yolk, heated, "hard-boiled" almost at once. We fed a portion of the hardboiled egg to a mouse. It survived.

I nibbled at another bit of it. Too small a quantity to taste, really, but it made me sick. Purely psychosomatic, I'm sure.

Boris W. Finley, of the Department of Biochemistry of Temple University—a department consultant—supervised these tests.

He said, referring to the hardboiling, "The ease with which the egg-proteins are heat-denatured indicates a partial denaturation to begin with and, considering the nature of the shell, the obvious guilt would lie at the door of heavy metal contamination."

So a portion of the yolk was analyzed for inorganic constitents, and it was found to be high in chloraurate ion, which is a singly-charged ion containing an atom of gold and four of chlorine, the symbol for which is $AuCl_4$. (The "Au" symbol for gold comes from the fact that the Latin word for gold is "aurum.") When I say the chloraurate ion content was high, I mean it was 3.2 parts per thousand, or 0.32 per cent. That's high enough to form insoluble complexes of "gold-protein" which would coagulate easily.

Finley said, "It's obvious this egg cannot hatch. Nor can any other such egg. It is heavy-metal poisoned. Gold may be more glamorous than lead but it is just as poisonous to proteins."

I agreed gloomily. "At least it's safe from decay, too."

"Quite right. No self-respecting bug would live in this chlorauriferous soup."

The final spectrographic analysis of the gold of the shell came in virtually pure. The only detectable impurity was iron, which amounted to 0.23 per cent of the whole. The iron content of the egg yolk had been twice normal, also. At the moment, however, the matter of the iron was neglected.

One week after Project Goose was begun, an expedition was sent into Texas. Five biochemists went—the accent was still on biochemistry, you see—along with three truckloads of equipment, and a squadron of army personnel. I went along, too, of course.

As soon as we arrived, we cut MacGregor's farm off from the world.

That was a lucky thing, you know—the security measures we took right from the start. The reasoning was wrong, at first, but the results were good.

The Department wanted Project Goose kept quiet at the start simply because there was always the thought that this might still be an elaborate hoax and we couldn't risk the bad publicity, if it were. And if it weren't a hoax, we couldn't risk the newspaper hounding that would definitely result over any goose-and-golden-egg story.

It was only well after the start of Project Goose, well after our arrival at MacGregor's farm, that the real implications of the matter became clear.

Naturally, MacGregor didn't like the men and equipment settling down all about him. He didn't like being told The Goose was government property. He didn't like having his eggs impounded.

He didn't like it but he agreed to it—if you can call it agreeing when negotiations are being carried on while a machine gun is being assembled in a man's barnyard and ten men, with bayonets fixed, are marching past while the arguing is going on.

He was compensated, of course. What's money to the government?

The Goose didn't like a few things, either—like having blood samples taken. We didn't dare anaesthetize it for fear of doing anything to alter its metabolism, and it took two men to hold it each time. Ever try to hold an angry goose?

The Goose was put under a twenty-four-hour guard with the threat of summary court-martial to any man who let anything happen to it. If any of those soldiers read this article, they may get a sudden glimmering of what was going on. If so they will probably have the sense to keep shut about it. At least, if they know what's good for them, they will.

Paté de Foie Gras

The blood of The Goose was put through every test conceivable.

It carried 2 parts per hundred thousand (0.002 per cent) of chloraurate ion. Blood taken from the hepatic vein was richer than the rest, almost 4 parts per hundred thousand.

Finley grunted. "The liver," he said.

We took X rays. On the X-ray negative, the liver was a cloudy mass of light gray, lighter than the viscera in its neighborhood, because it stopped more of the X rays, because it contained more gold. The blood vessels showed up lighter than the liver proper and the ovaries were pure white. No X rays got through the ovaries at all.

It made sense and in an early report, Finley stated it as bluntly as possible. Paraphrasing the report it went, in part:

"The chloraurate ion is secreted by the liver into the blood stream. The ovaries act as a trap for the ion, which is there reduced to metallic gold and deposited as a shell about the developing egg. Relatively high concentrates of unreduced chloraurate ion penetrate the contents of the developing eggs.

"There is little doubt that The Goose finds this process useful as a means of getting rid of the gold atoms which, if allowed to accumulate, would undoubtedly poison it. Excretion by eggshell may be novel in the animal kingdom, even unique, but there is no denying that it is keeping The Goose alive.

"Unfortunately, however, the ovary is being locally poisoned to such an extent that few eggs are laid, probably not more than will suffice to get rid of the accumulating gold, and those few eggs are definitely unhatchable."

That was all he said in writing, but to the rest of us, he said, "That leaves one peculiarly embarrassing question."

I knew what it was. We all did.

Where was the gold coming from?

No answer to that for a while, except for some negative evidence. There was no perceptible gold in The Goose's feed, nor were there any gold-bearing pebbles about that it might have swallowed. There was no trace of gold anywhere in the soil of the area and a search of the house and grounds revealed nothing. There were no gold coins, gold jewelry, gold plate, gold watches or gold anything. No one on the farm even had as much as gold fillings in this teeth.

There was Mrs. MacGregor's wedding ring, of course, but she had only had one in her life and she was wearing that one.

So where was the gold coming from?

The beginnings of the answer came on August 16, 1955.

Albert Nevis, of Purdue, was forcing gastric tubes into The Goose—another procedure to which the bird objected strenuously—with the idea of testing the contents of its alimentary canal. It was one of our routine searches for exogenous gold.

Gold *was* found, but only in traces, and there was every reason to suppose those traces had accompanied the digestive secretions and were, therefore, endogenous—from within, that is—in origin.

However, something else showed up, or the lack of it, anyway.

I was there when Nevis came into Finley's office in the temporary building we had put up overnight—almost—near the goosepen.

Nevis said, "The Goose is low in bile pigment. Duodenal contents show about none."

Finley frowned and said, "Liver function is probably knocked loop-the-loop because of its gold concentration. It probably isn't secreting bile at all."

"It *is* secreting bile," said Nevis. "Bile acids are present in normal quantity. Near normal, anyway. It's just the bile pigments that are missing. I did a fecal analysis and that was confirmed. No bile pigments."

Let me explain something at this point. Bile acids are steroids secreted by the liver into the bile and *via* that are poured into the upper end of the small intestine. These bile acids are detergentlike molecules which help to emulsify the fat in our diet—or The Goose's—and distribute them in the form of tiny bubbles through the watery intentional contents. This distribution, or homogenization, if you'd rather, makes it easier for the fat to be digested.

Bile pigments, the substance that was missing in The Goose, are something entirely different. The liver makes them out of hemoglobin, the red oxygen-carrying protein of the blood. Worn-out hemoglobin is broken up in the liver, the heme part being split away. The heme is made up of a squarish molecule—called a "porphyrin"—with an iron atom in the center. The liver takes the iron out and stores it for future use, then breaks the squarish molecule that is left. This broken porphyrin is bile pigment. It is colored browning or greenish—depending on further chemical changes—and is secreted into the bile.

The bile pigments are of no use to the body. They are poured into the bile as waste products. They pass through the intestines and come out with the feces. In fact, the bile pigments are responsible for the color of the feces.

Finley's eyes began to glitter.

Nevis said, "It looks as though porphyrin catabolism isn't following the proper course in the liver. Doesn't it to you?"

It surely did. To me, too.

There was tremendous excitement after that. This was the first metabolic abnormality, not directly involving gold, that had been found in The Goose!

We took a liver biopsy (which means we punched a cylindrical sliver out of The Goose reaching down into the liver). It hurt The Goose but didn't harm it. We took more blood samples, too.

This time, we isolated hemoglobin from the blood and small quantities of the cytochromes from our liver samples. (The cytochromes are oxidizing enzymes that also contain heme.) We separated out the heme and in acid solution some of it precipitated in the form of a brilliant orange substance. By August 22, 1955, we had 5 micrograms of the compound.

The orange compound was similar to heme, but it was not heme. The iron in heme can be in the form of a doubly charged ferrous ion (Fe + +) or a triply charged ferric ion (Fe + + +), in which later case, the compound is called hematin. (Ferrous and ferric, by the way, come from the Latin word for iron, which is "ferrum.")

The orange compound we had separated from heme had the porphyrin portion of the molecule all right, but the metal in the center was gold, to be specific, a triply charged auric ion (Au + + +). We called this compound "aureme," which is simply short for "auric heme."

Aureme was the first naturally occurring gold-containing organic compound ever discovered. Ordinarily, it would rate headline news in the world of biochemistry. But now it was nothing; nothing at all in comparison to the further horizons its mere existence opened up.

The liver, it seemed, was not breaking up the heme to bile pigment. Instead it was converting it to aureme; it was replacing iron with gold. The aureme, in equilibrium with chloraurate ion, entered the blood stream and was carried to the ovaries where the gold was separated out and the porphyrin portion of the molecule disposed of by some as-yet-unidentified mechanism.

Further analyses showed that 29 percent of the gold in the blood of The Goose was carried in the plasma in the form of chloraurate ion. The remaining 71 percent was carried in the red blood corpuscles in the form of "automoglobin." An attempt was made to feed The Goose traces of radioactive gold so that we could pick up radioactivity in plasma and corpuscles and see how readily the auremoglobin molecules were handled in the ovaries. It seemed to us the auremoglobin should be much more slowly disposed of than the dissolved chloraurate ion in the plasma.

The experiment failed, however, since we detected no radioactivity. We put it down to inexperience since none of us were isotope men which was too bad since the failure was highly significant, really, and by not realizing it, we lost several weeks.

The auremoglobin was, of course, useless as far as carrying oxygen was concerned, but it only made up about 0.1 percent of the total hemoglobin of the red blood cells so there was no interference with the respiration of The Goose.

This still left us with the question of where the gold came from, and it was Nevis who first made the crucial suggestion.

"Maybe," he said, at a meeting of the group held on the evening of August 25, 1955, "The Goose doesn't replace the iron with gold. Maybe it *changes* the iron to gold."

Before I met Nevis personally that summer, I had known him through his publications—his field is bile chemistry and liver function—and had always considered him a cautious, clear-thinking person. Almost overcautious. One wouldn't consider him capable for a minute of making any such completely ridiculous statement.

It just shows the desperation and demoralization involved in Project Goose.

The desperation was due to the fact that there was nowhere, literally nowhere, that the gold could come from. The Goose was excreting gold at the rate of 38.9 grams of gold a day and had been doing it over a period of months. That gold had to come from somewhere and, failing that—absolutely failing that—it had to be made from something.

The demoralization that led us to consider the second alternative was due to the mere fact that we were face to face with The Goose That Laid The Golden Eggs; the undeniable GOOSE. With that, everything became possible. All of us were living in a fairy-tale world and all of us reacted to it by losing all sense of reality.

Finley considered the possibility seriously. "Hemoglobin," he said, "enters the liver and a bit of auremoglobin comes out. The gold shell of the eggs has iron as its only impurity. The egg yolk is high in only two things; in gold, of course, and also, somewhat, in iron. It all makes a horrible kind of distorted sense. We're going to need help, men."

We did and it meant a third stage of the investigation. The first stage had consisted of myself alone. The second was the biochemical taskforce. The third, the greatest, the most important of all, involved the invasion of the nuclear physicists.

On September 5, 1955, John L. Billings of the University of California arrived. He had some equipment with him and more arrived in the following weeks. More temporary structures were going up. I could see that within a year we would have a whole research institution built about The Goose.

Billings joined our conference the evening of the 5th.

Finley brought him up to date and said, "There are a great many serious problems involved in this iron-to-gold idea. For one thing, the total quantity of iron in The Goose can only be of the order of half a gram, yet nearly 40 grams of gold a day are being manufactured."

Billings had a clear, high-pitched voice. He said, "There's a worse problem than that. Iron is about at the bottom of the packing fraction curve. Gold is much higher up. To convert a gram of iron to a gram of gold takes just about as much energy as is produced by the fissioning of one gram of U-235."

Finley shrugged. "I'll leave the problem to you."

Billings said, "Let me think about it."

He did more than think. One of the things done was to isolate fresh samples of heme from The Goose, ash it, and send the iron oxide to Brookhaven for isotopic analysis. There was no particular reason to do that particular thing. It was just one of a number of individual investigations, but it was the one that brought results.

When the figures came back, Billings choked on them. He said, "There's no Fe^{56}."

"What about the other isotopes?" asked Finley at once.

"All present," said Billings, "in the appropriate relative rations, but no detectable Fe^{56}."

I'll have to explain again: Iron, as it occurs naturally, is made up of four different isotopes. These isotopes are varieties of atoms that differ from one another in atomic weight. Iron atoms with an atomic weight of 56, or Fe^{56}, makes up 91.6 percent of all the atoms in iron. The other atoms have atomic weights of 54, 57 and 58.

The iron from the heme of The Goose was made up only of Fe^{54}, Fe^{57} and Fe^{58}. The implication was obvious. Fe^{56} was disappearing while the other isotopes weren't and this meant a nuclear reaction was taking place. A nuclear reaction could take one isotope and leave others be. An ordinary chemical reaction, any chemical reaction at all, would have to dispose of all isotopes equally.

"But it's energetically impossible," said Finley.

He was only saying that in mild sarcasm with Billings's initial remark in mind. As biochemists, we knew well enough that many reactions went on in the body which required an input of energy and that this was taken care of by coupling the energy-demanding reaction with an energy-producing reaction.

However, chemical reactions gave off or took up a few kilocalories per mole. Nuclear reactions gave off or took up millions. To supply energy for an energy-demanding nuclear reaction required, therefore, a second and energy-producing nuclear reaction.

We didn't see Billings for two days.

When he did come back, it was to say, "See here. The energy-producing reaction must produce just as much energy per nucleon involved as the energy-demanding reaction uses up. If it produces even slightly less, then the overall reaction won't go. If it produces even slightly more, then considering the astronomical number of nucleons involved, the excess energy produced would vaporize The Goose in a fraction of a second."

"So?" said Finley.

"So the number of reactions possibly is very limited. I have been able to find only one plausible system. Oxygen-18, if converted to iron-56, will produce enough energy to drive the iron-56 on to gold-197. It's like going down one side of a roller-coaster and then up the other. We'll have to test this."

"How?"

"First, suppose we check the isotopic composition of the oxygen in The Goose."

Oxygen is made up of three stable isotopes, almost all of it O^{16}. O^{18} makes up only one oxygen atom out of 250.

Another blood sample. The water content was distilled off in vacuum and some of it put through a mass spectrograph. There was O^{18} there but only one oxygen atom out of 1300. Fully 80 per cent of the O^{18} we expected wasn't there.

Billings said, "That's corroborative evidence. Oxygen-18 is being used up. It is being supplied constantly in the food and water fed to The Goose, but it is still being used up. Gold-197 is being produced. Iron-56 is one intermediate and since the reaction that uses up iron-56 is faster than the one that produces it, it has no chance to reach significant concentration and isotopic analysis shows its absence."

We weren't satisfied, so we tried again. We kept The Goose on water that had been enriched with O^{18} for a week. Gold production went up almost at once. At the end of a week, it was producing 45.8 grams a day while the O^{18} content of its body water was no higher than before.

"There's no doubt about it," said Billings.

He snapped his pencil and stood up. "That Goose is a living nuclear reactor."

The Goose was obviously a mutation.

A mutation suggested radiation among other things and radiation brought up the thought of nuclear tests conducted in 1952 and 1953 several hundred miles away from the site of MacGregor's farm. (If it occurs to you that no nuclear tests have been conducted in Texas, it just shows two things; I'm not telling you everything and you don't know everything.)

I doubt that at any time in the history of the atomic era was background radiation so thoroughly analyzed and the radioactive content of the soil so rigidly sifted.

Back records were studied. It didn't matter how top-secret they were. By this time, Project Goose had the highest priority that had ever existed.

Even weather records were checked in order to follow the behavior of the winds at the time of the nuclear tests.

Two things turned up.

One: The background radiation at the farm was a bit higher than normal. Nothing that could possibly do harm, I hasten to add. There were indications, however, that at the time of the birth of The Goose, the farm had been subjected to the drifting edge of at least two fallouts. Nothing really harmful, I again hasten to add.

Second: The Goose, alone of all geese on the farm, in fact, alone of all living creatures on the farm that could be tested, including the humans, showed no radioactivity at all. Look at it this way: *everything* shows traces of radioactivity; that's what is meant by background radiation. But The Goose showed none.

Finley sent one report on December 6, 1955, which I can paraphrase as follows:

"The Goose is a most extraordinary mutation, born of a high-level radioactivity environment which at once encouraged mutations in general and which made this particular mutation a beneficial one.

"The Goose has enzyme systems capable of catalying various nuclear reactions. Whether the enzyme system consists of one enzyme or more than one is not known. Nor is anything known of the nature of the enzymes in question. Nor can any theory be yet advanced as to how an enzyme can catalyze a nuclear reaction, since these involve particular interactions with forces five orders of magnitude higher than those involved in the ordinary chemical reactions commonly catalyzed by enzymes.

"The overall nuclear change is from oxygen-18 to gold-197. The oxygen-18 is plentiful in its environment, being present in signficant amount in water and all organic foodstuffs. The gold-197 is excreted via the ovaries. One known intermediate is iron-56 and the fact that auremoglobin is formed in the process leads us to suspect that the enzyme or enzymes involved may have heme as a prothetic group.

"There has been considerable thought devoted to the value this overall nuclear change might have to the goose. The oxygen-18 does it no harm and the gold-197 is troublesome to be rid of, potentially poisonous, and a cause of its sterility. Its formation might possibly be a means of avoiding greater danger. This danger—"

But just reading it in the report, friend, makes it all seem so quiet, almost pensive.

Paté de Foie Gras

Actually, I never saw a man come closer to apoplexy and survive than Billings did when he found out about our own radioactive gold experiments which I told you about earlier—the ones in which we detected no radioactivity in the goose, so that we discarded the results as meaningless.

Many times over he asked how we could possibly consider it unimportant that we had lost radioactivity.

"You're like the cub reporter," he said, "who was sent to cover a society wedding and on returning said there was no story because the groom hadn't shown up."

"You fed The Goose radioactive gold and lost it. Not only that, you failed to detect any natural radioactivity about The Goose. Any carbon-14. Any potassium-40. And you called it failure."

We started feeding The Goose radioactive isotopes. Cautiously, at first, but before the end of January of 1956 we were shoveling it in.

The Goose remained nonradioactive.

"What it amounts to," said Billings, "is that this enzyme-catalyzed nuclear process of The Goose manages to convert any unstable isotope into a stable isotope."

"Useful," I said.

"Useful? It's a thing of beauty. It's the perfect defense against the atomic age. Listen, the conversion of oxygen-18 to gold-197 should liberate eight and a fraction positrons per oxygen atom. That means eight and a fraction gamma rays as soon as each positron combines with an electron. No gamma rays either. The Goose must be able to absorb gamma rays harmlessly."

We irradiated The Goose with gamma rays. As the level rose, The Goose developed a slight fever and we quit in panic. It was just fever, though, not radiation sickness. A day passed, the fever subsided, and The Goose was as good as new.

"Do you see what we've got?" demanded Billings.

"A scientific marvel," said Finley.

"Man, don't you see the practical applications? If we could find out the mechanism and duplicate it in the test tube, we've got a perfect method of radioactive ash disposal. The most important drawback preventing us from going ahead with a full-scale atomic economy is the headache of what to do with the radioactive isotopes manufactured in the process. Sift them through an enzyme preparation in large vats and that would be it.

"Find out the mechanism, gentlemen, and you can stop worrying about fallouts. We would find a protection against radiation sickness.

"Alter the mechanism somehow and we can have Geese excreting any element needed. How about uranium-235 eggshells?

"The mechanism! The mechanism!"

We sat there, all of us, staring at The Goose.

If only the eggs would hatch. If only we could get a tribe of nuclear-reactor Geese.

"It must have happened before," said Finley. "The legends of such Geese must have started somehow."

"Do you want to wait?" asked Billings.

If we had a gaggle of such Geese, we could begin taking a few apart. We could study its ovaries. We could prepare tissue slices and tissue homogenates.

That might not do any good. The tissue of a liver biopsy did not react with oxygen-18 under any conditions we tried.

But then we might perfuse an intact liver. We might study intact embryos, watch for one to develop the mechanism.

But with only one Goose, we could do none of that.

We don't dare kill The Goose That Lays The Golden Eggs.

The secret was in the liver of that fat Goose.

Liver of fat goose! *Pate de foie gras!* No delicacy to us!

Nevis said, thoughtfully, "We need an idea. Some radical departure. Some crucial thought."

"Saying it won't bring it," said Billings despondently.

And in a miserable attempt at a joke, I said, "We could advertise in the newspapers," and that gave *me* an idea.

"Science fiction!" I said.

"What?" said Finley.

"Look, science-fiction magazines print gag articles. The readers consider it fun. They're interested." I told them about the thiotimoline articles Asimov wrote and which I had once read.

The atmosphere was cold with disapproval.

"We won't even be breaking security regulations," I said, "because no one will believe it." I told them about the time in 1944 when Cleve Cartmill wrote a story describing the atom bomb one year early and the F.B.I. kept its temper.

"And science-fiction readers have ideas. Don't underrate them. Even if they think it's a gag article, they'll send their notions in to the editor. And since we have no ideas of our own; since we're up a dead-end street, what can we lose?"

They still didn't buy it.

So I said, "And you know— The Goose won't live forever."

That did it, somehow.

We had to convince Washington; then I got in touch with John Campbell and he got in touch with Asimov.

Now the article is done. I've read it, I approve, and I urge you all not to believe it. Please don't.

Only—

Any ideas? ■

PEEK! I SEE YOU
by Poul Anderson

Illustration by John Sanchez.
Copyright © 1968 by The Conde Nast Publications, Inc.

The father of Sean F. X. Lindquist was an amiable, easygoing Boston Swede. His mother was, as might be guessed, an O'Kelly with a will of her own. Their genes combined to produce a son who was good-natured, a bit raffish, intelligent, disinclined to toil—but, on occasion, stubborn as Lucifer. And thereby hangs a tale.

Being expelled from college, for reasons having less to do with his grades than the president's daughter, he was drafted. Presently he was shipped to Asia. Though the general truce there had now lasted for several years, it was chronically unstable and everyone concerned maintained large forces close to hand. In due course, however, and with a certain feeling of mutual relief, the Army gave Lindquist his honorable discharge. He was enchanted with Bangkok, where he had been spending his leaves, and pulled wires to be demobbed in that city.

The enchantment wore off—she married someone else—and he made a leisurely way home around the world. Whenever his funds ran out, he did odd jobs. Some were very odd indeed. He was twenty-six before he reached the States again, and long out of touch. So he might have caught up on newspapers and technical journals; but he went instead to Las Vegas and updated himself in other fields. A true cliché calls luck a lady, apt to smile most upon men who do not pursue her. Lindquist departed with several thousand dollars in his pocket.

At this time the southwestern tourist boom was entering the steep part of its exponential curve. Lindquist remembered boyhood camping trips in the area. It occurred to him that he could make a pleasant living, and have his winters free, by starting an airferry service. The Four Corners country is famous for the grandeur and solitude of its uplands. But the time, effort, and expense of packing into those roadless mountains discouraged most potential visitors. Now if they and their gear could be flown in, and out again at an agreed-on time—if the pilot was available by radio in the meanwhile, to handle emergencies like lost can openers . . .

He took lessons and got his license. Then he bought himself a used VTOL aircraft and went to scout the territory.

Thus it was that he saw the spaceship.

He was droning leisurely along at about twelve thousand feet. The peaks were not extremely far below him. Their landscape was awesome; vast, steep, ragged, a ruddiness slashed by mineral ochers and blues, a starkness little relieved by scattered mesquite, greasewood, and sagebrush. Here and there, a streamlet turned the bottom of a canyon green. But mostly this was desert land, people-empty land, hawk, buzzard, jackrabbit, and coyote land. The sun was westering in a deep, almost purple sky. Updrafts boomed briefly and trickily, shaking the plane in its course.

Lindquist's lean, sandy-haired, shabby-clad form sat relaxed. He puffed a corncob pipe and hummed a bawdy song. But alertness was in him. Before he tried carrying passengers, he must get familiar with this kind of flying. And he needed a place to roost for the night, preferably containing water and firewood. His eyes roved.

The vision slanted down before him. It moved at incredible speed, banked at impossible angles. Yet its passage was so silent that his own motor, his very pulse hammered at him. The shape, as nearly as he could tell, was roughly like a disk thickened in the middle. But the lambent, shifting colors that played across it, enveloped it in aurora, made such things hard to gauge.

It swung around, slid near, and his magnetic compass went crazy. For a moment he stared at what seemed to be a row of ports, glowing as if furnaces burned behind them. Far in the back of his mind, a reckoner clicked: *Diameter something like a hundred feet*. Otherwise he felt sandbagged.

The thing spun off. He grew aware that the pipe had dropped from his jaws. No matter. His hands were a-dance across the radar controls. He locked on. Reflection, yes! His compass steadied again. The vision dwindled . . . a mile away, two miles, three, shrinking to a rainbow dot, like the diffraction dots you see when you look sunward through your lashes . . . vanishing to nothing against mountain flanks and canyon shadows.

But it was real. Not just his rocking mind said so. His instruments did.

Other memories from boyhood and youth boiled up. "Judas priest," he whispered. "That's a sho-nuff flying saucer."

He opened the throttle. His plane leaped forward, roaring and shivering with power. He hadn't a chance of overhauling in a flat-out chase. But the thing did seem to be on a long downward track. Could he but stay within range, would it but land—

"Well, what then, bimbo?" he challenged himself.

He didn't know. But he relived vividly the arguments that had once fascinated him. The radicals had insisted that flying saucers were ships from outer space, operated by benevolent though green little men. The conservatives denied that anyone had ever seen anything. In this hour he, S. F. X. Lindquist, had been handed a chance to investigate personally. He had nothing to lose, and perhaps—if he could solve the mystery—a great deal to gain. Like fame and money.

Though no intellectual, he followed the news around him. Had he not spent the past several years in out-of-the-way places, he would have known that pursuit was a waste of time, that the riddle had, in fact, already been answered. But no one had mentioned this to him. Quite simply and naïvely, he lined out after the vision.

In the different cultures of the galaxy, Dorek's Law is known by many different names. Some call it Shepalour's Rule, some the Basic Law of Thermodynamics, some the Principle of Most Effort, and so on for millions of languages. But the formulation is invariant, because we all inhabit the same universe.

"Everything that can go wrong, will."

On their present voyage, the partners in the hypership had seen it in full glorious operation. There is no need to detail their woes with rickety hull, asthmatic engines, and senile computer. Nor need one describe what cargoes they carried, with what infinite trouble, from planet to planet. A tramp has to take anything she can get, and this is apt to be stuff too weird for the sleek cargo liners.

But they did think their fortunes had turned when they reached Zandar. A message from the brokers lay waiting for them. After discharging their load of sandorads—and, hopefully, getting most of the mercaptan odor out of the vessel—they were to pick up some machine tools for New Ystanikkinikkitantuvo. Plain machine tools, harmless crated metal! Of course, the destination was far out on the Rim. So much the better, though. It would be a peaceful haul, with lovely pay accumulating; and then, having been gone as long as they'd signed for, they would head home, loaded or not; and the fleshpots of the Core had better be filled in advance for them.

But a summons came from the port coordinator.

Pazilliwheep Finnison went along to the office. The coordinator was not of any species he recognized, possessing three eyes and a good many tentacles. They studied each other for a few seconds.

The spacefarer was from Ensikt. He was a diopt himself, though the eyes were quite large and dark, contrasting with blue stripes upon glabrous orange skin. (The air being thicker, wetter, and hotter than he was used to, he went nude except for a musette bag.) His body was slender, centauroid, with a gracefully waving tail. He breathed through rows of gill-like organs on either side of his long neck, which alternated with aural tympani. Albeit he thus had no nose, he did sport a muscular trunk above his mouth. It split into two arms that ended in boneless four-fingered hands. This was entirely practical on Ensikt, where gravity is comparatively weak and animals comparatively small. Pazilliwheep stood three feet high at the rump.

"Ah . . . Navigator Pilot Finnison, H/S *Grumdel Castle* . . . yes, yes. Welcome," said the coordinator in Interlingo-5 with a flatulent accent. He punched a button on his data screen and regarded what appeared. "Yes. Correct what I was informed. You are clearing for . . . yes, that part of the Rim . . . with a stopover at . . . what is the name of the planet?"

Pazilliwheep automatically jerked his tail, then said in haste: "My gesture indicated indifference."

"Were you afraid it might be objectionable in my culture? No, we have no tails. Now about this . . . yes . . . confounded planet. Never heard of it till the other day. Catalogued as— But what's the name?"

"Tierra, Earth, Mir, Jorden, die Erde, et cetera, et cetera." Pazilliwheep's vocal apparatus formed the sounds rather well, except for a lack of nasal quality. "Hundreds of autocthonous words. Most of them translate as 'Dirt.' "

"So. Yes. I see." The coordinator had kept one eye on the unrolling data. "Primitive world. What do you call it?"

"Restocking Station 143."

The coordinator waved a tentacle in the air. "I indicate assent and understanding. Well, Navigator Pilot, this is quite fortunate. Yes, fortunate. You came at, shall we say, the strategic moment. You are, therefore, able to be of material assistance to the Galactic Federation. Intergovernmental Department of Planetary Development, Bureau of Supervisions, to be exact."

Oh, oh! thought Pazilliwheep, and braced himself for bad news. But it was worse than he feared:

"Yes, you can, and, therefore, you . . . are herewith instructed to . . . furnish transportation and every necessary assistance . . . to the sector inspector."

"No!" Pazilliwheep cried. His four hooves clattered on the floor when he sprang backward. "Not the sector inspector!"

"Yes. The sector inspector. New one, you know. Anxious to make a good showing in . . . this latest assignment. Came here to check local records. Found no official investigation of that particular planet had been made for a long time. Yes, much overdue. Entire intelligent species being neglected. Perhaps, even, slyly exploited by the less scrupulous. Eh?"

"Exploited, my lowest left operculum!" Pazilliwheep protested. "What the entropy would there *be* to exploit? Besides, their principal culture belongs to the Federation. If they have any complaints, they can go through regular channels, can't they? And say, why doesn't the inspector go in his own ship?"

Remorselessly, the coordinator answered: "Economy drive at GHQ. Inspectors for outlying regions do not, shall we say, rate their own vessels any longer. They use available transporation. Yes, I know, they're always behindhand anyway. Too many planets. And a sector like this—not even important enough for records on it to clutter central data banks on any Core world—do you see?"

"But . . . listen, the *Grumdel*'s an old wreck. We've got the stingiest owners in the galaxy. My engineer's trying to repair a fusion tube right now. The interior maintenance units keep breaking down, too. Our top hyperspeed is a hypercrawl. Anything would be better!"

"No doubt. No doubt. But nothing else available. Not soon. Every other vessel due here within the next several weeks is a liner or else on time charter. Or, of course, not crewed by oxygen breathers. You may be old, Navigator Pilot Finnison; you may be rusty; you may be underpowered, vermin-infested, and all but certifiably unspaceworthy; but you are the best I can do for the sector inspector. And, yes, my own career—promotion off this dreary mudball—his reports to GHQ—you understand. Yes. You are hereby commandeered." And the coordinator handed over the official orders with a flourish.

Thus Hypership *Grumdel Castle* departed Zandar with a third being aboard.

The inspector was a good fellow at heart: young, inclined to take himself and his work overly seriously, but well intentioned. He apologized for the trouble he was causing, and reminded his hosts that their owners would be compensated according to law. His hosts showed no great enthusiasm at this. He explained that a major reason for his having picked their ship was that she was already scheduled to lay over on 143— "And might I inquire, out of a wish to become more intimately acquainted with my companions as well as for the technical information itself, not to mention simple curiosity, what activities you have planned on this planet?"

He used Interlingo-12 rather than any language of his own world, Ittatik. Unfortunately, Pazilliwheep did not speak Interlingo-12. Engineer Supercargo Urgo the Red did, more or less, and translated into his version of Interlingo-7.

"He says what're we gonna do there?"

"Well, no reason not to tell him the truth," Pazilliwheep replied. "Unless you've got some other little racket you haven't told me about."

"When we touch maybe once in three years? Don't make me laugh. It hurts."

In point of fact, Pazilliwheep had a racket of his own. It was a mild one, and might even be legal, for all he knew. He swapped small quantities of ondon oil, which had turned out to have powerful aphrodisiac effects on the natives of 143, for kitchenware. The latter was unusual and artistic enough to command good prices on several more advanced worlds. This was one reason he did his restocking on 143 whenever possible.

"Let's answer his question by reciting common, elementary knowledge," he suggested to Urgo. "Might put him to sleep, at least."

"Is any knowledge common?" wondered the engineer supercargo. "Like, it's a big galaxy. I never heard o' whatzisname's muckin' civilization till now. And still he says it fills a whole muckin' star cluster! Maybe he don't know how we operate in this spiral arm."

"Oh, I suppose the basic procedures are similar everywhere. If nothing else, in the course of ten thousand years or however long it's been around, wouldn't the Federation have had some leveling influence on the member species?" Pazilliwheep tail-shrugged. "We haven't anything better to do. Suppose you translate as I talk." He filled his lungs and began:

"It's a long way between stars in this thin outer part of the galaxy. And it's even longer between up-to-date systems that are normal ports of call. So ships are apt to need fresh supplies en route. Maybe the deuterium runs low, or the protein, or—lots of things. Or else, because no ship has perfect biochemical balance, it's necessary to stop on a homelike world and flush out accumulated by-products with fresh air. Planets suitable for the various types of space-going life-forms are listed in the 'Pilot's Data Bank and Ephemerides' for each region."

"He says we gotta tank up," Urgo told the inspector.

Klak't'klak of Ittatik nodded, signifying assent in the same way as most 143an cultures. The head he used for this purpose also resembled the 143an, and those of both his shipmates, in that it had two eyes and a mouth. However, mouth and nostrils were set in a beak that brought the narrow skull to a point. A fleshy aileron grew from the top, counterpart to the rudderlike fluke at the end of a thin tail. The body in between had, like Pazilliwheep's, evolved from a hexapod. But on Ittatik the rear limbs had become legs terminating in claws to grasp branches; the middle limbs had become skinny arms with six-digited hands; the forelimbs were now leathery wings. A keelbone jutted from the deep-chested torso. When he stood erect, Klak't'klak's nude gray-skinned frame was of slightly less stature than Pazilliwheep's; but his wingspan was easily twelve feet. Nonetheless, he could not fly here. The ship's G-field was set lower than his home gravity, but the air was so much thinner that he couldn't stay healthy without artificial help. This took the form of a pomander which he kept lifting to this face. The oxygen-generating biochemicals within smelled like rich swamp ooze.

"The requirement is understood," he said, "and obviously biological maintenance problems alone suffice to compel your descent into the planetary atmosphere. The point, however, which it was desired to make, is that a primary reason for the selection of this vessel as my transport was that you were, indeed, planning to restock on the world in question. Furthermore, your cargo is not perishable nor urgently required by the consignee. Thus the sum total of inconvenience and delay is minimized. Admittedly, I may be the cause of your remaining for more than the few 37.538-hour periods you presumably reckoned with. But if all appears to be in order, if there is no clear need at this point in time for further investigation of the possibility that ameliorative action may be required somewhere upon the globe, then we should be able to proceed within two or three months. I will not insist upon being returned to Zandar, but will rather continue with you to the Rim, where I shall debark in order to instigate a study of conditions prevailing upon that frontier."

"Oh," said Urgo. To Pazilliwheep: "He says we'll be stuck there for at least two or three months."

"Oh!" said the navigator pilot, rather more pungently. "Will you ask his unblessed bureaucratship why the inferno he wants to excrete away so loving much time on one unseemly little ball of fertilizer?" Likewise rather more pungently.

"No fair," grumbled Urgo. "I can't talk to him like that."

Klak't'klak explained. He wasn't really much interested in 143. His primary mission was to make sure that things were going well on the civilized planets of the Rim, and recommend remedies to the Federation authorities for whatever he found amiss. Still, 143 was overdue for inspection—seeing that it housed one nation that belonged to the great confraternity.

Such membership confers certain privileges. They are not many, because a galactic-scale league is necessarily a loose one, little more than a set of agencies serving the common interests of wildly diverse cultures. But a member is entitled to some things; for example, technical assistance if it wishes to modernize in any way.

"No," said Pazilliwheep, "our friends on 143 aren't what you would call the go-getter type. They're content to sell us their services, use of landing space, a few kinds of goods. Mainly they take biologicals in exchange—you know, longevity pills and, uh, other medicines. Ask them yourself if you doubt my word."

"I do not, of course," Klak't'klak answered through Urgo. "But I gather the planet holds numerous cultures. Perhaps they are being treated unfairly. Might they not, for example, be worthy of Federation membership too?"

"Chaos, no!" Pazilliwheep paused. "Well, I suppose they're no worse than some I could name. But no better, either. We do make spot checks, we traders, in the hope of finding new potential markets. But the majority of 143ans haven't shown an improvement in the better than two centuries that the blob's been visited. They've got a drab, fragmented, quarrelsome, early-mechanical kind of civilization. Last time I was there, we noticed traces of manned landings on the single moon. That indicates the stage they're at. If they learned the Federation exists—"

"They would have to be admitted to membership if they asked."

"Exactly! And can you imagine the results? Those dismal characters would yell for so much technical assistance that their whole planet would be one gigantic college for the next fifty years. Sector taxes would go up ten percent, I'll bet, to finance it. We'd have to stop using our base, probably, because of their confounded nationalistic regulations about passports and I don't know what other nonsense. And there isn't as handy a planet for us within a hundred light-years." Pazilliwheep gestured violently. "And all this sacrifice on our part for what? To add one more lousy space-traveling species—competing right in our trade lanes to the Rim!"

"You are satisfied with the status quo, then?"

"Right. The 143ans who do know about us and do have membership are friendly, dignified, unaggressive, mind-their-own-business people who'll work for us when we need help at an honest wage for honest labor, and who produce salable handicrafts. Do you wonder that we hide our existence from everyone else?"

"No. Frankly, I cannot help suspecting you underpay your native help; that is what 'honest wage for honest labor' usually means. But I am more concerned with ascertaining whether the planet has other civilizations that would, on balance, prove an asset to the Federation. Rather than read the sporadic reports of untrained and biased observers, I want to investigate and decide for myself."

Even through Urgo's translation, Pazilliwheep noted how Klak't'klak had dropped his elegant periods for shorter sentences in a sharper tone. The navigator pilot sighed and resigned his soul. All right, he'd be hung up for a while on 143, chauffeuring the sector inspector around, assisting with instruments, catching natives for interviews. (This was done in such wise that, after they were released, no one believed their story. Experience had shown that the best ploy on 143 was the Benign Observers of Elder Race.) He and Urgo would be at once busy and bored.

Yet . . . eventually they'd start drawing overtime pay. And the mission on 143 wouldn't likely be prolonged. If nothing else, *Grumdel Castle* was uncomfortable. Her cramped cabins, vibrating decks, rusty metal, chipped plastic, wheezy ventilators, and uninspired galley saw to that. In addition, she carried so few books and tapes suitable for Klak't'klak that he would have them memorized in weeks. Pazilliwheep and Urgo always laid in recreational materials before a voyage. But what use to an Ittatikan were Ensiktan murder mysteries and Bontuan pornography?

And so *Grumdel Castle* creaked and groaned the long dark way to the Solar System. She took up orbit around the third planet while Pazilliwheep checked for indications of excessive radioactivity, smog, and other hazards of an early-mechanical culture. Meanwhile Urgo the Red went outside to install camouflage tubes on the hull.

His shipmates saw his fur as bright blue; but then, they didn't use a visual spectrum identical with the Bontuan. The engineer supercargo was a tailless biped, eight feet tall and broad to match. His head was round, short-muzzled, big-eyed, fuzzy, and rather endearing. His hands were five-fingered, his feet four-toed. In spite of his hirsute skin, he affected white coveralls, sandals, and an ornate belt.

He clumped in again and shed his spacesuit. "Guess they'll hang together a while," he reported, "but if the owners don't spring for a new set when we get home, I'm gonna look for another berth. How's the planet doin'?"

"About as before. I note more air traffic each time, though, damn it," Pazilliwheep said. "Also, today, what appears to be a manned orbital satellite. We'll have to wait here till the stupid thing's on the opposite side of the globe."

Klak't'klak inquired why they lingered. Urgo explained. *Grumdel Castle* used a camouflage standard on worlds of this atmospheric type, where it was desired to fly unbeknownst. The natives could not detect an operating hyperdrive; if they had that capability, they'd soon be making their own star ships! And antiradiation screens served to control air molecules as well as atomic particles, making even the fastest travel soundless. But you were still stuck with the fact that your ship was a solid, visible, radar-reflecting object.

So you wrapped her in the gaudiest ionized gas-discharge effect you could generate. You added powerful magnetic and electrostatic fields, and varied them randomly. You sailed in, alerting every eye and every instrument for a hundred miles around—

Just like a natural traveling plasmoid.

But since those erratic masses of molecules and electrons occur in atmosphere, and the ship was in space, she must first sneak down.

Presently she did. Near her destination, she spied a native aircraft. At Klak't'klak's request, she veered close so he could get a good look. Then she headed off for the home of that 143an people who, during the past two hundred years, had been members in good standing of the Galactic Federation.

On the assumption that the flying saucer would continue in a straight line, Sean Lindquist zigzagged along the same general path. After half an hour he was rewarded. He crossed above an immense red ridge. Its farther slope tumbled into a canyon whose bottom was the most vivid green he'd spied in a long while. Squarish adobe buildings were stacked against one rock wall, overlooking a stream lined with trees. But what made his pulses jump afresh was the object that lay before the houses. The dazzling, confusing play of colors was gone; the shape had definite outlines and a dark gray hue; but it was surely the thing that had buzzed him. And by all the saints and any heathen gods who cared to join in—it *was* a vessel!

He tilted his airplane's wings, crammed on power, and whipped back the way he had come. A thermal nearly tossed him from control. But he must get out of sight before he was observed and —

And what? Some kind of ray gun shot him down? He ran his tongue across lips gone sandpapery. The ship had to be from outer space: real outer space, the unimaginable abysses that held the stars. He'd followed the progress of flybys and landings within the solar system. Hence he knew that, while the saucerians might be little and emerald-colored, they were not from any neighborhood planet. He also knew enough aerodynamics to be sure no terrestrial organization was experimenting with stuff that advanced. Even if he had been ignorant of the engineering requirements, he was learned in the ways of public relations offices . . . "Stop maundering, will you?" he croaked.

What to do?

He kept the plane wobbling back and forth on the far side of the mountain while, feverishly, he studied his charts and tried to discover where he was. Uh, yes . . . "Wuwucimti," plus the symbol for Population 0-1000 . . . evidently a pueblo, and lonely as hell, to judge from the fact that nothing led away from it except a dim mule trail . . . Numbly, like parts of a machine rather than a body, his fingers activated the radio. If he could raise, oh, Gallup or Durango or wherever . . . make his location known, so it wouldn't do the aliens any good to destroy him . . . A distant

Peek! I See You

seething filled his earphones. Whether atmospherics or They were responsible, he couldn't get through.

He got his pipe off the floor, reloaded and relit it, and fumed himself into a measure of calm. A long gulp from a bottle that lived in his sleeping bag was equally helpful. *Consider, Lindquist,* he thought. *You've stumbled on a secret to shake the world. But this is hardly our first visit from yonder. Leaving aside the mistakes, the hoaxes, and the claims of the nut cults, there always was a certain amount of saucer observation that couldn't be explained away. At least, it was easier to believe in spaceships than in some of those concatenations of coincidences that the orthodox scientists postulated! And now you've got proof that the ship hypothesis is right. Only, who's going to take your unsupported word? Supposing you could go fetch witnesses, the thing's bound to be gone when you return. You'd get classed with Adamski and his breed.*

For which same reason, you'll keep your mouth shut.

Hey! he reflected with rising eagerness. *How many people have actually met saucerians, and been disbelieved afterward? And, on that account, how many more have met them and—not wanting to be laughed at—simply kept mum?*

After all . . . what little consistent evidence there is—indicates the saucerians aren't evil. They're shy, or snobbish, or something, but I can't remember anyone ever claiming that they do any deliberate harm. So maybe, this time, I can—

Allowing himself no second thoughts, Lindquist brought the plane about. He roared back over the mountain, chose his position, tilted wings, and commenced vertical descent.

Updrafts were tricky; and this was a somewhat battered, cranky craft he had. For a while he was too occupied with controls, instruments, hiss and shudder around him, to heed much else. He did see how the saucer squatted imperturbable in the bright late sunlight. Tawny mud-brick walls, red canyon sides, deep blue sky, green meadows and cornfields, green cottonwoods and willows along the quicksilver stream, dusty sage and juniper farther back—and in the middle, a spaceship from the stars!

His landing gear touched. He cut the power. Silence hit him like a thunderclap. He unharnessed, opened the door, and sprang shakily forth. The air was thin, dry, pungent with resinous odors. Except for a breeze, tinkle of water, bleating from a pasture shared by sheep and goats, the silence continued.

It was not broken by the approaching locals. They were ordinary Pueblo types, a few hundred medium-sized dark-complexioned folk of every apparent age. Men and women both wore their hair in braids. Clothing varied, from more or less traditional breechclouts, gowns, and blankets, to levis and sports shirts. Lindquist's sharpened perceptions noted that the people were better clad, seemed more healthy and prosperous, than the average southwest Indian. And they were strangely uncordial. Not that they threatened him. But they drew up in a kind of phalanx, and stared, and said never a word. Even the littlest children sucked their thumbs in a marked manner.

Lindquist gulped. "Uh . . . hello," he said. His voice sounded very small to him. "I'm afraid I, uh, don't speak your language." They might know Spanish. *"Buenos días, mis amigos."* Trouble was, that damn near exhausted his Spanish.

A grizzled, weather-beaten man called softly, "Sikyabotoma." Lindquist said, "I beg your pardon?" but decided it was the name of a young man who stepped to the elder. They put heads together and conferred in mutters.

Lindquist gulped again, nodded, pasted on a smile, and started toward the flying saucer. At once he grew so conscious of it—so astonished, for instance, at the pitted, corroded metal of what had once been a smooth unitized shape—that the Indians faded from his mind. Colliding with them was a shock. Several had moved to intercept him.

They were embarrassed. The pueblo dwellers are among the politest beings on Earth. They smiled, in a forced way, bobbed their heads and waved their hands. They pushed gently on Lindquist's arms, as if to urge him toward their houses.

Anger flared. "No, thanks!" he snapped, and planted his heels.

The young man rescued the situation. He was among those who wore modern clothes, including the gaudiest sombrero Lindquist had ever met. He sauntered forth, tapped the newcomer on the back, and said, "Excuse me, buddy. That's not the way."

"What?" Lindquist whirled to confront him.

"Welcome to Wuwucimti Pueblo," the Indian said. "I'm Sikyabotoma. But in the Army I used the name Joe Andrews. Picked that because it's handy being near the head of the alphabet. So if you want, call me Joe. Come on inside and have a drink."

"I . . . I thought . . . you—"

"You needn't be surprised. Sure, the Hopi don't approve of liquor as a rule. But they need somebody like me, who's equipped to handle white men. Like, I interpret when we take the mules to town and stock up on things. And I did do a military hitch. So I've gotten a few outside habits. It's good bourbon."

"But . . . I mean—" Lindquist twisted his neck to goggle at what lay now behind his back. "I never imagined—"

"Yes, it is unusual," Sikyabotoma agreed cordially. He linked arms with Lindquist, who must needs come along as he ambled in the direction of the village. "We're the most isolated pueblo in the country. Not awful old. A bunch of Shoshonean-speaking Hopi moved here to get away from the Spaniards after the revolt of 1680 was put down. So we have a tradition of minding our own affairs, and we discourage visitors. Nothing rude, you understand. We just don't do anything interesting when the anthropologists come. And we got rid of the missionaries by telling the last padre who showed that we'd already been converted to hard-shell Baptists."

The other Indians trailed after at some distance. They kept their silence. "Please don't think we're hostile," Sikyabotoma urged. "We're only satisfied. We combine the old and the new as suits us best; and we do quite well for ourselves, on the whole; and everybody among us knows it. Regular contact with the outside world would upset our applecart. So we act pretty unanimously to defend our privacy. Unanimity comes natural in the Hopi culture anyhow. If you're in trouble, we'll help you, Mr., uh . . ."

"Lindquist," said Lindquist feebly.

"We'll do what we can for you. But if you dropped in out of curiosity, well, I hate to sound inhospitable, but the fact is you'd find Wuwucimti a mighty dull place.

Lively young fellow like you, huh? I'd suggest you proceed right away. And, uh, I'd take it as a favor if you don't mention this stop you made. We're not after tourist business and that's that. You savvy?"

"*Dull?*" Lindquist tore loose. He spun, flung out both arms toward the great spaceship, and shouted, "You call that dull?" so echoes rang.

"Well, not to me, of course," Sikyabotoma said. "I get my kicks. And the average pueblo dweller is staid by nature."

"Flying saucers and . . . and . . ."

Sikyabotoma regarded Lindquist narrowly. "Do you feel O.K.?" he asked.

"Sure, I feel O.K.! What about that flying saucer over there?"

Sikyabotoma squinted. "What flying saucer?"

"What do you mean? I . . . I . . . I chased it . . . to here . . . and there it sits!"

"Awa-Tsireh," called Sikyabotoma, "do you see a flying saucer?"

A middle-aged Indian looked solemnly back and shook his head. "No," he grunted. "No see fly saw-suh."

"I'll ask the others in Hopi if you want," Sikyabotoma offered. "But you know, Mr. Lindquist, when people aren't used to this thin air and sun glare, they can mistake mirage effects for some of the damndest things. I'd be careful about that if I were you. Flitting around in an airplane, a guy has to be mighty sure what's real and what's an optical illusion. Doesn't he?"

Lindquist stared for an entire minute into the broad bland face. The others moved closer, and had also begun to smile and murmur soothing words. Briefly, in his tottering mind, he wondered if he was not indeed the crazy one.

No! He sprang back and launched himself. His legs flew. Dust spurted, the footfalls slammed through his shins, and he made an end run around the tribe. Meanwhile he bawled:

"Do radars have illusions? Do compasses? By heaven . . . let me . . . at my instruments . . . and I'll show you!"

He reached the ship. Its curve swelled immense above him, casting a knife-edge shadow. He snatched a rock and pounded the metal. It boomed. A lizard ran away. The sandstone crumbled under repeated impacts. "Is that optical?" he screamed.

The Hopi had been running toward him. But once more they halted at a distance. Sikyabotoma came nearer. The young Indian stopped, regarded Lindquist, and sighed.

"O.K.," he said. "I didn't really expect it'd work. Have your way, Charlie."

He semaphored with his arms.

Lindquist stepped back from the ship, panting, sweating, trembling. The canyon brooded in a quiet immense and eternal; only the wind had voice. Then came a rusty creak.

Someone had been watching from inside, through some kind of television. And in some fashion, a part of the hull detached itself on three sides and unrolled, to make a gangway to the ground. Three creatures came forth. Lindquist saw them and strangled on an oath that was half a prayer.

Sikyabotoma took a philosophical attitude. "You ought to see what membership in the Galactic Federation has done to our kachina dolls," he remarked. "The real ones, that we don't show the anthropologists."

"This is most annoying," Klak't'klak said. He flapped his wings. They made a parchment rustle where he squatted in the sunshine, under the spaceship, confronting the bug-eyed 143an.

"Sure is," Urgo the Red agreed. "We gotta get rid of this bum. And then we gotta stay away from here for several days—prob'ly go into orbit—in case he does somehow talk somebody into comin' back with him. Right when I was hopin' to get that Number Three regulator tuned!"

"I was thinking more personally," the inspector admitted. "I am not prepared to conduct interviews. That is, my translating computer has not yet assimilated the records of this planet's dominant languages which the autochthons brought me from their . . . ah . . . what did they call it? . . . their kiva. And I hate working through interpreters."

"So don't."

"No, as long as we have captured this being, I feel my duty is to examine him for whatever information he can give. And, too, I should endeavor to allay his fears. To this poor unsophisticated semi-savage, we must resemble veritable demons. Consider how he staggered to his aircraft for that bottle of tranquilizing medication he now clutches so tightly."

Urgo waved a massive blue hand. Pazilliwheep trotted over, using his nose-tendrils in turn to summon one of the Indians. "I don't speak this barbarian's jabber," the navigator pilot explained, "but Sikyabotoma does." Urgo passed on the datum.

The galactics, including the pueblo man, formed a semicircle confronting Lindquist. The rest of the village watched aloofly. Klak't'klak lifted one gaunt arm. "Greeting to you, O native," he said in Interlingo-12. "Rest assured that you are in the grasping organs of civilized and benevolent entities who intend you no harm; who may, indeed, prove to be the promoters of a benign revolution upon your planet. Whether this eventuality materializes or not is dependent upon my official judgement as to whether a general announcement of the existence of a galaxy-wide Federation of technologically and sociologically advanced races will serve the larger good, including your own good. Hence the outcome is to a small extent dependent upon what you yourself, individually, today, choose to give me in the way of information. May I therefore initially request—request, mind you; we shall not compel you—and advise that you relate to me in circumstantial detail what I wish to be apprised of, beginning with the events which led to your untoward arrival."

"He wants to know how the bum got here," Urgo said in Interlingo-7.

"The honorable envoy of the Federation's guiding council asks what gods led hither the stranger's path," Pazilliwheep said in Hopi.

"The pterodactyl character is a kind of inspector," Sikyabotoma said in English. "He won't hurt you, but he would like to know a few things, like how come you stopped by."

Lindquist took another pull on his bottle. "I . . . I saw the flying saucer . . . and followed it," he whispered.

"Yeah, sure. Look, pal, I don't believe you can tell him a thing that I can't. But let's go through with the game and make him happy. O.K.? The other two are plain merchant sailors. Old buddies of mine; I even made a voyage with 'em once, to help establish an outplanet market for our local handicrafts. But Beak-and-Wings, he's come to find out whether the galactics ought to let the rest of Earth know about them; whether they should invite every country to join their Federation. In other words, he's one of those do-gooder types."

"You . . . don't think . . . we should join?" Lindquist got forth.

"Frankly, no." Sikyabotoma shrugged. "Not that this pueblo is selfish, or holds a deep grudge against the white man, or anything. However, you can't expect we'll fall over ourselves to do the white man a favor, can you? Especially when that'd end our own comfortable monopoly on trade and services with the galaxy. We're not ostentatious about it, and, of course, we're pretty small potatoes in the Federation . . . but you'd be surprised at some of the stuff we keep in our adobes."

Lindquist braced himself. "*I* look at the matter differently," he said. "Can I trust you to give him my side of the story?"

"Sure. I may be prejudiced, but I'm honest. Besides, he figures to study the whole planet. Don't loft your hopes, though. One dollar gets you ten that he turns thumbs down."

"How can he?" Lindquist cried.

Sikyabotoma looked closer. "I'll be damned, you're right. He has thumbs on both sides of his palms . . . oh. You mean how can he refuse the U.S.A., and the U.S.S.R., and France, and Britain, and China, and— Well, it's easy. They haven't anything unique to offer. Not in a galaxy loaded with civilizations. All that Wuwucimti has, really, is a convenient location, and people who don't swarm over every ship that lands, stealing things and asking stupid questions. You start letting in the riffraff, and first you've got to disestablish institutions like war, and then you've got to give them technical assistance, and then— Anyhow, it's a mess. That's why secrecy is preserved, you know. If you guys ever found out the truth, collectively, you'd have to be invited to join. Otherwise, the do-gooders say, your precious little egos would be so bruised that what culture you have would fall to pieces." The Hopi checked himself. "Sorry. I didn't mean to sound smug. Or malicious. It's just the way the ball bounces."

"How about my ego?" Lindquist demanded, close to tears.

Sikyabotoma patted his shoulder. "Nothing personal, Charlie," he said. "Individual humans who got interviewed in the past don't seem to've suffered harm. Look at it this way: you won't be any worse off than you were. Huh?"

"I'll tell the world!" Lindquist said furiously. "I'll call in the F.B.I., the news reporters, the—"

"For both our sakes," the Indian answered, "I wish you wouldn't. You'd only make a fool of yourself. At most, you'd bring in somebody else, and the village 'ud have to go through the same old cover-up as before. You wouldn't do that to us, would you, now? A nice guy like you?"

"No, I'll keep watch—" Lindquist snapped his mouth shut.

"Till another ship arrives, eh?" Sikyabotoma chuckled. "You'd wait a mighty long time, podner."

"Not many come?"

"Well, it varies. With thousands of shipping outfits plying these lanes, we can expect several craft per year to stop by, though we never know in advance. However, what we do know is if anybody's within twenty-thirty miles. A little gadget that detects thoughts. So you can't monitor us unbeknownst. We can warn off ships; they do radio us from orbit before landing. Chances are they'd come down anyway, but maintain camouflage. All you'd observe, or photograph, would be a colored blur like ordinary ball lightning. If worst comes to worst, a bunch of us can deal with a spy. Nothing violent, understand. We'll kind of escort him away, no more. If we have to break his camera, we'll pay him full value. You see, we're Federation members, so we live by Federation rules."

The inspector spoke words which went along the chain of interpreters. Sikyabotoma nodded and sat down on his haunches. "You might as well relax," he said. "Over here, in the shade. You're about to be interviewed."

Time passed. Shadows lengthened. The Pueblo women cooked dinner. They brought some to Lindquist. It was Hopi food, based on cornmeal tortillas, but the filling was like nothing on Earth. Quite literally so. Sikyabotoma explained that a lot of interstellar trade was in spices.

When the sun went below the mountains, stars leaped arrogantly forth. Coyotes yipped across a gigantic silence. Lindquist stared heavenward, shivering in the cold.

Sikyabotoma rose, yawning. "That's that," he said. "They'll fly you out now, to make sure you don't hang around. Any special place you'd like to go?"

"Colorado Springs?" Lindquist faltered.

"I wouldn't. NORAD headquarters, remember. If they spot your plane on their radars without any flight plan filed, they might get a little unpleasant."

"That's my problem." Lindquist could scarcely keep his tone level. He had not dared hope his precarious plan would work to this extent.

"O.K., so 'tis. Hm-m-m, I think I'll ride along. You might enjoy being shown around a genuine hypership. Something to tell your grandchildren, if you don't mind 'em thinking you're an awful liar."

The three aliens embarked. Lindquist and Sikyabotoma followed, after the village elders had bidden the former good-bye with every ritual courtesy. A larger opening gaped elsewhere in the hull; the aircraft rose on some silent, invisible beam of force; it was stowed aboard. The great ship closed herself. Soundlessly, but swathed again in rainbow haze, she lifted and swung north.

Inside, she was less impressive. In fact, she was grimy, battered, noisy, and ill-smelling. Sikyabotoma shrugged when Lindquist dared remark on it. "So what do you expect in an old tramp with cheapskate owners? Red plush toilet seats? C'mon, we better stash you in your plane. Be over Pike's Peak soon."

When Lindquist was harnessed, the Hopi stuck a hand through the open cabin door of the aircraft. His brown face was bent in a wry smile. "Shake," he offered. "I hope there aren't any hard feelings. You're a right guy. I could damn near wish Birdbrain does certify this whole planet for membership. But I know he won't. So long, Charlie, and good luck to you."

He closed the door. For a minute Lindquist sat alone, in the thrumming, coldly lit cavern of the hold. The hull opened. Stars glittered in the aperture, brilliant against crystalline black. Air puffed outward, popping his eardrums, and cold flowed inward. He started his engine. But it was the impalpable force beam that carried him forth and released him.

Town lights glittered far beneath. The spaceship hovered close, like a swirling, shifting, many-hued light-fog. She departed, gathering speed until no human-built rocket could have paced her. Night swallowed the vision.

Lindquist shuddered. His radio earphones squawked with challenge. An interceptor jet winged toward him. "Sure," he said. "I'll come down. Any place you want." Excitement torrented through him. "And then . . . take me to your leader!"

In the morning they turned him over to Lieutenant Harold Quimby. Maybe that press officer could get rid of him.

Sunlight slanted through a window, beyond which stretched the neat buildings and walked the neat personnel of a United States Air Force base. Light glowed on immaculate office furniture, on Quimby's polished insignia and practiced toothpaste smile. Lindquist grew doubly aware of how unshaven, sweaty, and haggard he was. His eyes burned; the lids felt like sandpaper.

"Cigarette?" Quimby invited. "Coffee?"

"No," Lindquist grated. "Some common sense. That's all I ask. The common sense and common decency of listening to me."

"Why, surely our people—"

"Yeah, they grilled me. For most of the night. Oh, polite enough. But they kept after me and after me."

"Well, you must realize, Mr. Lindquist, when you suddenly appear over a sensitive area like this, you must expect that men charged with the national defense will ask for details."

"Damn it, I *gave* them details! Every last stinking detail I could dredge up. Look, the fact that I did appear, without your fool radars registering me till I was there . . . doesn't that mean anything?"

"It means that the plasmoid blanketed your approach. Not unknown. An unusually fine plasmoid, wasn't it?" Quimby leaned forward with a sympathetic air. "I can easily understand why you would follow such a beautiful and fascinating object. And, ah, how the interplay of colors . . . hypnotic, even epileptogenic effects . . . mistaking a vivid dream for reality— No, wait!" He lifted his hand. "The Air Force is not calling you a lunatic, Mr. Lindquist. What happened to you could happen to anyone. I talked with Major Williams of our psychiatric division before my appointment with you today. He assured me that illusion and confusion are the normal result of lengthy exposure to certain optical phenomena. We lodged you overnight precisely so that our intelligence officers could make a few phone calls, checking on your background and recent activities. I assure you, Mr. Lindquist, we are careful here. We have established that you are sane and well-intentioned. We appreciate the patriotism that led you to seek us out, even in your, ah, slightly delirious condition. You are free to go home, Mr. Lindquist, with the warmest thanks of the United States Air Force." Quimby paused for breath.

"But you saw the spaceship yourselves!" Lindquist groaned. "You radared the thing. You recorded electric and magnetic effects. Your technical man admitted as much to me. How can you call it an illusion?"

"We don't, sir, we don't," Quimby beamed. "It was absolutely real. The Air Force is not dogmatic; also the Air Force has been interested in this subject for many years. When the first so-called 'flying saucer' reports were made in the 1940s, the Air Force mounted its own official investigation. Here"—he handed Lindquist a glossy-paper pamphlet off a stack on his desk—"a brief summary of Project Blue Book. Certain people remained unsatisfied. They charged—quite wrongly, I assure you—distortion and suppression of evidence. Accordingly, to clear its good name, in the late 1960s the Air Force commissioned a new investigation by independent scientific organizations and reputable unaffiliated individuals. An unclassified project, mind you." He gave Lindquist another pamphlet. "Here is a history of that effort. It was crowned by success. Here is a summary of the technical findings. Here is a somewhat more popular account, and here is a reprint of what proved to be the key physical data, and here is a—"

Lindquist slumped. "I know," he said. "They told me last night what they believe. Ball lightning."

"Well, no, not exactly that," Quimby said. "The subject is pretty complicated. Yes, sir, pretty complicated, if I do say so myself. Flying saucer reports had many different sources. Early during the furor, it was shown that most were caused by sightings of weather balloons, or mirages, or reflections, or Venus, or any of several other things. There did remain a certain small percentage which could not be accounted for in that way. But then it was shown—about 1965 or '70, as I recall—that nature can generate plasmoids in the atmosphere. You know, traveling masses of ionized gas, held together for a few hours by a kind of self-generated magnetic bottle. Ball lightning is one kind of plasmoid. There are others. Including the kind that sines, produces erratic magnetic and electric fields, reflects radar, shuttles about at incredible speed but with never a sound, and is roughly disk-shaped. In short, the classical flying saucer apparition. This was *proven,* Mr. Lindquist. It was observed, analyzed, and reproduced in the laboratory. By now, any good electrophysicist who wanted to take the trouble could fake his own flying saucer. Here, take this account by the Nobel Prize winner Dr.—"

"Never mind," Lindquist mumbled. "I don't doubt there are natural neon signs zipping around. So the saucerians don't need anything for camouflage except a false one."

"Well, Mr. Lindquist," Quimby replied, the least bit severely, "don't you believe it's high time you looked at the matter like the reasonable man you are? You had a, ah, an involuntary psychedelic experience. You would not have had it if you had known the truth. Then you would have realized there was no point in chasing that plasmoid. Nobody does any more, you know. Because of your, ah, long foreign residence, you weren't kept up to date. But the truth is that the flying-saucer hysteria vanished years ago. Once the clear light of science was thrown on this murky subject, the American people realized that everything had been due to an easily explainable natural phenomenon. They turned their attention to better topics. You won't find anyone any longer who claims that flying saucers are, ah, spaceships crewed by little green men."

"Would you believe a surly blue giant?"

"No, Mr. Lindquist, I would not. Nor, ah, pterodactyls and centaurs with arms on their noses. Least of all that a bunch of poverty-stricken, mostly illiterate Pueblo Indians are— Well, you have a very imaginative subconscious mind, sir, but I'm afraid no one cares to listen. So you had better settle for reality."

Lindquist raised eyes in which hope still struggled with exhaustion. "No one?" he asked. "Absolutely no one in the world?"

"Oh, I suppose a few cranks are left, like in California," Quimby laughed. "People to whom the outer-space-visitors idea became a sort of religion that they still can't bear to give up." His tone sharpened. "It would not be advisable to prey on their gullibility. Not that you would, Mr. Lindquist. But some confidence man who, ah, tried to squeeze a dollar from those poor deluded souls . . . yes, I think the authorities might deal rather harshly with him."

Lindquist rose. "I know when I'm licked," he said bitterly. "I won't take any more of your time."

"Well, thank you, that's appreciated." Quimby stood, too—with almost indecent haste. "We are rather busy at the moment, preparing press kits about General Robinson's promotion to four-star rank."

Lindquist ignored the proffered hand and shambled toward the door. "Too busy to bring Earth into the Galactic Federation!" he spat.

"That's not the job of the Air Force," Quimby reminded him. "Foreign relations belong to the State Department."

The bar which Lindquist found was noisy with college students. He didn't mind that. For the most part he sat hunched over his beer. When his awareness did, occasionally, return from interstellar immensities—to order more beer—he got a little encouragement from the sight of coeds passing by. A universe which had produced girls couldn't be all bad.

Contrariwise, it must be a hell of a good universe. Rich, wonderful, various, exciting, mind-expanding, soul-uplifting: if only you could get out into it.

"Rats!" Lindquist muttered around his pipestem. "Got to be *some* way to make a buck with what I know."

He wasn't entirely cynical. The galactics were, he thought. They denied to the human race every marvel, opportunity, insight, help, comfort that a millennia-old science must have to give. Not that they were monsters. With—how many suns in the galaxy? A hundred billion? They rated intelligent species at a dime a dozen, and probably this was inevitable. Indeed, it was astonishing how altruistic they were. They could have conquered Earth in an afternoon. But instead, they slunk about in disguise for fear of what the knowledge of their presence might do to men . . . if, following the revelation, they did not promptly act to lift man to their own level.

Sure, you can't blame them. Why should they solve our problems for us? Especially when it'd be a lot of trouble and expense to them. What did we ever do for the galactics?

Lindquist fumed smoke into the racketing, beer-laden air. *That's not the point,* he thought grimly. *The point as far as I'm concerned is that I and my whole ever-lovin' species will keep on being poor, ignorant, war-plagued, tyrannized, restricted, short-lived, and I don't know what else—unless the Federation can be forced to take us in.*

Which it can be, if we the people of the United States learn for sure that the Federation exists.

How? The galactics, including those Injuns, understand how to keep us blindfolded. They didn't even bother to silence me. Who'd listen?

Maybe, momentarily, the chance had existed. In 1950, or whenever the flying saucer craze started, human civilization had advanced to the point where it could imagine extraterrestrial visitors; and it had not yet gotten the idea of plasmoids, or rather, it was denying that any such thing could be. So the standard spaceship disguise had been ineffective for a decade or two. Unfortunately, though, no one had happened to catch a sitting spaceship during those years. At least, not enough people had happened to do so, and their unsupported word was insufficient. Now research had established that flying saucers could be plasmoids. Therefore, humankind concluded, they were plasmoids. As the galactics had foreseen.

Today no one would believe the crazy truth. Except maybe some pathetic remnants of the discredited saucer cults. They might. But what could they do, except invite the narrator into their mutual admiration society?

What . . . could . . . they . . . do?

Sean Lindquist leaped to his feet. His table went over, scattering beer and broken glass. His pipe fell to the floor. "Eureka!" he bellowed.

The bartender approached. "You had enough, buster," he said ominously. "Start taking off your clothes and I call a cop."

The Reverend Jaxton Muir, pastor of the First United Church of the Cosmic Brotherhood, was a surprise. Though Lindquist had done considerable research beforehand, he had expected someone more, well, far out. Reverend Muir was soft-spoken, self-contained, and conventionally dressed—for Los Angeles, at least. He lived with his wife in a apartment near the shop that earned him his daily bread. The place could have belonged to any middle-class, middle-aged couple. Only the books were unusual. They formed probably as complete a library of sauceriana as existed anywhere on Earth.

"Please sit down, Mr. Lindquist," he invited. "Would you care for some coffee? Smoke if you wish. It's bad for the health, but until the Elder Brethren see fit to raise us to the next rung of evolution's ladder, we can't much help our frailties. Pardon me. I didn't intend to preach at you. You came to tell me something, not vice versa."

Lindquist wondered what his best gambit was. From what he could learn of the C. B. Church, its few-score active members, and its influence on several hundred saucerists of other kinds, he didn't believe that he could be entirely truthful. Muir's credo held that the extraterrestrials were the benevolent, well-nigh omnipotent agents of a civilization which was the chosen instrument of God. That wouldn't fit so well with a rusty old tramp ship, pinchpenny owners, and so forth. Would it?

"I've had an Experience," he said.

"Really?" Muir's tone did not alter. "Do you know, I never have been vouchsafed one. Few who were are left alive; and the last confirmed report of a talk with Them was fifteen years ago." His gaze was quite steady. Traffic noises came through the window, to underscore his voice with muted thunder. "Hoaxes are not unheard of."

Lindquist achieved a smile. "You're skeptical, Reverend?"

"Well, let us say I'm openminded. I've often stated, in sermons and articles, that I think the Elders have abandoned us for a while because we grew too skeptical. They will come back when faith has come back. But—forgive me—there have been deliberate frauds, and there have been far more honest mistakes. For your sake as well as ours, we must sift your story carefully—whatever you tell."

"You're very tactful, sir." Lindquist's lanky frame relaxed in the armchair. As he felt his way into the situation, he gained confidence. "And I might as well confess at the outset, I want money. Furthermore, I haven't a scrap of physical evidence. Only the recent sighting over Colorado Springs, which thousands of people saw." He drew a breath. "However, if I can get financing, your auditors will keep track of every nickel. What we need is to build and transport a certain device which the Elders have described to me. For this, we'll have to buy materials and hire expensive technicians. We'll have to do a little R & D, perhaps, because the Elders didn't give me any blueprint, only a general verbal account. We'll have to do this on the QT until we're ready to roll, or you can imagine what a field day the news media will have."

Muir opened his mouth. Lindquist hurried on:

"In earnest of my sincerity, as well as to help, I can mortgage what little I own and toss several thousand dollars into the kitty. If you can double that, I believe we'll have the necessary. I checked on your people before I phoned you. They're not rich by a long shot. But between your congregation and, uh, its sympathizers—if you launch an appeal yourself—a few dollars contributed per person—the thing can be swung financially without hurting any individual except me if it fails."

He paused. "I do not guarantee success," he finished.

Muir sat quiet for a long time. His eyes never left his visitor. Finally he whispered, "You're not a con artist. You may be a crank, but you're honest. Go on, in God's name."

Lindquist saw tears. However noble his purpose, he felt a touch guilty as he gave his doctored account. The benevolent Elders had returned. They found Earth in dire straits. Disaster was imminent. Yet they could not destroy the human spirit by acting as dictators. They could only work through such persons as had faith in them.

Nor could they linger here. Other planets also needed their attention. But if enough humans had faith—if the veritable mustard seed existed upon Earth—then they could manifest themselves at last, and lead mankind to salvation. To this end, let the faithful build a communication device such as they demonstrated and explained to Sean F. X. Lindquist. In time, they would receive its message and they would come.

Did no such call reach them, they would sadly know that man was beyond redemption.

Passing through the ship's observation verandah—an elegant phrase for a crummy little cabin outfitted with an exterior visiscreen and a few seats adjustable to most species—Urgo the Red saw Klak't'klak. The sector inspector stood hunched before the view that slid beneath. The scene was of high desert, raw mineral hues under a blazing sun. His winged shape was etched in black by contrast. And yet he looked so frail, bowed, utterly tired and discouraged, that Urgo's equivalent of a heart went out to him. The engineer supercargo had grumbled at length during the past tedious weeks. Nevertheless, against his will, he had come to like the official passenger. It hurt him, now, to see the little Ittatikan stand thus alone. He went and joined him.

"You're really quittin', huh?" he asked inanely.

Klak't'klak uttered a mournful whistle. "Yes. Not that the natives have no potential. They seem about average, insofar as any such concept is meaningful. But I could not justify a recommendation that missions be sent to elevate them."

"Troublemakers. Yeh, I could'a told you that right off," Urgo rumbled.

"No. Not really." Klak't'klak spread his wings and folded them again. "They would not be a detriment to the Federation. But neither would they be an outstanding asset, as far as I can judge on the basis of my examinations. They would, in short, be . . . merely one more member species. Therefore, as long as they remain in happy ignorance of us, I cannot honestly say that the Federation taxpayer should be burdened with the cost of incorporating them. Let them invent the hyperdrive for themselves, in a thousand or two years."

Urgo belched, which out of him corresponded to a sigh of relief. "That's the spirit, Inspector! I knew you'd decide right. But how come are you lookin' so down in the chops you haven't got?"

"I don't rightly know," Klak't'klak said. "Depression, I suppose. So much time, effort, expense, inconveniencing you and Navigator Pilot Finnison—you've been extraordinarily kind, you two, and I won't forget it when I write my official report—but for nothing."

Urgo spread his mighty arms. "Ah, don't worry. The job was a drag, sure, but it's over with now. We'll stop off at the pueblo to snatch a rest and some trade goods. Then ho for the Rim!"

At that moment, the buzzer sounded. Pazilliwheep's voice followed. *"Attenta!"* He had amused himself by acquiring a few 143an phrases as *Grumdel Castle* prowled around the globe. *"Pericolo!* All hands to stations!"

"What the blazes?" Urgo was already loping for the engine room. Klak't'klak flapped and hopped toward his quarters, where he would at least be out of the way. You don't argue when someone calls emergency on a hypership. The deck gonged to the engineer supercargo's footfalls. "What's'matter?" he roared.

"I don't know," Pazilliwheep said tautly over the intercom. "Electromagnetic field . . . variable . . . registered a few seconds ago. Might be a natural plasmoid, but we'd better have a look."

Urgo felt relieved. The news could have been something nasty, like the bottom dropping out of this hull. "Where are we, anyhow?" he asked.

"About fifty miles west of Wuwucimti. Which is to say, the emanations could be from a galactic ship in distress—a little ways beyond mind-detector range from the pueblo." Pazilliwheep swung his craft through a ninety-degree turn. The acceleration compensators were so badly out of phase that Urgo slipped on the deck and hit his nose.

Nevertheless, the engineer supercargo confined his remarks to a muttered *"Snagabagabartbats!"* That was cruel country below, especially for beings who had not evolved on this planet. A vessel grounded helpless in those arid mountains and canyons might soon be crewless. And that—aside from every moral consideration—invited the disaster of discovery by non-Hopi autochthons. It was well that *Grumdel Castle* had happened by in time.

Once in the engine room, Urgo activated his own visiscreen. He saw a wild landscape, heat shimmers and dust devils . . . and, yes, a saucer shape on a small mesa. Its outlines were blurred by a weak camouflage field, and neither he nor Pazilliwheep could identify the make of ship. But with millions of different makes—

"Why aren't they transmitting?" Pazilliwheep wondered.

"Transmitter busted, I guess," Urgo said. "They could'a lain here for, cometfire, days or weeks, you know. Aimin' to land at Wuwucimti but not makin' it. Expectin' somebody else'd come by eventually, and keeping' their field goin' so's they'd be detectable at a distance."

"But not daring to strike out on foot for the pueblo," Pazilliwheep added. "Right you are. Let's get down."

Grumdel Castle descended to the mesa and cut her own camouflage and her engines. The galactics emerged into brilliant, silent, sagebrush-pungent air. Hulking Urgo, graceful Pazilliwheep, broad-winged Klak't'klak moved across the sand toward the beached hypership.

Only, now that they were close, it looked less and less like a hypership. It looked more like—

"Surprise, surprise!" caroled a native voice. Sean F. X. Lindquist's lean form sprang from the false hull. He ran to meet them, arms spread in welcome, face wide open in a silly grin. "Am I glad to see you! Two weeks waiting! And you turn out to be the very same guys who— Come on and have a cold beer!"

Klak't'klak had brought his translator machine, which was keyed to several Federation as well as 143an languages. But it was his pomander behind which he retreated. His eyes rolled. He gasped. Urgo bawled, "Oh, no!" and Pazilliwheep looked ill.

Other humans emerged. So did a television camera on a dolly. "We alerted the news services," Lindquist said happily. "Of course they thought this was a lunatic-fringe project, but they did agree to stand by, in case we came up with anything good for laughs. Smile, you're on candid camera! Now we better break the news gently to my assistants, that you aren't quite the godlike beings most of them think you are." He stopped, blushed through his stubble, and beckoned to a companion. "Pardon me. I was so excited I forgot. Here's Professor Rostovtsev from Colorado U. He speaks Hopi."

Klak't'klak had already adjusted his machine to English. He turned it off for a minute, while he expressed himself in his own tongue. Then he closed the circuit again.

"Never mind," he said resignedly. "Welcome to the Galactic Federation." ∎

THE EXHALTED

by L. Sprague de Camp

Illustration by Edd Cartier.
Copyright 1940 by Street & Smith Publications, Inc.; renewed 1967 by The Conde Nast Publications, Inc.

The storklike man with the gray goatee shuffled the twelve black billets about on the table top. "Try it again," he said.

The undergraduate sighed. "O.K., Professor Methuen." He looked apprehensively at Johnny Black, sitting across the table with one claw on the button of the stop clock. Johnny returned the look impassively through the spectacles perched on his yellowish muzzle.

"Go," said Ira Methuen.

Johnny depressed the button. The undergraduate started the second run of his wiggle-block test. The twelve billets formed a kind of three-dimensional jigsaw puzzle; when assembled they would make a cube. But the block had originally been sawn apart on wavy, irregular lines, so that the billets had to be put together just so.

The undergraduate fiddled with the billets, trying this one and that one against one he held in his hand. The clock ticked round. In four minutes he had all but one in place. This one, a corner piece, simply would not fit. The undergraduate wiggled it and pushed it. He looked at it closely and tried again. But its maladjustment remained.

The undergraduate gave up. "What's the trick?" he asked.

Methuen reversed the billet end for end. It fitted.

"Oh, heck," said the undergraduate. "I could have gotten it if it hadn't been for Johnny."

Instead of being annoyed, Johnny Black twitched his mouth in a bear's equivalent of a grin. Methuen asked the student why.

"He distracts me somehow. I know he's friendly and all that, but . . . it's this way, sort of. Here I came to Yale to get to be a psychologist. I hear all about testing animals, chimps and bears and such. And when I get here I find a bear testing *me*. It's kind of upsetting."

"That's all right," said Methuen. "Just what we wanted. We're after, not your wiggly-block score by itself, but the effect of Johnny's presence on people taking the test. We're getting Johnny's distraction factor—his ability to distract people. We're also getting the distraction factor of a lot of other things, such as various sounds and smells. I didn't tell you sooner because the knowledge might have affected your performance."

"I see. Do I still get my five bucks?"

"Of course. Good day, Kitchell. Come on, Johnny; we've just got time to make Psychobiology 100. We'll clean up the stuff later."

On the way out of Methuen's office, Johnny asked: "Hey, boss! Do you feer any effec' yet?"

"Not a bit," said Methuen. "I think my original theory was right: that the electrical resistance of the gaps between human neurons is already as low as it can be, so the Methuen injections won't have any appreciable effect on a human being. Sorry, Johnny, but I'm afraid your boss won't become any great genius as a result of trying a dose of his own medicine."

The Methuen treatment had raised Johnny's intelligence from that of a normal black bear to that of—or more exactly to the equivalent of that of—a human being. It had

The Exhalted

enabled him to carry out those spectacular coups in the Virgin Islands and the Central Park Zoo. It had also worked on a number of other animals in the said zoo, with regrettable results.

Johnny grumbled in his urso-American accent: "Stirr, I don't sink it is smart to teach a crass when you are furr of zat stuff. You never know—"

But they had arrived. The class comprised a handful of grave graduate students, on whom Johnny's distraction factor had little effect.

Ira Methuen was not a good lecturer. He put in too many uh's and er's, and tended to mumble. Besides, Psychobiology 100 was an elementary survey, and Johnny was pretty well up in the field himself. So he settled himself to a view of the Grove Street Cemetery across the street, and to melancholy reflections on the short life span of his species compared with that of men.

"Ouch!"

R. H. Wimpus, B.S., '68, jerked his backbone from its normally nonchalant arc into a quivering reflex curve. His eyes were wide with mute indignation.

Methuen was saying: "—whereupon it was discovered that the . . . uh . . . paralysis of the pes resulting from excision of the corresponding motor area of the cortex was much more lasting among the Simiidae than among the other catarrhine primates; that it was more lasting among these than among the platyrrhines—Mr. Wimpus?"

"Nothing," said Wimpus. "I'm sorry."

"And that the platyrrhines, in turn, suffered more than the lemuroids and tarsioids. When—"

"Unh!" Another graduate student jerked upright. While Methuen paused with his mouth open, a third man picked a small object off the floor and held it up.

"Really, gentlemen," said Methuen, "I thought you'd outgrown such amusements as shooting rubber bands at each other. As I was saying when—"

Wimpus gave another grunt and jerk. He glared about him. Methuen tried to get his lecture going again. But, as rubber bands from nowhere continued to sting the necks and ears of the listeners, the classroom organization visibly disintegrated like a lump of sugar in a cup of weak tea.

Johnny had put on his spectacles and was peering about the room. But he was no more successful than the others in locating the source of the bombardment.

He slid off his chair and shuffled over to the light switch. The daylight through the windows left the rear end of the classroom dark. As soon as the lights went on, the source of the elastics was obvious. A couple of the graduates pounced on a small wooden box on the shelf beside the projector.

The box gave out a faint whir, and spat rubber bands through a slit, one every few seconds. They brought it up and opened it on Methuen's lecture table. Inside was a mass of machinery apparently made of the parts of a couple of alarm clocks and a lot of hand-whittled wooden cams and things.

"My, my," said Methuen. "A most ingenious contraption, isn't it?"

The machine ran down with a click. While they were still examining it, the bell rang.

Methuen looked out the window. A September rain was coming up. Ira Methuen pulled on his topcoat and his rubbers and took his umbrella from the corner. He never wore a hat. He went out and headed down Prospect Street, Johnny padding behind.

"Hi!" said a young man, a fat young man in need of a haircut. "Got any news for us, Professor Methuen?"

"I'm afraid not, Bruce," replied Methuen. "Unless you call Ford's giant mouse news."

"What? What giant mouse?"

"Dr. Ford has produced a three-hundred-pound mouse by orthogonal mutation. He had to alter its morphological characteristics—"

"Its *what?*"

"Its shape, to you. He had to alter it to make it possible for it to live—"

"Where? Where is it?"

"Osborn Labs. If—" But Bruce Inglehart was gone up the hill toward the science buildings. Methuen continued: "With no war on, and New Haven as dead a town as it always has been, they have to come to us for news, I suppose. Come on, Johnny. Getting garrulous in my old age."

A passing dog went crazy at the sight of Johnny, snarling and yelping. Johnny ignored it. They entered Woodbridge Hall.

Dr. Wendell Cook, president of Yale University, had Methuen sent in at once. Johnny, excluded from the sanctum, went up to the president's secretary. He stood up and put his paws on her desk. He leered—you have to see a bear leer to know how it is done—and said: "How about it, kid?"

Miss Prescott, an unmistakable Boston spinster, smiled at him. "Suttinly, Johnny. Just a moment. She finshed typing a letter, opened a drawer, and took out a copy of Hecht's "Fantazius Mallare." This she gave Johnny. He curled up on the floor, adjusted his glasses, and read.

After a while he looked up, saying, "Miss Prescott, I am halfway srough zis, and I stirr don't see why zey cawr it obscene. I sink it is just dirty. Can't you get me a *rearry* dirty book?"

"Well, really, Johnny, I don't run a pornography shop, you know. Most people find that quite strong enough."

Johnny sighed. "Peopre get excited over ze funnies' sings."

Meanwhile, Methuen was closeted with Cook and Dalrymple, the prospective endower, in another of those interminable and indecisive conferences. R. Hanscom Dalrymple looked like a statue that the sculptor had never gotten around to finishing. The only expression the steel chairman ever allowed himself was a canny, secretive smile. Cook and Methuen had a feeling he was playing them on the end of a long and well-knit fish line made of U.S. Federal Reserve notes. It was not because he wasn't willing to part with the damned endowment, but because he enjoyed the sensation of power over these oh-so-educated men. And in the actual world, one doesn't lose one's temper and tell Croesus what to do with his loot. One says: "Yes, Mr. Dalrymple. My, my, that *is* a brilliant suggestion, Mr. Dalrymple! Why didn't we think of it ourselves?" Cook and Methuen were both old hands at this game. Methuen, though otherwise he considered Wendell Cook a pompous ass, admired the president's endowment-snagging ability. After all, wasn't Yale University named after a retired merchant on the basis of a gift of five hundred and sixty-two pounds twelve shillings?

"Say, Dr. Cook," said Dalrymple, "why don't you come over to the Taft and have lunch on me for a change? You, too, Professor Methuen."

The academics murmured their delight and pulled on their rubbers. On the way out Dalrymple paused to scratch Johnny behind the ears. Johnny put his book away, keeping the title on the cover out of sight, and restrained himself from snapping at the steel man's hand. Dalrymple meant well enough, but Johnny did not like people to take such liberties with his person.

So three men and a bear slopped down College Street. Cook paused now and then, ignoring the sprinkle, to make studied gestures toward one or another of the units of the great soufflé of Georgian and Collegiate Gothic architecture. He explained this and that. Dalrymple merely smiled his blank little smile.

Johnny, plodding behind, was the first to notice that passing undergraduates were pausing to stare at the president's feet. The word "feet" is meant literally. For Cook's rubbers were rapidly changing into a pair of enormous pink bare feet.

Cook himself was quite unconscious, until quite a group of undergraduates had collected. These gave forth the catarrhal snorts of men trying unsuccessfully not to laugh. By the time Cook had followed their stares and looked down, the metamorphosis was complete. That he should be startled was only natural. The feet were startling enough. His face gradually matched the feet in redness, making a cheerful note of color in the gray landscape.

R. Hanscom Dalrymple lost his reserve for once. His howls did nothing to save prexy's now-apoplectic face. Cook finally stooped and pulled off the rubbers. It transpired that the feet had been painted on the outside of the rubbers and covered over with lampblack. The rain had washed the lampblack off.

Wendell Cook resumed his walk to the Hotel Taft in gloomy silence. He held the offensive rubbers between thumb and finger as if they were something unclean and loathsome. He wondered who had done this dastardly deed. There hadn't been any undergraduates in his office for some days, but you never wanted to underestimate the ingenuity of undergraduates. He noticed that Ira Methuen was wearing rubbers of the same size and make as his own. But he put suspicion in that direction out of his mind before it had fully formed. Certainly Methuen wouldn't play practical jokes with Dalrymple around, when he'd be the head of the new Department of Biophysics when—if—Dalrymple came through with the endowment.

The next man to suspect that the Yale campus was undergoing a severe pixillation was John Dugan, the tall thin one of the two campus cops. He was passing Christ

Church—which is so veddy high-church Episcopal that they refer to Charles I of England as St. Charles the Martyr—on his way to his lair in Phelps Tower. A still small voice spoke in his ear: "Beware, John Dugan! Your sins will find you out!"

Dugan jumped and looked around. The voice repeated its message. There was nobody within fifty feet of Dugan. Moreover, he could not think of any really serious sins he had committed lately. The only people in sight were a few undergraduates and Professor Methuen's educated black bear, trailing after his boss as usual. There was nothing for John Dugan to suspect but his own sanity.

R. Hanscom Dalrymple was a bit surprised at the grim earnestness of the professors in putting away their respective shares of the James Pierpont dinner. They were staying the eternal gnaw of hunger that afflicts those who depend on a college commissary for sustenance. Many of them suspected a conspiracy among college cooks to see that the razor edge wasn't taken off students' and instructors' intellects by over-feeding. They knew that conditions were much the same in most colleges.

Dalrymple sipped his coffee and looked at his notes. Presently Cook would get up and say a few pleasant nothings. Then he would announce Dalrymple's endowment, which was to be spent in building a Dalrymple Biophysical Laboratory and setting up a new department. Everybody would applaud and agree that biophysics had floated in the void between the domains of the departments of zoölogy, psychology, and the physiological sciences long enough. Then Dalrymple would get up and clear his throat and say—though in much more dignified language: "Shucks, fellas, it really isn't nothing."

Dr. Wendell Cook duly got up, beamed out over the ranked shirt fronts, and said his pleasant nothings. The professors exchanged nervous looks when he showed signs of going off into his favorite oration, there-is-no-conflict-between-science-and-religion. They had heard it before.

He was well launched into Version 3A of this homily, when he began to turn blue in the face. It was not the dark purplish-gray called loosely "blue" that appears on the faces of stranglees, but a bright, cheerful cobalt. Now, such a color is all very well in a painting of a ship sailing under a clear sky, or in the uniform of a movie-theater doorman. But it is distinctly out of place in the face of a college president. Or so felt the professors. They leaned this way and that, their boiled shirts bulging, popping and gaping as they did so, and whispered.

Cook frowned and continued. He was observed to sniff the air as if he smelled something. Those at the speakers' table detected a slight smell of acetone. But that seemed hardly an adequate explanation of the robin's-egg hue of their prexy's face. The color was now quite solid on the face proper. It ran up into the area where Cook's hair would have been if he had had some. His collar showed a trace of it, too.

Cook, on his part, had no idea of why the members of his audience were swaying in their seats like saplings in a gale and whispering. He thought it very rude of them. But his frowns had no effect. So presently he cut Version 3A short. He announced the endowment in concise, businesslike terms, and paused for the expected thunder of applause.

There was none. To be exact, there was a feeble patter that nobody in his right mind would call a thunder of anything.

Cook looked at R. Hanscom Dalrymple, hoping that the steel man would not be insulted. Dalrymple's face showed nothing. Cook assumed that this was part of his general reserve. The truth was that Dalrymple was too curious about the blue face to notice the lack of applause. When Cook introduced him to the audience, it took him some seconds to pull himself together.

He started rather lamely: "Gentlemen and members of the Yale faculty . . . uh . . . I mean, of course, you're *all* gentlemen . . . I am reminded of a story about the poultry farmer who got married— I mean, I'm not reminded of *that* story, but the one about the divinity student who died and went to—" Here Dalrymple caught the eye of the dean of the divinity school. He tacked again: "Maybe I'd . . . uh . . . better tell the one about the Scotchman who got lost on his way home and—"

It was not a bad story, as such things go. But it got practically no laughter. Instead, the professors began swaying, like a roomful of boiled-shirted Eastern ascetics at their prayers, and whispering again.

Dalrymple could put two and two together. He leaned over and hissed into Cook's ear: "Is there anything wrong with me?"

"Yes, your face has turned green."

"Green?"

"Bright green. Like grass. Nice young grass."

"Well, you might like to know that yours is blue."

Both men felt their faces. There was no doubt; they were masked with coatings of some sort of paint, still wet.

Dalrymple whispered: "What kind of gag is this?"

"I don't know. Better finish your speech."

Dalrymple tried. But his thoughts were scattered beyond recovery. He made a few remarks about how glad he was to be there amid the elms and ivy and traditions of old Eli, and sat down. His face looked rougher-hewn than ever. If a joke had been played on him—well, he hadn't signed any checks yet.

The lieutenant governor of the State of Connecticut was next on the list. Cook shot a question at him. He mumbled: "But if I'm going to turn a funny color when I get up—"

The question of whether his honor should speak was never satisfactorily settled. For at that moment a thing appeared on one end of the speakers' table. It was a beast the size of a St. Bernard. It looked rather the way a common bat would look if, instead of wings, it had arms with disk-shaped pads on the ends of the fingers. Its eyes were as big around as luncheon plates.

There was commotion. The speaker sitting nearest the thing fell over backward.

The lieutenant governor crossed himself. An English zoölogist put on his glasses and said: "By Jove, a spectral tarsier! But a bit large, what?"

A natural-sized tarsier would fit in your hand comfortably, and is rather cute if a bit spooky. But a tarsier the size of this one is not the kind of thing one can glance at and then go on reading the adventures of Alley Oop. It breaks one's train of thought. It disconcerts one. It may give one the screaming meemies.

This tarsier walked gravely down the twenty feet of table. The diners were too busy going away from there to observe that it upset no tumblers and kicked no ashtrays about; that it was, in fact, slightly transparent. At the other end of the table it vanished.

Johnny Black's curiosity wrestled with his better judgment. His curiosity told him that all these odd happenings had taken place in the presence of Ira Methuen. Therefore, Ira Methuen was at least a promising suspect. "So what?" said his better judgment. "He's the only man you have a real affection for. If you learned that he was the pixie in the case, you wouldn't expose him, would you? Better keep your muzzle out of this."

But in the end his curiosity won, as usual. The wonder was that his better judgment kept on trying.

He got hold of Bruce Inglehart. The young reporter had a reputation for discretion.

Johnny explained: "He gave himserf ze Messuen treatment—you know, ze spinar injection—to see what it would do to a man. Zat was a week ago. Should have worked by now. But he says it had no effec'. Maybe not. But day after ze dose, awr zese sings start happening. Very eraborate jokes. Kind a crazy scientific genius would do. If it's him, I mus' stop him before he makes rear troubre. You wirr he'p me?"

"Sure, Johnny. Shake on it."

Johnny extended his paw.

It was two nights later that Durfee Hall caught fire. Yale had been discussing the erasure of this singularly ugly and useless building for forty years. It had been vacant for some time, except for the bursar's office in the basement.

About ten o'clock an undergraduate noticed little red tongues of flame crawling up the roof. He gave the alarm at once. The New Haven fire department was not to be blamed for the fact that the fire spread as fast as if the building had been soaked in kerosene. By the time they, and about a thousand spectators, had arrived, the whole center of the building was going up with a fine roar and crackle. The assistant bursar bravely dashed into the building and reappeared with an armful of papers, which later turned out to be a pile of quite useless examination forms. The fire department squirted enough water onto the burning section to put out Mount Vesuvius. Some of them climbed ladders at the ends of the building to chop holes in the roof.

The water seemed to have no effect. So the fire department called some more apparatus, connected up more hoses, and squirted more water. The undergraduates yelled:

"Rah, rah, fire department! Rah, rah, fire! Go get 'em, department! Hold that line, fire!"

Johnny Black bumped into Bruce Inglehart, who was dodging about in the crowd with a pad and pencil, trying to get information for his New Haven *Courier*. Inglehart asked Johnny whether he knew anything.

Johnny, in his deliberate manner, said, "I know one sing. Zat is ze firs' heatress fire I have seen."

Inglehart looked at Johnny, then at the conflagration. "My gosh!" he said. "We ought to feel the radiation here, oughtn't we? Heatless fire is right. Another super-scientific joke, you suppose?"

"We can rook around," said Johnny. Turning their backs on the conflagration, they began searching among the shrubbery and railings along Elm Street.

"Woof! said Johnny. "Come here, Bruce!"

In a patch of shadow stood Professor Ira Methuen and a tripod whereon was mounted a motion-picture projector. It took Johnny a second to distinguish which was which.

Methuen seemed uneasily poised on the verge of flight. He said: "Why, hello, Johnny, why aren't you asleep? I just found this . . . uh . . . this projector—"

Johnny, thinking fast, slapped the projector with his paw. Methuen caught it as it toppled. Its whir ceased. At the same instant the fire went out, vanished utterly. The roar and crackle still came from the place where the fire had been. But there was no fire. There was not even a burned place in the roof, off which gallons of water were still pouring. The fire department looked at one another foolishly.

While Johnny's and Inglehart's pupils were still expanding in the sudden darkness, Methuen and his projector vanished. They got a glimpse of him galloping around the College Street corner, lugging the tripod. They ran after him. A few undergraduates ran after Johnny and Inglehart, being moved by the instinct that makes dogs chase automobiles.

They caught sight of Methuen, lost him, and caught sight of him again. Inglehart was not built for running, and Johnny's eyesight was an affair of limited objectives. Johnny opened up when it became evident that Methuen was heading for the old Phelps mansion, where he, Johnny, and several unmarried instructors lived. Everybody in the house had gone to see the fire. Methuen dashed in the front door three jumps ahead of Johnny and slammed it in the bear's face.

Johnny padded around in the dark with the idea of attacking a window. But while he was making up his mind, something happened to the front steps under him. They became slicker than the smoothest ice. Down the steps went Johnny, *bump-bump-bump*.

Johnny picked himself up in no pleasant mood. So this was the sort of treatment he got from the one man— But then, he reflected, if Methuen was really crazy, you couldn't blame him.

Some of the undergraduates caught up with them. These crowded toward the mansion—until their feet went out from under them as if they were wearing invisible roller skates. They tried to get up, and fell again, sliding down the slight grade of the crown of the road into heaps in the gutter. They retired on hands and knees, their clothes showing large holes.

A police car drove up and tried to stop. Apparently neither brakes nor tires would hold. It skidded about, banged against the curb once, and finally stopped down the street beyond the slippery zone. The cop—he was a fairly important cop; a captain—got out and charged the mansion.

He fell down, too. He tried to keep going on hands and knees. But every time he applied a horizontal component of force to a hand or knee, the hand or knee simply slid backward. The sight reminded Johnny of the efforts of those garter snakes to crawl on the smooth concrete floor of the Central Park Zoo monkey house.

When the police captain gave up and tried to retreat, the laws of friction came back on. But when he stood up, all his clothes below the waist, except his shoes, disintegrated into a cloud of textile fibers.

"My word!" said the English zoölogist, who had just arrived. "Just like one of those Etruscan statues, don't you know!"

The police captain bawled at Bruce Inglehart: "Hey, you, for gossakes gimme a handkerchief!"

"What's the matter: got a cold?" asked Inglehart innocently.

"No, you dope! You know what I want it for!"

Inglehart suggested that a better idea would be for the captain to use his coat as an apron. While the captain was knotting the sleeves behind his back, Inglehart and Johnny explained their version of the situation to him.

"Hm-m-m," said the captain. "We don't want nobody to get hurt, or the place to get damaged. But suppose he's got a death ray or sumpon?"

"I don't sink so," said Johnny "He has not hurt anybody. Jus' prayed jokes."

The captain thought for a few seconds of ringing up headquarters and having them send an emergency truck. But the credit for overpowering a dangerous maniac single-handed was too tempting. He said: "How'll we get into the place if he can make everything so slippery?"

They thought. Johnny said: "Can you get one of zose sings wiss a wood stick and a rubber cup on end?"

The captain frowned. Johnny made motions. Inglehart said, "Oh, you mean the plumber's friend! Sure. You wait. I'll get one. See if you can find a key to the place."

The assault on Methuen's stronghold was made on all fours. The captain, in front, jammed the end of the plumber's friend against the rise of the lowest front step. If Methuen could abolish friction, he had not discovered how to get rid of barometric pressure. The rubber cup held, and the cop pulled himself, Inglehart, and Johnny after him. By using the instrument on successive steps, they mounted them. Then the captain anchored them to the front door and pulled them up to it. He hauled himself to his feet by the door handle, and opened the door with a key borrowed from Dr. Wendell Cook.

At one window, Methuen crouched behind a thing like a surveyor's transit. He swiveled the thing toward them, and made adjustments. The captain and Inglehart, feeling their shoes grip the floor, gathered themselves to jump. But Methuen got the contraption going, and their feet went out from under them.

Johnny used his head. He was standing next to the door. He lay down, braced his hind feet against the door frame, and kicked out. His body whizzed across the frictionless floor and bowled over Methuen and his contraption.

The professor offered no more resistance. He seemed more amused than anything, despite the lump that was growing on his forehead. He said: "My, my, you fellows *are* persistent. I suppose you're going to take me off to some asylum. I thought you and you"—he indicated Inglehart and Johnny—"were friends of mine. Oh, well, it doesn't matter."

The captain growled: "What did you do to my pants?"

"Simple. My telelubricator here neutralizes the interatomic bonds on the surface of any solid on which the beam falls. So the surface, to a depth of a few molecules, is put in the condition of a supercooled liquid as long as the beam is focused on it. Since the liquid form of any compound will wet the solid form, you have perfect lubrication."

"But my pants—"

"They were held together by friction between the fibers, weren't they? And I have a lot more inventions like that. My soft-speaker and my three-dimensional projector, for instance, are—"

Inglehart interrupted: "Is that how you made that phony fire, and that whatchamacallit that scared the people at the dinner? With a three-dimensional projector?"

"Yes, of course, though, to be exact, it took two projectors at right angles, and a phonograph and amplifier to give the sound effect. It was amusing, wasn't it?"

"But," wailed Johnny, "why do you *do* zese sings? You trying to ruin your career?"

Methuen shrugged. "It doesn't matter. Nothing matters, Johnny, as you'd know if you were in my . . . uh . . . condition. And now, gentlemen, where do you want me to go? Wherever it is, I'll find something amusing there."

Dr. Wendell Cook visited Ira Methuen on the first day of his incarceration in the New Haven Hospital. In ordinary conversation Methuen seemed sane enough, and quite agreeable. He readily admitted that he had been the one responsible for the jokes. He explained: "I painted your and Dalrymple's face with a high-powered needle sprayer I invented. It's a most amusing little thing. Fits in your hand and discharges through a ring on your finger. With your thumb you can regulate the amount of acetone mixed in with the water, which in turn controls the surface tension and therefore the point at which the needle spray breaks up into droplets. I made the spray break up just before it reached your face. You were a sight, Cook, especially when you found out what was wrong with you. You looked almost as funny as the day I painted those feet on my rubbers and substituted them for yours. You react so beautifully to having your dignity pricked. You always were a pompous ass, you know."

Cook puffed out his cheeks and controlled himself. After all, the poor man was mad. These absurd outbursts about Cook's pompousness proved it. He said sadly:

"Dalrymple's leaving tomorrow night. He was most displeased about the face painting episode, and when he found that you were under observation, he told me that no useful purpose would be served by his remaining here. I'm afraid that's the end of our endowment. Unless you can pull yourself together and tell us what's happened to you and how to cure it."

Ira Methuen laughed. "Pull myself together? I am all in one piece, I assure you. And I've told you what's the matter with me, as you put it. I gave myself my own treatment. As for curing it, I wouldn't tell you how even if I knew. I wouldn't give up my present condition for anything. I at last realize that nothing really matters, including endowments. I shall be taken care of, and I will devote myself to amusing myself as I see fit."

Johnny had been haunting Cook's office all day. He waylaid the president when the latter returned from the hospital.

Cook told Johnny what had happened. He said: "He seems to be completely irresponsible. We'll have to get in touch with his son, and have a guardian appointed. And we'll have to do something about you, Johnny."

Johnny didn't relish the prospect of the "something." He knew he had no legal status other than that of a tamed wild animal. The fact that Methuen technically owned him was his only protection if somebody took a notion to shoot him during bear-hunting season. And he was not enthusiastic about Ralph Methuen. Ralph was a very average young schoolteacher without his father's scientific acumen or whimsical humor. Finding Johnny on his hands, his reaction would be to give Johnny to a zoo or something.

He put his paws on Miss Prescott's desk and asked: "Hey, good-rooking, wirr you cawr up Bruce Ingrehart at ze *Courier*?"

"Johnny," said the president's secretary, "you get fresher every day."

"Ze bad infruence of ze undergraduates. Wirr you cawr Mr. Ingrehart, beautifur?" Miss Prescott, who was not, did so.

Bruce Inglehart arrived at the Phelps mansion to find Johnny taking a shower. Johnny was also making a horrible bawling noise. *"Waaaaa!"* he howled. *"Hooooo! Yrrrrrrr! Waaaaaa!"*

"Whatcha doing?" yelled Inglehart.

"Taking a bass," replied Johnny. *"Wuuuuuuh!"*

"Are you sick?"

"No. Jus' singing in bass. People sing whire taking bass; why shouldn't I? *Yaaaaaaaaa!"*

"Well, for Pete's sake don't. It sounds like you were having your throat cut. What's the idea of three bath towels spread all over the floor?"

"I show you." Johnny came out of the shower, lay down on the bath towels, and rolled. When he was more or less dry, he scooped the towels up in his forepaws and hove them into a corner. Neatness was not one of Johnny's strong points.

He told Inglehart about the Methuen situation. "Rook here, Bruce," he said, "I sink I can fix him, but you wirr have to he'p me."

"O.K. Count me in."

Pop!

The orderly looked up from his paper. But none of the buttons showed a light. So, presumably, none of the patients wanted attention. He went back to his reading.

Pop!

It sounded a little like a breaking light bulb. The orderly sighed, put away his paper, and began prowling. As he approached the room of the mad professor, No. 14, he noticed a smell of limburger.

Pop!

There was no doubt that the noise came from No. 14. The orderly stuck his head in.

At one side of the room sat Ira Methuen. He held a contraption made of a length of glass rod and assorted wires. At the other side of the room, on the floor, lay a number of crumbs of cheese. A cockroach scuttled out of the shadows and made for the crumbs. Methuen sighted along his glass rod and pressed a button. *Pop!* A flash, and there was no more cockroach.

Methuen swung the rod toward the orderly. "Stand back, sir! I'm Buck Rogers, and this is my disintegrator!"

"Hey," said the orderly feebly. The old goof might be crazy, but after what happened to the roach— He ducked out and summoned a squad of interns.

But the interns had no trouble with Methuen. He tossed the contraption on the bed, saying: "If I thought it mattered, I'd raise a hell of a stink about cockroaches in a supposedly sanitary hospital."

One of the interns protested: "But I'm sure there aren't any here."

"What do you call that?" asked Methuen dryly, pointing at the shattered remains of one of his victims.

"It must have been attracted in from the outside by the smell of that cheese. *Phew!* Judson, clean up the floor. What *is* this, professor?" He picked up the rod and the flashlight battery attached to it.

Methuen waved a deprecating hand. "Nothing important. Just a little gadget I thought up. By applying the right e.m.f. to pure crown glass, it's possible to raise its index of refraction to a remarkable degree. The result is that light striking the glass is so slowed up that it takes weeks to pass through it in the ordinary manner. The light that is thus trapped can be released by making a small spark near the glass. So I simply lay the rod on the window sill all afternoon to soak up sunlight, a part of which is released by making a spark with that button. Thus I can shoot an hour's accumulated light-energy out the front end of the rod in a very small fraction of a second. Naturally when this beam hits an opaque object, it raises its temperature. So I've been amusing myself by luring the roaches in here and exploding them. You may have the thing; its charge is about exhausted."

The intern was stern. "That's a dangerous weapon. We can't let you play with things like that."

"Oh, can't you? Not that it matters, but I'm only staying here because I'm taken care of. I can walk out any time I like."

"No you can't, professor. You're under a temporary commitment for observation."

"That's all right, son. I still say I can walk out whenever I feel like it. I just don't care much whether I do or not." With which Methuen began tuning the radio by his bed, ignoring the interns.

Exactly twelve hours later, at 10 A.M., Ira Methuen's room in the hospital was found to be vacant. A search of the hospital failed to locate him. The only clue to his disappearance was the fact that his radio had been disemboweled. Tubes, wires and condensers lay in untidy heaps on the floor.

The New Haven police cars received instructions to look for a tall thin man with gray hair and goatee, probably armed with death rays, disintegrators, and all the other advanced weapons of fact and fiction.

For hours they scoured the city with screaming sirens. They finally located the menacing madman, sitting placidly on a park bench three blocks from the hospital and reading a newspaper. Far from resisting, he grinned at them and looked at his watch. "Three hours and forty-eight minutes. Not bad, boys, not bad, considering how carefully I hid myself."

One of the cops pounced on a bulge in Methuen's pocket. The bulge was made by another wire contraption. Methuen shrugged. "My hyperbolic solenoid. Gives you a conical magnetic field, and enables you to manipulate ferrous objects at a distance. I picked the lock of the door to the elevators with it."

When Bruce Inglehart arrived at the hospital about four, he was told Methuen was asleep. That was amended to the statement that Methuen was getting up, and could see a visitor in a few minutes. He found Methuen in a dressing gown.

Methuen said: "Hello, Bruce. They had me wrapped up in a wet sheet, like a mummy. It's swell for naps; relaxes you. I told 'em they could do it whenever they liked. I think they were annoyed about my getting out."

Inglehart was slightly embarrassed.

Methuen said: "Don't worry; I'm not mad at you. I realize that nothing matters, including resentments. And I've had a most amusing time here. Just watch them fizz the next time I escape."

"But don't you care about your future?" said Inglehart. "They'll transfer you to a padded cell at Middletown—"

Methuen waved a hand. "That doesn't bother me. I'll have fun there, too."

"But how about Johnny Black, and Dalrymple's endowment?"

"I don't give a damn what happens to them."

Here the orderly stuck his head in the door briefly to check up on this unpredictable patient. The hospital, being short-handed, was unable to keep a continuous watch on him.

The Exhalted

Methuen continued: "Not that I don't like Johnny. But when you get a real sense of proportion, like mine, you realize that humanity is nothing but a sort of skin disease on a ball of dirt, and that no effort beyond subsistence, shelter, and casual amusement is worth while. The State of Connecticut is willing to provide the first two for me, so I shall devote myself to the third. What's that you have there?"

Inglehart thought. "They're right; he's become a childishly irresponsible scientific genius." Keeping his back to the door, the reporter brought out his family heirloom, a big silver pocket flask dating back to the fabulous prohibition period. His aunt Martha had left it to him, and he himself expected to will it to a museum.

"Apricot brandy," he murmured. Johnny had tipped him off to Methuen's tastes.

"Now, Bruce, that's something sensible. Why didn't you bring it out sooner, instead of making futile appeals to my sense of duty?"

The flask was empty. Ira Methuen sprawled in his chair. Now and then he passed a hand across his forehead. He said: "I can't believe it. I can't believe that I felt that way half an hour ago. O Lord, what have I done?"

"Plenty," said Inglehart.

Methuen was not acting at all drunk. He was full of sober remorse.

"I remember everything—those inventions that popped out of my mind, everything. But I didn't care. How did you know alcohol would counteract the Methuen injection?"

"Johnny figured it out. He looked up its effects, and discovered that in massive doses it coagulates the proteins in the nerve cells. He guessed it would lower their conductivity to counteract the increased conductivity through the gaps between them that your treatment causes."

"So," said Methuen, "when I'm sober I'm drunk and when I'm drunk I'm sober. But what'll we do about the endowment—my new department and the laboratory and everything?"

"I don't know. Dalrymple's leaving tonight; he had to stay over a day on account of some trustee business. And they won't let you out for a while yet, even when they know about the alcohol counter-treatment. Better think of something quick, because the visiting period is pretty near up."

Methuen thought. He said, "I remember how all those inventions work, though I couldn't possibly invent any more of them unless I went back to the other condition." He shuddered. "There's the soft-speaker, for instance—"

"What's that?"

"It's like a loud-speaker, only it doesn't speak loudly. It throws a supersonic beam, modulated by the human voice to give the effect of audible sound-frequencies when it hits the human ear. Since you can throw a supersonic beam almost as accurately as you can throw a light beam, you can turn the soft-speaker on a person, who will then hear a still small voice in his ear apparently coming from nowhere. I tried it on Dugan one day. It worked. Could you do anything with that?"

"I don't know. Maybe."

"I hope you can. This is terrible. I thought I was perfectly sane and rational. Maybe

I was—Maybe nothing *is* important. But I don't feel that way now, and I don't want to feel that way again—"

The omnipresent ivy, of which Yale is so proud, affords splendid handholds for climbing. Bruce Inglehart, keeping an eye peeled for campus cops, swarmed up the big tower at the corner of Bingham Hill. Below, in the dark, Johnny waited.

Presently the end of a clothesline came dangling down. Johnny inserted the hook in the end of the rope ladder into the loop in the end of the line. Inglehart hauled the ladder up and secured it, wishing that he and Johnny could change bodies for a while. That climb up the ivy had scared him and winded him badly. But he could climb ivy, and Johnny couldn't.

The ladder creaked under Johnny's five hundred pounds. A few minutes later it slid slowly, jerkily up the wall, like a giant centipede. Then Inglehart, Johnny, ladder, and all were on top of the tower.

Inglehart got out the soft-speaker and trained the telescopic sight on the window of Dalrymple's room in the Taft, across the intersection of College and Chapel Streets. He found the yellow rectangle of light. He could see into about half the room. His heart skipped a few beats until a stocky figure moved into his field of vision. Dalrymple had not yet left. But he was packing a couple of suitcases.

Inglehart slipped the transmitter clip around his neck, so that the transmitter nestled against his larynx. The next time Dalrymple appeared, Inglehart focused the crosshairs on the steel man's head. He spoke: "Hanscom Dalrymple!" He saw the man stop suddenly. He repeated: "Hanscom Dalrymple!"

"Huh?" said Dalrymple. "Who the hell are you? Where the hell are you?" Inglehart could not hear him, of course, but he could guess.

Inglehart said, in solemn tones: "I am your conscience."

By now Dalrymple's agitation was evident even at that distance. Inglehart continued: "Who squeezed out all the common stockholders of Hephaestus Steel in that phony reorganization?" Pause. "You did, Hanscom Dalrymple!

"Who bribed a United States senator to swing the vote for a higher steel tariff, with fifty thousand dollars and a promise of fifty thousand more, which was never paid?" Pause. "You did, Hanscom Dalrymple!

"Who promised Wendell Cook the money for a new biophysics building, and then let his greed get the better of him and backed out on the thin excuse that the man who was to have headed the new department had had a nervous breakdown?" Pause, while Inglehart reflected that "nervous breakdown" was merely a nice way of saying "gone nuts." "You did, Hanscom Dalrymple!

"Do you know what'll happen to you if you don't atone, Dalrymple? You'll be reincarnated as a spider, and probably caught by a wasp and used as live fodder for her larvæ. How will you like that, *heh-heh?*

"What can you do to atone? Don't be a sap. Call up Cook. Tell him you've changed your mind, and are renewing your offer!" Pause. "Well, what are you waiting for? Tell him you're not only renewing it, but doubling it!" Pause. "Tell him—"

But at this point Dalrymple moved swiftly to the telephone. Inglehart said, "Ah, that's better, Dalrymple," and shut off the machine.

Johnny asked: "How did you know awr zose sings about him?"

"I got his belief in reincarnation out of his obit down at the shop. And one of our rewrite men who used to work in Washington says everybody down there knows about the other things. Only you can't print a thing like that unless you have evidence to back it up."

They lowered the rope ladder and reversed the process by which they had come up. They gathered up their stuff and started for the Phelps mansion. But as they rounded the corner of Bingham they almost ran into a familiar storklike figure. Methuen was just setting up another contraption at the corner of Welch.

"Hello," he said.

Man and bear gaped at him. Inglehart asked, "Did you escape again?"

"Uh-huh. When I sobered up and got my point of view back, it was easy, even though they'd taken my radio away. I invented a hypnotizer, using a light bulb and a rheostat made of wire from my mattress, and hypnotized the orderly into giving me his uniform and opening the doors for me. My, my, that *was* amusing."

"What are you doing now?" Inglehart became aware that Johnny's black pelt had melted off into the darkness.

"This? Oh, I dropped around home and knocked together an improved soft-speaker. This one'll work through masonry walls. I'm going to put all the undergraduates to sleep and tell 'em they're monkeys. When they wake up, it will be most amusing to see them running around on all fours and scratching and climbing the chandeliers. They're practically monkeys to begin with, so it shouldn't be difficult."

"But you can't, professor! Johnny and I just went to a lot of trouble getting Dalrymple to renew his offer. You don't want to let us down, do you?"

"What you and Johnny do doesn't matter to me in the slightest. Nothing matters. I'm going to have my fun. And don't try to interfere, Bruce." Methuen pointed another glass rod at Inglehart's middle. "You're a nice young fellow, and it would be too bad if I had to let you have three hours' accumulation of sun-ray energy all at once."

"But this afternoon you said—"

"I know what I said this afternoon. I was drunk and back in my old state of mind, full of responsibility and conscientiousness and such bunk. I'll never touch the stuff again if it has that effect on me. Only a man who has received the Methuen treatment can appreciate the futility of all human effort."

Methuen shrank back into the shadows as a couple of undergraduates passed. Then he resumed work on his contraption, using one hand and keeping Inglehart covered with the other. Inglehart, not knowing what else to do, asked him questions about the machine. Methuen responded with a string of technical jargon. Inglehart wondered desperately what to do. He was not an outstandingly brave young man, especially in the face of a gun or the equivalent. Methuen's bony hand never wavered. He made the adjustments on his machine mostly by feel.

"Now," he said, "that ought to be about right. This contains a sonic metronome that will send them a note of frequency of 349 cycles a second, with 68.4 pulses of sound a minute. This, for various technical reasons, has the maximum hypnotic effect. From here I can rake the colleges along College Street—" He made a final adjustment. "This will be the most amusing joke yet. And the cream of it is that, since Connecticut is determined to consider me insane, they can't do anything to me for it! Here goes, Bruce—*Phew*, has somebody started a still here, or what? I've been smelling and tasting alcohol for the last five minutes—*ouch!*"

The glass rod gave one dazzling flash, and then Johnny's hairy black body catapulted out of the darkness. Down went Ira Methuen, all the wind knocked out of him.

"Quick, Bruce!" barked Johnny. "Pick up zat needre spray I dropped. Unscrew ze container on ze bottom. Don't spirr it. Zen come here and pour it down his sroat!"

This was done; with Johnny holding Methuen's jaws apart with his claws, like Sampson slaying the lion, only conversely.

They waited a few minutes for the alcohol to take effect, listening for sounds that they had been discovered. But the colleges were silent save for the occasional tick of a typewriter.

Johnny explained: "I ran home and got ze needre sprayer from his room. Zen I got Webb, ze research assistant in biophysics, to ret me in a raboratory for ze arcohor. Zen I try to sneak up and squirt a spray in his mouse whire he talks. I get some in, but I don't get ze sprayer adjusted right, and ze spray hit him before it breaks up, and stings him. I don't have fingers, you know. So we have to use what ze books cawr brute force."

Methuen began to show signs of normalcy. As without his glass rod he was just a harmless old professor, Johnny let him up. His words tumbled out: "I'm so glad you did, Johnny—you saved my reputation, maybe my life. Those fatheads at the hospital wouldn't believe I had to be kept full of alcohol, so, of course, I sobered up and went crazy again. Come on: let's get back there quickly. If they haven't discovered my absence, they might be willing to keep this last escape quiet. When they let me out, I'll work on a permanent cure for the Methuen treatment. I'll find it, if I don't die of stomach ulcers from all the alcohol I'll have to drink."

Johnny waddled up Temple Street to his home, feeling rather smug. Maybe Methuen, sober, was right about the futility of it all. But if such a philosophy led to the upsetting of Johnny's pleasant existence, Johnny preferred Methuen drunk.

He was glad Methuen would soon be well and coming home. Methuen was the only man he had any sentimental regard for. But as long as Methuen was shut up, Johnny was going to take advantage of that fact. When he reached the Phelps mansion, instead of going directly in, he thrust a foreleg around behind the hedge next to the wall. It came out with a huge slab of chewing tobacco. Johnny bit off about half the slab, thrust the rest back in its cache, and went in, drooling happily. Why not? ■

GONE WITH THE GODS
by Andrew Offutt

I was gagging my way through the day's third Gothic novel, trying to get myself into perpetrating one of the damned things so some artist could perpetrate another cover with an uptight-looking young woman in the foreground and a castle or old house in the background—with a light in one window. It was one of those times when any sort of interruption was welcome, even a ringing phone.

The phone rang.

I bounced "The Castle of Malfoie" off the far wall and reached for a cigarette with my right hand. My left went after the phone. I am totally incapable of handling a

Illustration by Kelly Freas.
Copyright © 1974 by The Conde Nast Publications, Inc.

telephone without a cigarette. I try to control the nasty things, but on those days when I have to answer and place several calls, the tobacco industry gets a break. And I wake up next day with a throat like a piece of old harness leather.

"Hello, this is Harvey Moss," I said, wiping a book of matches off the desk.

"Harvey sweetheart, howsa boy?"

"Doing my damnedest to get into an Otranto mood, Mark," I said, with plenty of put-upon weariness in my voice. Mark Ventnor's voice, naturally, was one I recognized instantly. I hunched my left shoulder to hold the phone against my ear while I tore off a match and lit up.

"Otranto? Otranto?"

I sighed smokily. "The grandaddy of all Gothic novels, Mark. Very old novelette, by a gent named Walpole, may his soul sizzle sickly!"

"Oh yeah, oh yeah, *that* Otranto," Mark Ventnor said in that raspy high voice of his. Sounds like Ed McMahon doing W.C. Fields, sober. With a cold. And about to cry. "Well, forget that Gothic jazz, Harvey sweetheart. I got something I need you to do."

"Last week you needed me to do a Gothic," I reminded him. "By the first."

"That was last week. I just had a really weird phone call, Harvey. A really odd call."

"Me too," I muttered, "this one." More loudly I said, not without trepidation, "Tell me about it, Mark."

"Yeah. Listen Harve, I just had a call from an old fraternity brother of mine, Dr.—"

"Hey, I never knew you were in a fraternity," I said, reaching for the ashtray and not quite making it. If it's true that ashes are good for rugs, I should keep one on my desk instead of a blotter. The ash is always longer than it should be; the tray is always a few centimeters too far away.

"Uh yeah, yeah, I was," he said, half blown away by the interruption. "Sure I was. It was a long time ago," the cueball-headed boss of Morpheus Books added unnecessarily. "So an old fraternity brother, Dr. Ben Corrick, called me today."

"Marvy," I said, "and you want me to ghost a book about his earthshaking new diet plan, right?"

There was a brief accusing silence, heavy with hurt. Then: "Harvey, this call is costing me money. It's my nickel, remember. Things are not so good I should listen to you shoot off your mouth every time I open mine—and before I close it. I—"

"Right, Mark. Sorry."

I heard his sigh. Oh Lord. I'd done it again. I resisted apologizing for having interrupted to apologize. The silence just sort of sat there for awhile, surly.

"Ben Corrick isn't a medical doctor," Mark said in the manner of the teacher in a retarded-I-mean-exceptional class. "He has one of those PhD's. You know. In physics. Like . . . ah, you know, physics. He's stayed on at the old school all these years while I've been working my ass off up here in New York, and he's been working on an *invention*."

I curbed the automatic impulse to comment. An invention. Oh boy.

"You still reading all those hardcore science articles the way a kid reads funnybooks, Harvey?"

"Sure. What's the invention?"

"Well, see, he's had this grant, he and his department. But he's been at work on a private project for years too, see. He calls it a, ah, temporal traverser."

"A temporal traverser," I echoed, dry as the landscape around Sinai.

"Right," Mark said, with escalating excitement in his foice. "D'you think it's possible, Harvey?"

"The word 'impossible,' " I said, "won't be in Webster's Fourth. But how do I know, what's it supposed to—a *temporal traverser?"*

"Right!"

"Mark? Time travel?"

"Right! Right!" I could practically see him and his belly jiggling up and down in his excitement.

"You sure he's not putting you on, Mark?"

"I don't think so, but that's what I want to find out, Harve boy. Can you get over to Chinchilla, Pennsylvania and find out for me?"

"Can I—you sending me a plane ticket, Mark? *Chinchilla!"*

"I'll cover it, Harvey. Just try to hold it down, OK? Times are hard."

I ignored that. Mark Ventnor is a hyper, not to mention a shucker. He is also publisher, president, editor, and bigot-in-charge of Morpheus Books, which he founded. He's tried dozens of times—literally—to get a really Big Book out there, opportunistically, exploitatively jumping aboard every topical express to come down the track. It's never happened. I know; I've written most of the books for him. And so Mark sings the blues, constantly—although the old phony *does* have money. Part of the reason is he hangs onto it the way fans hoard old magazines and books. I know. I've done fifty-seven books for Mark Ventnor in the past six years, with advances ranging from an embarrassing-to-admit seven hundred and fifty dollars to a decent thirty-five hundred, using eleven pen names. Subject matter has been very broad indeed: attempt after attempt at get-rich exploitation, each about as effective as government economic plans.

Not one of those books has ever sold enough to earn me any royalties beyond the advance. Or so Mark Ventnor says, anyhow, and he's the one with the ledgers. And his mainstay, a seemingly endless stream of Gothics. They *sell*.

And now I knew we were off again.

But Mark was talking. "You know how academic-types are, Harve, Ben had a, ah, little accident. They, ah . . . he isn't with the university any more. And he—"

"A little accident?"

"Ben'll tell you all about it, Harve. Dr. Corrick. Just get over there. I've got money at stake."

So then, while I lit another cigarette, Mark Ventnor dropped the rest of it on me. There'd been a fair crowd on hand the day Dr. Ben Corrick was at last ready to demonstrate his device. He explained, re-explained, blinked, and finally closed the switch. Nothing happened. He then went across the big lab-sort-of room in which he'd constructed his . . . Thing. And he plugged it in.

Fortuitous, his being on the other side of that big room. The temporal traverser did absolutely nothing for a moment or so. Then it removed, in a manner most noisy, the better part of the south and east walls of ivied old Smoire Hall, not to mention a large assortment of glass items in the surrounding area.

The t.t. was not amid the rubble.

Shamed, castigated, attacked, called charlatan and worse, Ben Corrick, PhD, was forcibly sabbaticalized.

Now, months later, he had called his old fraternity brother. The working model of his Mark Two t.t. was nearly finished. But his bank account and savings were *totally* finished. All he needed to finish the device was another ten thousand dollars. And everybody knows publishers have lots of money.

Ventnor didn't have to tell me that he then relieved himself of a sermon on money, inflation, hungry writers, and grasping, incompetent distributors, inflation, prices, union printers, inflation . . . and so on. I'd heard it several times from Mark; it's improved signally since the advent of the recent unlamented Administration.

But somehow Ventnor succumbed. Somehow Corrick persuaded and convinced him to check out the temporal traverser, at least. And so Mark Ventnor, actually giving consideration to parting (after due tearfulness and lectures) with ten thousand clams, told Corrick to hold tight. And Mark called in Harvey Moss.

Me.

I'm a writer. It's all I do. I make a living at it and from it. There are several ways that can be done. You can write a book about a garbage-eating bird with a sixth-grade philosophy, for instance, and be rich forever because that's one grade above *Reader's Digest* readers, who are easily impressed. Or do a sort of fact novel about a couple convicted murderers, and be rich and drop names forever. Or you can write science fiction, and stay hungry. You can perpetrate Gothics for whoever it is that reads them, and know that every word you write will sell, instantly and easily.

Or you can do what I do. I make a nice comfortable living the same way the A&P does: on volume. I write a lot, and I've never been late for a contract deadline. Fifty-seven books for Ventnor in the last six years, as I said, and all on time. Dependable, that's me. Always dependable; a pussycat. And always hungry. OK, I admit it: I have the usual booze 'n' broads habit. Sure, writers get groupies; writing's almost show biz, you know. And we have to get down at the end of a day, after hyping up on ideas and coffee all day. So—broads and booze, right? It cuts into the old finances.

I've also written some decent science fiction, and I read pure science articles just as Mark said, constantly. Presumably, then, I know a few things. Certainly to a guy like Mark Ventnor, who knows *very* few.

So he called to sic me onto Corrick. To study his notes and his schematics and to look at the Thing in the garage behind his Chinchilla, Pennsylvania cottage, and to make a judgment, and to report back to Daddy Warbucks Ventnor in Manhattan. He would then decide whether to risk ten of his thousands on Corrick's alleged temporal traverser.

Flattering? I guess so; Mark trusted me and my knowledge. Also a drag. After all—a *time machine!* Didn't John Campbell prove the total impossibility of time travel?

But . . . maybe, I thought, there was a science-fiction idea in it, and that would beat having to do the damned Gothic, since I'd written only one book in the past five weeks. I was in great need of something to do a book about, and Gothics are icky, and writing pornography always makes me so damned horny!

So I journeyed to the town of Chinchilla, Pennsylvania to meet a kook named Corrick, Benjamin A., PhD, and listen to his nonsense, and tell Mark Ventnor what he should have known to do in the first place: save his ten thousand. Or give it to me as an advance to go and interview Clifford Oiving.

But that wasn't the way it turned out.

First I met Dr. Ben Corrick, who was a "call-me-Ben" sort of guy you couldn't dislike if you tried. About Ventnor's age, with hair, less weight, more wrinkles. Somehow he managed to look baggy and wrinkly and rumpled even in doubleknits—the trousers pockets stuffed so full of this and that they resembled army fatigues. Quite a bit of reddish hair, curly, above a high forehead that was obviously a lot higher than when he and Mark Ventnor had been fraternal brethren together. His blue eyes were of the sort usually called watery, set in a pleasant-enough face, almost a boy's face.

He was the sort of man you liked the moment you saw him. I had to remind myself to maintain a scientific attitude, to treat him not as a friend but as a charlatan.

But he wasn't. I studied, I pored, I re-studied and asked questions. Examined and re-examined the stuff in the garage. The temporal traverser, he called it.

And so did I, finally. I said so, to Mark Ventnor. He acted incredulous, but his delight and excitement glowed through the careful, questioning attitude like the sun through closed venetian blinds.

With Corrick practically having signed away his brithright (not to mention his burial plot, thus including his deathright as well), Mark Ventnor financed the project he dubbed *Project Fugit.* And time fled, while Ben Corrick worked away at finishing his brain-baby and while Mark Ventnor worked away at plotting, designing his Grand Scheme—to be rich and famous at last.

Me? To stay in money, I wrote "The Castle of Brandywine," gagging all the while. I had to cut the scene in which the hunchback raped the kitchen maid, too.

"The traverser," Ben Corrick told me in that strangely near-breathless way of his, "is ready for field-testing."

I blinked. "Ready? Really ready?"

He nodded, maintaining his solemnity despite the twinkle in his eyes and the smile that was trying to tug at each corner of his mouth. "It's really ready, Harve."

"And this time," I said, grinning, practically rubbing my hands together, "you're gonna do it from *inside,* hm-m-m?"

"Definitely! The other time there was the explosion, of course, and then the remote failed to work. I am convinced that the machine did work, and properly. That's why there was no sign of it amid the debris."

"Um. But suppose something goes wrong. Ben. You're a certified genius. You've got no business inside that thing before it's tested."

"It's *been* tested," Ben assured me. "It's lost somewhere, the Mark One. I mean, *somewhen.*"

"And it doesn't have to be plugged in, anymore? I mean, if you want to go back and have a talk with Ben Franklin, you're going to play hell finding a wallplug!"

"Of course. And now we hire a truck and take the temporal traverser, Mark Two, out for its field-test."

"Out?" I gave him a brows-up look. "Out? What do you mean? Out where?"

Ben Corrick smiled his boyish smile and made an uncharacteristically extravagant gesture. "Out into the open. Into a *field,* where else?" His watery eyes studied me, waiting anxiously for my reaction.

I saw that, and then I saw his joke. *"Field*-testing! In a field!"

"Of course."

So we got the truck, a big flatbed. And we got a couple of guys to help us load the t.t., although they were sure we were cracked wide open. We didn't tell them what it was. As a matter of fact we told them it was a kloosh; ever heard that old joke?

Then we drove the temporal traverser out into the country, off the highway onto a back road, and off the back road into a field, scaring the beak off a matronly bobwhite. The field was full of timothy that rose about halfway up my calves.

I was still frowning, having doubts, prickly in the armpits, when Ben entered the temporal traverser and buttoned up.

The t.t. Well, Ben had a real brainstorm this time, so as not to be too obtrusive when he materialized in the distant past or future. Very clever of him, really—and besides, he needed a power-source at hand. So he had built the temporal traverser into a yellow VW squareback station wagon. Lots of space in those things. It could even be driven.

But he wasn't driving it now. I waited, standing well back. Holding my breath, having palpitations. Staring at that yellow car atop the big red flatbed truck he'd insisted on, just in case the VW couldn't be driven back. Happy thought! He was certain, he said, that the t.t. would move from surface to surface, not materialize elsewhere some five feet off the ground and drop with one hell of an impact. I hoped he was right. What if he came down on a cow, I thought, and started to yell, and—

The explosion knocked me off my feet. It was the shock more than the shock *waves,* I feel sure. But it *was* a shock, and physical force or not it was just as effective as had it been shock wave. I went down, and now my heart wasn't palpitating, it was pounding. Once I got myself sort of untangled and looked, there was the truck. It appeared to be OK.

But there wasn't any VW on it.

"Well I'll be damned," I muttered. "He must have done it. He must be traveling in time. Darn . . . I didn't even think to ask where he was going. I mean when."

I glanced at my watch. During that glance, the VW reappeared. I stood frozen until he stepped out, beaming.

I blurted, "Are you all right?"

Sorry. It was the first thing I thought of. I realized I could have said something brilliant, such as "Mr. Watson, come here, I need you." I just hadn't thought about it in advance, as Neil Armstrong so obviously had. Or as Ben Corrick had done:

"One small step for mankind," Ben Corrick said, "one giant step for science." Then, "Of course I'm all right. I only went to tomorrow. Look at this."

"Oh brother," I said, commenting on his first words, not on what he showed me, although it was worth no fancier comment. I fornwed at it. "A button?"

Corrick nodded vigorously. "A button. Look familiar?"

No, but he soon showed me that it appeared to match those on my jacket. That didn't seem to prove anything, and I said so.

Ben blinked. "It proves that I went into the future," he said, dipping a hand into one stuffed pocket of his ever-baggy pants, "and brought you back this button from your coat. It was lying right there on the ground."

I checked. "Ben—I think we ought to be dancing, screaming, getting drunk, whatever. Instead we're standing here talking about a damn button—and there aren't any buttons missing from my jacket!"

"Of course there is, Harvey," Ben said, opening the knife he'd brought out of his pocket, and he cut the lowest button off the front of my coat.

"Hey!"

Smiling, Ben dropped the button into the grass. "I'm putting it there," he said, "so it'll be there tomorrow. And then I walk over from the temporal traverser, bend over like this, and pick it up." He straightened up to show me the two buttons in his palm. They appeared to be identical.

"Be damned," I said. "But Ben . . . this . . . this isn't *proof*. I mean . . . you could have, you know—hell, you're a scientist. This isn't any sort of scientific proof."

"Do you mean to stand there and—" He broke off. "You're right," he said slowly.

So he thought a moment, and then told me to take out my wallet and drop it on the ground, and I did, and off he went again, while I stood there and did as I was told. I stared at my wallet, lying there in the tall grass in the middle of someone's field of timothy. The wallet didn't move. Then Ben was back, and walking over to me, and handing me my wallet.

It was mine, all right. And it was still lying down there at my feet, too.

"Condition's not as good," Ben said as I examined it, "since it spent the rest of the afternoon and tonight here on the ground, and then got covered with dew tomorrow morning, which the sun baked off. And kept on baking until I picked it up."

I went through my wallet. The new one. I mean the second one; wallet$_2$. I now had two of everything. Very convenient—but the currency with the identical serial numbers, I thought, could be pretty dangerous. (Also a tempting way to "make" money. Put a wad of it down. Go to tomorrow and bring it back. Again . . . and again . . . and again! If there's a paradox there, I'm not going to worry about it. I can see that it *could* be the money that folded itself, somewhere up the line.)

I dropped the wallet beside its look-alike and hugged Ben Corrick. We danced around a little, and then I asked if he'd mind just going around again and picking up my wallet *earlier*, before it got ruined. Ben stared at me, then started laughing, and I realized how chickenshit ridiculous I was being, under the circumstances—the circumstances being that he had just successfully traveled in time—and we hugged and whooped and did our jig again.

We had ourselves a genuine bona-fide certified card-carrying *time machine!*

Ben went around again, as requested. Handed me my wallet again. (The second one vanished, with a minor bang.) I was still left with two, but he pointed out that I had to leave the original lying there. So it would be there for him to pick up tomorrow. Because he just had. Twice.

"What if I don't?" I asked, feeling sly.

"Please. Harvey."

"Right," I said, in manner businesslike. "Now what about next week, or next year, Ben?"

Ben tried, but this time he came back crestfallen. The VW wouldn't go past tomorrow. So then he went back to yesterday. That worked out, and he came back just fine. But he couldn't make the day after tomorrow. Or next week or next year; nothing past tomorrow.

Don't bother asking why. You can play with that sort of thing, theorizing, all day and into the middle of next month. Yesterday is there to visit, because it *was* there, remember? So we can go back to it. Tomorrow? I don't know. Maybe it follows naturally out of today. But the day *after* tomorrow just isn't there yet. It hasn't happened. Maybe it can be *changed,* which is why we can't go there (then). Because it is subject to change, and thus doesn't exist yet.

Buy it; you like the concept of freedom of choice, don't you? Would it be there if we could visit the future?

"Well," I said, a little dry in the mouth, "there went a lot of marvy get-rich-quick ideas! OK Ben, it's time to . . . find out, right?"

Ben and I stood there in the middle of that field of slighty-waving timothy, looking at each other. He blinked those pale, watery eyes, stared another couple of seconds into mine, and turned away. He waded through the timothy, and mounted the truck, and got into the VW. Then he and that strange VW wagon went away: *Bang!*

I squatted down and gazed at my wallet while I waited.

That was the explanation for the unfortunate, precipitate, and lamented demise of the south and east walls of poor old ivied Smoire Hall, I mused. The bang. Thunder. Suddenly there's a VW-sized hole in the air, and the air rushes in to fill it. *Bang!* He had thought of that, and that's why we were way the hell out in the middle of this field. Shaking up birds with bang after bang.

Then Dr. Corrick returned, obviously able to return to the same moment at which he'd left if he really wanted to, fine-tuning. He bore five *comic books*. Five, no less. All newsstand fresh, all identical: the June, 1938 edition of Action Comics.

Chortling, he explained. "I thought I might as well bring some *worthwhile* proof," he told me triumphantly. "This is the Origin of Superman issue! Each is worth a thousand dollars or more, in mint condition. And believe me, Harvey—these are in mint condition!"

The sound I made is what is known as a Comanche yell.

A few more little experiments taught us a few more little things. For one, there's a weight-loss, a nigh weightless factor in trans-time movement. Let's don't go into too many details, but Ben and I learned that the VW could transport enormous weights, so long as it was timejumping.

(Time-travel, Ben had postulated and now proven, is inextricably bound up with $\bar{c}$ and $e = mc^2$. That led me to point out that since we got it all together out in the middle of a field, we had proven the Corrick Unified Field Theorem.)

He did have a hard time selling those comic books, by the way. They were *so* perfect, so new, that dealers were decidedly wary. But he sold four of them at last—keeping one because he just couldn't "bear to part with it"—to some hotshot dealers out Dallas way. Some people kept insisting that those guys had been taken, and there was a lot of chatter in the dealers' magazines for awhile, about the Dallas con.

We let a hyper-excited Mark Ventnor know what we'd done, and he came down to Chinchilla to see, and then to try out the temporal traverser (which Ben and I by now referred to simply as "the veedub").

Mark came back from his fourth jaunt into the very distant past very shaken indeed. He had visited a consummately ancient gent named Abram, the same who later changed his name to Abraham. Much impressed, he indicated to his visitor that he was invited to dinner.

"Mutton?" Ben asked.

Mark nodded, frowning, unable to speak.

"Wow," I muttered.

Ben was obviously deep in thought about something else. At last he said, "But how is it that we can travel in time without covering enormous astronomical distances as well?"

Mark stared at him, frowning.

"Uh . . . we've proven that we're all tied up with $e = mc^2$," I said. "So . . . we *do* cover enormous astronomical distances. At faster-than-light speed."

Mark stared at me, frowning.

Ben made a helpless, somewhat anguished gesture with his hands.

"Perhaps—but if we've discovered FTL, it *isn't* taking us anywhere. We stay—or return to—Earth. Look, Harve . . . our Sun is moving along—*and* dragging the Earth with it—at something like two hundred kilometers a second."

I nodded. "OK. A little over four Astronomical Units a year."

Gone With the Gods

Mark stared at us, frowning.

"That's right," Ben said. "Four-point-two AU's, to be a bit more precise. So. Using a rough value of a hundred million kilometers for the AU . . . in, ah, say ten thousand years we've traveled *nearly a light-year!*"

I thought about that. "Meaning . . . if we go back ten thousand years, why the hell weren't we some four-point-two times, ah times . . . ."

". . . times ten to the twelfth," Ben supplied.

Mark stared at him, frowning.

"OK," I said, nodding. "But we *weren't*. So . . ."

"So we don't know all there is to know about what we're doing," Ben said quietly, and not without sadness. "So we're engineers, not scientists. We're doing it, but we don't know how and why!"

"Maybe, uh, gravity," I said, knowing how lame that was. But at least it was a comfortable scientific word. There's security in labels; so long as we can tack a scientific-sounding tag on it, we feel a lot better. A while back it was witchcraft. Now it's science. Come to think, both witchcraft and scientific problems tend to yield to the same sort of solution: a lot of Latin words.

Mark frowned at Ben, staring. "What are you two chattering about?"

"Mark," I began slowly, "you just went back into time a long, long way. Since the Sun and therefore the Earth are moving, all the time, we figure you shouldn't have, ah, 'landed' on Earth at all. You *should* have wound up somewhere like 4.2 × 10^{12} kilometers away from the Sun's position."

"My God," Mark said, staring and frowning.

Ben nodded. "Uh-huh. Is that what Abraham said?"

Maybe that was what gave Ventnor his Idea. Certainly he could have become rich merely by journeying relatively short distances into the past and bringing forward more comic books, postage stamps, or silver dollars. Or betting on Derbies, fights, and ball games. But that wasn't how he chose to make his mark. And what Mark chose to do was *it*. As noted, Ben Corrick did tend to overlook little things. Such as the fact that the temporal traverser was no longer his, but the property of Transtempus, Inc., seventy-three percent of the stock of which was owned by Marcus D. Ventnor. And Mrs. Ventnor.

Mark Ventnor overlooks damned little.

First we added the heavy-duty cables and huge sled-like runners to the veedub, making it resemble a bright yellow forklift with panache. That way, timejumping, it would be able to transport about anything.

Then we liberated the new device that Westinghouse developed for NASA to use in space: an electron beam generator or "gun." It was unfortunately too expensive to buy, but judicious use of the temporal traverser solved that problem. It is a great mystery, how the e-beam generator, Mark Two, just *vanished* one fine night . . . and was back in place by the time the watchman came a'running with the two superiors he'd run for.

How does something vanish for ten or so seconds, then reappear? And particularly when I tell you that I used it, in this time period and that, this place and that, for several *months?*

Right!

We also equipped the veedub with a thermal drill, a truly marvelous invention.

Although he wasn't ashamed to admit he wasn't sure how/why it worked, Corrick meanwhile came up with a means of calibrating the veedub to the Earth's movements. Look, the machine was obviously somehow "glued" to the planet and thus couldn't get left during Sol/Earth's race through space. Using that as a premise, Corrick modified things so that the traveler could get from one *place* in the world to another, by time-jumping.

I practiced. And practiced some more, until I could bring the veedub down on a dime, in any given minute of time, and could practically remove a splinter from my finger with the thermal drill. Practically. I learned how to make little jumps back and then forward, to land in different areas.

It was Ventnor's ball game. He had signed a contract with me, written me out a fat check. His money covered the drill and a few other little knickknacks I'd be taking with me on my mission into the past. Yes, *I* was going. Along with the detailed instructions Mark had written out.

And then the day came, and I slid into that extraordinary VW squareback, and I was off. Into the past. The *distant* past. I was equipped with a suit resembling an astronaut's, because certainly I didn't want to spread any modern diseases among my remote ancestors. Or bring any of theirs forward to our time!

It was no lark. Using the electron-beam generator and the thermal drill to dig all those smooth-walled tunnels and caverns was *work,* and a drag betimes. Too, I had to keep coming back for more fuel: power source. (My favorite place and time for buying more gasoline was Louisville, in 1961. Very little attention was paid to my car; there weren't that many VW's around then, for anyone to have seen enough to realize mine was a later model. And there was more gasoline. Besides, Mary was in Louisville in 1961, and I *deserved* those periods of R&R.)

Then back I went to create more tunnels with floors resembling trinitite. I incised some most interesting pictures and pictograms on the walls, too, while I was at it.

Then I went in search of pre-man. This time I was tightly suited up, and hopefully sterilized; I didn't want to be a carrier of something that would wipe out Man before he got off the ground—or rather, out of the trees and caves.

My sudden appearance and strange garb really shook up the first band of hominids I came upon. I endeared myself to that hairy host, though, after the manner of Dorothy of Kansas and Oz, by materializing precisely atop their big shaggy leader, who I soon learned had been the meanest sunuvabitch in the valley.

Bowing and genuflecting hadn't been invented then, but they let me know they were most deferential and subservient indeed. A bit obscene, that demonstration. Think of a dog, showing his deference and trust. I was just able to refrain from laughing.

My appearance and simultaneous ending of the tyrannical reign of Grunt made me both god and savior, which, I mused, would be a fine combination for religion-inventors to bear in mind in a few thousand years. . . .

I made that stooped, stupid, hairy, and homely lot understand, eventually and after much agonizing work that made me reaffirm my high respect for elementary school teachers. But I finally got the message across to those almost-men: I wanted them to continue my drawings and carvings, and to make a few more little items in my honor. I showed them models.

Their making themselves understood to me took considerably less time. My translation of their reply goes like this:

"Check, OK, right, whatever you say, god sir."

I rewarded them: taking time out from his busy schedule, god-sir zapped them a nice big critter that looked like a super-hirsute elephant with a glandular imbalance. A very big meal, and they were most grateful. I received the homage routine again. Although I didn't need petrol, I jumped straight up to 1961. I needed Mary.

Back I went, this time dropping in on a happy-enough tribe of considerably more advanced near-people. Their holy-mackerel-He's-back reaction let me know that stories about my previous visit had been handed down. They were just about to sacrifice a flagrantly bosomy virgin in my honor, before I stopped them. Though I considered making better use of her, I refrained. I said *near*-people.

Getting my new and revised message across to this more-developed gaggle of humanoid geese was just as hard as last time, but I prevailed. I had to do a lot of gesturing and a lot of scratching out symbols in the dirt before, with an obvious mixture of fear and awe, they began to get the message. I worked harder, and they showed they had it all, but weren't happy about it.

Here's what I told those poor progenitors of us all, liar that I am:

"Look, I am a Good Guy from the heavens, right? I came down here to this strange world among you in my skywalking thing, old yaller over there. I was fleeing some Bad Guys, I meal real hard cases and lots of 'em, who are after me. Now I am afraid that I may have gotten all you nice handsome (ugh) folks in a bit of a spot, because those bad dudes may track me here even as one tracks the foodbeasts. So, you folks'd better stand by to dig in for swift shelter in case you need it—from aerial attack."

Now that shook them a bit, but it also sounded like work. They weren't too darned happy about the Bad Sky-people, but they weren't too enchanted with the prospect of all that digging, either.

So I "told" them a few tales about the Followers. Communication was a problem, and it took a while. Signs and drawings and even postures and facial expressions served well, particularly inasmuch as I was obviously a god, anyhow.

Besides, I'm a writer, and everybody knows writers are brilliant and resourceful, right?

I punctuated the hair-raising tales (they raised the hairs all over the bodies of my audience) with bloodless little displays of god-power. The matches made them go goggle-eyed and back away. The cherry bombs I tossed—no, not *at* anyone—were even more effective. With the semi-automatic rifle, United States Army surplus (how can they sell these things so cheap?), I cut down a tree a hundred or so feet away. The thermal drill felled another, almost as spectacularly and far more aromatically. The small quantity of nitric acid I dribbled onto an animal-hide blanket brought more wide eyes and oohs and ahs.

Then, using the veedub and some find and careful settings, I moved some exceedingly weighty chunks of rock. The mighty BANG that accompanied each mini-jump didn't hurt my cause any.

My demonstrations, along with my tales of possible followers of the inimical persuasion, served, in a few words, to shake the shinola out of them.

Besides, I showed them how to set this kid's broken leg. . . .

Right willingly, they went to work.

Despite their sorrowful importunings, I departed—and "returned" a couple of years later. (Took me less than five minutes.)

"Oh-oh—god's back," their attitudes said, but I was taken on a little tour of inspection.

Fascinating. Caves and tunnels, miracles of hard work and applied genius. Interesting, though crude, drawings adorned the walls: drawings of me, in my atmosphere suit. All about them, as decor, had been traced pictogram representations of what I had scratched out in the dust in my efforts at communication. Circles for suns and planets, squiggles, beelines with arrowheads, this and that. I smiled with pride at the genius and hard work of *my people;* some of those pictures were very artistic indeed. Phidias and Michelangelo were on their way.

But their mandated labors were otherwise pretty much petering out. After all, two years, no sky people, no returning Good Guy. So I conferred with the high priest (of the Harvey Moss cult).

"Get their tails back to work on those tunnels and things," I laboriously conveyed to that pot-bellied high-rolling do-naught, "or I'll fry yours the same way I did that shrub!"

With a glance over at the burning bush, he got the message. In short order *our people* were back at work, digging and carving.

I time-jumped, returned to them one month after I'd left (a day and half later, my time), and gave them their reward: enough fresh game and exotic fruits to feast twice their number. I let the headman fire the rifle, too, and preserved his fragile dignity by blocking him as, taken by surprise by the recoil, he started going over backward. I'm sure he wore that bruise on his weighty shoulder like a badge, and lamented its passing.

(In a cavern deep beneath what is now Normandy there is a pictorial representation of a primitive man with a stick in his hand, belching fire, and with a great dark mark carefully traced out on his shoulder.)

It was work, but I had accepted the task and it was a fascinating job and even sort of fun. Feeling like poor overworked Herakles (he was a blond, by the way, with ridiculously big feet), I repeated this labor-organizing among other tribes, widely separated from the first. I even took one headman's daughter for a time-jump, which she didn't appreciate overmuch. But she was returned to her people happy.

My next jump was a long one, forward, and I had to bounce three times to get to the right time and place. *That* was some big river, in those days. These people were advanced, and those bronze swords and the faces behind them looked nasty. But I got myself conveyed to their king, without having to kill or maim, and we "talked." His wife also made eyes at me. Unfortunately she looked just like him; his sister, I assumed.

A lot of short-period bouncing around in time followed. He provided the slaves; the electron "gun" and the thermal drill easily carved out huge—I mean H*U*G*E—blocks of stone. The veedub transported them to the appointed place in no time, if you'll pardon the expression. All the slaves had to do was shove those megatherian building blocks onto the veedub's runners; it and I took over from there.

Piling them up in the proper form and shape was up to them and their ugly king, who was crazy about the whole idea. I provided a few instructions and suggestions, even diagrams (on clay tablets and papyrus, both of which I knew would never survive the centuries). Thus I started those Egyptians and their megalomanic king off on a nice project: the Great Pyramid. I think they did very nicely with it.

So did the Incas and Aztecs I started on the same project a few days (and several thousand years) later. In Peru, Mexico, and Ecuador I picked up some perfectly lovely groupies of both sexes, though I assured them I suffered from a hopeless heterosexual hangup. I'd had a vasectomy long ago; it seemed the thing to do. Now I was glad—Harvey Moss simply could *not* afford to have any Inca or Aztec offspring!

I did several other things, in several other times and places, but I think I've given the general flavor and manner of it. And then, with a lot of hair and a quite respectable beard, I returned to hometime, with more projects to my credit than Frank Lloyd Wright or even FDR ever envisioned.

I spent the next two months collecting and collating material on my activities from articles in newspapers, scientific and popular journals and worse; the range was from the Washington *Post* and the Louisville *Courier-Journal* to *The Morehead News* and the *L.A. Free Press;* from the *Smithsonian* through *Escapade* and "specialized" journals such as *Fate* magazine. I said material on *my* activities. Right. Except that none of the writers knew that the strange finds were *my* works. I was at first surprised to discover a lot of things I hadn't put there. But I smiled, realizing that I—carrying out the weird genius-plan of Marcus D. Ventnor—had fostered much of what we now call spinoffs.

That required two months, as I said. Then I wrote the book, with photographs. (Oh, they're *excellent!* Most of them I took on location while time-tripping. They are for the most part extraordinarily clear.) The actual writing of the book was the tedious part; writing that damned manuscript took three long weeks, man, and four more to edit and type it up pretty. Good writing, as Snoopy once observed, is hard work.

I didn't have to worry about finding a publisher; Ventnor was waiting for the ms.

with glowing eyes and dangling tongue. He rushed it into print, the bastard, using not the name I'd used as author—my own, for a change—but the French pen name you now know so well, Andre de Vrees. I dragged out our contract—and learned that I'd been a lot more excited about the advance and the prospect of my extended tripping into the past than ever-shrewd Ventnor. No wonder the advance had been so fat! It wasn't an advance against royalties at all; it was the sale price. Just as he owned the temporal traverser, Ventnor owned my book, totally.

You know what came of it. The book made a mint. Ventnor and the (invisible!) writer were hailed, kudoed, attacked, castigated. It was a work of genius; it was charlatanry. It was the discovery of the age; it was the work of the Anti-god.

It was also bought by nearly everyone in the United States. And overseas. It was also Ventnor making the money and the appearances on Today and Carson and Cavett, not me. Then there was the big television special; one hour long and a full page in *TV Guide*. MGM bought movie rights and immediately contacted and contracted Charlton Heston to play the part of the man from outer space the book postulated had visited Earth, so long ago.

"Mark, you slimy bastard, you're RICH!" I roared at the fat, hawknosed, bald man across his own desk—brand new brushed walnut. "You're *rich!* You're *famous*—dear god, why NOT share some of it with me—it was all MY work!"

Ventnor sighed exaggeratedly. "But *my* idea, Harve baby. And, as I pointed out to an equally screechy Ben Corrick just yesterday, *my* money financed the project. Come, look at it this way. I hired him to make it possible; I hired you to plant the evidence and write the book. And you were both paid."

"HIRED! You . . . you damned Jay Gould, I'll—"

He lurched forward in his swivel chair, so new it was squeakless. *"Don't,* Harvey. Whatever it is, *don't.* Try suing or making wild claims and I'll smash you. *We have a contract.* You've received the highest advance on a book you ever saw in your life!"

I tried not to splutter; my face felt as if I had a fever of 105. "ADVANCE! You mean PRICE! And that book's made MILLIONS!"

He shook his head. "Oh Harvey, Harvey. *Price,* then. But why quibble over terminology—when did you ever do a book that earned royalties? Come on; this is more than you ever made on a book in your *life!*"

OK, there was nothing to be done, aside from murder. I tried to get hold of Ben for some mutual commiseration; he linked me with Mark and wouldn't even talk with me. He did own twenty-seven percent of Transtemps, Inc. but unfortunately T.I. didn't publish the book. Morpheus Books, Inc., did. Transtempus had turned no profit. . . .

I sat down and started whanging out a science-fiction novel, since I didn't dare do an exposé. It was about this guy who went back in time and planted all the evidence in the de Vrees book—and it became obvious very quickly that no one wanted to publish it. So I thought, and thought, and my money dwindled. Then I hit upon a unique plan of vengeance, and practically cackled, in my laughter.

It took awhile, and it took some more of my dwindling assets. But I regained the veedub, and I went back again. On a mission of vengeance. Mark Ventnor would be the biggest laughingstock on the planet.

This time I labored long and hard over an enormous statue, a crude stone monstrosity that was a caricature of big-nosed, bald, Mark Ventnor of the basilisk eyes. More hard work: I placed it on a platform on the coast of an unpopulated island, facing inland. Then I hauled Polynesian settlers to that island, trio after trio, trip after trip. You can only get so many people into a VW. And I showed them how to catch fish more rapidly, so they wouldn't have to sweat food-gathering. Thus they'd have plenty of time, and I started them to work: creating duplications of my statue. More Mark Ventnor caricatures.

It required only a few hours, subjective time, to pop back on five occasions, thus throwing the fear of, ah, Moss into them and insuring that they would continue the project.

The next trick was to keep the veedub. I had liberated it from where Mark had it stashed in Manhattan. Now I set the controls carefully for two months *after* the date of my departure, so I'd materialize elsewhere. Near, as a matter of fact, Chinchilla, Pee-Ay. Then, chuckling at my colossal joke on that bastard Ventnor, I consulted the records: encyclopedias and so on. Yep! There were now *many* such stone busts on the *Isle de Pascua:* Easter Island.

So much for Mr. Marcus D. Ventnor!

Then I saw the copy of *Newstime* on the newsstand. It featured a story on the new book by Andre de Vrees, all about the Easter Island phenomena. And there was a picture of the man who must have churned out that second book, the bastard: Mark Ventnor. The miserable mother had used part of the first book's vast proceeds to get a nose-job, to root hair on his no-longer-cueball noggin, and he had raised a mustache!

I stood there staring at that picture, and I groaned. Mark Ventnor no longer bore the faintest resemblance to my Easter Island caricatures.

I didn't just nurse my wounds. I planned and plotted, again. I worked it all out carefully, and I admit to feeling like a genius. We're all afflicted—or blessed—with it at one time or another. This plan I even talked over with Ben Corrick; we were friends now, and allies.

I went back again.

Back, this time, to 1816. A bit of jockeying: June, 1816. A bit more: Switzerland, June 15, 1816. I hid the veedub pretty damned cleverly, I thought, and reached my destination in the midst of a cold nasty rain that I knew would continue for several days. And I knocked at a door, the door of the Maison Chappuis. Out back, I knew, was a vineyard and, about fifteen minutes' stroll away, the Villa Diodati.

Naturally they had had to take me in. I was obviously what passed for a gentleman in those days, and just as obviously a stranger in a strange land, not to mention of passing intelligence—and wetly bedraggled, and hungry. They were all there: Mary, Claire, George, Percy, and John. Claire, Mary's half-sister and George's mistress, obviously wished we'd all bug off and leave her and her lover alone so they could continue the relationship they'd begun in England.

We didn't. We talked constantly. (George kept writing down pieces of a long heroic poem he was working on and stuffing them into his pockets. I wondered if he'd ever get all that fire-starter sorted out and pieced together.)

Mary was a shy girl (yeah, you female sexists, *girl;* she was nineteen) who was manifestly content to listen to the rest of us. She exhibited the presence of a good brain though, and was well-read. Her husband and his friend were fervently interested in modern science—that is, what was modern then, and passed for science. Galvanism, for instance. No, no, not galvan*izing*. Galvanism, after Luigi Galvani, who'd died only eighteen years before. He had serendipitously discovered what he was to call "animal electricity," and learned how to create a metallic arc that caused the muscles of frogs' legs to contract so that they twitched.

The new discipline was still called "galvanism," although by the time of my visit to Maison Chappuis, Alessandro Volta had slipped paper soaked in salt-water between alternating plates of copper and zinc, and had been proclaimed a count by Napoleon, who also hung a gold medal on him.

"The point is," George said, gesturing with his glass of sherry, "that galvanism appears to enliven the limbs of the deceased. Now, might it not be possible, as some say, to impart life to the entire organism by the same means?"

John, whose father had been a countryman of both Volta and Galvani smiled, obviously making a small effort not to sneer. "George seeks little, friend Moss; he would but revive the dead, you see."

I sighed. "I agree that it seems not too likely," I admitted. "That a body can be made to jerk does not necessarily mean that it possesses *life*. Though perhaps in future, with more knowledge and more sophisticated machinery, electricity may provide means for, ah, treating sudden death."

"Dear God," said Percy the atheist, "what a phrase!"

"What a phrase indeed," John said. "And you actually believe that someday the dead might be raised by men of medicine—using these lightning-tools of Volta and Galvani—oh, and the American, Franken?"

"Franklin," I muttered, noting how Mary was sitting forward in a tense posture of concentration. "Perhaps, Doctor. Certainly there are more things in heaven and earth than are dreamt of in our simple philosophies . . . and what it pleases us to call science. Meanwhile . . . it would seem the only means at hand of raising the dead is through the East European superstition . . . vampirism."

Well, George confessed to being fascinated by that subject, though just now he was into Charlemagne pretty heavily, again. So we talked on. Outside, it was a proper night for such a conversation: the wind blew and cracked its cheeks, the rain sluiced down with viciousness. Eventually Percy was nodding off, and we had to call a halt. George and John stayed the night, though I think Claire slept alone. I did.

The following night we were reminded that Percy had on two occasions penned what were then Gothic romances (of the "Castle of Otranto" school, not like the

Gone With the Gods

"Gothics" of the twentieth century): "Zastrozzi," and "St. Irvyne or The Rosicrucian." That led us to the fact that John's father was guilty of having translated Walpole's "Otranto" into his native tongue. Ah, the interconnections! I tried to tell them Ruthven Todd's surrealist-tale of the boy who found himself in a sort of Erewhon and eventually turned into a Greak Auk, "The Lost Traveller." They weren't much interested, though John was taken with the name "Ruthven" and made a note of it.

This night was even worse; somehow we agreed to an appropriate reading of stories of the occult. There was one about the legend of poor old Prometheus, another, "History of the Inconstant Lover," about a man whose bride turned out to be either ancient or a corpse, I forget which.

Then, all excited George was suggesting that we all try our hands at a ghost story, or *something* supernatural. I suggested a vampire tale, with George excitedly interrupting the outline to embellish—and John assiduously making notes in his illegible physician's hand. Mary demurred; she had no supernatural ideas.

"Suppose," I said, "that a scientist of brilliant mind, a physician such as our esteemed friend here, were convinced that galvanism could be used to revive the dead—*or* impart life to a humanoid creature of his own devising!"

"There, dear," Percy said, yawning, "combine that with your fascination with Prometheus and perhaps you will unburden your sweet self of a story of surpassing horror."

So, George Gordon started his vampire story, halfheartedly, and Claire, too, started one, while John tinkered with the *wompyr* idea that was mine and George's. Eventually he wrote it, as a novella—about a vampire named Lord Ruthven, no less!—and for a while it was attributed to George. It was Mary, though, who commenced to skip meals and make her fingers sore, writing her yarn of "Prometheus Rebound, or The Strange Tale of Doktor Schmidt." It was I who suggested that the entire novel might be handled as a flashback. She thought that was very clever indeed, and hopped to it.

Convincing her that "Viktor Schmidt" was a nowhere name was rather more difficult.

"Why not the name of that American electricity man, Franken?" John suggested.

"Franklin," I muttered.

"Franklinson?" Claire amended.

"In German," enthusiastic George cried. "Frankenstein!"

"That's a nice name," Mary said.

At last the rains let up. I departed, with Mary thanking me profusely and all of them begging me to return. I promised.

And I did; that was part of my Master Plan. By that time, two years later, John Polidori had been canned as George's companion and tame physician and had published *The Vampyre* in London; George Gordon had abandoned his novel in favor of fitting together the scraps of paper into the third canto of "Childe Harold," which he signed Lord Byron as usual, and Mary Shelley's novel *Frankenstein or The Modern Prometheus* was doing very well indeed.

I was welcomed with open arms and bottles, naturally, and both Byron and Shelley agreed to what I wanted and had gone through the whole business to set up: personal interviews. I made sure never to goof up and let them hear any sounds from the tape recorder. Nor would Count Alessandro Volta, over Como way, have recognized its power source, the successor to the Voltaic pile and the Voltaic cell. Size C.

Once again I departed my dear friends George (of *course* we didn't call him Lord), Percy, Mary, and Claire, and let Twuman Capote top *that*.

I moved myself forward only a few years, to England in 1846. There/then, by divers devious means, I made the acquaintance of two lamentably homely and relentingly neurotic sisters. One thing led to another, according to plan, and each became a bit less neurotic, via method similar to that which the service station man means when he tells you your car needs to be taken out and have its carburetor adjusted.

Thus, a bit happier and more knowledgeable and having less trouble with their monthlies, at least, those two did *not* that year or any other year write the novels that were to be the progenitors of the modern flood of what *we* call Gothic romances; thus the Brontë sisters perpetrated neither *Jane Eyre* nor *Wuthering Heights*.

A quick bounce up to the end of that century showed me that Henry James, without those books as catalysis, never thought of his novella about the poor sweet governess who comes to the mysterious house inhabited by ghosts Out To Get Her and the children: *The Turn of the Screw*.

I had not only made the career of Boris Karloff, I had effectively stopped all those novels with girl + castle/mansion-with-one-lighted-window on the cover. The modern Gothic was stillborn!

My work was nearly done, except for the few weeks I took off to transcribe the notes and tapes of my conversations with Byron and Shelley.

Although we'd spent most of our time at Shelley's chalet, I called the book after Byron's, *Villa Diodati*. It hath a better ring and doth fall more trippingly off the tongue.

Published in 1954, *Villa Diodati* became *the* definitive work on those gentlemen. The movie starred Robert Taylor and Tyrone Power, with George Sanders as Polidori and Grace Kelly as Mary. Though it received far less critical acclaim than the book, and certainly nothing but the back-of-me-hand treatment from academia, the movie was a blockbuster. The gross was enormous, of which my ten percent was—well, we needn't get too specific, need we?

The publishing firm I then launched, beginning with my own novel based on the (unwritten) *Turn of the Screw*, not only prospered, but utterly swamped another firm that was being launched at the same time. Faced with bankruptcy, its owner/founder accepted my less than munificent terms. You know who it was, the bastard.

Mark Ventnor is the oldest slushpile reader in the publishing business.

As to Benjamin A. Corrick, PhD and now FRS . . . I financed his researches personally, when he was just beginning them. He was kind enough to give me a great deal of the credit last year when he received Honorable Mention in the Stockholm

Nobel ceremonies—for having proven graphically and conclusively the utter possibility of time travel. ∎

MAIL SUPREMACY
by Hayford Peirce

Illustration by Kelly Freas.
Copyright © 1975 by The Conde Nast Publications, Inc.

It all seems so inevitable, now that mankind is spreading out through the galaxy. The only question is: Why wasn't it done sooner? Why did the road to the stars have to wait until 1984, when an Anglo-Chinese merchant fell to musing over his correspondence? But perhaps all of mankind's greatest advances, from fire through the wheel, from penicillin through hydrogen fusion, seem inevitable only in retrospect.

Who remembers the faceless thousands who unlocked the secret of nuclear energy, the man who dropped the first atomic bomb? Mankind remembers Einstein.

Who remembers the faceless thousands who built the first moonship, the man who first stepped upon an alien world? Mankind remembers Verne and Ley and Campbell.

As mankind remembers Chap Foey Rider.

Chap Foey Rider's main offices were in New York, not far from Grand Central Station. From them he directed an import-export firm that blanketed the globe. On November 8, 1984, a Friday, his secretary brought him the day's mail. It was 11:34 in the morning.

Chap Foey Rider frowned. Nearly noon, and only now was the mail delivered. How many years had it been since there had been two deliveries a day, morning and afternoon? At least twenty-five. Where was the much-vaunted progress of the age of technology?

He remembered his childhood in London, long before the war, when there had been *three* daily deliveries. When his father would post a letter in the morning, asking an associate to tea. And receive a written reply before tea-time. It was enough to make a bloke shake his head.

Chap Foey Rider shook his head and picked up his mail.

There was a bill of lading from his warehouse in Brooklyn, seven miles away. Mailed eight days ago.

There was a portfolio print-out from his investment counselor in Boston, 188 miles away. Mailed seven days ago.

There was an inquiry from his customs broker in Los Angeles, 2,451 miles away. Mailed four days ago.

There was a price list from a pearl merchant in Papeete, Tahiti, 6,447 miles away. Mailed three days ago.

Chap Foey Rider reached for his slide rule.

He then called his branch manager in Honolulu. He told him to mail a letter to the branch manager in Capetown, 11,535 miles away.

The Capetown manager called Chap Foey Rider two days later to advise him that the letter from Honolulu had arrived. Although still Sunday in New York, it was early Monday morning in Capetown.

Chap Foey Rider pondered. The length of the equator was 24,901.55 miles. No spot on Earth could be farther than 12,450.78 miles from any other.

He reached for the World Almanac.

Bangkok was 12,244 miles from Lima. He smiled. He had offices in each city.

A letter from Bangkok reached Lima in a single day.

Chap Foey Rider returned to his slide rule.

The extrapolation was staggering.

One further test was required to prove his theory. He pursed his lips, then carefully addressed an envelope: *Occupant, 614 Starshine Boulevard, Alpha Centauri IV*. He looked at his watch: good, the post office was open for another hour. He personally pushed the envelope through the Out-of-Town slot and strolled home.

Returning to his office the next morning, he found in his stack of mail the envelope addressed to Alpha Centauri. Frowning, he picked it up. Stamped across the front in purple ink were the words: *Addressee Unknown, Returned to Sender.*

Chap Foey Rider lighted his first cigarette of the day and to conceal his discontent puffed perfect rings toward the ceiling. Was the test actually conclusive? True, the envelope had been returned. But with suspicious speed. He reviewed his chain of logic, then studied the envelope with a magnifying glass. There was, after all, nothing to indicate *which* post office had stamped it.

He ground the cigarette out and reached for a piece of paper. He wrote firmly, without hesitation:

The Rgt. Hon. Chairman
 of the Supreme Galactic Council
Sagittarius

Sir: I feel I must draw to your attention certain shortcomings in your General Post Office system. Only yesterday I mailed a letter . . .

Chap Foey Rider awaited the morning's delivery. Eventually it arrived.

There was an envelope-sized piece of thick creamy parchment, folded neatly and held together by a complex red seal. His name appeared on one side, apparently engraved in golden ink.

Expressionless, he broke the seal, unfolded the parchment, and read the contents. It was from the Executive Secretary, Office of the Mandator of the Galactic Confederation:

Dear Sir: In reply to yours of the 14th inst. the Mandator begs me to inform you that as per your speculation the Galactic Confederation does indeed exist as primarily a Postal Union, its purpose being to promote Trade and Commerce between its 27,000 members. Any civilization is invited to join our Confederation, the sole qualification of membership being the independent discovery of our faster-than-light Postal Union. His Excellency is pleased to note that you, on behalf of your fellow Terrans, have at long last fulfilled the necessary conditions, and in consequence, an Ambassador-Plenipotentiary from the Galactic Confederation will be arriving on Terra within the next two days. Please accept, Mr. Rider, on behalf of the Mandator, the expression of his most distinguished sentiments.

". . . . to promote Trade and Commerce . . ."

Chap Foey Rider restrained himself from rubbing his hands together in glee. Instead he pushed a buzzer to summon his four sons to conference. The stars were coming to mankind. Rider Factoring, Ltd. would be ready for them; he called the mailroom to tell them to be on the alert for a large package from Sagittarius. ■

THE GENTLE EARTH

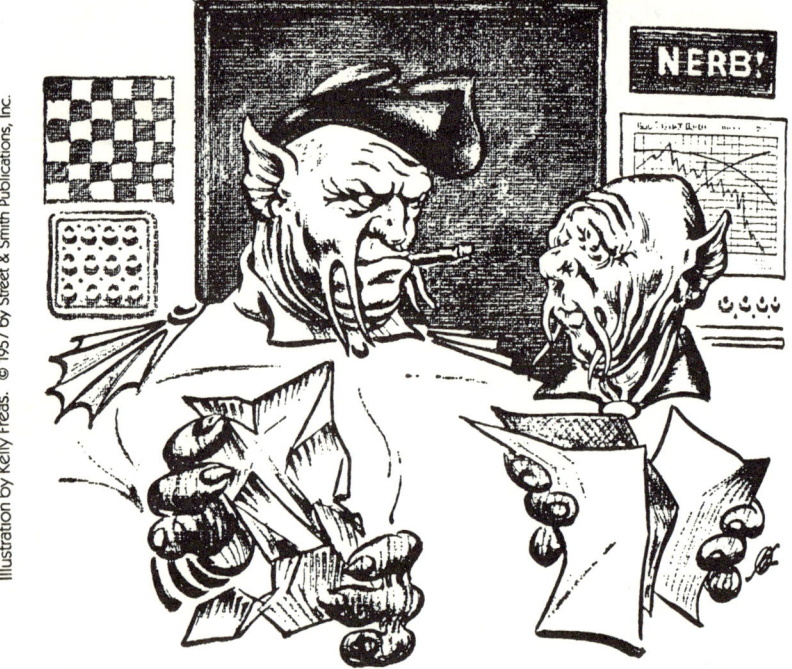

by Christopher Anvil

Tlasht Bade, Supreme Commander of Invasion Forces, drew thoughtfully on his slim cigar. "The scouts are all back?"

Sission Runckel, Chief of the Supreme Commander's Staff, nodded. "They all got back safely, though one or two had difficulties with some of the lower life forms."

"Is the climate all right?"

Runckel abstractedly reached in his tunic, and pulled out a thing like a short piece of thick tarred rope. As he trimmed it, he scowled. "There's some discomfort, apparently because the air is too dry. But on the other hand there's plenty of oxygen near the planet's surface, and the gravity's about the same as it is back home. We can live there."

Bade glanced across the room at a large blue, green, and brown globe, with irregular patches of white at top and bottom. "What are the white areas?"

"Apparently, chalk. One of our scouts landed there, but he's in practically a state of shock. The brilliant reflectivity in the area blinded him, a huge white furry animal attacked him, and he barely got out alive. To cap it all, his ship's insulation apparently broke down on the way back, and now he's in the sick bay with a bad case of spacegripe. All we can get out of him is that he had severe prickling sensations in the feet when he stepped out onto the chalk dust. Probably a pile of little spiny shells."

"Did he bring back a sample?"

"He claims he did. But there's only water in his sample box. I imagine he was delirious. In any case, this part of the planet has little to interest us."

Bade nodded. "What about the more populous regions?"

"Just as we thought. A huge web of interconnecting cities, manufacturing centers, and rural areas. Our mapping procedures have proved to be accurate."

"That's a relief. What about the natives?"

"Erect, land-dwelling, ill-tempered bipeds," said Runckel. "They seem to have little or no planet-wide unity. Of course, we have large samplings of their communications media. When these are all analyzed, we'll know a lot more."

"What do they dook like?"

"They're pink or brown in color, quite tall, but not very broad or thick through the chest. A little fur here and there on their bodies. No webs on their hands or feet, and their feet are fantastically small. Otherwise, they look quite human."

"Their technology?"

Runckel sucked in a deep breath and sat up straight. "Every bit as bad as we thought." He picked up a little box with two stiff handles, squeezed the handles hard, and touched a glowing wire on the box to his piece of black rope. He puffed violently.

Bade turned up the air-conditioning. Billowing clouds of smoke drew away from Runckel in long streamers, so that he looked like an island looming through heavy mist. His brow was creased in a foreboding scowl.

"Technologically," he said, "they are deadly. They've got fission and fusion, indirect molecular and atomic reaction control, and a long-reaching development of electron flow and pulsing devices. So far, they don't seem to have anything based on deep rearrangement or keyed focusing. But who knows when they'll stumble on that? And then what? Even now, properly warned and ready they could give us a terrible struggle."

Runckel knocked a clinker off his length of rope and looked at Bade with the tentative, judging air of one who is not quite sure of another's reliability. Then he said, loudly and with great firmness, "We have a lot to be thankful for. Another five or ten decades' delay getting the watchships up through the cloud layer, and they'd have had us by the throat. We've got to smash them before they're ready, or *we'll* end up as *their* colony."

Bade's eyes narrowed. "I've always opposed this invasion on philosophical grounds. But it's been argued and settled. I'm willing to go along with the majority opinion." Bade rapped the ash off his slender cigar and looked Runckel directly in the eyes. "But it you want to open the whole argument up all over again—"

"No," said Runckel, breathing out a heavy cloud of smoke. "But our micromapping and radiation analysis shows a terrific rate of progress. It's hard to look at those figures and even breathe normally. They're gaining on us like a shark after a minnow."

"In that case," said Bade, "let's wake up and hold our lead. This business of attacking the suspect before he has a chance to commit a crime is no answer. What about all the other planets in the universe? How do we know what they might do some day?"

"This planet is right beside us."

"Is murder honorable as long as you do it only to your neighbor? Your argument is self-defense. But you're straining it."

"Let it strain, then," said Runckel angrily. "All I care about is that chart showing our comparative levels of development. Now *we* have the lead. I say, frag them out by their necks and let them submit or we'll thrust their heads underwater and have done with them. And anyone who says otherwise is a doubtful patriot!"

Bade's teeth clamped, and he set his cigar carefully on a tray.

Runckel blinked, as if he only appreciated what he had said by echo.

Bade's glance moved over Runckel deliberately, as if stripping away the emblems and insignia. Then Bade opened the bottom drawer of his desk, and pulled out a pad of dun-colored official forms. As he straightened, his glance caught the motto printed large on the base of the big globe. The motto had been used so often in the struggle to decide the question of invasion that Bade seldom noticed it any more. But now he looked at it. The motto read:

THEM OR US

Bade stared at it for a long moment, looked up at the globe that represented the mighty planet, then down at the puny motto. He glanced at Runckel, who looked back dully but squarely. Bade glanced at the motto, shook his head in disgust, and said, "Go get me the latest reports."

Runckel blinked. "Yes, sir," he said, and hurried out.

Bade leaned forward, ignored the motto, and thoughtfully studied the globe.

Bade read the reports carefully. Most of them, he noted, contained a qualification. In the scientific reports, this generally appeared at the end:

" . . . Owing to the brief time available for these observations, the conclusions presented herein must be regarded as only provisional in character."

In the reports of the scouts, this reservation was usually presented in bits and pieces:

" . . . And this thing, that looked like a tiny crab, had a pair of pincers at one end, and I didn't have time to see if this was the end it got me with, or if it was the other end. But I got a jolt as if somebody squeezed a lighter and held the red-hot wire against my leg. Then I got dizzy and sick to my stomach. I don't know for sure if this was what did it, or if there are many of them, but if there are, and if it did, I don't see how a man could fight a war and not be stung to death when he wasn't looking. But I wasn't there long enough to be sure . . . "

Another report spoke of a "Crawling army of little six-legged things with a set of oversize jaws on one end, that came swarming through the shrubbery straight for the ship, went right up the side and set to work eating away the superplast binder around the viewport. With that gone, the ship would leak air like a fishnet. But when I tried to clear them away, they started in on me. I don't know if this really proves anything, because Rufft landed not too far away, and he swears the place was like a paradise. Nevertheless, I have to report that I merely set my foot on the ground, and I almost got marooned and eaten up right on the spot."

Bade was particularly uneasy over reports of a vague respiratory difficulty some of the scouts noticed in the region where the first landings were planned. Bade commented on it, and Runckel nodded.

"I know," said Runckel. "The air's too dry. But if we take time to try to provide for that, at the same time they may make some new advance that will more than nullify whatever we gain. And right now their communications media show a political situation that fits right in with our plans. We can't hope for that to last forever."

Bade listened as Runckel described a situation like that of a dozen hungry sharks swimming in a circle, each getting its jaws open for a snap at the next one's tail. Then Runckel described his plan.

At the end, Bade said, "Yes, it may work out as you say. But listen, Runckel, isn't this a little too much like one of those whirlpools in the Treacherous Islands? If everything works out, you go through in a flash. But one wrong guess, and you go around and around and around and around and you're lucky if you get out with a whole skin."

Runckel's jaw set firmly. "This is the only way to get a clear-cut decision."

Bade studied the far wall of the room for a moment. "I'm sorry I didn't get a hand at these plans sooner."

"Sir," said Runckel, "you would have, if you hadn't been so busy fighting the whole idea." He hesitated, then asked, "Will you be coming to the staff review of plans?"

"Certainly," said Bade.

"Good," said Runckel. "You'll see that we have it all worked to perfection."

Bade went to the review of plans and listened as the details were gone over minutely. At the end, Runckel gave an overall summary:

"The Colony Planet," he said, rapping a pointer on maps of four hemispheric views, "is only seventy-five per cent water, so the land areas are immense. The chief land masses are largely dominated by two hostile power groups, which we may call East and West. At the fringes of influence of these power groups live a vast mass of people not firmly allied to either.

"The territory of this uncommitted group is well suited to our purposes. It contains many pleasant islands and comfortable seas. Unfortunately, analysis shows that the dangerous military power groups will unite against us if we seize this territory directly. To avoid this, we will act to stun and divide them at one stroke."

Runckel rapped his pointer on a land area lettered "North America" and said, "On this land mass is situated a politico-economic unit known as the U.S. The U.S.

is the dominant power both in the Western Hemisphere and in the West power group. It is surrounded by side seas that separate it from its allies.

"Our plan is simple and direct. We will attack and seize the central plain of the U.S. This will split it into helpless fragments, any one of which we may crush at will. The loss of the U.S. will, of course, destroy the power balance between East and West. The East will immediately seize the scraps of Western power and influence all over the globe.

"During this period of disorder we will set up our key-tools factories and a light-duty forceway network. In rapid stages will then come ore-converters, staging plants, fabricators, heavy-duty forceway stations, and self-operated production units. With these last we will produce energy-conversion units and storage piles by the million in a network to blanket the occupied area. The linkage produced will power our damper units and blot out missile attacks that may now begin in earnest.

"We will thus be solidly established on the planet itself. Our base will be secure against attack. We will now turn our energies to the destruction of the U. S. S. R. as a military power." He reached out with his pointer to rap a new land mass.

"The U.S.S.R. is the dominant power of the East power group. This will by now be the only hostile power group remaining on the planet. It will be destroyed in stages.

"In Stage I we will confuse the U.S.S.R. by propaganda. We will profess friendship while we secretly multiply our productive facilities to the highest possible degree.

"In Stage II, we will seize and fortify the western and northern islands of Britain, Novaya Zemlya, and New Siberia. We will also seize and heavily fortify the Kamchatka Peninsula in the extreme eastern U.S.S.R. We will now demand that the U.S.S.R. lay down its arms and surrender.

"In the event of refusal, we will, from our fortified bases, destroy by missile attack all productive facilities and communication centers in the U.S.S.R. The resulting paralysis will bring down the East power group in ruins. The planet will now lie open before us."

Runckel looked at each of his listeners in turn.

"Everything has been done to make this invasion a success. To crush out any possible miscalculation, we are moving with massive reserves close behind us. Certain glory and a mighty victory await us.

"Let us raise our heads in prayer, then join in the Oath of Battle."

The first wave of the attack came down like an avalanche on the central U.S. Multiple transmitters went into action to throw local radar stations into confusion. Stull-gas missiles streaked from the landing ships to explode over nearby cities. Atmospheric flyers roared off to intercept possible enemy attacks. A stream of guns, tanks, and troop carriers rolled down the landing ways and fanned out to seize enemy power plants and communications centers.

The commander of the first wave reported: "Everything proceeding according to plan. Enemy resistance negligible."

Runckel ordered the second wave down.

Bade, watching it on a number of giant viewscreens in the operations room of a ship coming down, had a peculiar feeling of numbness, such as might follow a deep cut before the pain is felt.

Runckel, his face intense, said: "Their position is hopeless. The main landing site is secure and the rest will come faster than the eye can see." He turned to speak into one of a bank of microphones, then said, "Our glider missiles are circling over their capital."

A loud-speaker high on the wall said, "Landing minus three. Take your stations, please."

The angle of vision of one of the viewscreens tilted suddenly, to show a high, dome-topped building set in a city filled with rushing beetle shapes—obviously ground-cars of some type. Abruptly these cars all pulled to the sides of the streets.

"That," said Runckel grimly, "means their capital is out of business."

The picture on the viewscreen blurred suddenly, like the reflection from water ruffled by a breeze. There was a clang like a ten-ton hammer hitting a twenty-ton gong. Walls, floor, and ceiling of the room danced and vibrated. Two of the viewscreens went blank.

Bade felt a prickling sensation travel across his shoulders and down his back. He glanced sharply at Runckel.

Runckel's expression looked startled but firm. He reached out and snapped orders into one of his microphones.

There was an intense, high-pitched ringing, then a clap like a nuclear cannon of six paces distance.

The wall loud-speaker said, "Landing minus two."

An intense silence descended on the room. One by one, the viewscreens flickered on. Bade heard Runckel say, "The ship is totally damped. They haven't anything that can get through it."

There was a dull, low-pitched thud, a sense of being snapped like a whip, and the screens went blank. The wall loud-speaker dropped, and jerked to a stop, hanging by its cord.

Then the ship set down.

Runckel's plan assumed that the swift-moving advance from the landing site would overrun a sizeable territory during the first day. With this maneuvering space quickly gained, the landing site itself would be safe from enemy ground attack by dawn of the second day.

Now that they were down, however, Bade and Runckel looked at the operations room's big viewscreen and saw their vehicles standing still all over the landscape. The troops crowded about the rear of the vehicles to watch cursing drivers pull the motors up out of their housings and spread them out on the ground. Here and there a stern officer argued with grim-faced troops who stared stonily ahead as if they didn't hear. Meanwhile, the tanks, trucks, and weapons carriers stood motionless.

Runckel, infuriated, had a cluster of microphones gripped in his hand and was pronouncing death by strangling and decapitation on any officer who failed to get his unit in motion right away.

Bade studied the baffled expressions on the faces of the drivers, then glanced at the enemy ground-cars abandoned at the side of the road. He turned to see a tall officer with general's insignia stagger through the doorway and grip Runckel by the arm. Bade recognized Rast, General Forces Commander.

"Sir," said Rast, "it can't be done."

"It has to be done," said Runckel grimly. "So far we've decoyed the enemy missiles to a false site. Before they spot us again, *those troops have got to be spread out!*"

"They won't ride in the vehicles!"

"It's that or get killed!"

"Sir," said Rast, "you don't understand. I came back here in a gun carrier. To start with, the driver jammed the speed lever all the way to the front shield, and nothing happened. He got up to see what was wrong. The carrier shot ahead with a flying leap, threw the driver into his back and almost snapped our heads off. Then it coasted to a stop. We pulled ourselves together and turned around to get the cover off the motor box.

"*Wham!* The carrier took off, ripped the cover out of our hands, threw us against the rear shield and knocked us senseless. Then it rolled to a stop.

"That's how we got here. Jump! Roll. Stop. Wait. Jump! Roll. Stop. Wait. On one of those jumps, the gun went out the back of the carrier, mount, bolts, and all. The driver swore he'd turn off the motor, and fangjaw take the planet and the whole invasion. We aren't going to win a war with troops in that frame of mind."

Runckel took a deep breath.

Bade said, "What about the enemy's ground-cars? Will they run?"

Rast blinked. "I don't know. Maybe—"

Bade snapped on a microphone lettered "Aerial Rec." A little screen in a half-circle atop the microphone lit up to show an alert, harried-looking officer. Bade said, "You've noticed our vehicles are stopped?"

"Yes, sir."

"Were the enemy's ground-cars affected at the same time as ours?"

"No sir, they were still moving after ours were stuck."

"Any motor trouble in Atmospheric Flyer Command?"

"None that I know of, sir."

Bade glanced at Rast. "Try using the enemy ground-cars. Meanwhile, get the troops you can't move back under cover of the ships' dampers."

Rast saluted, whirled, and went out at a staggering run.

Bade called Atmospheric Flyer Command, and Ground Forces Maintenance, and arranged for the captured enemy vehicles to be identified by a large yellow X painted across the top of the hood. Then he turned to Runckel and said, "We're going to need all the support we can get. See if we can bring Landing Force 2 down late today instead of tomorrow."

"I'll try," said Runckel.

It seemed to Bade that the events of the next twenty-four hours unrolled like the scenes of a nightmare.

Before the troops were all under cover, an enemy reconnaissance aircraft leaked in very high overhead. The detector screens of Atmospheric Flyer Command were promptly choked with enemy aircraft coming in low and fast from all directions.

These aircraft were of all types. Some heaved their bombs in underhand, barreled over and streaked home for another load. Others were flying hives of anti-aircraft missiles. A third type were suicide bombers or winged missiles; these roared in head-on and blew up on arrival.

While the dampers labored and overheated, and Flyer Command struggled with enemy fighters and bombers overhead, a long-range reconnaissance flyer spotted a sizable convoy of enemy ground forces rushing up from the southwest.

Bade and Runckel concentrated first on living through the air attack. It soon developed that the enemy planes, though extremely fast, were not very maneuverable. The enemy's missiles did not quite overload the dampers. The afternoon wore on in an explosive violence that was severe, but barely endurable. It began to seem that they might live through it.

Toward evening, however, a small enemy missile streaked in on the end of a wire and smashed the grid of an auxiliary damper unit. Before this unit could be repaired, a heavy missile came down near the same place, and overloaded the damper network. Another missile streaked in. One of the ships tilted, and fell headlong. The engines of this ship were ripped out of the circuit that powered the dampers. With the next enemy missile strike, another ship was heaved off its base. This ship housed a large proportion of Flyer Command's detector screens.

Bade and Runckel looked at each other. Bade's lips moved, and he heard himself say, "Prepare to evacuate."

At this moment, the enemy attack let up.

It took an instant for Bade to realize what had happened. He canceled his evacuation order before it could be transmitted, then had the two thrown ships linked back into the power circuit. He turned around, and his glance fell on one of the viewscreens showing the shadowy plain outside. A brilliant flash lit the screen, and he saw dark low shapes rushing in toward the ships. Bade immediately gave orders to defend against ground attack, but not to pursue beyond range of the dampers.

A savage, half-lit struggle developed. The enemy, whose weapons failed to work in range of the dampers, attacked with bayonets, and used guns, shovels, and picks in the manner of clubs and battle axes. In a spasm of bloody violence they fought their way in among the ships, then, confused in the dimness, were thrown back with heavy losses. As night settled down, the enemy dug in to make a fortified ring close around the landing site.

The enemy missile attack failed to recover its former violence.

Bade gave silent thanks for the deliverance. As the comparative quiet continued, it seemed clear that the enemy high command was holding back to avoid hitting their own men dug in nearby.

It occurred to Bade that now might be a good time to get a little sleep. He turned to go to his cot, and there was a rush of yellow dots on Flyer Command's pilot screen. As he stared wide-eyed, auxiliary screens flickered on and off to show a ghostly dish-shaped object that led his flyers on a wild chase all over the sky, then vanished at an estimated speed twenty times that the enemy planes were thought capable of doing.

Runckel said, "Landing Force 2 can get here at early dawn. That's the best we can manage."

Bade nodded dully.

The ground screens now lit in brilliant flashes as the enemy began firing monster rockets at practically point-blank range.

Night passed in a continuous bombardment.

At early dawn of the next day, Bade put in all his remaining missiles, and bomber and interceptor flyers. For a brief interval of time, the enemy bombardment was smothered.

Landing Force 2 set down beside Landing Force 1.

Bade ordered the stull-gas missiles of Landing Force 2 exploded near the enemy ground troops. In the resulting confusion, the ground forces moved out and captured large numbers of enemy troops, weapons, and vehicles. The captured vehicles were marked and promptly put to use.

Bade spoke briefly with General Rast, commanding the ground forces.

"Now's your chance," said Bade. "Move fast and we can capture supplies and reinforcements flowing in, before they realize we've broken their ring."

Under the protection of the flyers of Landing Force 2, Rast's troops swung out onto the central plain of the North American continent.

The advance moved fast. Enemy troops and supply convoys were caught off guard on the road. When the enemy fought, his resistance was patchy and confused.

Bade, feeling drugged from lack of sleep, lay down on his cot for a nap. He awoke feeling fuzzy-brained and dull.

"They're whipped," said Runckel gleefully. "We've got back the time we lost yesterday. There's no resistance to speak of. And we've just made a treaty with the East bloc."

Bade sat up dizzily. "That's wonderful," he said. He glanced at the clock. "Why wasn't I called sooner?"

"No need," said Runckel. "It's all just a matter of form. Landing Force 3 is coming down tonight. The war's over." Runckel's face, as he said this, had a peculiar shine.

Bade frowned. "Isn't the enemy making any reaction at all?"

"Nothing worth mentioning. We're driving them ahead of us like a school of minnows."

Bade got to his feet uneasily. "It can't be this simple." He stepped out into the operations room and detected unmistakable signs of holiday jubilation. Nearly everyone was grinning, and gawkers were standing in a thick ring before the screen showing the map room's latest plot.

Bade said sharply, "Don't these men have anything to do?" His voice carried across the room with the effect of a shark surfacing in the midst of a ladies' swimming party. Several of the men at the map jumped. Others glanced around jerkily. There was a concerted bumping of elbows, and the ring of gawkers evaporated briskly in all directions. In every part of the room there was abruptly something approaching a businesslike atmosphere.

Bade looked around angrily and sat down at his desk. Then he saw the map. He squeezed his eyes shut, then looked again.

In the center of the map of North America was a big blot, as if a bottle of red ink had been thrown at it. Bade turned to Runckel and asked harshly, "Is that map correct?"

"Absolutely," said Runckel, his face shining with satisfaction.

Bade looked back at the map and performed a series of rapid calculations. He glanced at the viewscreens, and saw that those which would normally show the advanced ground troops weren't in use. This, he supposed, meant that the advance had outrun the technical crews.

Bade snapped on a microphone lettered "Supply, Ground." In the half-circle atop the microphone appeared an officer in the last stage of sleepless exhaustion. The officer's eyes twitched, and his skin had a drawn dull look. His head was slumped on his hand.

"Supply?" said Bade in alarm.

"Sorry," mumbled the officer, "we can't do it. We're overstretched already. Try Flyer Command. Maybe they'll parachute it to you."

Bade switched off, and glanced at the map again. He turned to Runckel. "Listen, what are we using for transport?"

"The enemy ground-cars."

"Fast, aren't they?"

Runckel smiled cheerfully. "They are built for speed. Rast grabbed a whole fleet of them to start with, and they've worked fine ever since, A few wrecks, some bad cases of kinkfoot, but that's all."

"What the devil is 'kinkfoot'?"

"Well, the enemy have tiny feet with little toes and no webs at all. Some of their ground-car controls are on the floor. There just isn't much space so our men's feet get cramped. It's just a mild irritation." Runckel smiled vaguely. "Nothing to worry about."

Bade squinted hard at Runckel. "What's Supply using for transport?"

"Steam trucks, of course."

"Do they work all right, or do they jump?"

Runckel smiled dreamily. "They work fine."

The Gentle Earth

Bade snapped on the Supply microphone. The same weary officer appeared, his head in his hands, and mumbled, "Sorry. We're overloaded. Try Flyer Command."

Bade said angrily, "Wake up a minute."

The man raised his head, blinked at Bade, then straightened as if hauled by the back of the collar.

"Sir?"

"What's the overall supply picture?"

"Sir, it's awful. Terrible."

"What's the matter?"

"The advance is so fast, and the units are all mixed up, and when we get to a place, they've already pulled out. Worse yet, the steam trucks—" He hesitated, as if afraid to go on.

"Speak up," snapped Bade. "What's wrong with the trucks? Is it the engine? Fuel? Running gear? What is it?"

"It's . . . the water, sir."

"The water?"

"Sir, there's that constant loss of steam out the exhaust. At home, we just throw a few more buckets of water in the tank and go on. But here—"

"Oh," said Bade, the situation dawning on him.

"But around here, sir," said the officer, "they've had something called a 'severe drought.' The streams are dry."

"Can you dig down?"

"Sir, at best there's just muck. We *know* there's water here somewhere, but meanwhile our trucks are stalled all over the country with the men dug down out of sight, and the natives standing around shaking their heads, and *sure*, there's *got* to be water down there somewhere, but what do we use right now?"

Bade took a deep breath. "What about the enemy trucks? Can't you use them?"

"If we'd started off with them, I suppose we could have. But Ground Forces has requisitioned most of them. Now we're spread out in all directions with the front getting farther away all the time."

Bade switched off and got in touch with Ground Forces, Maintenance. A sprucelooking major appeared. Bade paused a moment, then asked, "How's your workload, major? Are you behind schedule?"

The major looked shocked. "No, sir. Far from it. We're away ahead of schedule."

"Aren't these enemy vehicles giving you any trouble? Any difficulties in repair?"

The major laughed. "Fangjaw, general, we don't repair them! When they burn out, we throw them away. We pried up the hoods of some of them, pulled off the top two or three layers of machinery, and took a good look underneath. That was enough. There are hundred of parts, all shapes and sizes. And dozens of different kinds of motors. Half of the parts are stuck so they won't move when you try to get them out, and, to top it all, there isn't enough room in there to squeeze in an extra grain of sand. So what's the use? If something goes wrong with one of those things, we give it a shove off the road and forget it. There are plenty of others."

"I see," said Bade. "Do you send your repair crews out to shove the ground-cars off the road?"

"Oh, no, sir," said the major. looking startled. "Like the colonel says, 'Let the Ground Forces do it.' Sir, it doesn't take any skill to do that. It's just that that's our *policy*. Don't repair 'em. Throw 'em away."

"What about *our* vehicles, then? Have you found out what's wrong?"

The major looked uncomfortable. "Well, the difficulty is that the vehicles work satisfactorily *inside* the ship, and for a little while *outside*. But then, after they've been out a while, a malfunction occurs in the mechanism. That's what causes the trouble." He looked at Bade hopefully. "Was there anything else, sir?"

"Yes," said Bade dryly, "it's the malfunction I'm interested in. What *is* it that goes wrong?"

The major looked unhappy. "Well, sir, we've had the motors apart and put back together I don't know how many times, and the fact is, there's nothing at all wrong with them. There's nothing wrong but they still won't work. That's not our department. We've handed the whole business over to the Testing Lab."

"Then," said Bade, "you actually don't have any work to do?"

The major jumped. "Oh, no sir, I didn't say that. We . . . we're holding ourselves in readiness, sir, and we've got our shops in order, and some of the men are doing some very, ah, very important research on the . . . the structure of the enemy ground-car, and—"

"Fine," said Bade. "Get your colonel on this line." When the colonel appeared, Bade said, "Ground Forces Supply has its steam trucks out of service for lack of water. Get in touch with their H.Q., find out the location of the trucks, and get out there with the water. Find out where they can replenish in the future. Take care of this as fast as you can."

The colonel worked his mouth in a way that suggested a weak valve struggling to hold back a large quantity of compressed air. Bade looked at him hard. The colonel's mouth blew open, and "Yes, sir!" came out. The colonel looked startled.

Bade immediately switched back to Supply and said, "Ground Forces Maintenance is going to help you water your trucks. Why didn't you get in touch with them yourselves? It's the obvious thing."

"Sir, we did, hours ago. They said water supply wasn't in *their* department."

Bade seemed to see the bursting of innumerable bubbles before his eyes. It dawned on him that he was bogged down in petty details while big events rushed on unheeded. He switched back to the colonel briefly and when he switched off the colonel was plainly vibrating with energy from head to toe. Then Bade looked forebodingly at the map and ordered Liaison to get General Rast for him.

This took a long time, which Bade spent trying to anticipate the possible enemy reaction if Supply broke down completely, and a retirement became necessary. By

The Gentle Earth

the time Rast appeared on the screen, Bade had thought it over carefully, and could see nothing but trouble ahead. There was a buzz, and Bade looked up to see a fuzzy picture of Rast.

Rast, as far as Bade could judge, had a look of victory and exhilaration. But the communicator's reception was uncommonly bad, and Rast's image had a tendency to flicker, fade, and slide up and down. Judging by the trend of the conversation, Bade decided reception must be worse yet on the other end.

Bade said, "Supply is in a mess. You'd better choose some sort of defensible perimeter and halt."

Rast said, "Thank you. The enemy is in full flight."

"Listen," said Bade. "Supply is stopped. We can't get supplies to you. Supply can't catch up with you."

"We'll pursue them day and night," said Rast.

"Listen to me," said Bade. "Break off the pursuit! We can't get supplies to you!"

Rast's form slowly dimmed and expanded till it filled the screen, then burst, and reappeared as a brilliant image the size of a man's thumb. His voice cut off, then came through as a crackle.

"Siss kissis sissis," said the image, expanding again, "hisss sisss kississ sikississ." This noise was accompanied by earnest gestures on the part of Rast, and a very determined facial expression. The image grew huge and dim, and burst, then started over again.

Bade spat out a word he had promised himself never to say again under any circumstances whatever. Then he sat helpless while the image, large and clear, leaned forward earnestly and pounded one huge fist into the other.

"Hiss! Siss! Fississ!"

"Listen," said Bade, "I can't make out a word you're saying." He leaned forward. 'WE CAN'T GET SUPPLIES TO YOU!"

The image burst and started over, bright and small.

Bade sucked in a deep breath. He grabbed the Communications microphone. "Listen," he snapped, "I've got General Rast on the screen here and I can't hear anything but a crackle. The image constantly expands and contracts."

"I know, sir," said a gray-smocked technician with a despairing look. "I can see the monitor screen from here. It's the best we can do, sir."

Out of the corner of his eye, Bade could see Rast's image growing huge and dim. "Hiss! Siss!" said Rast earnestly.

"What causes this?" roared Bade.

"Sir, all we can guess is some terrific electrical discharge between here and General Rast's position. What such a discharge might be, I can't imagine."

Bade scowled, and looked at a thumb-sized Rast. Bade opened his mouth to roar out that there was no way to get supplies through. Rast's image suddenly vibrated like a twanged string, then stopped expanding.

Rast's voice came through clearly. "Will you repeat that, sir?"

"WE CAN'T SUPPLY YOU," said Bade. "Halt your advance. Pick a good spot and HALT!"

Rast's image was expanding again. "Siss hiss," he said, and saluted. His image vanished.

Bade immediately snapped on the Communications microphone. "Do you have anyone down there who can read lips?" he demanded.

"Read *lips?* Sir, I—" The technician squinted suddenly and swung off the screen. He was back in a moment, his face clear and hopeful. "Sir, we've got a man in the section. that's a fanatic on communications methods. The other men think he *can* read lips, and I've sent for him."

"Good," said Bade. "Set him to work on the record of that conservation with General Rast. Another thing—is there any way you can get a message through to Rast?"

The technician looked doubtful. "Well, sir . . . I don't know—" His face cleared slightly. "We can try, sir."

"Good," said Bade. "Send 'Supply situation bad. Strongly suggest you halt your advance and consolidate position.' " Bade's glance fell on the latest plot from the map room. Glumly he asked himself how Rast or anyone else could hope to consolidate the balloonlike situation that was coming about.

"Sir," asked the technician, "is that all?"

"Yes," said Bade, "and let me know when you get through to Rast."

"Yes, sir."

Bade switched off, and turned to ask Runckel for the exact time Landing Force 3 would be down. Bade hesitated, then squinted hard at Runckel.

Runckel's face had an unusually bright, animated look. He was glancing rapidly through a sheaf of reports, quickly scribbling comments on them, and tossing them to an excited-looking clerk, who rushed off to slap them on the desks of various exhilarated officers and clerks. These men eagerly transmitted them to their various sections. This procedure was normal, but the faces of the men all looked too excited. Their movements were jerky and fast.

Bade became aware of the sensation of watching a scene in a lunatic asylum.

The excited-looking clerk rushed to Runckel's desk to snatch up a sheaf of reports, and Bade snapped, "Bring those here."

The clerk jumped, rushed to Bade's desk, halted with a jerky bounce, and saluted snappily. He flopped the papers on the desk, whirled around and raced off toward the desks of the officers who usually got the reports Bade was now holding. The clerk stopped suddenly, looked at his empty hands, spun around, stared at Runckel's desk, then at Bade's. A look of enlightenment passed across his face. "Oh," he said, with a foolish grin. He teetered back and forth on his heels, then rushed over to look at the latest plot from the map room.

Bade set his jaw and glanced at the reports Runckel had marked.

The top two or three reports were simple routing and had merely been initialed.

The next report, however, was headed: "Testing Lab. Report on Cause of Vehicle Failure; Recommendations."

Bade quickly glanced over several sheets of technical diagrams and figures, and turned to the summary. He read:

"In short, the breakdown of normal function, and the resultant slow violent pulsing action of the motor, is caused by the abnormally low conductivity of Surface Conduction Layer S-3. The pulser current, which would normally flow across this layer, is blocked, and instead builds up on projection L-26. Eventually a sufficient charge accumulates, and arcs across air gap B. This throws a shock current through the exciter such as is normally experienced only during violent acceleration. The result is that the vehicle shoots ahead from a standing start, then rolls to a stop while the current again slowly accumulates. The root cause of this malfunction is the fantastically low moisture content of the atmosphere on this planet. It is this that causes the loss of conductivity across Layer S-3.

"Recommended measures to overcome this malfunction include:

a) Artificial humidification of the air entering the motor, by means of sprayer and fan.

b) Sealing of the motor unit.

c) Coating of surface condition layer S-3 with a top-sealed permanent conducting film.

"A) or b) probably can be carried out as soon as the requisite devices and materials are obtainable. This, however, may involve a considerable delay. c), on the other hand, will require a good deal of initial testing and experimentation, but may then be carried into effect very quickly, as the requisite tools and materials are already at hand. We will immediately carry out the initial measures for whichever plan you deem preferable."

Bade looked the report over again carefully, then glanced at Runckel's scrawled comment:

"Good work! Carry this out immediately! S. R."

Bade glared. Carry *what* out immediately?

Bade glanced angrily at Runckel, then sat up in alarm. Runckel's hands clenched the side of his desk. Runckel's back was straight as a rod. His chest was inflated to huge dimensions, and he was slowly drawing in yet more air. His face bore a fixated, inward-turned look that might indicate either horror or ecstasy.

Bade shoved his chair back and glanced around for help.

His glance stopped at the map screen, where the huge overblown blot in the center of the continent had sprouted a long narrow pencil reaching out toward the west.

There was a quick low gonglike sound, and the semicircular rim atop the Communications microphone lit up in red. Bade snapped the microphone on and a scared-looking technician said, "Sir, we've worked out what General Rast said."

"What?" Bade demanded.

At Bade's side, there was a harsh scraping noise. Bade whipped around.

Runckel lurched to his feet, his face tense, his eyes shut, his mouth half open and his hands clenched.

Runckel twisted. There was a gagging sound, then a harsh roar:

   Ka   Ka   Ka   KACHOOOOO!!

Bade sat down in a hurry and grabbed the microphone marked "Medical Corps."

A crowd of young doctors and attendants swarmed around Runckel with pulse-beat snoopers, bloodpressure gauges, little lights on long rubber tubes, and bottles and jars which they filled with fluid sucked out of the suffering Runckel with long hollow needles. They whacked Runckel, pinched him, and thumped him, then jumped for cover as he let out another blast.

"Sir," said a young doctor wearing a "Medical-Officer-On-Duty" badge, "I'm afraid I shall have to quarantine this room and all its occupants. That includes you, sir." He said this in a gentle but firm voice.

Bade glanced at the doorway. A continuous stream of clerks, officers, and messengers moved in and out on necessary business. Some of these officers, Bade noticed, were speaking in low angry tones to idiotically smiling members of the staff. As one of the angry officers slapped a sheaf of papers on a desk, the owner of the desk came slowly to his feet. His chest inflated to gigantic proportions, he let out a terrific blast, reeled back against a wall, and let out another.

The young medical officer spun around excitedly. "Epidemic!" he yelled. "Seal that door! Back, all of you!" His face had a faint glow as he turned to Bade. "We'll have this under control in no time, sir." He went briskly to the door, his hand came up and plastered a red and yellow sticker over the joint where door and wall came together. He faced the room. "Everyone here is quarantined. It's death to break that seal."

From Bade's desk came an insistent ringing, and the small voice of the communications technician pleaded, "Sir . . . please, sir . . . this is important!" On the map across the room the bloated red space now had two sizable dents driven into it, such as might be expected if the enemy were opening a counteroffensive. The thin pencil line reaching toward the west was wobbling uncertainly at its far end.

Bade became aware of a fuzzy quality in his own thinking, and struggled to fix his mind on the scene around him.

The young doctor and his assistants hustled Runckel toward the door. As Bade stared, the doctor and assistants went out the door without breaking the quarantine seal. The sticker was plastered over the joint on the hinge side of the door. The seal bent as the door opened, then straightened out unhurt as the door shut.

"*Phew*," said Bade. He picked up the Communications microphone. "What did General Rast say?"

"Sir, he said, 'I can't reach the coast any faster than a day-and-a-half!' "

"The *coast!*"

"That's what he said, sir."

"Did you get that message to him?"

"Not yet, sir. We're trying."

Bade switched off and tried to think. His army was stretched out like a rubber balloon. His headquarters machinery was falling apart fast. An epidemic was loose among his men and plainly spreading fast. The base was still secure. But without sane men to man it, the enemy could be expected to walk in any time.

Bade's eyes were watering. He blinked, and glanced around for some sane face in the sea of hysterically cheerful people. He spotted an alert-looking officer with his back against the wall and a chair leg in his hand. Bade called to him. The officer looked around.

Bade said, "Do you know when Landing Force 3 is coming down?"

"Sir, they're coming down right now."

Bade stayed conscious long enough to watch the beginning of the enemy's counteroffensive, and also to see the start of the exploding sickness spread through the landing site. He grimly summarized the situation to the man he chose to take over command.

This man was the leader of Landing Force 3, a general by the name of Kottek. General Kottek was a fanatic, a man with a rough hypnotic voice and a direct unblinking stare. General Kottek's favorite drink was pure water. Food was a matter of indifference to him. His only known amusements were regular physical exercise and the dissection of military problems. To hesitate to obey a command of General Kottek's was unheard of. To bungle in the performance of it was as pleasant as to sit down in the open mouth of shark. General Kottek's officers were usually recognizable by their lean athletic appearance, and a tendency to jump at unexpected noises. General Kottek's men were nearly always to be seen in a state of good order and high spirits.

As soon as Bade, aching and miserable, summarized the situation and ordered Kottek to take over, Kottek gave a sharp precise salute, turned, and immediately began snapping out orders.

Heavily armed troops swung out to guard the site. Military police forced wandering gangs of sick men back to their ships. The crews of Landing Force 3 divided up to bring the depleted crews of the other ships up to minimum standards. The ships' damper units were turned to full power, and the outside power network and auxiliary damper units were disassembled and carried into the ships. Word came that a large enemy force had made an air-borne landing not far away. Kottek's troops marched in good order back to their ships. The ships of all three landing forces took off. They set down together in the center of the largest mass of Rast's encircled troops. The next day passed embarking these men under the protection of Kottek's fresh troops and the ships' dampers. Then the ships took off and repeated the process.

In this way, some sixty-five percent of the surrounded men were saved in the course of the week. Two more landing forces came down General Rast and a small body of guards were found unconscious partway up an unbelievably high hill in the west. The situation at this point became hopelessly complicated by the exploding sickness.

This sickness, which none of the doctors were able to cure or even relieve, manifested itself in various forms. The usual form began by exhilarating the victim. In this state, the patient generally considered himself capable of doing anything, however foolhardy, and regardless of difficulties. This lasted until the second phase set in with violent contractions of the chest and a sudden outrush of air from the lungs, accompanied by a blast like a gun going off. This second stage might or might not have complications such as digestive upset, headache, or shooting pains in the hands and feet. It ended when the third and last phase set in. In this phase the victim suffered from mental depression, considered himself a hopeless failure, and was as likely as not to try to end his life by suicide.

As a result of this suicidal impulse there were nightmarish scenes of soldiers disarming other soldiers, which brought the whole invasion force into a state of quaking uncertainty. At this critical point, and despite all precautions, General Kottek himself began to come down with the sickness. With him, the usual exhilaration took the form of a stream of violent and imperative orders.

Troops who should have retreated were ordered to fight to the death where they stood. Savage counterattacks for worthless objectives were driven home "to the last drop of blood." Because General Kottek ordered it, people obeyed without thought. The hysterical light in his eye was masked by the fanatical glitter that had been there to begin with. The general himself only realized what was wrong when his chest tightened up, his body tensed, and a racking concatenation of explosions burst from his chest. He immediately brought his body to the position of attention, and crushed out by sheer will a series of incipient tickling sensations way down in his throat. General Kottek handed the command over to General Runckel and reported himself to sick bay.

Runckel, by this time, had recovered enough from the third phase to be untied and allowed to walk around with only two guards. As he had not fully recovered his confidence, however, he immediately went to see Bade.

Bade's illness took the form of nausea, weakness, cold hands and feet, and a sensation of severe pressure in the small of the back. Bade was lying on a cot when Runckel came in, followed by his two watchful guards.

Bade looked up and saw the two guards lean warily against the wall, their eyes narrowed as they watched Runckel. Runckel paused at the foot of Bade's bed. "How do you feel?" Runckel asked.

"Except for yesterday and the day before," said Bade, "I never felt worse in my life. How do you feel?"

"All right most of the time." He cleared his throat. "Kottek's down with it now."

"Did he know in time?"

"No, I'm afraid he's left things in a mess."

Bade shook his head. "Do we have a general officer who *isn't* sick?"

"Not in the top brackets."

"Who did Kottek hand over to?"

"Me." Runckel looked a little embarrassed. "I'm not sure I can handle it yet."

"Who's in actual charge right now?"

"I've got the pieces of our own staff and the staff of Landing Force 2 working on it. Kottek's staff is hopeless. Half of them are talking about sweeping the enemy off the planet in two days."

Bade grunted. "What's your idea?"

"Well," said Runckel, "I still get . . . a little excited now and then. If you could possibly provide a sort of general supervision—"

Bade looked away weakly. "How's Rast?"

"Tied to his bunk with half-a-dozen men sitting on him."

"What about Vokk?"

"Tearing his lungs out every two or three minutes."

"Sokkis, then?"

Runckel shook his head grimly. "I'm afraid they didn't hear the gun go off in time. The doctors are still working on him, though."

"Well . . . is Frotch all right?"

"Yes, thank heaven. But then he's Flyer Command. And, worse yet, there's nobody to put in his place."

"All right, how about Sozzle?"

"Well," said Runckel, "Sozzle may be a good propaganda man, but personally I wouldn't trust him to command a platoon."

"Yes," said Bade, rolling over to try to ease the pain in his back, "I see your point." He took a deep breath. "I'll try to supervise the thing." He swung gingerly to a sitting position.

Runckel watched him, then his face twisted. "This whole thing is all my fault," he said. He choked. "I'm just no goo—"

The two guards sprang across the room, grabbed Runckel by the arms and rushed him out the door. Harsh grunts and solid thumping sounds came from the corridor outside. There was a heavy crash. Somebody said, "All right, get the general by the feet, and I'll take him by the shoulders. *Phew!* Let's go."

Bade sat dizzily on the edge of the bed. For a moment, he had a mental image of Runckel before the invasion, leaning forward and saying impressively, "Certain glory and a mighty victory await us."

Bade took several slow deep breaths. Then he got up carefully found a towel, and cautiously went to wash.

It took Bade almost a week to disentangle the troops from the web of indefensible positions and hopeless last stands Kottek had commanded them to in a day-and-a-half of peremptory orders. The enemy, meanwhile, took advantage of opportunity, using ground and air attacks, rockets, missiles and artillery in such profusion as to stun the mind. It was not until Bade's men and officers had recovered from circulating attacks of the sickness and another landing force had come down, that it was possible to temporarily resume the offensive. Another two weeks, and another sick landing force recovered, saw the invasion army in control of a substantial part of the central plain of the continent. Bade now had some spare moments to squint at certain reports that were piled up on his desk. Exasperatedly, he called a meeting of high officers.

Bade was standing with Runckel at a big map of the continent when their generals came in. Bade and Runckel each looked grim and intense. The generals looked uniformly dulled and worn down.

Bade took a last hard look at the map, then he and Runckel turned around. Bade glanced at Veth, Landing Site Commander. "What's your impression of the way things are going?"

Veth scowled. "Well, we're still getting eight to ten sizable missile hits a day. Of course, there's no predicting when they'll come in. With the men working outside the ships, any single hit could vaporize large numbers of essential technical personnel. Until we get the underground shelters built, the only way around this is to have the whole site damped out all the time." He shook his head. "This takes a lot of energy."

Bade nodded, and turned to Rast, Ground Forces Commander.

"So far," said Rast frowning, "our situation on paper looks not too bad. Morale is satisfactory. Our weapons are superior. We have strong forces in a reasonable large central area, and in theory we can shift rapidly from one front to the other, and be superior anywhere. But in practice, the enemy has so many missiles, of all types and sizes, that we can't take advantage of the position.

"Suppose, for instance, that I order XX and XXII Tank Armies from the eastern to the western front. They can't go under their own power, because of fuel expenditure, the wear on their tracks, and the resulting delay for repairs. They can't go by forceway network because there isn't any built yet. The only way to send them is by the natives' iron track roads. That would be fine, except that the iron track roads make beautiful targets for missile attacks. Thanks to the enemy, every bridge and junction either is, has been, or will be blown up and not once, either. The result is, we have to use slow filtration of troops from one front to the other, or we have to accept very heavy losses on route. In addition, we now know that the enemy has formidable natural defenses in the east and west, especially in the west. There's a range of hills there that surpasses anything I've ever seen or heard of. Not only is the difficulty of the terrain an obstacle but as our men go higher, movement finally becomes practically impossible. I know this from personal experience. The result of it is, the enemy need only guard the passes and he has a natural barrier behind which he can mass for attack at any chosen point."

Bade frowned. "Don't the hills have the same harmful effect on the enemy?"

"No sir, they don't."

"Why not?"

"I don't know. But that and their missiles put us in a nasty spot."

Bade absorbed this, then turned to General Frotch, head of Atmospheric Flyer Command.

Frotch said briskly, "Sir, so far as the enemy air forces are concerned, we have the situation under control. And various foreign long-range reconnaissance aircraft that might been filtering in from distant native countries, have also successfully batted out of the sky. However, as far as . . . ah . . . missiles . . . are concerned, the situation is a little strained."

Bade snapped, "Go on."

"Well, sir," said Frotch, "The enemy has missiles that can be fired at the fastest atmospheric flyers, that can be made to blow up near them, that can be guided to them, and even that can be made to chase and catch them."

"What about our weapons?"

"They're fine, on a percentage basis. But the enemy has a lot more missiles than we have pilots."

"I see," said Bade. "Well—" He turned to speak to the Director of Intelligence, but Frotch went on:

"Moreover, sir, we are having atmospheric troubles."

" 'Atmospheric troubles'? What's that?"

"For one thing, gigantic traveling electrical displays that disrupt plane-to-ground and ground-to-plane communications, and have to be avoided, or else the pilots either don't come out, or else come out fit for nothing but a rest cure. Then there are mass movements of air traveling from one part of the planet to another. Like land breezes and sea breezes at home. But here the breezes can be pretty forceful. The effect is to put an unpredictable braking force on all our operations."

Bade nodded slowly. "Well, we'll have to make the best of it." He turned to General Sozzle, who was Disseminator of Propaganda.

Sozzle cleared his throat. "I can make my report short and to the point. Our propaganda is getting us nowhere. For one thing, the enemy is apparently used to being ambushed daily by something called 'advertising,' which seems to consist of a series of subtle propaganda traps. By comparison our approach is so crude it throws them into hysterics."

Bade glanced at the Director of Intelligence, who said dully, "Sir, it's too early to say for certain how our work will eventually turn out. We've had some successes; but, so far, we've been handicapped by translation difficulties."

Bade frowned. "For instance?"

"Take the single word, 'snow,' " said the Intelligence Director. "You can't imagine the snarl my translators get into over that word. It apparently means 'white solid which falls in crystals from the sky.' Figure that out."

Bade squinted, then looked relieved. "Oh. It means, 'dust.' "

"That's the way the interpreters translated it. Now consider this sentence from a schoolbook. 'When April comes, the dust all turns to water and flows into the ground to fill the streams.' "

"That doesn't make any sense at all."

"No. But that's what happens if you accept 'dust' as the translation for 'snow.' There are other words such as: 'winter,' 'blizzard,' 'tornado.' Ask a native for an explanation, and with a straight face he'll give you a string of incomprehensible nonsense that will stand you on your ear. Not that it's important in itself. But it seems to show something about the native psychology that I can't quite figure out. You can fight your enemy best when you can understand him. Well, from this angle they're completely incomprehensible."

"Keep working on it," said Bade, after a short silence. He turned to Runckel.

Runckel said, "The overall situation looks about the same from my point of view. Namely, the natives are driven back, but by no means defeated. What we have to remember is that we never expected to have them defeated at this stage. True, our time schedule has been set back somewhat, but this was due not to enemy action, but to purely accidental circumstances. That is, first the atmosphere was so deficient in moisture that our ground vehicles were temporarily out of order, and, second, we were disabled by an unexpected disease. But these troubles are over with. My point is that we can now begin the decisive phase of operations."

"Good," said Bade. "But to do that we have to firmly hold the ground we have. I want to know if we can do this. On the surface, perhaps, it looks like it. But there are signs here I don't like. As the old saying goes, 'A shark shows you his fin, not his teeth. Take warning from the fin; when you see the teeth, it's too late.' "

"Yes," said Frotch, turning excitedly to Rast, "that's the thought exactly. "Now, will *you* mention it, or shall I?"

"Holy fangjaw," growled Rast, "maybe it doesn't really mean anything."

"The Supreme Commander," said Runckel angrily, "was trying to talk."

Bade said, "What is it, Rast? Speak up."

"Well—" Rast hesitated, glanced uneasily at Runckel, then thrust out his jaw, "Sir, it looks like the whole master plan of the invasion may have come unhinged." Runckel angrily started to speak. Bade glanced at Runckel, took out a long slender cigar, and sat down on the edge of the table to watch Runckel. He lit the cigar and put down the lighter. As far as Bade was concerned, his face was expressionless. Things seemed to have an unnatural clarity, however, as he looked at Runckel and waited for him to speak.

Runckel looked at Bade, swallowed hard and said nothing.

Bade glanced at Rast.

Rast burst out, "Sir, for the last ten days or so, we've been wondering how long the enemy could keep up his missile attacks. Flyer Command has blasted factories vital to missile manufacture, and destroyed all their known stockpiles. Well, grant we didn't get all their stockpiles. That's logical enough. Grant that they had tremendous stocks stored away. Even grant that before we got here they made missiles all the time for the sheer love of making them. Maybe every man, woman, and child in the country had a missile, like a pet. Still, there's got to be an end *somewhere*."

Bade nodded soberly.

"Well, sir," said Rast, "we get these missiles fired at us all the time, day after day after day, one missile after the other, like an army of men tramping past in an endless circle forever. It's inconceivable that they'd use their missiles like this unless their supply is inexhaustible. Frotch gets hit with them, I get hit with them, Veth gets hit with them. For every job there's a missile. We put our overall weapons superiority in one pan of the balance. They pour an endless heap of missiles in the other pan. *Where do all these missiles come from?"*

For an instant Rast was silent, then he went on. "At first we thought 'Underground factories.' Well, we did our best to find them and it was no use. And whenever we managed to spot moving missiles, they seemed to be coming from the coast.

"About this time, some of my officers were trying to convert a bunch of captives to our way of thinking. One of the officers noticed a peculiar thing. Whenever he clinched his argument by saying, "Moreover, you are alone in the world; you cannot defeat us alone—" the captives would all look very serious. Most of them would be very still and attentive, but here and there among them, a few would choke, gag, make sputtering noises, and shake all over. The other soldiers would secretively kick these men, and jab them with their elbows until they were still and attentive. Now, however, the question arose, what did all this mean? The actions were described to Intelligence, who said they meant exactly what they seemed to mean, 'suppressed mirth.'

"In other words, whenever we said, 'You can't win; you're alone in the world,' they wanted to burst out laughing, My officers now varied the technique. They would say, for instance, 'The U.S.S.R. is our faithful ally.' Our captives would sputter, gasp, and almost strangle to death. Put this together with their inexhaustible supply of missiles and the thing takes on a sinister look."

"You think," said Bade, "that the U.S.S.R. and other countries are shipping missiles to the U.S. by sea?"

General Frotch cleared his throat apologetically. "Sir, excuse me. I have something new to add to this. I've set submerger planes down along all three of their coasts. Not only are the ports alive with shipping. But some of our men swam into the harbors at night and hid, and either they're the victims of mass-hypnosis or else those ships are unloading missiles like a fish unloads spawn."

Bade looked at Runckel.

Runckel said dully, "In that case, we have the whole planet to fight. That was what we had to avoid at any cost."

This comment produced a visible deterioration of morale. Before this attitude had a chance to set, Bade said forcefully and clearly, "I was never in favor of this attack. And this fortifies my original views. But from a strictly military point of view, I believe we can still win."

He went to the map, and speaking to each of the generals in turn, he explained his plan.

In the three following days, each of the three remaining landing forces set down. The men of each landing force, as expected, became violently ill with the exploding sickness. With the usual course of the sickness known, it proved possible to care for this new horde of patients with nothing worse than extreme inconvenience for the invasion force as a whole.

The enemy, meanwhile, strengthened his grip around the occupied area, and at the same time cut troop movements within the area to a feeble trickle. Day after day, the enemy missiles fell in an increasingly heavy rain on the road and rail centers. During the height of this bombardment, Bade succeeded in gradually filtering all of Landing Force 3 back to the protection of the ships.

Rast now reported that the enemy attacks were mounting in force and violence, and requested permission to fall back and contract the defense perimeter.

Bade replied that help would soon come, and Rast must make only small local withdrawals.

Landing Forces 7, 8, and 9, cured of the exploding sickness, now took off. Immediately afterward, Landing Force 3 took off.

Landing Forces 3 and 7, under General Kottek, came down near the base of the Upper Peninsula of Michigan, and struck south and west to rip up communications in the rear of the main enemy forces attacking General Rast.

Landing Force 8 split, its southern section seizing the western curve of Cuba to cut the shipping lanes of the Gulf of Mexico. Its northern sections seized Long Island, to block shipping entering the port of New York, and to subject shipping in the ports of Boston, Philadelphia, Baltimore, and Washington to heavy attack from the air.

Landing Force 9 remained aloft until the enemy's reaction to General Kottek's thrust from the rear became evident. This reaction proved to be a quickly improvised simultaneous attack from north and south, to pinch off the flow of supplies from Kottek's base to the point of his advance. Landing Force 9 now set down, broke the attack of the southern pincer, then struck southeastward to that road and rail supplying the enemy's northern armies. The overall situation now resembled two large, roughly concentric circles, each very thick in the north, and very thin in the south. A large part of the outer circle, representing the enemy's forces, was now pressed between the inner circle and the inverted Y of Kottek's attack from the north.

A large percentage of the enemy missile-launching sites were now overrun, and Rast for the first time found it possible to switch his troops from place to place without excessive losses. The enemy opened violent attacks in both east and west to relieve the pressure on their trapped armies in the north, and Rast fell back slowly, drawing forces from both these fronts and putting them into the northern battle.

The outcome hung in a treacherous balance until the enemy's supplies gave out in the north. This powerful enemy force then collapsed, and Rast swung his weary troops to the south.

Three weeks after the offensive began, it ended with the fighting withdrawal of the enemy to the east and west. The enemy's long eastern and southern coasts were now sealed against all but a comparative trickle of supplies from overseas. General Kottek held the upper peninsula of Michigan in a powerful grip. From it he dominated huge enemy industrial regions, and threatened the flank of potential enemy counterattacks from north or east.

Within the main occupied region itself, the forceway network and key-tools factories were being set up.

Runckel was only expressing the thought of nearly the whole invasion army when he walked into the operations room, heaved a sigh of relief and said to Bade, "Well, thank heaven *that's* over!"

Bade heard this and gave a noncommittal growl. He had felt this way himself some time before. During Runckel's absence, however, certain reports had come to Bade's desk and left him feeling like a man who goes down a flight of steps in the dark, steps off briskly, and finds there was one more step than he thought.

"Look at this," said Bade. Runckel leaned over his shoulder, and together they looked at a report headed, "Enemy Equipment." Bade passed over several pages of drawings and descriptions devoted to enemy knives, guns, grenades, helmets, canteens, mess equipment and digging tools, then paused at a section marked "Enemy clothing: 1) Normal enemy clothing consists of light two-piece underwear, an inner and an outer foot-covering, and either a light two-piece or light one-piece outer covering for the arms, chest, abdomen and legs. 2) However, capture of enemy supply trains in the recent northern offensive uncovered the following fantastic variety; a) thick inner and outer hand coverings; b) heavy one-piece undergarment covering legs, arms, and body; c) heavy upper outer garment; d) heavy lower outer garment; e) heavy inner foot covering; f) massive outer footcovering; g) additional heavy outer garment; h) extraordinarily heavy outer garment designed to cover entire body with exception of head, hands, and lower legs. In addition, large extra quantities of the heavy cover normally issued to the troops for sleeping purposes were also found. The purpose of all this clothing is difficult to understand. Insofar as the activity of a soldier encased in all these garments would be cut to a minimum, it can only be assumed that all these coverings represent body-shielding against some abnormal condition. The presence of poisonous chemicals in large quantities seems a likely possibility. Yet with the exception of the massive outer foot-covering, these garments are not impermeable."

Bade looked at Runckel. "They do have war chemicals?"

"Of course," said Runckel, frowning. "But we have protective measures and our own war chemicals, if trouble starts."

Bade nodded thoughtfully, slid the report aside, and picked up one headed, "Medical Report on Enemy Skin Condensation."

Runckel shook his head. "I can never understand those. We've had a flood of reports like that from various sources. At most, I just initial them and send them back."

"Well," said Bade, "read the summary, at least."

"I'll try," growled Runckel, and leaned over Bade's shoulder to read:

"To summarize these astonishing facts, enemy captives have been observed to form, on the outer layer of their skin, a heavy beading of moisture. This effect is similar to that observed with laboratory devices maintained at depressed temperatures—that is, at reduced degrees of heat. The theory was, therefore, formed that the enemy's skin is, similarly, maintained at a temperature lower than that of his surroundings. Complex temperature-determining apparatus were set up to test this theory.

As a result, this theory was disproved, but an even more astonishing state of affairs was discovered: The enemy's internal temperature varied very little, regardless of considerable experimental variation of the temperature of his environment.

"The only possible conclusion was that the enemy's body contains some built-in mechanism that actually controls the degree of heat and maintains it at a constant level.

"Now, according to Poff's widely accepted Principle, no complex bodily mechanism can long maintain itself in the absence of need or exercise. And what is the need for a bodily mechanism that has the function of holding body temperature constant despite wide external fluctuation? What is the need for a defense against something unless the something exists?

"We are forced to the conclusion that the degree of heat on this planet is subject to variations sufficiently severe as to endanger life. A new examination of what has hitherto been considered to be the enemy's mythology indicates that, contrary to conditions on our own planet, this planet is subject to remarkable fluctuations of temperature, that alternately rise to a peak, then fall to an incredible low.

"According to this new theory, our invasion force arrived as the temperature was approaching its maximum. Since then, it has reached and passed its peak, and is now falling. All this has passed unnoticed by us, partly because the maximum here approaches the ordinary condition on our home planet. The danger, of course, is that the minimum on this planet would prove insupportable to our form of life."

This was followed by a qualifying phrase that further tests would have to be made, and the conclusions could not be considered final.

Bade looked at Runckel. Runckel snapped, "What do you do with a report like that? I'd tear it up, but why waste strength? It's easier to throw them in the wastebasket and go on."

"Wait a minute," said Bade. "If this report just happens to be right, then where are we?"

"Frankly," said Runckel, "I don't know or care. 'Skin condensation.' These scientists should keep their minds on things that have some chance of being useful. It would help if they'd figure out how to cut down flareback on our subtron guns. Instead they talk about 'skin condensation.'"

Bade wrote on the report, "This may turn out to be important. List on no more than two sheets of paper possible defenses against reduced degree of heat. Get it to me as soon as possible. Bade."

Bade signaled to a clerk. "Snap a copy of this, send the original out, and bring me the copy."

"Yes, sir."

"Now," said Bade, "We have one more report."

"Well, I have to admit," said Runckel, "that I can't see that either of these reports were of any value."

"Well, read this one, then."

Runckel shook his head in disgust, and leaned over. His eyes widened. This paper was headed, "For the Supreme Commander only. Special Report of General Kottek."

The report began, "Sir: It is an officer's duty to state, plainly and without delay, any matter that requires the immediate attention of his superior. I, therefore, must report to you the following unpleasant but incontrovertible facts:

"1) Since their arrival in this region, my troops have on three recent occasions displayed a strikingly low level of performance. Two simulated night attacks revealed feeble command and exaggerated sluggishness on the part of the troops. A defense exercise carried out at dawn to repulse a simulated amphibious landing was a complete failure; troops and officers alike displayed insufficient energy and initiative to drive the attack home.

"2) On other occasions, troops and officers have maintained a high, sometimes strikingly high, level of energy and activity.

"3) No explanation of this variability of performance has been forthcoming from the medical and technical personnel attached to my command. Neither have I any assurance that these fluctuations will not take place in the future.

"4) It is, therefore, my duty to inform you that I cannot assure the successful performance of my mission. Should the enemy attack with his usual energy during a period of low activity on the part of my troops, the caliber of my resistance will be that of wax against steel. This is no exaggeration, but plain fact.

"5) This situation requires the immediate attention of the highest military and technical authorities. What is in operation here may be a disease, an enemy nerve gas, or some natural factor unknown to us. Whatever its nature, the effect is highly dangerous.

"6) A mobile, flexible defense in these circumstances is impossible. A rigid linear defense is worthless. A defense by linked fortifications requires depth. I am therefore constructing a deep fortified system in the western section of the region under my control. This is no cure, but a means of minimizing disaster.

"7) Enemy missile activity since the defeat of their northern armies has been somewhat less than forty percent of that expected."

Runckel's face was somber. "This is serious," he said. "When Kottek yells for help, we've got trouble. We'll have to put all our attention on this thing and get it out of the way as fast as we can."

Bade nodded, and reached over to take a message from a clerk. He glanced at it and scowled. The message was from Atmospheric Flyer Command. It read:

"Warning! Tornado sighted approaching main base!"

Runckel leaned over to read the message. "What's this?" he said angrily. " 'Tornado' is just a myth. Everybody knows that."

Bade snapped on the microphone to Aerial Reconnaissance. "What's this 'tornado' warning?" he demanded. "What's a 'tornado'?"

"Sir, a tornado is a whirling severe breeze of destructive character, conjoined with a dark cloud in the shape of a funnel, with the smaller end down."

Runckel gave an inarticulate snarl.

Bade squinted. "This thing is dangerous?"

"Yes, sir. The natives dig holes in the ground, and jump in when one comes along. A tornado will smash houses and ground-cars to bits, sir."

"Listen," snarled Runckel, "it's just *air*, isn't it?"

Bade snapped on Landing Site Command. "Get all the men back in the ships," he ordered. "Turn the dampers to full power."

"Holy fangjaw!" Runckel burst out. "Air can't hurt us. What's bad about a breeze, anyway?" He seized the Aerial Reconnaissance microphone and snarled. "Stand up, you! What have you been drinking?"

Bade took Runckel by the arm. "Look there!"

On the nearest wall screen, a wide black cloud warped across the sky, and stretched down a long arc to the ground. The whole thing grew steadily larger as they watched.

Bade seized the Landing Site Command microphone. "Can we lift ships?"

"No, sir. Not without tearing the power and damper networks to pieces."

"I see," said Bade. He looked up. The cloud overspread the sky. The screen fell dark. There was a heavy clang, a thundering crash, the ship trembled, tilted, heeled, and slowly, painfully, settled back upright as Bade hung onto the desk and Runckel dove for cover. The sky began to lighten. Bade gripped the microphone and asked what had happened. He listened blank-faced as, after a moment, the first estimates of the damage came in.

One of the thousand-foot-long ships had been tipped off its base. In falling, it struck another ship, which also fell, striking a third. The third ship struck a fourth, which fell unhindered and split up the side like a bean pod. The mouth of the tornado's funnel then ran along the split, and the ship's inside looked as if it had been cleaned out with a vacuum hose. A few stunned survivors and scattered bits of equipment were clinging here and there. That was all.

The enemy chose this moment to land his heaviest missile strike in weeks.

It took the rest of the day, all night, and all the following day to get the damage moderately well cleaned up. Then a belated report came in that Forceway Station 1 had been subjected to a bombardment of desks, chairs, communications equipment, and odd bolts and nuts that had riddled the installation from one end to the other and set completion date back four weeks.

An intensive search now located most of the missing equipment and personnel—strewn over forty miles of territory.

"It was," said Runckel weakly, "only air, that's all."

"Yes," said Bade grimly. He looked up from a scientific report on the tornado. "A whirlpool is only water. Whirling water. Apparently this planet has traveling whirlpools of air."

Runckel groaned, then a sudden thought seemed to hit him. He reached into his wastebasket, fished around, and drew out a crumpled ball of paper. He smoothed it out, read for a while, then growled, "Scientific reports. Here's some kind of report that came in right in the middle of a battle. According to this thing, the native name for the place where we've set down is 'Cyclone Alley.' Is there some importance in knowing a thing like that?"

Bade felt severe prickling sensations across his back and neck. " 'Cyclone,' " he said. "Where did I hear that before? Give me that paper."

Runckel shrugged and tossed it over. Bade smoothed it out and read:

"In this prevalent fairy tale, the 'cyclone'—corresponding to our 'sea serpent,' or 'Ogre of the Deep'—makes recurrent visits to communities in certain regions, frightening the inhabitants terribly and committing all sorts of prankish violence. On some occasions, it carries its chosen victims aloft, to set them down again far away. The cyclone is a frightening giant, tall and dark, who approaches in a whirling dance.

"An interesting aspect is the contrast of this legend with the equally prevalent legend of Santa Claus. Cyclone comes from the south, Santa from the north. Cyclone is prankish, frightening. Santa is benign, friendly, and even brings gifts. Cyclone favors 'springtime,' but may come nearly any time except 'winter.' Santa comes only in 'winter.' Cyclone is secular. Santa reflects some of the holy aura of the religious festival, 'Christmas.'

" 'Christmas comes but once a year. When it comes, it brings good cheer.' Though Cyclone visits but a few favored towns at a time, Santa visits at once all, everyone, even the lowliest dweller in his humble shack. The natives are immensely earnest about both of these legends. An amusing aspect is that our present main base is almost ideally located for visits by that local Ogre of the Sea, 'Cyclone.' We are, in fact, situated in a location known as 'Cyclone Alley.' Perhaps the Ogre will visit us."

At the bottom of the page was a footnote: " 'Cyclone' is but one name for this popular Ogre. Another common name is 'Tornado.' "

Bade sat paralyzed for a moment staring at this paper. "Tornado Alley," he muttered. He grabbed the Flyer Command microphone to demand how the tornado warning system was coming. Then, groggily, he set the paper aside and turned his attention to the problem of General Kottek's special report. He looked up again as a nagging suspicion began to build up in him. He turned to Runckel. "How many of these 'myths' have we come across, anyway?"

Runckel looked as though a heavy burden were settling on him. He groped through his bulging wastebasket and fished out another crumpled ball of paper, then another. He located the one he wanted, smoothed it out, sucked in a deep breath, and read: "Cyclone, winter, spring, summer, hurricane, Easter bunny, autumn, blizzard, cold wave, Snow White and the Seven Dwarfs, lightning, Santa Claus, typhoon, mental telepathy, earthquake, levitation, volcano—" He looked up. "You want the full report on each of these things? I've got most of them here somewhere."

Bade looked warily at Runckel's overstuffed wastebasket. "No," he said. "But what about that report you're reading from? Isn't that an overall summary? Why didn't I get a copy of that?"

Runckel looked it over and growled, "Try to train them to send their reports to the right place. Yes, it's an overall summary. Here, want it?"

"Yes," said Bade. He took the report, then stopped to wonder, where was that report he had asked for on "reduced degree of heat"? He reached for a microphone, then remembered General Kottek's special report. Bade first sent word to Kottek that he approved what Kottek was doing, and that the problem was getting close attention. Then he read the crumpled overall summary Runckel had given him, and ended up thinking he had been on a trip through fairyland. His memory of the details evaporated even as he tried to mentally review the paper. "Hallowe'en," he growled, "icebergs, typhoons—this planet must be a mass of mythology from one end to the other." He picked up a microphone to call his Intelligence Service.

A messenger hurried across the room to hand him a slip of paper. The paper was from Atmospheric Flyer Command. It read:

"Warning! Tornado sighted approaching main base!"

This time, the tornado roared past slightly to the west of the base. It hit, instead, Forceway Station 1, and scattered sections of it all over the countryside.

For good measure, the enemy fired in an impressive concentration of rockets and missiles. The attack did only slight harm to to the base, but it finished off Forceway Station 1.

An incoherent report now came in from the occupied western end of Cuba, to the effect that a "hurricane" had just gone through.

Bade fished through Runckel's wastebasket to find out exactly what a "hurricane" might be. He looked up at the end of this, pale and shaken, and sent out a strong force to put his Cuban garrison back on its feet.

Then he ordered Intelligence and some of his technical and scientific departments to get together right away and break down the so-called "myths" into two groups: harmful, and nonharmful. The nonharmful group was to be arranged in logical order, and each item accompanied by a brief, straightforward description.

As Bade sent out this order, General Kottek reported that, as a supplement to his fortified system, he was making sharp raids whenever conditions were favorable, in order to keep the enemy in his section offbalance. In one of these raids, his troops had captured an enemy document which had since been translated. The document was titled: "Characteristics of Unheatful-Blooded Animals." Kottek enclosed a copy:

"Unheatful-blooded animals have no built-in system for maintaining their bodily rate of molecular activity. If the surrounding temperature falls, so does theirs. This lowers their physical activity. They cannot move or react as fast as normally. Heatful-blooded animals, properly clothed, are not subject to this handicap.

"In practical reality, this means that as unheatful conditions set in, the Invader should always be attacked during the most unheatful period possible. Night attacks have much to recommend them. So do attacks at dusk or dawn. In general, avoid taking the offensive during heatful periods such as early afternoon.

"Forecasts indicate that winter will be late this year, but severe when it comes. Remember, there is no year on record when temperatures have not dropped severely in the depths of winter. In such conditions, it is expected that the Invader will be killed in large numbers by—untranslatable—of the blood.

"Our job is to make sure they are kept worn down until winter comes. Our job then will be to make sure none of them live through the winter."

Bade looked up feeling as if his digestive system were paralyzed. A messenger hurried across the room to hand him a thick report hastily put together by the Intelligence Service. It was titled:

"Harmful Myths and Definitions."

Bade spent the first part of the night reading this spine-tingling document. The second part of the night he spent in nightmares.

Toward morning, Bade had one vivid and comparatively pleasant dream. A native wearing a simple cloth about his waist looked at Bade intently and asked, "Does the shark live in the air? Does a man breathe underwater? Who will eat grass when he can have meat?"

Bade woke up feeling vaguely relieved. This sensation was swept away when he reached the operations room and saw the expression on Runckel's face. Runckel handed Bade a slip of paper:

"Hurricane Hannah approaching Long Island Base."

Intercepted enemy radio and television broadcasts spoke of Hurricane Hannah as "the worst in thirty years." As Bade and Runckel sat by helplessly, Hurricane Hannah methodically pounded Long Island Base to bits and pieces, then swept away the pieces. The hurricane moved on up the shoreline, treating every village and city along the way like a personal enemy. When Hurricane Hannah ended her career, and retired to sink ships farther north, the Atlantic coast was a shambles from one end to the other.

Out of this shambles moved a powerful enemy force, which seized the bulk of what was left of Long Island Base. The remnant of survivors were trapped in the underground installations, and reported that the enemy was lowering a huge bomb down through the entrance.

In Cuba, the reinforced garrison was barely holding on.

A flood of recommendations now poured in on Bade:

1) Long Island Base needed a whole landing force to escape capture.

2) Cuba Base had to have at least another half landing force for reinforcements.

3) The Construction Corps required the ships of two full landing forces in order to power the forceway network. Otherwise, work on the key-tools factories would be delayed.

4) Landing Site Command would need the ships and dampers of three landing forces to barely protect the base if if the power supply of two landing forces were diverted to the Construction Corps.

5) The present main base was now completed and should be put to efficient use at once.

6) The present main base was worthless, because Forceway Station 1 could not be repaired in time to link the base to the forceway network.

7) Every field commander except General Kottek urgently needed heavy reinforcements without delay.

8) Studies by the Staff showed the urgent need of building up the central reserve without delay, at the expense of the field commanders, if necessary.

Bade gave up Long Island Base, ordered Cuba Base to hold on with what it had, told the Landing Site Commander to select a suitable new main base near some southern forceway station free of tornadoes, and threw the rest of the recommendations into the wastebasket.

Runckel now came over with a rope smoldering stub jutting out of the corner of his mouth. "Listen," he said to Bade, "we're going to have a disciplinary problem on our hands. That Cuban garrison has been living on some kind of native paint-remover called 'rum.' The whole lot of them have a bad case of the staggering lurch from it; not even the hurricane sobered them up. Poff knew what was going on. But he and his staff covered it over. His troops are worthless. Molch and the reinforcements are doing all the fighting."

Bade said, "Poff is still in command?"

"I put Molch in charge."

"Good. We'll have to courtmartial Poff and his staff. Can Molch hold the base?"

"He said he could. If we'd get Poff off his neck."

"Fine," said Bade. "One he gets things in order, ship the regular garrison to a temporary camp somewhere. We don't want Molch's troops infected."

Runckel nodded. A clerk apologized and stepped past Runckel to hand Bade a message. It was from General Frotch, who reported that all his atmospheric flyers based on Long Island had been lost in Hurricane Hannah. Bade showed the message to Runckel, who shook his head wearily.

As Runckel strode away, another clerk put a scientific report on Bade's desk. Bade read it through, got Frotch on the line, and arranged for a special mission by Flyer Command. Then he located his report on "Harmful Myths and Definitions." Carefully, he read the definition of winter:

"To the best of our knowledge, 'winter' is a severe periodic disease of plants, the actual onset of which is preceded by the vegetation turning various colors. The tall vegetables known as 'trees' lose their foliage entirely, except for some few which are immune and are known as 'evergreens.' As the disease progresses, the juices of the plants are squeezed out and crystallize in white feathery forms known as 'frost.' Sufficient quantities of this squeezed-out dried juice is 'snow.' The mythology refers to 'snow falling from the sky.' A possible explanation of this is that the large trees also 'snow,' producing a fall of dried juice crystals. These crystals are clearly poisonous. 'Frostbite,' 'chilblains,' and even 'freezing to death' are mentioned in the enemy's communication media. Even the atmosphere filled with the resulting vapor is said to be 'cold.' Totally unexplainable is the common reference to children rolling up balls of this poisonous dried plant juice and hurling them at each other. This can only be presumed to be some sort of toughening exercise. More research on this problem is needed."

Bade set this report down, reread the latest scientific report, then got up and slowly walked over to a big map of the globe. He gazed thoughtfully at various islands in the South Seas.

Late that day, the ships lifted and moved, to land again near Forceway Station 2. Power cables were run to the station across a sort of long narrow valley at the bottom of which ran a thin trickle of water. By early the morning of the next day, the Forceway network was in operation. Men and materials flashed thousands of miles in a moment, and work on the key-tools factories accelerated sharply.

Bade immersed himself in intelligence summaries of the enemy communications media. An item that especially interested him was "Winter Late This Year."

By now there were three viewpoints on "winter." A diehard faction doggedly insisted that it was a myth, a mere quirk of the alien mentality. A large and very authoritative body of opinion held the plant juice theory, and bolstered its stand with reams of data sheets and statistics. A small, vociferous group asserted the heretical water crystal hypotheses, and ate alone at small tables for doing so.

General Frotch called Bade to say that the special Flyer Command mission was coming in to report.

General Kottek sent word that enemy attacks were becoming more daring, that his troops' periods of inefficiency were more frequent, and that the vegetation in his district was turning color. He mentioned, for what it was worth, that troops within the fortifications seemed less affected than those outside. Troops far underground, however, seemed to be slowed down automatically, regardless of conditions on the surface, unless they were engaged in heavy physical labor.

Bade scowled and sent off inquiries to his scientific sections. Then he heard excited voices and looked up.

Four Flyer Command officers were coming slowly into the room, bright metal poles across their shoulders. Slung from the poles was a big plastic-wrapped bundle. The bundle was dripping steadily, and leaving a trail of droplets that led back out the door into the hall. The plastic was filmed over with a layer of tiny beads of moisture.

Runckel came slowly to his feet.

The officers, breathing heavily, set the big bundle on the floor near Bade's desk.

"Here it is, sir."

Bade's glance was fastened on the object.

"Unwrap it."

The officers bent over the bundle, and with clumsy fingers pulled back the plastic layer. The plastic stood up stiffly, and bent only with a hard pull. Underneath was something covered with several of the enemy's thick dark sleeping covers. The officers rolled the bundle back and forth and unwound the covers. An edge of some milky substance came into view. The officers pulled back the covers and a milky, semi-transparent block sat there, white vapor rolling out from it along the floor.

There was a concerted movement away from the block and the officers.

Bade said, "Was the whole place like that?"

"No, sir, but there was an awful lot of this stuff. And there was a compacted powdery kind of substance, too. We didn't bring enough of it back and it all turned to water."

"Did you wear the protective clothes we captured?"

"Yes, sir, but they had to be slit and zippered up the legs, because the enemy's feet are so small. The arms were a poor fit and there had to be more material across the chest."

"How did they work?"

"They were a great help, sir, as long as we kept moving. As soon as we slowed down, we started to stiffen up. The hand and foot gear was improvised and hard to work in, though."

Bade looked thoughtfully at the smoldering block, then got up, stepped forward, and spread his hand close to the block. A numbness gradually dulled his hand and moved up his arm. Then Bade straightened up. He found he could move his hand only slowly and painfully. He motioned to Runckel. "I think this is what 'cold' is. Want to try it?" Runckel got up, held his hand to the block, then straightened, scowling.

Bade felt a tingling sensation and worked his hand cautiously as Runckel, his face intent, slowly spread and closed his fingers.

Bade thoughtfully congratulated the officers, then had the block carried off to the Testing Lab.

The report on defense against "reduced degree of heat" now came in. Bade read this carefully several times over. The most striking point, he noticed, was the heavy energy expenditure involved.

That afternoon, several ships took off, separated, and headed south.

The next few days saw the completion of the first key-tool factory, the receipt of reports from insect-bitten scouts in various regions far to the south, and a number of terse messages from General Kottek. Bade ordered plans drawn up for the immediate withdrawal of General Kottek's army, and for the possible withdrawal by stages of other forces in the north. He ordered preparations made for the first completed factories to produce anti-reduced-degree-of-heat devices. He read a number of reports on the swiftly changing state of the planet's atmosphere. Large quantities of rain were predicted.

Bade saw no reason to fear rain, and turned to a new problem: The enemy's missiles had produced a superabundance of atomic debris in the atmosphere. Testing Lab was concerned over this, and suggested various ways to get rid of it. Bade approved the projects and turned to the immediate problem of withdrawing the bulk of General Kottek's troops from their strong position without losing completely the advantages of it.

Bade was considering the idea of putting a forceway station somewhere in Kottek's underground defenses, so that he could be reinforced or withdrawn at will. This would involve complicated production difficulties; but then Kottek had said the slowing-down was minimized under cover, and it might be worthwhile to hold an option on his position. While weighing the various intangibles and unpredictables, Bade received a report from General Rast. Rast was now noticing the same effect Kottek had reported.

Word came in that two more key-tools factories were now completed.

Intelligence reports of enemy atmospheric data showed an enormous "cold air mass moving down through Canada."

General Frotch, personally supervising high-altitude atmospheric tests, now somehow got involved in a rushing high-level air stream. Having the power of concentrating his attention completely upon whatever he was doing, Frotch got bound up in the work and never realized the speed of the air stream until he came down again—just behind the enemy lines.

When Bade heard of this, he immediately went over the list of officers, and found no one to replace Frotch. Bade studied the latest scientific reports and the disposition of his forces, then ordered an immediate switching of troops and aircraft through the forceway network toward the place where Frotch had vanished. A sharp thrust with local forces cut into the enemy defense system, was followed up by heavy reinforcements flowing through the forceway network, and developed an overpowering local superiority that swamped the enemy defenses.

Runckel studied the resulting dispositions and said grimly, "Heaven help us if they hit us hard in the right place just now.

"Yes," said Bade, "and heaven help us if we don't get Frotch back." He continued his rapid switching of forces, and ordered General Kottek to embark all his troops and set down near the main base.

Flyer Command meanwhile began to show signs of headless disorientation, the ground commanders peremptorily ordering the air forces around as nothing more than close-support and flying artillery. The enemy behind-the-lines communications network continued to function.

Runckel now reported to Bade that no reply had been received from Kottek's headquarters. Runckel was sending a ship to investigate.

Anguished complaints poured in from the technical divisions that their work was held up by the troops flooding the forceway network.

The map now showed Bade's men driving forward in what looked like a full-scale battle to break the enemy's whole defensive arrangements and thrust clear through to the sea. Reports came in that, with the enemy's outer defense belt smashed, signs of unbelievable weakness were evident. The enemy seemed to have nothing but local reserves and only a few of them. The general commanding on the spot announced that he could end the war if given a free hand.

Bade now wondered, if the enemy's reserves weren't there, where were they? He repeated his original orders.

Runckel now come over with the look of a half-drowned swimmer and motioned Bade to look at the two nearest viewscreens.

One of the viewscreens showed a scene in shades of white. A layer of white covered the ground, towering ships were plastered on one side with white, obstacles were heaped over with white, the air filled with horizontal streaks of white. Everything on the screen was white or turning white.

"Kottek's base," said Runckel dully.

The other screen gave a view of the long narrow valley just outside. This "valley" was now a rushing torrent of foaming water, sweeping along chunks of floating debris that bobbed a hand's breadth under the power cables from the ships to Forceway Station 2.

The only good news that day and the next was the recapture of General Frotch. In the midst of crumbling disorder, Flyer Command returned to normal.

Bade sent off a specially-equipped mission to try and find out what had happened to General Kottek. Then he looked up to see General Rast walking wearily into the room. Rast conferred with Runckel in low dreary tones, then the two of them started over toward Bade.

Bade returned his attention to a chart showing the location of the key-tools factories and the forceway network.

A sort of groan announced the arrival of Rast and Runckel. Bade looked up. Rast saluted. Bade returned the salute. Rast said stiffly, "Sir, I have been defeated. My army no longer exists."

Bade looked Rast over quickly, studying his expression and bearing.

"It's a plain fact," said Rast. "Sir, I should be relieved of command."

"What's happened?" said Bade. "I have no reports of any new enemy attack."

"No," said Rast, "there won't be any formal report. The whole northern front is anaesthetized from one end to the other."

"Snow?" said Bade.

"White death," said Rast.

A messenger stepped past the two generals to hand Bade a report. It was from General Frotch:

"1) Aerial reconnaissance shows heavy enemy forces moving south on a wide front through the snow-covered region. No response or resistance has been noted on the part of our troops.

"2) Aerial reconnaissance shows light enemy forces moving in to ring General Kottek's position. The enemy appears to be moving with extreme caution.

"3) It has so far proved impossible to get in touch with General Kottek.

"4) It must be reported that on several occasions our ground troops have, as individuals, attempted to seize from our flyer pilots and crews, their special protective anti-reduced-degree-of-heat garments. This problem is becoming serious."

Bade looked up at Rast. "You're Ground Forces Commander, not commander of a single front."

"That's so," said Rast. "I should be. But all I command now is a kind of mob. I've tried to keep the troops in order, but they know one thing after another is going wrong. Naturally, they put the blame on their leaders."

The room seemed to Bade to grow unnaturally light and clear. He said, "Have you had an actual case of mutiny, Rast?"

Rast stiffened. "No, sir. But it is possible for troops to be so laggardly and unwilling that the effect is the same. What I mean is that there is the steady growth of a cynical attitude everywhere. Not only in the the troops but in the officers."

Bade looked off at the far corner of the room for a moment. He glanced at Runckel. "What's the state of the key-tools factories?"

"Almost all completed. But the northern ones are now in the reduced-degree-of-heat zone. Part of the forceway network is, too. Using the key-tools plants remaining, it might be possible to patch together some kind of a makeshift. But the reduced-degree-of-heat zone is still moving south."

A pale clerk apologized, stepped around the generals and handed Bade two messages. The first was from Intelligence:

"Enemy propaganda broadcasts beamed at our troops announce General Kottek's unconditional surrender with all his forces. We have no independent information on Kottek's actual situation."

The second message was from the commander of Number 1 Shock Infantry Division. This report boiled down to a miserable confession that the commanding officer found himself unable to prevent:

1) Fraternization with the enemy.

2) The use of various liquid narcotics that rendered troops unfit for duty.

3) The unauthorized wearing of red, white, and blue buttons lettered, "Vote Republican."

4) An ugly game called "footbase," in which the troops separated into two long lines armed with bats, to hammer, pound, beat, and kick, a ball called "the officer," from one end of the field to the other.

Bade looked up at Rast. "How is it I only find out about this now?"

"Sir," said Rast, "each of the officers was ashamed to report it to his superior."

Bade handed the report to Runckel, who read it through and looked up somberly. "If it's hit the shock troops, the rest must have it worse."

"Yet," said Bade, "the troops fought well when we recaptured Frotch."

"Yes," said Rast, "but it's the damned planet that's driving them crazy. The natives are remarkable propagandists. And the men can plainly see that even when they win a victory, some freak like the exploding sickness, or some kind of atmospheric jugglery, is likely to take it right away from them. They're in a bad mood and the only thing that might snap them out of it is definite action. But if they go the other way, we're finished."

"This," said Bade, "is no time for you to resign."

"Sir, it's a mess, and I'm responsible. I have to make the offer to resign."

"Well," said Bade, "I don't accept it. But we'll have to try to straighten out this mess." Bade pushed over several sheets of paper. On the first, he wrote:

"Official News Bureau: 1) Categorically deny the capture of General Kottek and his base. State that General Kottek is in full control of the North, that the enemy has succeeded in infiltrating troops into the general region under cover of snow, but that he has been repulsed with heavy losses in all attacks on the base itself.

"2) State that the enemy announcement of victory in the area is a desperation measure, timed to coincide with their almost unopposed advance through the evacuated Northern Front.

"3) The larger part of the troops in the Northern Front were withdrawn prior to the attack and switched by forceway network to launch a heavy feinting attack against the enemy. State that the enemy, caught by surprise, appears to be rushing reserves from his northern armies to cover the areas threatened by the feint.

"4) Devoted troops who held the Northern Front to make the deception succeed have now been overrun by the enemy advance under cover of the snow. Their heroic sacrifice will not be forgotten.

"5) The enemy now faces the snowtime alone. His usual preventive measures have been drastically slowed down. His intended decisive attack has failed of its object. The snow this year is unusually severe, and is already working heavy punishment on the enemy.

"6) Secret measures are now for the first time being brought into the open that will place our troops far beyond the reach of snow."

On the second sheet of paper, Bade wrote:

"Director of Protocol: Prepare immediately: 1) Supreme Commander's Citation for Extraordinary Bravery and Resourcefulness in Action: To be awarded General Kottek. 2) Supreme Commander's Citation for Extraordinary Devotion to Duty: To be awarded singly, to each soldier on duty during the enemy attack on the entire Northern Front. 3) These awards are both to be mentioned promptly in the Daily Notices."

Bade handed the papers to Runckel, "Send these out yourself." As Runckel started off, Bade looked at Rast, then was interrupted by a messenger who stepped past Rast, and handed Bade two slips of paper. With an effort of will, Bade extended his hand and took the papers. He read:

"Sir: Exploration Team South 3 has located ideal island base. Full details follow. Frotch."

"Sir: We have finally contacted General Kottek. He and his troops are dug into underground warrens of great complexity beneath his his system of fortifications. Most of the ships above ground are mere shells, all removable equipment having been stripped out and carried below for the comfort of the troops. Most of the ships' engines have also been disassembled one at a time, carried below, and set up to run the dampers—which are likewise below ground—and the 'heating units' devised by Kottek's technical personnel. His troops appear to be in good order and high spirits. Skath, Co., A. F. C., forwarded by Frotch."

Bade sucked in a deep breath and gave silent thanks. Then he handed the two reports to Rast. Bade snapped on a microphone and got in touch with Frotch. "Listen, can you get pictures of Kottek and his men?"

Frotch held up a handful of pictures, spread like playing cards. "The men took them for souvenirs and gave me copies. You can have all you want."

Bade immediately called his photoprint division and gave orders for the pictures to be duplicated by the thousands. The photoprint division slaved all night, and the excited troops had the pictures on their bulletin boards by the next morning.

The Official News Service meanwhile was dinning Bade's propaganda into the troops' ears at every opportunity. The appearance of the pictures now plainly caught the enemy propaganda out on a limb.

Doubting one thing the enemy propaganda had said, the troops suddenly doubted all. A violent revulsion of feeling took place. Before anything else could happen, Bade ordered the troops embarked.

By this time, the apparently harmless rain had produced a severe flood, which repeatedly threatened the power cables supplying the forceway network. The troops had to use this network to get to the ships in time.

As Bade's military engineers blasted out alternate channels for the rising water, and a fervent headquarters group prayed for a drought, the troops poured through the still-operative forceway stations and marched into the ships with joyful shouts.

The enemy joined the celebration with a mammoth missile attack.

The embarkation, together with the disassembling of vital parts of the accessible key-tools factories, took several days. During this time, the enemy continued his steady methodical advance well behind the front of the cold air mass. The enemy, however, made no sudden thrust on the ground to take advantage of the embarkation. Bade pondered this sign of tiredness, then sent up a ship to radio a query home. When the answer came, Bade sent a message to the enemy government. The message began:

"Sirs: This scouting expedition has now completed its mission. We are now withdrawing to winter quarters, which may be: a) an unspecified distant location; b) California; c) Florida. If you are prepared to accept certain temporary armistice conditions, we will understand we must choose a). Otherwise, you will understand we must choose b) or c). If you are prepared to consider these armistice conditons, you are strongly urged to send a plenpotentiary without delay. The plenipotentiary should be prepared to consider both the temporary armistice and the matters of mutual benefit to us."

Bade waited tensely for the reply. He had before him two papers, one of which read:

" . . . the enemy-held peninsula of Florida has thus been found to be heavily infested with heartworm—parasites which live inside the heart, slow circulation, and lower vital activity sharply. While the enemy appears to be immune to infestation, our troops plainly are not. The four scouts who returned here have at last, we believe, been cured—but they have not as yet recovered their strength. The state of things in nearby Cuba is not yet known for certain. Possibly, the troops' enormous consumption of native 'rum' has interacted medicinally with our blood chemistry to retard infestation. If so, we have our choice of calamities. In any case, a landing in Florida would be ruinous."

As for California, the other report concluded:

". . . Statistical studies based on past experience lead us to believe that, myth or no myth, immediately upon our landing in California, there will be a terrific earthquake."

Bade had no desire to go to Florida or California. He fervently hoped the enemy would not guess this.

At length the reply came. Bade read through ominous references to the growing might of the United States of the World, then came to the operative sentence:

". . . Our plenipotentiary will be authorized to treat only with regard to an armistice; he is authorized only to transmit other information to his government. He is not empowered to make any agreement whatever on matters other than an armistice."

The plenipotentiary was a tall thin native, who constantly sponged water off his neck and forehead, and who looked at Bade as if he would like to cram a nuclear missile down his throat. Getting an agreement was hard work. The plenipotentiary finally accepted Bade's first condition—that General Kottek not be attacked for the duration of the armistice—but flatly refused the second condition allowing the continued occupation of western Cuba. After a lengthy verbal wrestling match, the plenipotentiary at last agreed to a temporary continuation of the western Cuban occupation, provided that the Gulf of Mexico blockade be lifted. Bade agreed to this and the plenipotentiary departed mopping his forehead.

Bade immediately lifted ships and headed south. His ships came down to seize sections of Sumatra, Java, and Borneo, with outposts on the Christmas and Cocoa Islands and on small islands in the Indonesian archipelago.

Bade's personal headquarters were on a pleasant little island conveniently located in the Sunda Strait between Java and Sumatra. The name of the island was Krakatoa.

Bade was under no illusion that the inhabitants of the islands welcomed his arrival. Fortunately, however, the armament of his troops outclassed anything in the vicinity, with the possible exception of a bristly-looking place called Singapore. Bade's scouts, after studying Singapore carefully, concluded it was not mobile, and if they left it alone, it would leave them alone.

The enemy plenipotentiary now arrived in a large battleship, and was greeted in the islands with frenzied enthusiasm. Bade was too absorbed in reports of rapidly improving morale and highly successful mass-swimming exercises to care about this welcome. Although an ominous document titled "War in the Islands: U.S.–Japan," sat among the translated volumes of history at Bade's elbow, and served as a constant reminder that this pleasant situation could not be expected to last forever, Bade intended to enjoy it while it did last.

Bade greeted the plenipotentiary in his pleasant headquarters on the leveled top of the tall picturesque cone-shaped hill that rose high above Krakatoa, then dropped off abruptly by the sea.

The plenipotentiary, on entering the headquarters, mopped his brow constantly, kept glancing furtively around, and was plainly ill at ease. The interpreters took their places, and the conversation opened.

"As you see," said Bade, "we are comfortably settled here for the winter."

The plenipotentiary looked around and gave a hollow laugh.

"We are," added Bade, "perfectly prepared to return next . . . ah . . .'summer' . . . and take up where we left off."

"By next summer," said the plenipotentiary, "the United States will be a solid mass of guns from one coast to the other."

Bade shrugged, and the plenipotentiary added grimly, "And *missiles*."

Despite himself, Bade winced.

One of Bade's clerks, carrying a message across the far end of the room, became distracted in his effort to be sure he heard everything. The clerk was busy watching Bade when he banged into the back of a tall filing case. The case tilted off-balance, then started to fall forward.

A second clerk sprang up to catch the side of the case. There was a low heavy rumble as all the drawers slid out.

The plenipotentiary sprang to his feet, and looked wildly around.

The filing case twisted out of the hands of the clerk and came down on the floor with a thundering crash.

The plenipotentiary snapped his eyes tightly shut, clenched his teeth, and stood perfectly still.

Bade and Runckel looked blankly at each other.

The plenipotentiary slowly opened his eyes, looked wonderingly around the room, jumped as the two clerks heaved the filing case upright, turned around to stare at the clerks and the case, turned back to look sharply at Bade, then clamped his jaw.

Bade, his own face as calm as he could make it, decided this might be a good a time as any to throw in a hard punch. He remarked, "You have two choices. You can make a mutually profitable agreement with us. Or you can force us to switch heavier forces and weapons to this planet and crush you. Which is it?"

"We," said the plenipotentiary coldly, "have the resources of the whole planet at our disposal. You have to bring everything from a distance. Moreover, we have captured a good deal of your equipment, which we may duplicate—"

"Lesser weapons," said Bade. "As if an enemy captured your rifles, duplicated them at great expense, and was then confronted with your nuclear bomb."

"This is our planet," said the plenipotentiary grimly, "and we will fight for it to the end."

"We don't want your planet."

The plenipotentiary's eyes widened. Then he burst into a string of invective that the translators couldn't follow. When he had finished, he took a deep breath and recapitulated the main point, "If you don't want it, what are you doing here?"

Bade said, "Your people are clearly warlike. After observing you for some time, a debate arose on our planet as to whether we should hit you or wait till you hit us. After a fierce debate, the first faction won."

"Wait a minute. How could *we* hit *you?* You come from another planet, don't you?"

"Yes, that's true. But it's also true that a baby shark is no great menace to anyone. Except that he will grow up into a big shark. That is how our first faction looked on Earth."

The plenipotentiary scowled. "In other words, you'll kill the suspect before he has a chance to commit the crime. Then you justify it by saying the man would have committed a crime if he'd lived."

"We didn't intend to kill you—only to disarm you."

"How does all this square with your telling us you're just a scout party?"

"Are you under the impression," said Bade, "that this is the main invasion force? Would we attack without a full reconnaissance first? Do you think we would merely make one sizable landing, on *one* continent? How could we hope to conquer in that way?"

The plenipotentiary frowned, sucked in a deep breath, and mopped his forehead. "What's your offer?"

"Disarm yourselves voluntarily. All hostilities will end immediately."

The plenipotentiary gave a harsh laugh.

Bade said, "What's your answer?"

"What's your real offer?"

"As I remarked," said Bade, "there were two factions on our planet. One favored the attack, as self-preservation. The other faction opposed the attack, on moral and political grounds. The second faction at present holds that it is now impossible to remain aloof, as we had hoped to before the attack. One way or the other, we are now bound up with Earth. We either have to be enemies, or friends. As it happens, I am a member of the bloc that opposed the attack. The bloc that favored the attack has lost support owing to the results of our initial operations. Because of this political shift, I have practically a free hand at the moment." Bade paused as the plenipotentiary turned his head slightly and leaned forward with an intent look.

Bade said, "Your country has suffered by far the most from our attack. Obviously, it should profit the most. We have a number of scientific advances to offer as bargaining counters. Our essential condition is that we retain some overt standing—some foothold—some way of knowing by direct observation that this planet—or any nation of it—won't attack us."

The plenipotentiary scowled. "Every nation on Earth is pretty closely allied as a result of your attack. We're a world of united states—all practically one nation. And all the land on the globe belongs to one of us or the other. While there's bound to be considerable regional rivalry even when we have peace, that's all. Otherwise we're united. As a result, there's not going to be any peace as long as you've got your foot on land belonging to any of us. That includes Java, Sumatra and even this . . . er . . . mountain we're on now." He looked around uneasily, and added, "We might let you have a little base, somewhere . . . maybe in Antarctica but I doubt it. We won't want any foreign planet sticking its nose in our business."

Bade said, "My proposal allows for that."

"I don't see how it could," said the plenipotentiary. "What is it?"

Bade told him.

The plenipotentiary sat as if he had been hit over the head with a rock. Then he let out a mighty burst of laughter, banged his hand on his knee and said, "You're serious?"

"Absolutely."

The plenipotentiary sprang to his feet. "I'll have to get in touch with my government. Who knows? Maybe— Who knows?" He strode out briskly.

About this time, a number of fast ships arrived from home. These ships were much in use during the next months. Delegations from both planets flew in both directions.

Runckel was highly uneasy. Incessantly he demanded, "Will it work? What if they flood our planet with a whole mob—"

"I have it on good authority," said Bade, "that our planet is every bit as uncomfortable for them as theirs is for us. We almost lost one of their delegates straight down through the mud on the last visit. They have to use dozens of towels for handkerchiefs every day, and that trace of ammonia in the atmosphere doesn't seem to agree with them. Some of them have even gotten fog-sick."

"Why should they go along with the idea, then?"

"It fits in with their nature. Besides, where else are they going to get another one? As one of their senators put it, 'Everything here on Earth is sewed up.' There's even a manifest destiny argument."

"Well, the idea has attractions, but—"

"Listen," said Bade, "I'm told not to prolong the war, because it's too costly and dangerous; not to leave behind a reservoir of fury to discharge on us in the future; not to surrender; not, in the present circumstances, to expect them to surrender. I am told to somehow keep a watch on them and bind their interests to ours; and not to forget the tie must be more than just on paper, it's got to be emotional was well as legal. On top of that, if possible, I'm supposed to open up commercial opportunities. Can you think of any other way?"

"Frankly, no," said Runckel.

There was a grumbling sound underneath them, and the room shivered slightly.

"What was that?" said Runckel.

Bade looked around, frowning. "I don't know."

A clerk came across the room and handed Runckel a message and Bade another message. Runckel looked up, scowling. "The sea water here is beginning to have an irritating effect on our men's skin."

"Never mind," said Bade, "their plenipotentiary is coming. We'll know one way or the other shortly."

Runckel looked worried, and began searching through his wastebasket.

The plenipotentiary came in grinning. "O.K.," he said, "the Russians are a little burned up, and I don't think Texas is any too happy, but nobody can think of a better way out. You're in."

He and Bade shook hands fervently. Photographers rushed in to snap pictures. Outside, Bade's band was playing "The Star-Spangled Banner."

"Another state," said the plenipotentiary, grinning expansively. "How's it feel to be a citizen?"

Runckel erupted from his wastebasket and bolted across the room.

"Krakatoa is a *volcano!*" he shouted. "And here's what a volcano is!"

There was a faint but distinct rumble underfoot.

The room emptied fast.

On the way home, they were discussing things.

Bade was saying, "I don't claim it's perfect, but then our two planets are so mutually uncomfortable there's bound to be little travel either way till we have a chance to get used to each other. Yet, we *can* go back and forth. Who has a better right than a citizen? And there's a good chance of trade and mutual profit. There's a good emotional tie." He frowned. "There's just one thing—"

"What's that?" said Runckel.

Bade opened a translated book to a page he had turned down. He read silently. He looked up perplexedly.

"Runckel," he said, "there are certain technicalities involved in being a citizen."

Runckel tensed. "What do you mean?"

"Oh— Well, like this." He looked back at the book for a moment.

"What is it?" demanded Runckel.

"Well," said Bade, "what do you suppose 'income tax' is?"

Runckel looked relieved. He shrugged.

"Don't worry about it." he said. "It's too fantastic. Probably it's just a myth."

■

The Gentle Earth

A !TANGLED WEB
by Joe Haldeman

Your spaceport bars fall into two distinct groups, the ones for the baggage and the ones for the crew. I was baggage, this trip, but didn't feel like paying the prices that people who space for fun can afford. The Facilities Directory listed under "Food and Drink" four establishments: The Hartford Club (inevitably), The Silver Slipper Lounge, Antoine's, and Slim Joan's Bar & Grill.

I went to a currency exchange booth first, assuming that Slim Joan was no better at arithmetic than most bartenders, and cashed in a hundredth-share of Hartford stock. Then I took the drop-lift down to the bottom level. That the bar's door was right at the drop-lift down to the exit would be a dead giveaway even if its name had been The Bell, Book, and Candle. Baggage don't generally like to fall ten stories, no matter how slowly.

It smelled right, stir-fry and stale beer, and the low lighting suggested economy

Illustration by Jack Gaughan.
© 1981 by Davis Publications, Inc.

rather than atmosphere. Slim Joan turned out to be about a hundred thousand grams of transvestite. Well, I hadn't come for the scenery.

The clientele seemed about evenly mixed between humans and others, most of the aliens being !tang, since this was Alberio III. I've got nothing against the company of aliens, but if I was going to spend all next week wrapping my jaws around !tangish, I preferred to mix my drinking with some human tongue.

"Speak English?" I asked Slim Joan.

"Some," he/she/it growled. "You would drink something." I'd never heard a Russian-Brooklyn accent before. I ordered a double saki, cold, in Russian, and took it to an empty booth.

One of the advantages of being a Hartford interpreter is that you can order a drink in a hundred different languages and dialects. Saves money; they figure if you can speak the lingo you can count your change.

I was freelancing this trip, though, working for a real-estate cartel that wanted to screw the !tang out of the few thousand square kilometers of useless seashore property. It wouldn't stay useless, of course.

Alberio III is a real garden of a planet, but most people never see it. The tachyon nexus is down by Alberio I, which we in the trade refer to as "Armpit," and not many people take the local hop out to III (Armpit's the stopover on the Earth-Sammler run). Starlodge, Limited, was hoping to change that situation.

I couldn't help eavesdropping on the !tangs behind me. (I'm not a snoop; it's a side effect of the hypnotic-induction learning process.) One of them was leaving for Earth today, and the other was full of useful advice. "He"—they have seven singular pronoun classes, depending on the individual's age and estrous condition—was telling "her" never to make any reference to human body odor, no matter how vile it may be. He might also tell her not to breathe on anyone. One of the byproducts of their metabolism was butyl nitrite, which smells like well-aged socks and makes humans get all faint and cross-eyed.

I've worked with !tangs a few times before, and they're some of my favorite people. Very serious, very honest, and their logic is closer to human logic than most. But they *are* strange-looking. Imagine a perambulating haystack with an elephant trunk protruding. They have two arms under the pile of yellow hair, but it's impolite to take them out in public unless one is engaged in physical work. They do have sex in public, constantly, but it takes a zoologist with a magnifying glass to tell when.

He wanted her to bring back some Kentucky bourbon and Swiss chocolate. Their metabolism parts company with ours over proteins and fats, but they love our carbohydrates and alcohol. The alcohol has a psychedelic sort of effect on them, and sugar leaves them plastered.

A human walked in and stood blinking in the half-light. I recognized him and shrank back into the booth. Too late.

He strode over and stuck out his hand. "Dick Navarro!"

"Hello, Pete." I shook his hand once. "What brings you here? Hartford business?" Pete was also an interpreter.

—Oh, no, he said in Arabic. —Only journeying.

—Knock it off, I said in Serbo-Croatian. —Isn't your native language English? I added in Greek.

"Sure it is. Yours?"

"English or Spanish. Have a seat." I smacked my lips twice at Slim Joan, and she came over with a menu. "To be eating you want?"

"Nyet," he said. "Vodka." I told her I'd take another.

"So what are you doing here?" Pete asked.

"Business."

"Hartford?"

"Nope."

"Secret."

"That's right." Actually, they hadn't said anything about it being secret. But I knew Peter Lafitte. He wasn't just passing through.

We both sat silently for a minute, listening to the !tangs. We had to smile when he explained to her how to decide which public bathroom to use when. This was important to humans, he said. Slim Joan came with the drinks and Pete paid for both, a bad sign.

"How did that Spica business finally turn out?" he asked.

"Badly." Lafitte and I had worked together on a partition-of-rights hearing on Spica IV, with the Confederación actually bucking Hartford over an alien-rights problem. "I couldn't get the humans to understand that the minerals had souls, and I couldn't get the natives to believe that refining the minerals didn't affect their spiritual status. It came to a show of force and the natives backed down. I wouldn't like to be there in twenty years, though."

"Yeah. I was glad to be recalled. Arcturus all over."

"That's what I tried to tell them." Arcturus wasn't a regular stop any more, not since a ship landed and found every human artistically dismembered. "You're just sight-seeing?"

"This has always been one of my favorite planets."

"Nothing to do."

"Not for you city boys. The fishing is great, though."

Ah ha. "Ocean fishing?"

"Best in the Confederación."

"I might give it a try. Where do you get a boat?"

He smiled and looked directly at me. "Little coastal village, Pa'an!al."

Smack in the middle of the tribal territory I'd be dickering for. I dutifully repeated the information into my ring.

I changed the subject for a while. Then I excused myself, saying I was time-lagging and had to get some sleep. Which was true enough, since the shuttle had stayed on Armpit time, and I was eight hours out of phase with III. But I bounced straight to the Hartford Courier office.

The courier on duty was Estelle Dorring, whom I knew slightly. I cut short the pleasantries. "How long to get a message to Earth?"

She studied the clock on the wall. "You're out of luck if you want it hand-carried. I'm not going to Armpit until tomorrow. Two days on the shuttle and I'll miss the Earth run by half-a-day.

"If broadcast is all right, you can beam to Armpit and the courier there can take it along on the Twosday run. That leaves in 72 minutes. Call it 19 minutes' beam time. You know what you want to say?"

"Yeah. Set it up." I sat down at the customers' console.

STARLODGE, LIMITED
642 EASTRIVER
NEW YORK, NEW YORK 100992
ATTENTION: PATRICE DUVAL

YOU MAY HAVE SOME COMPETITION HERE. NOTHING OPEN YET, BUT A GUY WE CALL PETER RABBIT IS ON THE SCENE. CHECK INTERPRETERS GUILD AND SEE WHO'S PAYING PETER LAFITTE. CHANGE TERMS OF SALE? PLEASE REPLY NEXT SAMMLER RUN—RICARDO NAVARRO/RM 2048/ALBERIO HILTON.

I wasn't sure what good the information would do me, unless they also found how how much he was offering and authorized me to outbid him. At any rate, I wouldn't hear for three days, earliest. Sleep.

Alberio III—it's real name is !ka'al—rides a slow sweeping orbit aroung Alberio A, the brighter of the two suns that make up the Alberio system (Alberio A is a close double star itself, but its white dwarf companion hugs so close that it's lost in the glare). At this time of day, Alberio B was visible low in the sky, a hard blue diamond too bright to stare at, and A was right overhead, a bloated golden ball. On the sandy beach below us the flyer cast two shadows, dark blue and faint yellow, which raced to come together as we landed.

Pa'an!al is a fishing village thousands of years old, on a natural harbor formed where a broad jungle river flows into the sea. Here on the beach were only a few pole huts with thatched roofs, where the fishers who worked the surf and shallow pools lived. Pa'an!al proper was behind a high stone wall, which protected it on one side from the occasional hurricane, and on the other from the interesting fauna of the jungle.

I paid off my driver and told him to come back at second sundown. I took a deep breath and mounted the steps. There was an open-cage Otis elevator beside the stairs, but people didn't use it, only fish.

The !tang are compulsive about geometry. This wall was a precise 1:2 rectangle, and the stairs mounted from one corner to the opposite in a satisfyingly Euclidian 26.5 degrees. A guardrail would have spoiled the harmony. The stairs were just wide enough for two !tang to pass, and the rise of each step was a good half-meter. By the time I got to the top I was both tired and slightly terrified.

A spacefaring man shouldn't be afraid of heights, and I'm not, so long as I'm in a vehicle. But when I attained the top of the wall and looked down the equally long and perilous flight of stairs to the ground level, I almost swooned. Why couldn't they simply have left a door in the wall?

I sat there for a minute and looked down at the small city. The geometrical regularity *was* pleasing. Each building was either a cube or a stack of cubes, and the rock from which the city was built had been carefully sorted, so that each building was a uniform shade. They went from white marble through sandy yellow and salmon to pearly gray and obsidian. The streets were a regular matrix of red brick. I walked down, hugging the wall.

At the bottom of the steps a !tang sat on a low bench, watching the nonexistent traffic. —Greetings, I clicked and snorted at him, —it certainly is a pleasant day.

—Not everywhere, he grunted and wheezed back. An unusually direct response.

—Are you waiting for me?

—Who can say? I am waiting. His trunk made a philosophical circle in the air.

—If you had not come, who knows for what I would have been waiting?

—Well that's true, that's true. He made a circle in the other direction, which I think meant What else? I stood there for a minute while he looked at me or the ground or the sky. You could never tell.

—I hope this isn't a rude question, he said. —Will you forgive me if this is a rude question?

—I certainly will try.

—Is your name !ica'o Iva!o?

That was admirably close. —It certainly is.

—You could follow me. He got up. —or enjoy the pleasant day.

I followed him closely down the narrow street. If he got in a crowd I'd lose him for sure. I couldn't tell an estrous-four female from a neuter, not having sonar (they tell each other apart by sensing body cavities, very romantic).

We went through the center of town, where the well and the market square were. A few dozen !tang bargained over food, craft items, or abstractions. They were the most mercantile race on the planet, although they had sidestepped the idea of money in favor of labor-equivalence: for those two ugly fish I will trade you an original sonnet about your daughter and three vile limericks for your next affinity-group meeting. Four limericks, tops.

We went into a large white building that might have been City Hall. It was evidently guarded, at least symbolically, since two !tang stood by the door with their arms exposed.

It was a single large room similar to a Terran mosque, with a regular pattern of square columns holding up the ceiling. The columns supported shelving in neat squares, up to about two meters; on the shelves were neat stacks of accordion-style books. Although the ceiling had inset squares of glass and gave adequate light, there was a strong smell of burnt fish oil, which meant the building was used at night. (We had introduced them to electricity, but they used it only for heavy machinery and toys.)

The !tang led me to the farthest corner, where a large haystack was bent over a book, scribbling. They had to read or write with their heads a few centimeters from the book, since their light-eyes were only good for close work.

—It has happened as you foretold, Uncle. (Not too amazing a prophecy, as I'd sent a messenger over yesterday.)

Uncle waved his nose in my direction. —Are you the same one who came four days ago?

—No. I have never been to this place. I am Ricardo Navarro, from the Starlodge tribe.

—I grovel in embarrassment. Truly it is difficult to tell one human from another. To my poor eyes you look exactly like Peter Lafitte.

(Peter Rabbit is bald and ugly, with terrible ears. I have long curly hair with only a trace of grey, and women have called me attractive.) —Please do not be embarrassed. This is often true when different peoples meet. Did my brother say what tribe he represented?

—I die. O my hair falls out and my flesh rots and my bones are cracked by the hungry ta!a'an. He drops me behind him all around the forest and nothing will grow where his excrement from my marrow falls. As the years pass the forest dies from the poison of my remains. The soil washes into the sea and poisons the fish, and all die. O the embarrassment.

—He didn't say?

—He did but said not to tell you.

That was that. —Did he by some chance say he was interested in the small morsel of land I mentioned to you by courier long ago?

—No, he was not interested in the land.

—Can you tell me what he was interested in?

—He was interested in *buying* the land.

Verbs. —May I ask a potentially embarrassing question?

He exposed his arms. —We are businessmen.

—What were the terms of his offer?

—I die. I breathe in and breathe in and cannot exhale. I explode all over my friends. They forget my name and pretend it is dung. They wash off in the square and the well becomes polluted. All die. O the embarrassment.

—He said not to tell me?

—That's right.

—Did you agree to sell him the land?

—That is a difficult question to answer.

—Let me rephrase the question: is it possible that you might sell the land to my tribe?

—It is possible, if you offer better terms. But only possible, in any case.

—This is embarrassing. I, uh, die and, um, the last breath from my lungs is a terrible acid. It melts the seaward wall of the city and a hurricane comes and washes it away. All die. O the embarrassment.

—You're much better at that than he was.

—Thank you. But may I ask you to amplify as to the possibility?

—Certainly. Land is not a fish or an elevator. Land is something that keeps you from falling all the way down. It gives the sea a shore and makes the air stop. Do you understand?

—So far. Please continue.

—Land is like time but not in a mercantile sense. I can say "In return for the time it takes me to decide which one of you is the guilty party, you must give me such-and-so." But how can I say "In return for the land I am standing on you must give me this-and-that"? Nobody can step off the time, you see, but I can step off the land, and then what is it? Does it even exist? In a mercantile sense? These questions and corrolaries to them have been occupying some of our finest minds ever since your courier came long ago.

—May I make a suggestion?

—Please do. Anything might help.

—Why not just sell it to the tribe that offers the most?

—No, you don't see. Forgive me, you Terrans are very simple-minded people, for all your marvelous Otis elevators and starships (this does not embarrass me to say because it is meant to help you understand yourself; if you were !tang you would have to pay for it). You see, there are three mercantile classes. Things and services may be of no worth, of measurable worth, or of infinite worth. Land has never been classified before and it may belong in any of the categories.

—But Uncle! The Lafitte and I have offered to buy the land. Surely that eliminates the first class.

—O you poor Terran. I would hate to see you try to buy a fish. You must think of all the implications.

—I die. I, uh, have a terrible fever in my head and it gets hotter and hotter until my head is a fire, a forge, a star. I set the world on fire and everybody dies. O the embarrassment. What implications?

—Here is the simplest. If the land has finite value, when at best all it does is keep things from falling all the way down, how much is air worth? Air is necessary for life, and it makes fires burn. If you pay for land do you think we should let you have air for free?

—An interesting point, I said, thinking fast and !tangly. —But you have answered it yourself. Since air is necessary for life it is of infinite value, and not even one breath can be paid for with all the riches of the universe.

—O poor one, how can you have gotten through life without losing your feet? Air would be of infinite worth to us only if *life* were of infinite worth, and even so little as I know of your rich and glorious history proves conclusively that you place very little value on life. Other people's lives, at any rate. Sad to say, our own history contains a similarly bonehungry period.

—Neither are we that way now, Uncle.

—I die. My brain turns to hungry maggots . . .

* * *

I talked with Uncle for an hour or so, but got nothing out of it save a sore soft palate. When I got back to the hotel there was a message from Peter Lafitte, asking whether I would like to join him at Antoine's for dinner. No, I would not *like* to, but under the circumstances it seemed prudent. I had to rent a formal tunic from the bellbot.

Antoine's has all the *joie de vivre* of a frozen halibut, which puts it on a par with every other French restaurant off Earth. We started with an artichoke *vinaigrette* that should have been left to rot in the hydroponics tank. Then a filet of "beef" from some local animal that I doubt was even warmblooded. All this served by a waiter who was a Canadian with a fake Parisian accent.

But we also had a bottle of phony Pouilly-Fuisse followed by a bottle of ersatz Burgundy followed by a bottle of synthetic Chateau-d'Yquem. Then they cleared the table and set a bottle of brandy between us, and the real duel began. Short duel, it turned out.

"So how long is your vacation going to last?" I made a gesture that was admirably economical. "Not long at these prices."

"Well, there's always Slim Joan's." He poured himself a little brandy and me a lot. "How about yourself?"

"Ran into a snag," I said. "Have to wait until I hear from Earth."

"They're not easy to work with, are they?"

"Terrans? I'm one myself."

"The !tang, I mean." He stared into his glass and swirled the liquor. "Terrans as well, though. Could I set to you a hypothetical proposition?"

"My favorite kind," I said. The brandy stung my throat.

"Suppose you were a peaceable sort of fellow."

"I am." Slightly fuzzy, but peaceable.

"And you were on a planet to make some agreement with the natives."

I nodded seriously.

"Billions of bux involved. Trillions."

"That would really be something," I said.

"Yeah. Now further suppose that there's another Terran on this planet who, uh, is seeking to make the same sort of agreement."

"Must happen all the time."

"For trillions, Dick? Trillions?"

"Hyp'thetical trillions." Bad brandy, but strong.

"Now the people who are employing you are ab—solute—ly ruthless."

"*Ma!ryso'ta,*" I said, the !tang word for "bonehungry." Close to it, anyhow.

"That's right." He was starting to blur. More wine than I'd thought. "Stop at nothing. Now how would you go about warning the other Terran?"

My fingers were icy cold and the sensation was crawling toward my elbows. My chin slipped off my hand and my head was so heavy I could hardly hold it up. I stared at the two fuzzy images across the table. "Peter." The words came out slowly, and then not at all: "You aren't drinking. . . ."

"Terrible brandy, isn't it." My vision went away, although it felt as if my eyes were still open. I heard my chin hit the table.

"Waiter?" I heard the man come over and make sympathetic noises. "My friend has had a little too much to drink. Would you help me get him to the bellbot?" I couldn't even feel them pick me up. "I'll take this brandy. He might want some in the morning." Jolly.

I finally lapsed into unconsciousness while we were waiting for the elevator, the bellbot lecturing me about temperance.

I woke up the next afternoon on the cold tile floor of my suite's bathroom. I felt like I had been taken apart by an expert surgeon and reassembled by an amateur mechanic. I looked at the tile for a long time. Then I sat for a while and studied the interesting blotches of color floating between my eyes and my brain. When I thought I could survive it, I stood up and took four Hangaways.

I sat and started counting. Hangaways hit you like a piledriver. At eighty the adrenaline shock came. Tunnel vision and millions of tiny needles being pushed out through your skin. Rivers of sweat. Cathedral bells tolling, your head the clapper. Then the dry heaves and it was over.

I staggered to the phone and ordered some clear soup and a couple of cold beers. Then I stood in the shower and contemplated suicide. By the time the soup came I was contemplating homicide.

The soup stayed down and by the second beer I was feeling almost human, Neanderthal anyhow. I made some enquiries. Lafitte had checked out. No shuttle had left, so he was either still on the planet or he had his own ship, which was possible if he was working for the outfit I suspected he was working for. I invoked the holy name of Hartford, trying to find out to whom his expenses had been billed. Cash.

I tried to order my thoughts. If I reported Lafitte's action to the Guild he would be disbarred. Either he didn't care, because They were paying him enough to retire in luxury—for which I knew he had a taste—or he actually thought I was not going to get off the planet alive. I discarded the dramatic second notion. Last night he could have more easily killed me than warned me. Or had he actually *tried* to kill me, the talk just being insurance in case I didn't ingest a fatal dose? I had no idea what the poison could have been. That sort of knowledge isn't relevant to my line of work.

I suppose the thoroughly rational thing would have been to sit tight and let him have the deal. The fortunes of Starlodge were infinitely less important to me than my skin. He could probably offer more than I, anyhow.

The phone chimed. I thumbed the vision button and a tiny haystack materialized over the end table.

—Greetings. How is the weather?
—Indoors, it's fine. Are you Uncle?
—Not now. Inside the Council Building I am Uncle.
—I see. Can I perform some worthless service for you?
—For yourself, perhaps.

—Pray continue.

—Our Council is meeting with the Lafitte this evening, with the hope of resolving this question about the mercantile nature of land. I would be embarrassed if you did not come too. The meeting will be at *ala'ang in the Council Building.

—I would not cause you embarrassment. But could it possibly be postponed?

He exposed his arms. —We are meeting.

He disappeared and I spent a few minutes translating *ala'ang into human time. The !tang divide their day into a complicated series of varying time intervals depending on the position of the suns and state of appetite and estrous condition. Came to a little before ten o'clock, plenty of time.

I could report Lafitte, and probably should, but decided I'd be safer not doing so, retaining the threat of exposure for use as a weapon. I wrote a brief description of the situation—and felt a twinge of fear on writing the word "Syndicate"—and sealed it in an envelope. I wrote the address of the Hartford Translators' Guild across the seal and bounced up to the courier's office.

Estelle Dorring stared at me when I walked into the office. "Ricardo! You look like a corpse warmed over."

"Rough night," I said. "Touch of food poisoning."

"I never eat that Tang stuff."

"Good policy." I set the envelope in front of her. "I'm not sure whether to send this or not. If I don't come get it before the next shuttle, take it to Armpit and give it to the next Earth courier."

She nodded slowly and read the address. "Why so mysterious?"

"Just a matter of Guild ethics. I wanted to write it down while it was still fresh. Uh . . ." I'd never seen a truly penetrating stare before. "But I might have more information tonight that would invalidate it."

"If you say so, Ricardo." She slipped the envelope into a drawer. I backed out mumbling something inane.

Down to Slim Joan's for a sandwich of stir-fried vegetables in Syrian bread. Slightly rancid and too much curry, but I didn't dare go to the Council meeting on an empty stomach. !tang sonar would scan it and they would make a symbolic offer of bread, which couldn't be refused. Estelle was partly right about "Tang" food: one bit of the bread contained enough mescaline to make you see interesting things for hours. I'd had enough of that for a while.

I toyed with the idea of taking a weapon. There was a rental service in the pharmacy, to accommodate the occasional sporting type, and I could pick up a laser or a tranquilizer there. But there would be no way to conceal it from the !tang sonar. Besides, Lafitte isn't the kind of person who would employ direct violence.

But if it actually were the Syndicate behind Lafitte, they might well have sent more than one person here; they certainly could afford it. A hitter. But then why would Lafitte set up the elaborate poisoning scene? Why not simply arrange an accident?

My feet were taking me toward the pharmacy. Wait. Be realistic. You haven't fired a gun in twenty years. Even then, you couldn't hit the ground with a rock. If it came to a burnout, you'd be the one who got crisped. Better to leave their options open.

I decided to compromise. There was a large clasp-knife in my bag, that would at least help me psychologically. I went back up to my room.

I thumbed the lock and realized that the cube I'd heard playing was my own. The door slid open and there was Lafitte, lounging on my sofa, watching an old movie.

"Dick. You're looking well."

"How the hell did you get in here?"

He held up his thumb and stripped a piece of plastic off the fleshy part. "We have our resources." He sat up straight. "I hear you're taking a flyer out to Pa'an!al. Shall we divide the cost?"

There was a bottle of wine in a bucket of ice at his feet. I got a glass out of the bathroom and helped myself. "I suppose you charged this to my room." I turned off the cube.

He shrugged. "You poked me for dinner last night, *mon frère*. Passing out like that."

I raised the glass to my lips, flinched, and set it down untouched. "Speaking of resources, what was in that brandy? And who are these resourceful friends?"

"The wine's all right. You seemed agitated; I gave you a calmative."

"A *horse* calmative! Is it the Syndicate?"

He waved that away. "The Syndicate's a myth. You—"

"Don't take me for an idiot. I've been doing this for almost as long as you have." Every ten years or so there was a fresh debunking. But the money and bodies kept piling up.

"You have indeed." He concentrated on picking at a hangnail. "How much is Starlodge willing to pay?"

I tried not to react. "How much is the Syndicate?"

"If the Syndicate existed," he said carefully, "and if it were they who had retained me, don't you think I would try to use that fact to frighten you away?"

"Maybe not directly—last night, you said 'desperate men.' "

"I was drunk." No, not Peter Rabbit, not on a couple bottles of wine. I just looked at him. "All right," he said, "I was told to use any measures short of violence—"

"Poisoning isn't violence?"

"Tranquilizing, not poisoning. You couldn't have died." He poured himself some wine. "Top yours off?"

"I've become a solitary drinker."

He poured the contents of my glass into his. "I might be able to save you some trouble, if you'll only tell me what terms—"

"A case of Jack Daniels and all they can eat at Slim Joan's."

"That might do it," he said unsmilingly, "but I can offer 1500 shares of Hartford."

That was 150 million dollars, half again what I'd been authorized. "Just paper to them."

"Or a million cases of booze, if that's the way they want it." He checked his watch. "Isn't our flyer waiting?"

I supposed it would be best to have him along, to keep an eye on him. "The one who closes the deal pays for the trip?"

"All right."

On the hour-long flyer ride I considered various permutations of what I could offer. My memory had been jammed with the wholesale prices of various kinds of machinery, booze, candy, and so forth, along with their mass and volume, so I could add in the shipping costs from Earth to Armpit to Alberio III. Lafitte surely had similar knowledge; I could only hope that his figure of 1500 shares was a bluff.

(I had good incentive to bargain well. Starlodge would give me a bonus of up to ten percent of the difference between a thousand shares and whatever the settlement came to. If I brought it in at 900, I'd be a millionaire.)

We were turning inland; the walls of the city made a pink rectangle against the towering jungle. I tapped the pilot on the shoulder. "Can you land inside the city?"

"Not unless you want to jump from the top of a building. I can set you on the wall, though." I nodded.

"Can't take the climb, Dick? Getting old?"

"No need to waste steps." The flyer was a little wider than the wall, and it teetered as we stepped out. I tried to look just at my feet.

"Beautiful from up here," Lafitte said. "Look at that sunset." Half the large sun's disk was visible on the jungle horizon, a deeper red than Earth's Sun ever shone. The bloody light stained the surf behind us purple. It was already dark in the city below; the smell of rancid fish oil burning drifted up to us.

Lafitte managed to get the inside lane of the staircase. I tried to keep my eyes on him and the wall as we negotiated the high steps.

"Believe me," he said (a phrase guaranteed to inspire trust), "it would make both our jobs easier if I could tell you who I'm representing. But I really am sworn to secrecy."

An oblique threat deserves an oblique answer: "You know I can put you in deep trouble with the Standards Committee. Poisoning a Guild brother."

"Your word against mine. And the bellbot's, the headwaiter's, the wine steward's . . . you did have quite a bit to drink."

"A couple of bottles of wine won't knock me out."

"Your capacity is well known. I don't think you want a hearing investigating it, though, not at your age. Two years 'til retirement?"

"Twenty months."

"I was rounding off," he said. "Yes, I did check. I wondered whether you might be in the same position as I am. My retirement's less than two months away; this is my last big-money job. So you must understand my enthusiasm."

I didn't answer. He wasn't called Rabbit for lack of "enthusiasm."

As we neared the bottom, he said, "Suppose you weren't to oppose me too vigorously. Suppose I could bring in the contract at a good deal less than—"

"Don't be insulting."

In the dim light from the torches sputtering below I couldn't read his expression. "Ten percent of my commission wouldn't be insulting."

I stopped short; he climbed down another step. "I can't believe even *you*—"

"*Verdad.* Just joking." He laughed unconvincingly. "Everyone knows how starchy you are, Dick. I know better than most." I'd fined him several times during the years I was head of the Standards Committee.

We walked automatically through the maze of streets, our guides evidently having taken identical routes. Both of us had eidetic memories, of course, that being a minimum prerequisite for the job of interpreter. I was thinking furiously. If I couldn't out-bargain the Rabbit I'd have to somehow finesse him. Was there anything I knew about the !tang value system that he didn't? Assuming that this Council would decide that land was something that could be bought and sold.

I did have a couple of interesting proposals in my portfolio, that I'd written up during the two-week trip from Earth. I wondered whether Lafitte had seen them. The lock didn't appear to have been tampered with, and it was the old-fashioned magnetic key type. You can pick it but it won't close afterwards.

We turned a corner and there was the Council Building at the end of the street, impressive in the flickering light, its upper reaches lost in darkness. Lafitte put his hand on my arm, stopping. "I've got a proposition."

"Not interested."

"Hear me out, now; this is straight. I'm empowered to take you on as a limited partner."

"How generous. I don't think Starlodge would like it."

"What I *mean* is Starlodge. You hold their power of attorney, don't you?"

"Unlimited, on this planet. But don't waste your breath; we get an exclusive or nothing at all." Actually, the possibility had never been discussed. They couldn't have known I was going into a competitive bidding situation. If they had, they certainly wouldn't have sent me here slow freight. For an extra fifty shares I could have gone first class and been here a week before Peter Rabbit; could have sewn up the thing and been headed home before he got to Armpit.

Starlodge had a knack for picking places that were about to become popular—along with impressive media power, to make sure they did—and on dozens of worlds they did have literally exclusive rights to tourism. Hartford might own a spaceport hotel, but it wasn't really competition, and they were usually glad to hand it over to Starlodge anyhow. Hartford, with its ironclad lock on the tachyon drive, had no need to diversify.

There was no doubt in my mind that this was the pattern Starlodge had in mind for Alberio III. It was a perfect setup, the beach being a geological anomaly: there wasn't another decent spot for a hotel within two thousand kilometers of the spaceport. Just bleak mountaintops sprouting occasionally out of jungles full of large and hungry animals. But maybe I could lead the Rabbit on. I leaned up against a post that supported a guttering torch. "At any rate, I certainly couldn't consider entering into an agreement without knowing who you represent."

He looked at me impassively for a second. "Outfit called A. W. Stoner Industries."

I laughed out loud. "Real name, I mean." I'd never heard of Stoner, and I do keep in touch.

"That's the name I know them by."

"No concern not listed in *Standard, Poor and Tueme* could come up with nine figures for extraterrestrial real estate speculation. No legitimate concern, I mean."

"There you go again," he said mildly. "I believe they're a coalition of smaller firms."

"I don't. Let's go."

Back in my luggage I had a nasal spray that deadened the sense of smell. Before we even got inside, I knew I should have used it.

The air was grey with fish-oil smoke, and there were more than a hundred !tang sitting in neat rows. I once was treated to a "fish kill" in Texas, where a sudden ecological disaster had resulted in windrows of rotting fish piled up on the beach. This was like walking along that beach using an old sock for a muffler. By Lafitte's expression, he was also unprepared. We both walked forward with slightly greenish cheerfulness.

A !tang in the middle of the first row stood up and approached us. —Uncle? I ventured, and he waved his snout in affirmation.

—We have come to an interim decision, he said.

—Interim? Lafitte said. —Were my terms unacceptable?

—I die. My footprints are cursed. I walk around the village not knowing that all who cross where I have been will stay in estrous zero, and bear no young. Eventually, all die. O the embarrassment. We want to hear the terms of Navarro's tribe. Then perhaps a final decision may be made.

That was frighteningly direct. I'd tried for an hour to tell him our terms before, but he'd kept changing the subject.

—May I hear the terms of Lafitte's tribe? I asked.

—Certainly. Would Lafitte care to state them, or should I?

—Proceed, Uncle, Lafitte said, and then in Spanish, "Remember the possibility of a partnership. If we get to haggling . . ."

I stopped listening to Rabbit as Uncle began a long litany of groans, creaks, pops, and whistles. I kept running total of wholesale prices and shipping costs. Bourbon, rum, brandy, gin. Candy bars, raw sugar, honey, pastries. Nets, computers, garbage composters, water purifying plant, hunting weapons. When he stopped I had a total of only H620.

—Your offer, Navarro? Could it include these things as a subset?

I had to be careful. Lafitte was probably lying about the 1500, but I didn't want to push him so hard he'd be able to go over a thousand on the next round. And I didn't want to bring out my big guns until the very end.

—I can offer these things and three times the specified quantity of rum—(the largest rum distillery in the world was a subsidiary of Starlodge)—and furthermore free you from the rigors of the winter harvest, with 26 fully programmed mechanical farm laborers. (The winters here were not even cool by Earth standards, but something about the season made the local animals restless enough occasionally to jump over the walls that normally protected farmland.)

—These mechanical workers would not be good to eat? For the animals?

—No, they would be very hard for the animals even to damage.

There was a lot of whispered conversation. Uncle conferred with the !tang at the front of each row, then returned.

—I die. Before I die my body turns hair-side-in. People come from everywhere to see the insides of themselves. But the sight makes them lose will, and all die. O the embarrassment. The rum is welcome but we cannot accept the mechanical workers. When the beast eats someone he sleeps, and can be killed, and eaten in turn. If he does not eat he will search, and in searching destroy crops. This we know to be true.

—Then allow me to triple the quantities of gin, bourbon, and brandy. I will add two tonnes each of vermouth and hydrochloric acid, for flavoring. (That came to about H710.)

—This is gratefully accepted. Does your tribe, Lafitte, care to include these as a subset of your final offer?

—Final offer, Uncle?

—Two legs, two arms, two eyes, two mouths, two offers.

—I die. Lafitte said. —Where they bury me, the ground caves in. It swallows up the city and all die. O the embarrassment. Look, Uncle, that's the market law for material objects. You can't move land around; its ownership is an abstraction.

Uncle exposed one arm—the Council tittered—and reached down and thumped the floor twice. —The land is solid, therefore material. You can move it around with your machines; I myself saw you do this in my youth, when the spaceport was built. The market law applies.

Lafitte smiled slowly. —Then the Navarro's tribe can no longer bid. He's had two.

Uncle turned to the Council and gestured toward Rabbit, and said, —Is he standing on feet? And they cracked and snuffled at the joke. To Lafitte he said, —The Navarro's offer was rejected, and he made a substitution. Yours was not rejected. Do you care to make his amended offer a subset of yours?

If mine is rejected, can I amend it?

This brought an even louder reaction. —Poor one, Uncle said. —No feet, no hands. That would be a third offer. You must see that.

—All right. Lafitte began pacing. He said he would start with my amended offer and add the following things. The list was very long. It started with a hydroelectric generator and proceeded with objects of less and less value until he got down to individual bottles of exotic liqueurs. By then I realized he was giving me a message: he was coming down as closely as he could to exactly a thousand shares of Hartford.

So we both had the same limit. When he finished he looked right at me and raised his eyebrows.

Victory is sweet. If the Rabbit had bothered to spend a day or two in the marketplace, watching transactions, he wouldn't have tried to defeat me by arithmetic; he wouldn't have tried by accretion to force me into partnership.

Uncle looked at me and bared his arms for a split second. —Your tribe, Navarro? Would you include this offer as a subset of your final offer?

What Rabbit apparently didn't know was that this bargaining by pairs of offers was a formalism: if I did simply add to his last offer, the haggling would start over again, with each of us allowed another pair. And so on and on. I unlocked my briefcase and took out two documents.

—No. I merely wish to add two inducements to my own previous offer (sounds of approval and expectation). Lafitte stared, his expression unreadable.

—These contracts are in Spanish. Can you read them, Uncle?

—No, but there are two of us who can.

—I know how you like to travel. I handed him one of the documents. —This allows each of five hundred !tang a week's vacation on the planet of its choice; any planet where Starlodge has facilities.

"What?" Lafitte said, in English. "How the hell can you do that?"

"Dead-heading," I said.

One of the Council abruptly rose. "Pardon me," he said in a weird parody of English, "we have to be dead to take this vaction? That seems of little value."

I was somewhat startled at that, in view of the other inducement I was going to offer. I told him it was an English term that had nothing to do with heads or death. —Most of the Hartford vessels that leave this planet are nearly empty. It is no great material loss to Hartford to take along non-paying guests, so long as they do not displace regular passengers. And Hartford will ultimately benefit from an increase in tourism to !ka'al, so they were quite willing to make this agreement with my tribe.

—The market value of this could be quite high, Uncle said.

—As much as five or six hundred shares, I said, —depending on how distant each trip is.

—Very well. And what is your other inducement?

—I won't say. (I had to grin.) —It is a gift.

The Council chittered and tweeted in approval. Some even exposed their arms momentarily in a semi-obscene gesture of fellowship. "What kind of game are you playing?" Peter Rabbit said.

"They like surprises and riddles." I made a polite sound requesting attention and said, —There is one thing I will tell you about this gift: it belongs to all three mercantile classes. It is of no value, of finite value, and infinite value, all at once, and to all people.

—When considered as being of infinite value, Uncle said, —how much is it worth in terms of Hartford stock?

—Exactly one hundred shares.

He rustled pleasantly at that, and went to confer with the others. "You're pretty clever, Dick," Rabbit said. "What, they don't get to find out what the last thing is unless they accept?"

"That's right. It's done all the time; I was rather surprised that you didn't do it."

He shook his head. "I've only negotiated with !tang off-planet. They've always been pretty conventional."

I didn't ask him about all the fishing he had supposedly done here. Uncle came back and stood in front of us.

—There is unanimity. The land will go to the Navarro's tribe. Now what is the secret inducement, please? How can it be every class at once, to all people?

I paused to parse out the description in !tangish. —Uncle, do you know of the Earth corporation, or tribe, Immortality Unlimited?

—No.

Lafitte made a strange noise. I went on. —This Immortality Unlimited provides a useful service to humans who are apprehensive about death. They offer the possibility of revival. A person who avails himself of this service is frozen solid as soon as possible after death. The tribe promises to keep the body frozen until such time as science discovers a way to revive it.

—The service is expensive. You pay the tribe one full share of Hartford stock. They invest it, and take for themselves one tenth of the income, which is their profit. A small amount is used to keep the body frozen. If and when revival is possible, the person is thawed, and cured of whatever was killing him, and he will be comparatively wealthy.

—This has never been done with nonhumans before, but there is nothing forbidding it. Therefore I purchased a hundred "spaces" for !tang; I leave it to you to decide which hundred will benefit.

—You see, this is of no material value to any living person, because you must die to take advantage of it. However, it is also of finite worth, since each space costs one share of Hartford. It is also of infinite worth, because it offers life beyond death.

The entire Council applauded, a sound like a horde of locusts descending. Peter Rabbit made the noise of attention, and then he made it again, impolitely loud.

—This is all very interesting, and I do congratulate the Navarro for his cleverness. However, the bidding is not over.

There was a low, nervous whirring. "Better apologize first, Rabbit," I whispered.

He bulled ahead. —Let me introduce a new mercantile class: negative value.

"Rabbit, don't—"

—This is an object or service that one does *not* want to have. I will offer not to give it to you if you accept my terms rather than the Navarro's.

—Many kilometers up the river there is a drum full of a very powerful poison. If I touch the button that opens it, all of the fish in the river, and for a great distance out into the sea, will die. You will have to move or . . .

He trailed off.

One by one, single arms snaked out, each holding a long, sharp knife.

"Poison again, Rabbit? You're getting predictable in your old age."

"Dick," he said hoarsely. "They're completely nonviolent. Aren't they?"

"Except in matters of trade." Uncle was the last one to produce a knife. They moved toward us very slowly. "Unless you do something fast, I think you're about to lose your feet."

"My God! I thought that was just an expression."

"I think you better start apologizing. Tell them it was a joke."

—I die! he shouted, and they stopped advancing. —I, um . . .

"You play a joke on your friends and it backfires," I said in Greek.

Rapidly: —I play a joke on my good friends and it backfires. I, uh . . . "Christ, Dick, help me."

"Just tell the truth and embroider it a little. They know about negative value, but it's an obscenity."

—I was employed by . . . a tribe that did not understand mercantilism. They asked me, of all things, to introduce terms of negative value into a trivial transaction. My friends know I must be joking and they laugh. They laugh so much they forget to eat. All die. O the embarrassment.

Uncle made a complicated pass with his knife and it disappeared into his haybale fur. All the other knives remained in evidence, and the !tang moved into a circle around us.

—This machine in your pocket, Uncle said, —it is part of the joke?

Lafitte pulled out a small gray box. —It is. Do you want it?

—Put it on the floor. The fun would be complete if you stayed here while the Navarro took one of your marvelous floaters up the river. How far would he have to go to find the rest of the joke?

—About twelve kilometers. On an island in midstream.

Uncle turned to me and exposed his arms briefly. —Would you help us with our fun?

The air outside was sweet and pure. I decided to wait a few hours, for light.

That was some years ago, but I still remember vividly going into the Council Building the next day. Uncle had divined that Peter Rabbit was getting hungry, and they'd filled him up with !tang bread. When I came in, he was amusing them with impersonations of various Earth vegetables. The effect on his metabolism was not permanent, but when he left Alberio III he was still having mild attacks of cabbageness.

By the time I retired from Hartford, Starlodge had finished its hotel and sports facility on the beach. I was the natural choice to manage it, of course, and though I was wealthy enough not to need employment, I took the job with enthusiasm.

I even tried to hire Lafitte as an assistant—people who can handle !tangish are rare—but he had dropped out of sight. Instead, I found a young husband-and-wife team who have so much energy that I hardly have to work at all.

I'm not crazy enough to go out in the woods, hunting. But I do spend a bit of time fishing off the dock, usually with Uncle, who has also retired. Together we're doing a book that I think will help our two cultures understand one another. The human version is called *Hard Bargain*. ■

DESPOILERS OF THE GOLDEN EMPIRE
by David Gordon

Illustration by Kelly Freas.
© 1959 by Street & Smith Publications, Inc.

I

In the seven centuries that had elapsed since the Second Empire had been founded on the shattered remnants of the First, the nobles of the Imperium had come slowly to realize that the empire was not to be judged by the examples of its predecessor. The First Empire had conquered most of the known universe by political intrigue and sheer military strength; it had fallen because that same propensity for political intrigue had gained over every other strength of the Empire, and the various branches and sectors of the First Empire had begun to use it against one another.

The Second Empire was politically unlike the First; it tried to balance a centralized government against the autonomic governments of the various sectors, and had almost succeeded in doing so.

But, no matter how governed, there are certain essentials which are needed by any governmental organization.

Without power, neither Civilization nor the Empire could hold itself together, and His Universal Majesty, the Emperor Carl, well knew it. And power was linked solidly to one element, one metal, without which Civilization would collapse as surely as if it had been blasted out of existence. Without the power metal, no ship could move or even be built; without it, industry would come to a standstill.

In ancient times, even as far back as the early Greek and Roman civilizations, the metal had been known, but it had been used, for the most part, as decoration and in the manufacture of jewelry. Later, it had been coined as money.

It had always been relatively rare, but now, weight for weight, atom for atom, it was the most valuable element on Earth. Indeed, the most valuable in the known universe.

The metal was Element Number Seventy-nine—gold.

To the collective mind of the Empire, gold was the prime object in any kind of mining exploration. The idea of drilling for petroleum, even if it had been readily available, or of mining coal or uranium would have been dismissed as impracticable and even worse than useless.

Throughout the Empire, research laboratories worked tirelessly at the problem of transmuting commoner elements into Gold-197, but thus far none of the processes was commercially feasible. There was still, after thousands of years, only one way to get the power metal: extract it from the ground.

So it was that, across the great gulf between the worlds, ship after ship moved in search of the metal that would hold the far-flung colonies of the Empire together. Every adventurer who could manage to get aboard was glad to be cooped up on a ship during the long months it took to cross the empty expanses, was glad to endure the hardships on alien terrain, on the chance that his efforts might pay off a thousand or ten thousand fold.

Of these men, a mere handful were successful, and of these one or two stand well above the rest. And for sheer determination, drive, and courage, for the will to push on toward his goal, no matter what the odds, a certain Commander Frank had them all beat.

II

Before you can get a picture of the commander—that is, as far as his personality goes—you have to get a picture of the man physically.

He was enough taller than the average man to make him stand out in a crowd, and he had broad shoulders and a narrow waist to match. He wasn't heavy; his was the hard, tough, wirelike strength of a steel cable. The planes of his tanned face showed that he feared neither exposure to the elements nor exposure to violence; it was seamed with fine wrinkles and the thin white lines that betray scar tissue. His mouth was heavy-lipped, but firm, and the lines around it showed that it was unused to smiling. The commander could laugh, and often did—a sort of roaring explosion that burst forth suddenly whenever something struck him as particularly uproarious. But he seldom just smiled; Commander Frank rarely went halfway in anything.

His eyes, like his hair, were a deep brown—almost black, and they were set well back beneath heavy brows that tended to frown most of the time.

Primarily, he was a military man. He had no particular flair for science, and, although he had a firm and deep-seated grasp of the essential philosophy of the Universal Assembly, he had no inclination towards the kind of life necessarily led by those who would become higher officers of the Assembly. It was enough that the Assembly was behind him; it was enough to know that he was a member of the only race in the known universe which had a working knowledge of the essential, basic Truth of the Cosmos. With a weapon like that, even an ordinary soldier had little to fear, and Commander Frank was far from being an ordinary soldier.

He had spent nearly forty of his sixty years of life as an explorer-soldier for the Emperor, and during that time he'd kept his eyes open for opportunity. Every time his ship had landed, he'd watched and listened and collected data. And now he knew.

If these data were correct—and he was certain that they were—he had found his strike. All he needed was the men to take it.

III

The Expedition had been poorly outfitted and undermanned from the beginning.

The commander had been short of money at the outset, having spent almost all he could raise on his own, plus nearly everything he could beg or borrow, on his first two probing expeditions, neither of which had shown any real profit.

But they *had* shown promise; the alien population of the target which the commander had selected as his personal claim wore gold as ornaments, but didn't seem to think it was much above copper in value, and hadn't even progressed to the point of using it as coinage. From the second probing expedition, he had brought back two of the odd-looking aliens and enough gold to show that there must be more where that came from.

The old, hopeful statement, "There's gold in them thar hills," should have brought the commander more backing than he got, considering the Empire's need of it and the commander's evidence that it was available; but people are always more ready to bet on a sure thing than to indulge in speculation. Ten years before, a strike had been made in a sector quite distant from the commander's own find, and most of the richer nobles of the Empire preferred to back an established source of the metal than to sink money into what might turn out to be the pursuit of a wild goose.

Commander Frank, therefore, could only recruit men who were willing to take a chance, who were willing to risk anything, even their lives, against tremendously long odds.

And, even if they succeeded, the Imperial government would take twenty percent of the gross without so much as a by-your-leave. There was no other market for the metal except back home, so the tax could not be avoided; gold was no good whatsoever in the uncharted wilds of an alien world.

Because of his lack of funds, the commander's expedition was not only dangerously undermanned, but illegally so. It was only by means of out-and-out trickery that he managed to evade the official inspection and leave port with too few men and too little equipment.

There wasn't a scientist worthy of the name in the whole outfit, unless you call the navigator, Captain Bartholomew, an astronomer, which is certainly begging the question. There was no anthropologist aboard to study the semibarbaric civilization of the natives; there was no biologist to study the alien flora and fauna. The closest thing the commander had to physicists were engineers who could take care of the ship itself—specialist technicians, nothing more.

There was no need for armament specialists; each and every man was a soldier, and, as far as his own weapons went, an ordnance expert. As far as Commander Frank was concerned, that was enough. It had to be.

Mining equipment? He took nothing but the simplest testing apparatus. How, then, did he intend to get the metal that the Empire was screaming for?

The commander had an answer for that, too, and it was as simple as it was economical. The natives would get it for him.

They used gold for ornaments, therefore, they knew where the gold could be found. And, therefore, they would bloody well dig it out for Commander Frank.

IV

Due to atmospheric disturbances, the ship's landing was several hundred miles from the point the commander had originally picked for the debarkation of his troops. That meant a long, forced march along the coast and then inland, but there was no help for it; the ship simply wasn't built for atmospheric navigation.

That didn't deter the commander any. The orders rang through the ship: "All troops and carriers prepare for landing!"

Half an hour later, they were assembled outside the ship, fully armed and armored, and with full field gear. The sun, a yellow G-O star, hung hotly just above the towering mountains to the east. The alien air smelled odd in the men's nostrils, and the weird foliage seemed to rustle menacingly. In the distance, the shrieks of alien fauna occasionally echoed through the air.

A hundred and eighty-odd men and some thirty carriers stood under the tropic blaze for forty-five minutes while the commander checked over their equipment with minute precision. Nothing faulty or sloppy was going into that jungle with him if he could prevent it.

When his hard eyes had inspected every bit of equipment, when he had either passed or ordered changes in the manner of its carrying or its condition, when he was fully satisfied that every weapon was in order—then, and only then, did he turn his attention to the men themselves.

He climbed atop a little hillock and surveyed them carefully, letting his penetrating gaze pass over each man in turn. He stood there, his fists on his hips, with the sunlight gleaming from his burnished armor, for nearly a full minute before he spoke.

Then his powerful voice rang out over the assembled adventurers.

"My comrades-at-arms! We have before us a world that is ours for the taking! It contains more riches than any man on Earth ever dreamed existed, and those riches, too, are ours for the taking. It isn't going to be a picnic, and we all knew that when we came. There are dangers on every side—from the natives, from the animals and plants, and from the climate.

"But there is not one of these that cannot be overcome by the onslaught of brave, courageous, and determined men!

"Ahead of us, we will find the Four Horsemen of the Apocalypse arrayed against our coming—Famine, Pestilence, War, and Death. Each and all of these we must meet and conquer as brave men should, for at their end we will find wealth and glory!"

A cheer filled the air, startling the animals in the forest into momentary silence.

The commander stilled it instantly with a raised hand.

"Some of you know this country from our previous expeditions together. Most of you will find it utterly strange. And not one of you knows it as well as I do.

"In order to survive, you must—and *will*—follow my orders to the letter—and beyond.

"First, as to your weapons. We don't have an unlimited supply of charges for them, so there will be no firing of any power weapons unless absolutely necessary. You have your swords and your pikes—use them."

Several of the men unconsciously gripped the hafts of the long steel blades at their sides as he spoke the words, but their eyes never left the commanding figure on the hummock.

"As for food," he continued, "we'll live off the land. You'll find that most of the animals are edible, but stay away from the plants unless I give the O.K.

"We have a long way to go, but, by Heaven, I'm going to get us there alive! Are you with me?"

A hearty cheer rang from the throats of the men. They shouted the commander's name with enthusiasm.

"All right!" he bellowed. "There is one more thing! Anyone who wants to stay with the ship can do so; anyone who feels too ill to make it should consider it his duty to stay behind, because sick men will simply hold us up and weaken us more than if they'd been left behind. Remember, we're not going to turn back as a body, and an individual would never make it alone." He paused.

"Well?"

Not a man moved. The commander grinned—not with humor, but with satisfaction. "All right, then: let's move out."

V

Of them all, only a handful, including the commander, had any real knowledge of what lay ahead of them, and that knowledge only pertained to the periphery of the area the intrepid band of adventurers was entering. They knew that the aliens possessed a rudimentary civilization—they did not, at that time, realize they were entering the outposts of a powerful barbaric empire—an empire almost as well-organized and well-armed as that of First Century Rome, and, if anything, even more savage and ruthless.

It was an empire ruled by a single family who called themselves the Great Nobles; at their head was the Greatest Noble—the Child of the Sun Himself. It has since been conjectured that the Great Nobles were mutants in the true sense of the word; a race apart from their subjects. It is impossible to be absolutely sure at this late date, and the commander's expedition, lacking any qualified geneticists or genetic engineers, had no way of determining—and, indeed, no real *interest* in determining—whether this was or was not true. None the less, historical evidence seems to indicate the validity of the hypothesis.

Never before—not even in ancient Egypt—had the historians ever seen a culture like it. It was an absolute monarchy that would have made any medieval king except the most saintly look upon it in awe and envy. The Russians and the Germans never even approached it. The Japanese tried to approximate it at one time in their history, but they failed.

Secure in the knowledge that theirs was the only civilizing force on the face of the planet, the race of the Great Nobles spread over the length of a great continent, conquering the lesser races as they went.

Physically, the Great Nobles and their lesser subjects were quite similar. They were, like the commander and his men, human in every sense of the word. That this argues some ancient, prehistoric migration across the empty gulfs that separate the worlds cannot be denied, but when and how that migration took place are data lost in the mists of time. However it may have happened, the fact remains that these people *were* human. As someone observed in one of the reports written up by one of the officers: "They could pass for Indians, except their skins are of a decidedly redder hue."

The race of the Great Nobles held their conquered subjects in check by the exercise of two powerful forces: religion and physical power of arms. Like the feudal organizations of Medieval Europe, the Nobles had the power of life and death over their subjects, and to a much greater extent than the European nobles had. Each family lived on an allotted parcel of land and did a given job. Travel was restricted to a radius of a few miles. There was no money; there was no necessity for it, since the government of the Great Nobles took all produce and portioned it out again according to need. It was communism on a vast and—incomprehensible as it may seem to the modern mind—*workable* scale. Their minds were as different from ours as their bodies were similar; the concept "freedom" would have been totally incomprehensible to them.

They were sun-worshipers, and the Greatest Noble was the Child of the Sun, a godling subordinate only to the Sun Himself. Directly under him were the lesser Great Nobles, also Children of the Sun, but to a lesser extent. They exercised absolute power over the conquered peoples, but even they had no concept of freedom, since they were as tied to the people as the people were tied to them. It was a benevolent dictatorship of a kind never seen before or since.

At the periphery of the Empire of the Sun-Child lived still-unconquered savage tribes, which the Imperial forces were in the process of slowly taking over. During the centuries, tribe after tribe had fallen before the brilliant leadership of the Great Nobles and the territory of the Empire had slowly expanded until, at the time the invading Earthmen came, it covered almost as much territory as had the Roman Empire at its peak.

The Imperial Army, consisting of upwards of fifty thousand troops, was extremely mobile in spite of the handicap of having no form of transportation except their own legs. They had no cavalry; the only beast of burden known to them—the flame-beasts—were too small to carry more than a hundred pounds, in spite of their endurance. But the wide, smooth roads that ran the length and breadth of the Empire enabled a marching army to make good time, and messages carried by runners in relays could traverse the Empire in a matter of days, not weeks.

And into this tight-knit, well-organized, powerful barbaric world marched Commander Frank with less than two hundred men and thirty carriers.

VI

It didn't take long for the men to begin to chafe under the constant strain of moving through treacherous and unfamiliar territory. And the first signs of chafing made themselves apparent beneath their armor.

Even the best-designed armor cannot be built to be worn for an unlimited length of time, and, at first, the men could see no reason for the order. They soon found out.

One evening, after camp had been made, one young officer decided that he had spent his last night sleeping in full armor. It was bad enough to have to march in it, but sleeping in it was too much. He took it off and stretched, enjoying the freedom from the heavy steel. His tent was a long way from the center of camp, where a small fire flickered, and the soft light from the planet's single moon filtered only dimly through the jungle foliage overhead. He didn't think anyone would see him from the commander's tent.

The commander's orders had been direct and to the point: "You will wear your armor at all times; you will march in it, you will eat in it, you will sleep in it. During such times as it is necessary to remove a part of it, the man doing so will make sure that he is surrounded by at least two of his companions in full armor. There will be no exceptions to this rule!"

The lieutenant had decided to make himself an exception.

He turned to step into his tent when a voice came out of the nearby darkness.

"Hadn't you better get your steel plates back on before the commander sees you?"

The young officer turned quickly to see who had spoken. It was another of the junior officers.

"Mind your own business," snapped the lieutenant.

The other grinned sardonically. "And if I don't?"

There had been bad blood between these two for a long time; it was an enmity that went back to a time even before the expedition had begun. The two men stood there for a long moment, the light from the distant fire flickering uncertainly against their bodies.

The young officer who had removed his armor had not been foolish enough to remove his weapons too; no sane man did that in hostile territory. His hand went to the haft of the blade at his side.

"If you say a single word—"

Instinctively, the other dropped his hand to his own sword.

"Stop! Both of you!"

And stop they did; no one could mistake the crackling authority in that voice. The commander, unseen in the moving, dim light, had been circling the periphery of the camp, to make sure that all was well. He strode toward the two younger men, who stood silently, shocked into immobility. The commander's sword was already in his hand.

"I'll pit the first man that draws a blade," he snapped.

His keen eyes took in the situation at a glance.

"Lieutenant, what are you doing out of armor?"

"It was hot, sir, and I—"

"Shut up!" The commander's eyes were dangerous. "An asinine statement like that isn't even worth listening to! Get that armor back on! *Move!*"

He was standing approximately between the two men, who had been four or five yards apart. When the cowed young officer took a step or two back toward his tent, the commander turned toward the other officer. "And as for you, if—"

Despoilers of the Golden Empire

He was cut off by the yell of the unarmored man, followed by the sound of his blade singing from its sheath.

The commander leaped backwards and spun, his own sword at the ready, his body settling into a swordsman's crouch.

But the young officer was not drawing against his superior. He was hacking at something ropy and writhing that squirmed on the ground as the lieutenant's blade bit into it. Within seconds, the serpentine thing gave a convulsive shudder and died.

The lieutenant stepped back clumsily, his eyes glazing in the flickering light. "Dropped from th' tree," he said thickly. "Bit me."

His hand moved to a dark spot on his chest, but it never reached its goal. The lieutenant collapsed, crumpling to the ground.

The commander walked over, slammed the heel of his heavy boot hard down on the head of the snaky thing, crushing it. Then he returned his blade to its sheath, knelt down by the young man, and turned him over on his face.

The commander's own face was grim.

By this time, some of the nearby men, attracted by the yell, had come running. They came to a stop as they saw the tableau before them.

The commander, kneeling beside the corpse, looked up at them. With one hand, he gestured at the body. "Let this be a lesson to all of you," he said in a tight voice. "This man died because he took off his armor. That"—he pointed at the butchered reptile—"thing is full of as deadly a poison as you'll ever see, and it can move like lightning. *But it can't bite through steel!*

"Look well at this man and tell the others what you saw. I don't want to lose another man in this idiotic fashion."

He stood up and gestured.

"Bury him."

VII

They found, as they penetrated deeper into the savage-infested hinterlands of the Empire of the Great Nobles, that the armor fended off more than just snakes. Hardly a day passed but one or more of the men would hear the sharp *spang!* of a blowgun-driven dart as it slammed ineffectually against his armored back or chest. At first, some of the men wanted to charge into the surrounding forest, whence the darts came, and punish the sniping aliens, but the commander would have none of it.

"Stick together," he ordered. "They'll do worse to us if we're split up in this jungle. Those blowgun darts aren't going to hurt you as long as they're hitting steel. Ignore them and keep moving."

They kept moving.

Around them the jungle chattered and muttered and, occasionally, screamed. Clouds of insects, great and small, hummed and buzzed through the air. They subsided only when the drizzling rains came, and then lifted again from their resting places when the sun came out to raise steamy vapors from the moist ground.

It was not an easy march. Before many days had passed, the men's feet were cracked and blistered from the effects of fungus, dampness, and constant marching. The compact military marching order which had characterized the first few days of march had long since deteriorated into a straggling column, where the weaker were supported by the stronger.

Three more men died. One simply dropped in his tracks. He was dead before anyone could touch him. Insect bite? Disease? No one knew.

Another had been even less fortunate. A lionlike carnivore had leaped on him during the night and clawed him badly before one of his companions blasted the thing with a power weapon. Three days later, the wounded man was begging to be killed; one arm and one leg were gangrenous. But he died while begging, thus sparing any would-be executioner from an unpleasant duty.

The third man simply failed to show up for roll call one morning. He was never seen again.

But the rest of the column, with dauntless courage, followed the lead of their commander.

It was hard to read their expressions, those reddened eyes that peered at him from swollen, bearded faces. But he knew his own face looked no different.

"We all knew this wasn't going to be a fancy-dress ball when we came," he said. "Nobody said this was going to be the easiest way in the world to get rich."

The commander was sitting on one of the carriers, his eyes watching the men, who were lined up in front of him. His voice was purposely held low, but it carried well.

"The marching has been difficult, but now we're really going to see what we're made of.

"We all need a rest, and we all deserve one. But when I lie down to rest, I'm going to do it in a halfway decent bed, with some good, solid food in my belly.

"Here's the way the picture looks: An hour's march from here, there's a good-sized village." He swung partially away from them and pointed south. "I think we have earned that town and everything in it."

He swung back, facing them. There was a wolfish grin on his face. "There's gold there, too. Not much, really, compared with what we'll get later on, but enough to whet our appetites."

The men's faces were beginning to change now, in spite of the swelling.

"I don't think we need worry too much about the savages that are living there now. With God on our side, I hardly see how we can fail."

He went on, telling them how they would attack the town, the disposition of men, the use of the carriers, and so forth. By the time he was through, every man there was as eager as he to move in. When he finished speaking, they set up a cheer:

"For the Emperor and the Universal Assembly!"

The natives of the small village had heard that some sort of terrible beings were approaching through the jungle. Word had come from the people of the forest that the strange monsters were impervious to darts, and that they had huge dragons with them which were terrifying even to look at. They were clad in metal and made queer noises as they moved.

The village chieftain called his advisers together to ponder the situation. What should they do with these strange things? What were the invaders' intentions?

Obviously, the things must be hostile. Therefore, there were only two courses open—fight or flee. The chieftain and his men decided to fight. It would have been a good thing if there had only been some Imperial troops in the vicinity, but all the troops were farther south, where a civil war was raging over the right of succession of the Greatest Noble.

Nevertheless, there were two thousand fighting men in the village—well, two thousand men at any rate, and they would certainly all fight, although some were rather young and a few were too old for any really hard fighting. On the other hand, it would probably not come to that, since the strangers were outnumbered by at least three to one.

The chieftain gave his orders for the defense of the village.

The invading Earthmen approached the small town cautiously from the west. The commander had his men spread out a little, but not so much that they could be separated. He saw the aliens grouped around the square, boxlike buildings, watching and waiting for trouble.

"We'll give them trouble," the commander whispered softly. He waited until his troops were properly deployed, then he gave the signal for the charge.

The carriers went in first, thundering directly into the massed alien warriors. Each carrier-man fired a single shot from his power weapon, and then went to work with his carrier, running down the terrified aliens, and swinging a sword with one hand while he guided with the other. The commander went in with that first charge, aiming his own carrier toward the center of the fray. He had some raw, untrained men with him, and he believed in teaching by example.

The aliens recoiled at the onslaught of what they took to be horrible living monsters that were unlike anything ever seen before.

Then the commander's infantry charged in. The shock effect of the carriers had been enough to disorganize the aliens, but the battle was not over yet by a long shot.

There were yells from other parts of the village as some of the other defenders, hearing the sounds of battle, came running to reinforce the home guard. Better than fifteen hundred men were converging on the spot.

The invading Earthmen moved in rapidly against the armed natives, beating them back by the sheer ferocity of their attack. Weapons of steel clashed against weapons of bronze and wood.

The power weapons were used only sparingly; only when the necessity to save a life was greater than the necessity to conserve weapon charges was a shot fired.

The commander, from the center of the fray, took a glance around the area. One glance was enough.

"They're dropping back!" he bellowed, his voice carrying well above the din of the battle. "Keep 'em moving!" He singled out one of his officers at a distance, and yelled: "Hernan! Get a couple of men to cover that street!" He waved toward one of the narrow streets that ran off to one side. The others were already being attended to.

The commander jerked around swiftly as one of the natives grabbed hold of the carrier and tried to hack at the commander with a bronze sword. The commander spitted him neatly on his blade and withdrew it just in time to parry another attack from the other side.

By this time, the reinforcements from the other parts of the village were beginning to come in from the side streets, but they were a little late. The warriors in the square—what was left of them—had panicked. In an effort to get away from the terrible monsters with their deadly blades and their fire-spitting weapons, they were leaving by the same channels that the reinforcements were coming in by, and the resultant jam-up was disastrous. The panic communicated itself like wildfire, but no one could move fast enough to get away from the sweeping, stabbing, glittering blades of the invading Earthmen.

"All right," the commander yelled, "we've got 'em on the run now! Break up into squads of three and clear those streets! Clear 'em out! Keep 'em moving!"

After that, it was the work of minutes to clear the town.

The commander brought his carrier to a dead stop, reached out with his sword, and snagged a bit of cloth from one of the fallen native warriors. He began to wipe the blade of his weapon as Lieutenant Commander Hernan pulled up beside him.

"Casualties?" the commander asked Hernan without looking up from his work.

"Six wounded, no dead," said Hernan. "Or did you want me to count the aliens, too?"

The commander shook his head. "No. Get a detail to clear out the carrion, and then tell Frater Vincent I want to talk to him. We'll have to start teaching these people the Truth."

VIII

"Have you anything to say in your defense?" the commander asked coldly.

For a moment, the accused looked nothing but hatred at the commander, but there was fear behind that hatred. At last he found his voice. "It was mine. You promised us all a share."

Lieutenant Commander Hernan picked up a leather bag that lay on the table behind which he and the commander were sitting. With a sudden gesture, he upended it, dumping its contents on the flat, wooden surface of the table.

"Do you deny that this was found among your personal possessions?" he asked harshly.

"No," said the accused soldier. "Why should I? It's mine. Rightfully mine. I fought for it. I found it. I kept it. It's mine." He glanced to either side, towards the two guards who flanked him, then looked back at the commander.

The commander ran an idle finger through the pound or so of golden trinkets that

Hernan had spilled from the bag. He knew what the trooper was thinking. A man had a right to what he had earned, didn't he?

The commander picked up one of the heavier bits of primitive jewelry and tossed it in his hand. Then he stood up and looked around the town square.

The company had occupied the town for several weeks. The stored grains in the community warehouse, plus the relaxation the men had had, plus the relative security of the town, had put most of the men back into condition. One had died from a skin infection, and another from wounds sustained in the assault on the town, but the remainder were in good health.

And all of them, with the exception of the sentries guarding the town's perimeter, were standing in the square, watching the courtmartial. Their eyes didn't seem to blink, and their breathing was soft and measured. They were waiting for the commander's decision.

The commander, still tossing the crude golden earring, stood tall and straight, estimating the feeling of the men surrounding him.

"Gold," he said finally. "Gold. That's what we came here for, and that's what we're going to get. Five hundred pounds of the stuff would make any one of you wealthy for the rest of his life. Do you think I blame any one of you for wanting it? Do you think I blame this man here? Of course not." He laughed—a short, hard bark. "Do I blame myself?"

He tossed the bauble again, caught it. "But wanting it is one thing; getting it, holding it, and taking care of it wisely are something else again.

"I gave orders. I have expected—and still expect—that they will be obeyed. But I didn't give them just to hear myself give orders. There was a reason and a good one.

"Suppose we let each man take what gold he could find. What would happen? The lucky ones would be wealthy, and the unlucky would still be poor. And then some of the lucky ones would wake up some morning without the gold they'd taken because someone else had relieved them of it while they slept.

"And others wouldn't wake up at all, because they'd be found with their throats cut.

"I told you to bring every bit of the metal to me. When this thing is over, every one of you will get his share. If a man dies, his share will be split among the rest, instead of being stolen by someone else or lost because it was hidden too well."

He looked at the earring in his hand, then, with a convulsive sweep of his arm, he tossed it out into the middle of the square.

"There! Seven ounces of gold! Which of you wants it?"

Some of the men eyed the circle of metal that gleamed brightly on the sunlit ground, but none of them made any motion to pick it up.

"So." The commander's voice was almost gentle. He turned his eyes back toward the accused. "You know the orders. You knew them when you hid this." He gestured negligently toward the small heap of native-wrought metal. "Suppose you'd gotten away with it. You'd have ended up with your own share, *plus* this, thereby cheating the others out of—" He glanced at the pile. "Hm-m-m—say, twenty-five each. And that's only a little compared with what we'll get from now on."

He looked back at the others. "Unless the shares are taken care of *my* way, the largest shares will go to the dishonest, the most powerful, and the luckiest. Unless the division is made as we originally agreed, we'll end up trying to cut each other's heart out."

There was hardness in his voice when he spoke to the accused, but there was compassion there, too.

"First: You have forfeited your share in this expedition. All that you have now, and all that you might have expected, will be divided among the others according to our original agreement.

"Second: I do not expect any man to work for nothing. Since you will not receive anything from this expedition, there is no point in your assisting the rest of us or working with us in any way whatsoever.

"Third: We can't have anyone with us who does not carry his own weight."

He glanced at the guards. "Hang him." He paused. "Now."

As he was led away, the commander watched the other men. There was approval in their eyes, but there was something else there, too—a wariness, a concealed fear.

The condemned man turned suddenly and began shouting at the commander, but before he could utter more than three syllables, a fist smashed him down. The guards dragged him off.

"All right, men," said the commander carefully, "let's search the village. There might be more gold about; I have a hunch that this isn't all he hid. Let's see if we can find the rest of it." He sensed the relief of tension as he spoke.

The commander was right. It was amazing how much gold one man had been able to stash away.

IX

They couldn't stay long in any one village; they didn't have the time to sit and relax any more than was necessary. Once they had reached the northern marches of the native empire, it was to the commander's advantage to keep his men moving. He didn't know for sure how good or how rapid communications were among the various native provinces, but he had to assume that they were top-notch, allowing for the limitations of a barbaric society.

The worst trouble they ran into on their way was not caused by the native warriors, but by disease.

The route to the south was spotted by great strips of sandy barrenness, torn by winds that swept the grains of sand into the troopers' eyes and crept into the chinks of their armor. Underfoot, the sand made a treacherous pathway; carriers and men alike found it heavy going.

The heat from the sun was intense; the brilliant beams from the primary seemed to penetrate through the men's armor and through the insulation underneath, and made the marching even harder.

Even so, in spite of the discomfort, the men were making good time until the disease struck. And that stopped them in their tracks.

What the disease was or how it was spread is unknown and unknowable at this late date. Virus or bacterium, amoeba or fungus—whatever it was, it struck.

Symptoms: Lassitude, weariness, weakness, and pain.

Signs: Great, ulcerous, wartlike, blood-filled blisters that grew rapidly over the body.

A man might go to sleep at night feeling reasonably tired, but not ill, and wake up in the morning to find himself unable to rise, his muscles too weak to lift him from his bed.

If the blisters broke, or were lanced, it was almost impossible to stop the bleeding, and many died, not from the toxic effect of the disease itself, but from simple loss of blood.

But like many epidemics, the thing had a fairly short life span. After two weeks, it had burned itself out. Most of those who got it recovered, and a few were evidently immune.

Eighteen men remained behind in shallow graves.

The rest went on.

X

No man is perfect. Even with four decades of training behind him, Commander Frank couldn't call the turn every time. After the first few villages, there were no further battles. The natives, having seen what the invaders could do, simply showed up missing when the commander and his men arrived. The villages were empty by the time the column reached the outskirts.

Frater Vincent, the agent of the Universal Assembly, complained in no uncertain terms about this state of affairs.

"As you know, commander," he said frowningly one morning, "it's no use trying to indoctrinate a people we can't contact. And you can't subject a people by force of arms alone; the power of the Truth—"

"I know, Frater," the commander interposed quickly. "But we can't deal with these savages in the hinterlands. When we get a little farther into this barbarian empire, we can take the necessary steps to—"

"The Truth," Frather Vincent interrupted somewhat testily, "if for all men. It works, regardless of the state of civilization of the society."

The commander looked out of the unglazed window of the native hut in which he had established his temporary headquarters, in one of the many villages he had taken—or, rather, walked into without a fight because it was empty. "But you'll admit, Frater, that it takes longer with savages."

"True," said Frater Vincent.

"We simply haven't the time. We've got to keep on the move. And, besides, we haven't even been able to contact any of the natives for quite a while; they get out of our way. And we have taken a few prisoners—" His voice was apologetic, but there was a trace of irritation in it. He didn't want to offend Frater Vincent, of course, but dammit, the Assemblyman didn't understand military tactics at all. Or, he corrected himself hastily, at least only slightly.

"Yes," admitted Frater Vincent, "and I've had considerable success with the prisoners. But remember—we're not here just to indoctrinate a few occasional prisoners, but to change the entire moral and philosophical viewpoint of an entire race."

"I realize that, Frater," the commander admitted. He turned from the window and faced the Assemblyman. "We're getting close to the Great Bay now. That's where our ship landed on the second probing expedition. I expect we'll be more welcome there than we have been, out here in the countryside. We'll take it easy, and I think you'll have a chance to work with the natives on a mass basis."

The Frater smiled. "Excellent, commander. I . . . uh . . . want you to understand that I'm not trying to tell you your business; you run this campaign as you see fit. But don't lose sight of the ultimate goal of life."

"I won't. How could I? It's just that my methods are not, perhaps, as refined as yours."

Frather Vincent nodded, still smiling. "True. You are a great deal more direct. And—in your own way—just as effective. After all, the Assembly could not function without the military, but there were armies long before the Universal Assembly came into being."

The commander smiled back. "Not any armies like this, Frater."

Frater Vincent nodded. The understanding between the two men—at least on that point—was tacit and mutual. He traced a symbol in the air and left the commander to his thoughts.

Mentally, the commander went through the symbol-patterns that he had learned as a child—the symbol-patterns that brought him into direct contact with the Ultimate Power, the Power that controlled not only the spinning of atoms and the whirling of electrons in their orbits, but the workings of probability itself.

Once indoctrinated into the teachings of the Universal Assembly, any man could tap that Power to a greater or lesser degree, depending on his mental control and ethical attitude. At the top level, a first-class adept could utilize that Power for telepathy, psychokinesis, levitation, teleportation, and other powers that the commander only vaguely understood.

He, himself, had no such depth of mind, such iron control over his will, and he knew he'd never have it. But he could and did tap that Power to the extent that his physical body was under near-perfect control at all times, and not even the fear of death could shake his determination to win or his great courage.

He turned again to the window and looked at the alien sky. There was a great deal yet to be done.

The commander needed information—needed it badly. He had to know what the government of the alien empire was doing. Had they been warned of his arrival? Surely they must have, and yet they had taken no steps to impede his progress.

For this purpose, he decided to set up headquarters on an island just offshore in the Great Bay. It was a protected position, easily defended from assault, and the natives, he knew from his previous visit, were friendly.

They even helped him to get his men and equipment and the carriers across on huge rafts.

From that point, he began collecting the information he needed to invade the central domains of the Greatest Noble himself. It seemed an ideal spot—not only protection-wise, but because this was the spot he had originally picked for the landing of the ship. The vessel, which had returned to the base for reinforcements and extra supplies, would be aiming for the Great Bay area when she came back. And there was little likelihood that atmospheric disturbances would throw her off course again; Captain Bartholomew was too good a man to be fooled twice.

But landing on that island was the first—and only—mistake the commander made during the campaign. The rumors of internal bickerings among the Great Nobles of the barbarian empire were not the only rumors he heard. News of more local treachery came to his ears through the agency of natives, now loyal to the commander, who had been indoctrinated into the philosophy of the Assembly.

A group of native chieftains had decided that the invading Earthmen were too dangerous to be allowed to remain on their island, in spite of the fact that the invaders had done them no harm. There were, after all, whisperings from the north, whence the invaders had come, that the armored beings with the terrible weapons had used their power more than once during their march to the south. The chieftains were determined to rid their island of the potential menace.

As soon as the matter was brought to the commander's attention, he acted. He sent out a patrol to the place where the ringleaders were meeting, arrested them, and sentenced them to death. He didn't realize what effect that action would have on the rest of the islanders.

He almost found out too late.

XI

"There must be three thousand of them out there," said Lieutenant Commander Hernan tightly, "and every one of them's crazy."

"Rot!" The commander spat on the ground and then sighted again along the barrel of his weapon. "I'm the one who's crazy. I'm a lousy politician; that's my trouble."

The lieutenant commander shrugged lightly. "Anyone can make a mistake. Just chalk it up to experience."

"I will, when we get out of this mess." He watched the gathering natives through hard, slitted eyes.

The invading Earthmen were in a village at the southern end of the eight-mile-long island, waiting inside the mud-brick huts while the natives who had surrounded the village worked themselves into a frenzy for an attack. The commander knew there was no sense in charging into them at that point; they would simply scatter and reassemble. The only thing to do was wait until they attacked—and then smash the attack.

"Hernan," he said, his eyes still watching the outside, "you and the others get out there with the carriers after the first volley. Cut them down. They're twenty-to-one against us, so make every blow count. Move."

Hernan nodded wordlessly and slipped away.

The natives were building up their courage with some sort of war dance, whooping and screaming and making threatening gestures toward the embattled invaders. Then the pattern of the dance changed; the islanders whirled to face the mud-brick buildings which housed the invading Earthmen. Suddenly the dance broke, and the warriors ran in a screaming charge, straight for the trapped soldiers.

The commander waited. His own shot would be the signal, and he didn't want the men to fire too quickly. If the islanders were hit too soon, they might fall back into the woods and set up a siege, which the little company couldn't stand. Better to mop up the natives now, if possible.

Closer. Closer—

Now!

The commander's first shot picked off one of the leaders in the front ranks of the native warriors, and was followed by a raking volley from the other power weapons, firing from the windows of the mud-brick buildings. The warriors in the front rank dropped, and those in the second rank had to move adroitly to keep from stumbling over the bodies of their fallen fellows. The firing from the huts become ragged, but its raking effect was still deadly. A cloud of heavy, stinking smoke rolled across the clearing between the edge of the jungle and the village, as the bright, hard lances of heat leaped from the muzzles of the power weapons toward the bodies of the charging warriors.

The charge was gone from the commander's weapon, and he didn't bother to replace it. As Hernan and his men charged into the melee with their carriers, the commander went with them.

At the same time, the armored infantrymen came pouring out of the mud-brick houses, swinging their swords, straight into the mass of confused native warriors. A picked group of sharpshooters remained behind in the concealment of the huts to pick off the warriors at the edge of the battle with their sporadic fire.

The commander's lips were moving a little as he formed the symbol-patterns of power almost unconsciously; a lifetime of habit had burned them into his brain so deeply that he could form them automatically while turning the thinking part of his mind to the business at hand.

He soon found himself entirely surrounded by the alien warriors. Their bronze weapons glittered in the sunlight as they tried to fight off the onslaught of the invaders. And those same bronze weapons were sheared, nicked, blunted, bent, and broken as they met the harder steel of the commander's sword.

Then the unexpected happened. One of the warriors, braver than the rest, made a grab for the commander's sword arm. At almost the same moment, a warrior on the other side of the carrier aimed a spear thrust at his side.

Either by itself would have been ineffectual. The spear clanged harmlessly from the commander's armor, and the warrior who had attempted to pull him from the carrier died before he could give much of a tug. But the combination, plus the fact that the heavy armor was a little unwieldy, overbalanced him. He toppled to the ground with a clash of steel as he and the carrier parted company.

Without a human hand at its controls, the carrier automatically moved away from the mass of struggling fighters and came to a halt well away from the battle.

The commander rolled as he hit and leaped to his feet, his sword moving in flickering arcs around him. The natives had no knowledge of effective swordplay. Like any barbarian, they conceived of a sword as a cutting instrument rather than a thrusting one. They chopped with them, using small shields to protect their bodies as they tried to hack the commander to bits.

But the commander had no desire to become mincemeat just yet. Five of the barbarians were coming at him, their swords raised for a downward slash. The commander lunged forward with a straight stop-thrust aimed at the groin of the nearest one. It came as a complete surprise to the warrior, who doubled up in pain.

The commander had already withdrawn his blade and was attacking the second as the first fell. He made another feint to the groin and then changed the aim of his point as the warrior tried to cover with his shield. A buckler is fine protection against a man who is trying to hack you to death with a chopper, because a heavy cutting sword and a shield have about the same inertia, and thus the same maneuverability. But the shield isn't worth anything against a light stabbing weapon. The warrior's shield started downward and he was unable to stop it and reverse its direction before the commander's sword pierced his throat.

Two down, three to go. No, four. Another warrior had decided to join the little battle against the leader of the invading Earthman.

The commander changed his tactics just slightly with the third man. He slashed with the tip of his blade against the descending sword-arm of his opponent—a short, quick flick of his wrist that sheared through the inside of the wrist, severing tendons, muscles, veins and arteries as it cut to the bone. The sword clanged harmlessly off the commander's shoulder. A quick thrust, and the third man died.

The other three slowed their attack and began circling warily, trying to get behind the commander. Instead of waiting, he charged forward, again cutting at the sword arm of his adversary, severing fingers this time. As the warrior turned, the commander's sword pierced his side.

How long it went on, he had no idea. He kept his legs and his sword-arm moving, and his eyes ever alert for new foes as man after man dropped beneath that snake-tonguing blade. Inside his armor, perspiration poured in rivulets down his skin, and his arms and legs began to ache, but not for one second did he let up. He could not see what was going on, could not tell the direction of the battle nor even allow his mind to wonder what was going on more than ten paces from him.

And then, quite suddenly, it seemed, it was all over. Lieutenant Commander Hernan and five other men pulled up with their carriers, as if from nowhere, their weapons dealing death, clearing a space around their commander.

"You hurt?" bawled Hernan.

The commander paused to catch his breath. He knew there was a sword-slash across his face, and his right leg felt as though there was a cut on it, but otherwise—

"I'm all right," he said. "How's it going?"

"They're breaking," Hernan told him. "We'll have them scattered within minutes."

Even as he spoke, the surge of battle moved away from them, toward the forest. The charge of the carriers, wreaking havoc on every side, had broken up the battle formation the aliens had had; the flaming death from the horrible weapons of the invaders, the fearless courage of the foot soldiers, and the steel-clad monsters that were running amuck among them shattered the little discipline they had. Panicky, they lost their anger, which had taken them several hours to build up. They scattered, heading for the forest.

Shortly the village was silent. Not an alien warrior was to be seen, save for the hundreds of mute corpses that testified to the carnage that had been wrought.

Several of the commander's men had been wounded, and three had died. Lieutenant Commander Hernan had been severely wounded in the leg by a native javelin, but the injury was a long way from being fatal.

Hernan gritted his teeth while his leg was being bandaged. "The angels were with us on that one," he said between winces.

The commander nodded. "I hope they stick with us. We'll need 'em to get off this island."

XII

For a while, it looked as though they were trapped on the island. The natives didn't dare to attack again, but no hunting party was safe, and the food supply was dropping. They had gotten on the island only by the help of the natives, who had ferried them over on rafts. But getting off was another thing, now that the natives were hostile. Cutting down trees to build rafts might possibly be managed, but during the loading the little company would be too vulnerable to attack.

The commander was seated bleakly in the hut he had taken as his headquarters, trying to devise a scheme for getting to the mainland, when the deadlock was finally broken.

There was a flurry of footsteps outside, a thump of heavy boots as one of the younger officers burst into the room.

"Commander!" he yelled. "Commander! Come outside!"

The commander leaped to his feet. "Another attack?"

"No, sir! Come look!"

The commander strode quickly to the door. His sight followed the line of the young officer's pointing finger.

There, outlined against the blue of the sky, was a ship!

The news from home was encouraging, but it was a long way from being what the commander wanted. Another hundred men and more carriers had been added to the original company of now-hardened veterans, and the recruits, plus the protection of the ship's guns, were enough to enable the entire party to leave the island for the mainland.

By this time, the commander had gleaned enough information from the natives to be able to plan the next step in his campaign. The present Greatest Noble, having successfully usurped the throne from his predecessor, was still not in absolute control of the country. He had won a civil war, but his rule was still too shaky to allow him to split up his armies, which accounted for the fact that, thus far, no action had been taken by the Imperial troops against the invading Earthmen.

The commander set up a base on the mainland, near the coast, left a portion of his men there to defend it, and, with the remainder, marched inland to come to grips with the Greatest Noble himself.

As they moved in toward the heart of the barbarian empire, the men noticed a definite change in the degree of civilization of the natives—or, at least, in the degree of technological advancement. There were large towns, not small villages, to be dealt with, and there were highways and bridges that showed a knowledge of engineering equivalent to that of ancient Rome.

The engineers of the Empire of the Great Nobles were a long way above the primitive. They could have, had they had any reason to, erected a pyramid the equal of great Khufu's in size, and probably even more neatly constructed. Militarily speaking, the lack of knowledge of iron hampered them, but it must be kept in mind that a well-disciplined and reasonably large army, armed with bronze-tipped spears, can make a formidable foe, even against a much better equipped group.

The Imperial armies were much better disciplined and much better armed than any of the natives the commander had thus far dealt with, and there were reputed to be more than ten thousand of them with the Greatest Noble in his mountain stronghold. Such considerations prompted the commander to plan his strategy carefully, but they did not deter him in the least. If he had been able to bring aircraft and perhaps a thermonuclear bomb or two for demonstration purposes, the attack might have been less risky, but neither had been available to a man of his limited means, so he had to work without them.

But now, he avoided fighting if at all possible. Working with Frater Vincent, the commander worked to convince the natives on the fertile farms and in the prosperous villages that he and his company were merely ambassadors of good will—missionaries and traders. He and his men had come in peace, and if they were received in peace, well and good. If not . . . well, they still had their weapons.

The commander was depending on the vagueness of the information that may have filtered down from the north. The news had already come that the invaders were fierce and powerful fighters, but the commander gave the impression that the only reason any battles had taken place was because the northern tribes had been truculent in the extreme. He succeeded fairly well; the natives he now met considered their brethren of the northern provinces to be little better than savages, and therefore to be expected to treat strangers inhospitably and bring about their own ruin. The southern citizens of the empire eyed the strangers with apprehension, but they offered very little resistance. The commander and his men were welcomed warily at each town, and, when they left, were bid farewell with great relief.

It took a little time for the commander to locate the exact spot where the Greatest Noble and his retinue were encamped. The real capital of the empire was located even farther south, but the Greatest Noble was staying, for the nonce, in a city nestled high in the mountains, well inland from the seacoast. The commander headed for the mountains.

The passage into the mountains wasn't easy. The passes were narrow and dangerous, and the weather was cold. The air became thinner at every step. At eight thousand feet, mountain climbing in heavy armor becomes more than just hard work, and at twelve thousand it becomes exhausting torture. But the little company went on, sparked, fueled, and driven by the personal force of their commander, who stayed in the vanguard, his eyes ever alert for treachery from the surrounding mountains.

When the surprise came, it was of an entirely different kind than he had expected. The commander's carrier came over a little rise, and he brought it to an abrupt halt as he saw the valley spread out beneath him. He left the carrier, walked over to a boulder near the edge of the cliff, and looked down at the valley.

It was an elongated oval of verdant green, fifteen miles long by four wide, looking like an emerald set in the rocky granite of the surrounding peaks that thrust upward toward the sky. The valley ran roughly north-and-south, and to his right, at the southern end, the commander could see a city, although it was impossible to see anyone moving in it at this distance.

To his left, he could see great clouds of billowing vapor that rolled across the grassy plain—evidently steam from the volcanic hot springs which he had been told were to be found in this valley.

But, for the moment, it was neither the springs nor the city that interested him most.

In the heart of the valley, spreading over acre after acre, were the tents and pavilions of a mighty army encampment. From the looks of it, the estimate of thirty thousand troops which had been given him by various officials along the way was, if anything, too small.

It was a moment that might have made an ordinary man stop to think and, having thought, to turn and go. But the commander was no ordinary man, and the sheer remorseless courage that had brought him this far wouldn't allow him to turn back. So far, he had kept the Greatest Noble off balance with his advancing tactics; if he started to retreat, the Greatest Noble would realize that the invaders were not invincible, and would himself advance to crush the small band of strangers.

The Greatest Noble had known the commander and his men were coming; he was simply waiting, to find out what they were up to, confident that he could dispose of them at his leisure. The commander knew that, and he knew he couldn't retreat now. There was no decision to be made, really—only planning to be done.

He turned back from the boulder to face the officers who had come to take a look at the valley.

"We'll go to the city first," he said.

XIII

The heavy tread of the invaders' boots as they entered the central plaza of the walled city awakened nothing but echoes from the stone walls that surrounded the plaza. Like the small villages they had entered farther north, the city seemed devoid of life.

There is nothing quite so depressing and threatening as a deserted city. The windows in the walls of the buildings seemed like blank, darkened eyes that watched—and waited. Nothing moved, nothing made a sound, except the troopers themselves.

The men kept close to the walls; there was no point in bunching up in the middle of the square to be cut down by arrows from the windows of the upper floors.

The commander ordered four squads of men to search the buildings and smoke out anyone who was there, but they turned up nothing. The entire city was empty. And there were no traps, no ambushes—nothing.

The commander, with Lieutenant Commander Hernan and another officer, climbed to the top of the central building of the town. In the distance, several miles away, they could see the encampment of the monarch's troops.

"The only thing we can do," the commander said, his face hard and determined, "is to call their bluff. You two take about three dozen men and go out there with the carriers and give them a show. Go right into camp, as if you owned the place. Throw a scare into them, but don't hurt anyone. Then, very politely, tell the Emperor, or whatever he calls himself, that I would like him to come here for dinner and a little talk."

The two officers looked at each other, then at the commander.

"Just like that?" asked Hernan.

"Just like that," said the commander.

The demonstration and exhibition went well—as far as it had gone. The native warriors had evidently been quite impressed by the onslaught of the terrifying monsters that had thundered across the plain toward them, right into the great camp, and come to a dead halt directly in front of the magnificent pavilion of the Greatest Noble himself.

The Greatest Noble put up a good face. He had obviously been expecting the visitors, because he and his lesser nobles were lined up before the pavilion, the Greatest Noble ensconced on a sort of portable throne. He managed to look perfectly calm and somewhat bored by the whole affair, and didn't seem to be particularly affected at all when Lieutenant Commander Hernan bowed low before him and requested his presence in the city.

And the Greatest Noble's answer was simple and to the point, although it was delivered by one of his courtiers.

"You may tell your commander," said the noble, "that His Effulgence must attend to certain religious duties tonight, since he is also High Priest of the Sun. However, His Effulgence will most graciously deign to speak to your commander tomorrow. In the meantime, you are requested to enjoy His Effulgence's gracious hospitality in the city, which has been emptied for your convenience. It is yours, for the nonce."

Which left nothing for the two officers and their men to do but go thundering back across the plain to the city.

The Greatest Noble did not bring his whole army with him, but the pageant of barbaric splendor that came tootling and drumming its way into the city the next evening was a magnificent sight. His Effulgence himself was dressed in a scarlet robe and a scarlet, turbanlike head covering with scarlet fringes all around it. About his throat was a necklace of emerald-green gems, and his clothing was studded with more of them. Gold gleamed everywhere. He was borne on an ornate, gilded palanquin, carried high above the crowd on the shoulders of a dozen stalwart nobles, only slightly less gorgeously dressed than the Greatest Noble. The nobility that followed was scarcely less showy in its finery.

When they came into the plaza, however, the members of the procession came to a halt. The singing and music died away.

The plaza was absolutely empty.

No one had come out to greet the Emperor.

There were six thousand natives in the plaza, and not a sign of the invaders.

The commander, hiding well back in the shadows in one of the rooms of the central building, watched through the window and noted the evident consternation of the royal entourage with satisfaction. Frater Vincent, standing beside him, whispered, "Well?"

"All right," the commander said softly, "they've had a taste of what we got when we came in. I suppose they've had enough. Let's go out and act like hosts."

The commander and a squad of ten men, along with Frater Vincent, strode majestically out of the door of the building and walked toward the Greatest Noble. They had all polished their armor until it shone, which was about all they could do in the way of finery, but they evidently looked quite impressive in the eyes of the natives.

"Greetings, Your Effulgence," said the commander, giving the Greatest Noble a bow that was hardly five degrees from the perpendicular. "I trust we find you well."

In the buildings surrounding the square, hardly daring to move for fear the clank of metal on metal might give the whole plan away, the remaining members of the company watched the conversation between their commander and the Greatest Noble. They couldn't hear what was being said, but that didn't matter; they knew what to do as soon as the commander gave the signal. Every eye was riveted on the commander's right hand.

It seemed an eternity before the commander casually reached up to his helmet and brushed a hand across it—once—twice—three times.

Then all hell broke loose. The air was split by one sound of power weapons throwing their lances of flame into the massed ranks of the native warriors. The gunners, safe behind the walls of the buildings, poured a steady stream of accurately directed fire into the packed mob, while the rest of the men charged in with their blades, thrusting and slashing as they went.

The aliens, panic-stricken by the sudden, terrifying assault, tried to run, but there was nowhere to run to. Every exit had been cut off to bottle up the Imperial cortege. Within minutes, the entrances to the square were choked with the bodies of those who tried to flee.

As soon as the firing began, the commander and his men began to make their way toward the Greatest Noble. They had been forced to stand a good five yards away during the parlay, cut off from direct contact by the Imperial guards. The commander, sword in hand, began cutting his way through to the palanquin.

The palanquin bearers seemed frozen; they couldn't run, they couldn't fight, and they didn't dare drop their precious cargo.

The commander's voice bellowed out over the carnage. "Take him prisoner! I'll personally strangle the idiot who harms him!" And then he was too busy to yell.

Two members of the Greatest Noble's personal guard came for him, swords out, determined to give their lives, if necessary, to preserve the sacred life of their monarch. And give them they did.

The commander's blade lashed out once, sliding between the ribs of the first guard. He toppled and almost took the sword with him, but the commander wrenched it free in time to parry the downward slash of the second guard's bronze sword. It was a narrow thing, because the bronze sword, though of softer stuff than the commander's steel, was also heavier, and thus hard to deflect. As it sang past him, the commander swung a chop at the man's neck, cutting it halfway through. He stepped quickly to one side to avoid the falling body and thrust his blade through a third man, who was aiming a blow at the neck of one of the commander's officers. There were only a dozen feet separating the commander from his objective, the palanquin of the Greatest Noble, but he had to wade through blood to get there.

The palanquin itself was no longer steady. Three of the twelve nobles who had been holding it had already fallen, and there were two of the commander's men already close enough to touch the royal person, but they were too busy fighting to make any attempt to grab him. The Greatest Noble, unarmed, could only huddle in his seat, terrified, but it would take more than two men to snatch him from his bodyguard. The commander fought his way in closer.

Two more of the palanquin bearers went down, and the palanquin itself began to topple. The Greatest Noble screamed as he fell toward the commander.

One of the commander's men spun around as he heard the scream so close to him, and, thinking that the Greatest Noble was attacking his commander, lunged out with his blade.

It was almost a disaster. Moving quickly, the commander threw out his left arm to deflect the sword. He succeeded, but he got a bad slash across his hand for his trouble.

He yelled angrily at the surprised soldier, not caring what he said. Meanwhile, the others of the squad, seeing that the Greatest Noble had fallen, hurried to surround him. Two minutes later, the Greatest Noble was a prisoner, being half carried, half led into the central building by four of the men, while the remaining six fought a rearguard action to hold off the native warriors who were trying to rescue the sacred person of the Child of the Sun.

Once inside, the Greatest Noble was held fast while the doors were swung shut.

Outside, the slaughter went on. All the resistance seemed to go out of the warriors when they saw their sacred monarch dragged away by the invading Earthmen. It was every man for himself and the Devil take the hindmost. And the Devil, in the form of the commander's troops, certainly did.

Within half an hour after it had begun, the butchery was over. More than three thousand of the natives had died, and an unknown number more badly wounded. Those who had managed to get out and get away from the city kept on going. They told the troops who had been left outside what had happened, and a mass exodus from the valley began.

Safely within the fortifications of the central building, the commander allowed himself one of his rare grins of satisfaction. Not a single one of his own men had been killed and the only wound which had been sustained by anyone in the company was the cut on his own hand. Still smiling, he went into the room where the Greatest Noble, dazed and shaken, was being held by two of the commander's men. The commander bowed—this time, very low.

"I believe, Your Effulgence, that we have an appointment for dinner. Come, the banquet has been laid."

And, as though he were still playing the gracious host, the commander led the half-paralyzed Child of the Sun to the room where the banquet had been put on a table in perfect diplomatic array.

"Your Effulgence may sit at my right hand," said the commander pleasantly.

XIV

As MacDonald said of Robert Wilson, "This is not an account of how Boosterism came to Arcadia." It's a devil of a long way from it. And once the high point of a story has been reached and passed, it is pointless to prolong it too much. The capture of the Greatest Noble broke the power of the Empire of the Great Nobles forever. The loyal subjects were helpless without a leader, and the disloyal ones, near the periphery of the Empire, didn't care. The crack Imperial troops simply folded up and went home. The Greatest Noble went on issuing orders, and they were obeyed; the people were too used to taking orders from authority to care whether they were really the Greatest Noble's own idea or not.

In a matter of months, two hundred men had conquered an empire with a loss of thirty-five or forty men. Eventually, they had to execute the old Greatest Noble and put his more tractable nephew on the throne, but that was a mere incident.

Gold? It flowed as though there were an endless supply. The commander shipped enough back on the first load to make them all wealthy.

The commander didn't go back home to spend his wealth amid the luxuries of the Imperial court, even though Emperor Carl appointed him to the nobility. That sort of thing wasn't the commander's meat. There he would be a fourth-rate noble. Here, he was the Imperial Viceroy, responsible only to the distant Emperor. There, he would be nothing; here, he was almost a king.

Two years after the capture of the Greatest Noble, he established a new capital on the coast and named it Kingston. And from Kingston he ruled with an iron hand.

As has been intimated, this was *not* Arcadia. A year after the founding of Kingston, the old capital was attacked, burned, and almost fell under siege, due to a sudden uprising of the natives under the new Greatest Noble, who had managed to escape. But the uprising collapsed because of the approach of the planting season; the warriors had to go back home and plant their crops or the whole of the agriculture-based country would starve—except the invading Earthmen.

Except in a few instances, the natives were never again any trouble.

But the commander—now the Viceroy—had not seen the end of his troubles.

He had known his limitations, and realized that the governing of a whole planet—or even one continent—was too much for one man when the population consists primarily of barbarians and savages. So he had delegated the rule of a vast area to the south to another—a Lieutenant Commander James, known as "One-Eye," a man who had helped finance the original expedition, and had arrived after the conquest.

One-Eye went south and made very small headway against the more barbaric tribes there. He did not become rich, and he did not achieve anywhere near the success that the Viceroy had. So he came back north with his army and decided to unseat the Viceroy and take his place. That was five years after the capture of the Greatest Noble.

One-Eye took Center City, the old capital, and started to work his way northward, toward Kingston. The Viceroy's forces met him at a place known as Salt Flats and thoroughly trounced him. He was captured, tried for high treason, and executed.

One would think that the execution ended the threat of Lieutenant Commander James, but not so. He had a son, and he had had followers.

XV

Nine years. Nine years since the breaking of a vast empire. It really didn't seem like it. The Viceroy looked at his hands. They were veined and thin, and the callouses were gone. Was he getting soft, or just getting old? A little bit—no, a *great deal* of both.

He sat in his study, in the Viceregal Palace at Kingston, chewing over the events of the past weeks. Twice, rumors had come that he was to be assassinated. He and two of his councilors had been hanged in effigy in the public square not long back. He had been snubbed publicly by some of the lesser nobles.

Had he ruled harshly, or was it just jealousy? And was it really, as some said, caused by the Southerners and the followers of Young Jim?

He didn't know. And sometimes, it seemed as if it didn't matter.

Here he was, sitting alone in his study, when he should have gone to a public function. And he had stayed because of fear of assassination.

Was it—

There was a knock at the door.

"Come in."

A servant entered. "Sir Martin is here, my lord."

The Viceroy got to his feet. "Show him in, by all means."

Sir Martin, just behind the servant, stepped in, smiling, and the Viceroy returned his smile. "Well, everything went off well enough without you," said Sir Martin.

"Any sign of trouble?"

"None, my lord; none whatsoever. The —"

"Damn!" the Viceroy interrupted savagely. "I should have known! What have I done but display my cowardice? I'm getting yellow in my old age!"

Sir Martin shook his head. "Cowardice, my lord? Nothing of the sort. Prudence, I should call it. By the by, the judge and a few others are coming over." He chuckled softly. "We thought we might talk you out of a meal."

The Viceroy grinned widely. "Nothing easier. I suspected all you hangers-on would come around for your handouts. Come along, my friend; we'll have a drink before the others get here."

There were nearly twenty people at dinner, all, presumably, friends of the Viceroy. At least, it is certain that they were friends in so far as they had no part in the assassination plot. It was a gay party; the Viceroy's friends were doing their best to cheer him up, and were succeeding pretty well. One of the nobles, known for his wit, had just essayed a somewhat off-color jest, and the others were roaring with laughter at the punch line when a shout rang out.

There was a sudden silence around the table.

"What was that?" asked someone. "What did—"

"Help!" There was the sound of footsteps pounding up the stairway from the lower floor.

"Help! The Southerners have come to kill the Viceroy!"

From the sounds, there was no doubt in any of the minds of the people seated around the table that the shout was true. For a moment, there was shock. Then panic took over.

There were only a dozen or so men in the attacking party; if the "friends" of the Viceroy had stuck by him, they could have held off the assassins with ease.

But no one ran to lock the doors that stood between the Viceroy and his enemies, and only a few drew their weapons to defend him. The others fled. Getting out of a window from the second floor of a building isn't easy, but fear can lend wings, and, although none of them actually flew down, the retreat went fast enough.

Characteristically, the Viceroy headed, not for the window, but for his own room, where his armor—long unused, except for state functions—hung waiting in the closet, with him went Sir Martin.

But there wasn't even an opportunity to get into the armor. The rebel band charged into the hallway that led to the bedroom, screaming: *"Death to the Tyrant! Long live the Emperor!"*

It was personal anger, then, not rebellion against the Empire which had appointed the ex-commander to his post as Viceroy.

"Where is the Viceroy? Death to the Tyrant!" The assassins moved in.

Swords in hand, and cloaks wrapped around their left arms, Sir Martin and the Viceroy moved to meet the oncoming attackers.

"Traitors!" bellowed the Viceroy. "Cowards! Have you come to kill me in my own house?"

Parry, thrust! Parry, thrust! Two of the attackers fell before the snake-tongue blade of the fighting Viceroy. Sir Martin accounted for two more before he fell in a flood of his own blood.

The Viceroy was alone, now. His blade flickered as though inspired, and two more died under its tireless onslaught. Even more would have died if the head of the conspiracy, a supporter of Young Jim named Rada, hadn't pulled a trick that not even the Viceroy would have pulled.

Rada grabbed one of his own men and shoved him toward the Viceroy's sword, impaling the hapless man upon that deadly blade.

And, in the moment while the Viceroy's weapon was buried to the hilt in an enemy's body, the others leaped around the dying man and ran their blades through the Viceroy.

He dropped to the floor, blood gushing from half a dozen wounds.

Even so, his fighting heart still had seconds more to beat. As he propped himself up on one arm, the assassins stood back; even they recognized that they had killed something bigger and stronger than they. A better man than any of them lay dying at their feet.

He clawed with one hand at the river of red that flowed from his pierced throat and then fell forward across the stone floor. With his crimson hand, he traced the great symbol of his Faith on the stone—the Sign of the Cross. He bent his head to kiss it, and, with a final cry of *"Jesus!"* he died. At the age of seventy, it had taken a dozen men to kill him with treachery, something all the hell of nine years of conquest and rule had been unable to do.

And thus died Francisco Pizarro, the Conqueror of Peru. ■

THE PRESENT STATE OF IGNEOS RESEARCH

by Gordon R. Dickson

Research—serious research, that is—into the subject of the large *igneoeructidae* known familiarly to scholars in the field as "igneos" and to the layman as "dragons," has always been hampered as much by lack of a place to publish results as by the general skepticism of the public—to say nothing of the skepticism of most present-day biologists and zoologists—concerning the existence of this species.

The effect of this has been that efforts to publish in the field have produced activities on the part of the researcher more resembling those of the hero in a late-night spy movie than those of someone engaged in ordinary scholarly investigation. Occasionally, of course, this unorthodox behavior has paid unexpected dividends, as in the discovery of new channels of information, such as the publication in which you are now reading this monograph. True to a long-standing policy of barring nothing from its pages which might be of interest to its admittedly highly selective readership, *Analog* has emerged as the one publication of the last several decades which has continuously striven to keep its readers up to date on the latest igneos research.

Occasionally, we must admit, this information has had to be presented in fictional form, even here. But I need not rehearse examples of excellent information on the igneos, reaching this publication's readers from highly qualified workers in the field such as Anne McCaffrey and Poul Anderson, to name only two. Having, however, cited this pair, who by their scholarship and renown are hardly in a position to be shaken by any ordinary attack, let us move along to the main topic. For the subject of this particular paper is not the conditions and problems surrounding igneos research, but a fortunate discovery of a piece of invaluable new evidence which bids fair to shine a powerful, valuable—if not revolutionary—light on the whole species.

This discovery consists of a manuscript that presents an account, in verse, of an encounter between an igneos and a human. It is not, however, merely the account of any random encounter, but details the exact actions of a member of the "Dragon-Runners' Guild" toward one particular igneos, in accordance with the rules of that Guild. The Dragon-Runners' Guild is an organization the existence of which has been long suspected by researchers into the igneos situation. Now, with this manuscript, proof has at last been obtained that the Guild did indeed exist—and may still, in fact, be not only in existence, but in active existence, even in our present era.

But more of that in a moment. Let us pass on to more solid matters. It is necessary before building conjecture upon fact to give a more precise description of the manuscript, and an account of the information to be deduced from it.

On first examination the narrative appears to be written in something very like Fourteenth Century Middle English. Closer scrutiny, however, reveals two puzzling inconsistencies. One, the chronicler who wrote it was clearly unused to the making of such chronicles. There are variances within the text that show that it was penned with a good deal of carelessness and little thought beyond that of setting down the immediate information it contained. Second, the language used, while it has some of the tricks of spelling common to Middle English in the period mentioned, also shows a meter and rhyme that is only consistent if the words set down are pronounced as a speaker of Modern English would pronounce them.

However, tests of the parchment on which the manuscript was written, and the ink used, have proved that neither parchment nor ink were of any more recent vintage than some five hundred years, and possibly much older. This has left only one possible conclusion, by anyone knowledgeable in the igneos field. That is, that while the manuscript had to be written by someone with a modern ear, it was nonetheless written by such a person while he or she was existing in the fourteenth century or earlier.

In short, we must assume that a case of temporal translation (i.e., time-traveling) was involved in the production of this manuscript.

Startling—even self-contradictory—as this may sound to those unacquainted with the work already done in this field, it is quite consistent with other evidence previously published. Those informed about the igneos will undoubtedly recall Ms. McCaffrey's references to, and descriptions of, the phenomenon of temporal translation as achieved by these remarkable creatures, in her earlier papers in this publication. It therefore becomes entirely conceivable that the author of this manuscript was originally of our own modern era.

Once this fact is accepted, the internal evidence of the manuscript delivers up that information which I have—and I believe justly—referred to as revolutionary. For centuries researchers have puzzled over what actually extinguished the race of the igneos. Naturally, among knowledgeable scholars, the mistaken folk-tale notion that the igneos were evil creatures destroyed by human heroes—the "St. George and the Dragon" legend, for example—has long been recognized for the cruel distortion of fact that it is. I, myself, have had a few words to say on this matter in another publication, some seventeen years ago ("St. Dragon and the George," *Fantasy and Science Fiction*, September 1957); and the georgists, I am confident, are a dying breed. For some centuries we in the field have been convinced that igneos-nature was just the opposite of evil; although it is only for the first time, in this manuscript, that we have documentary proof of the fact—documentary proof provided by a human writer.

I refer you to stanza twenty-four, lines one and two, of the manuscript:

"Ye whole world knowes—despyte hys fercer parte
How ech Dragon wythin hathe noble herte . . ."

The important information here lies in the words "... hathe noble herte." As I say, anyone expert in the field has long suspected this to be true. But we must ask ourselves, since igneos were noble-hearted, and known by humans to be so, how did canards like the St. George and the Dragon legend get started?

I believe the answer to that can be given simply, in one word. Guilt. As internal evidence in this manuscript makes clear, humans were indeed responsible for the disappearance of the igneos from among us; but not by force of arms. Rather by neglect and inattention, a treatment these noble-hearted creatures could not endure.

As a careful examination of the manuscript will show, a close association between man and igneos was originally considered not merely advantageous, but necessary to the igneos. Observe that the story set down in these lines is that of an igneos revived from a poor state of health by a human. Lacking such human association previously, the igneos, Shagoth, as it is noted near the beginning of the poem, has become "fatte" and "styffe," with a temper that "wasse notte gude." He has, in fact, become so debilitated as to lose his natural ability to fly.

Contrast this condition with the accounts of the same igneos, further on in the poem after he has been contacted and exercised by a comparably noble-hearted human—the Prentice (later Knight, still later Baron) Morlet:

> "... Above ye rockye strande and cruel sea,
> SHAGOTH bete upward, lyght as fethers bee;
> Swoopynge and makynge Turnes Immeleman,
> And Loope-ye-Loopes, all suche as Dragon canne..."

Note, also, how it is later remarked that the now-slim igneos continues to "ronne" and lift "hevie weightes to keep hym trim" although Morlet, in person, has already parted with him. Above all, note the extremely important lines emphasizing that, as a result of Shagoth keeping up these activities, "all other Dragones envie hym..."(!)

To the trained professional eye, lines and line-fragments such as these fit together to make certain unmistakable statements. Shagoth is not just one igneos, left to lead a solitary existence—but all igneos in such condition of human neglect. Morlet is not merely one human, but representative of a whole class of humans who have always concerned themselves with the welfare of the igneos. And the message, in brief, is plain. Igneos require human contact and assistance for their existence in this world. A lack of such contact in recent centuries was obviously a primary reason for their disappearance from among us.

But is this sad conclusion all we can learn from this manuscript? No. There is further information to be gleaned from the lines of poetry; and this indicates almost beyond a shadow of a doubt that the igneos need not be gone from among us for good.

For, I submit humbly, but with the certainty of all my years of scholarship in this field, that these lines, together with other evidence I have mentioned, reveal that the igneos, as a race, have not died out. What they have done is to withdraw temporally from us humans. They have literally hidden themselves somewhere in the temporal continuum, using their ability to travel there.

Where in the temporal continuum are they hiding? The answer to this question must await further research. But no one of intelligence can doubt that the answer is there waiting for us. I submit to you two inescapable conclusions:

One, that this manuscript was clearly written by a modern hand.

Two, that the Dragon-Runners' Guild is proved beyond any reasonable doubt to exist.

The deduction from these conclusions is obvious. The writer of the manuscript must have been himself or herself a member of the Guild—a modern member who was able to return through time to the fourteenth century or earlier. Such temporal translations could only have been accomplished with the help of one or more igneos—which means that their race must still exist, in some area removed from our modern present, but from which they are in contact with the Guild. Such Guild-contact can only indicate that the igneos have not completely given up on humanity.

This being the case, however, we may well ask ourselves—can the igneos ever be brought back into contact with the rest of our race, and if so, how?

The poem itself offers an answer. It was the lack with association with noble-hearted humans that caused the igneos to disappear from view, it tells us. But it avoids suggesting that there were no longer any noble-hearted humans in existence. I propose, rather, that it was the noisy vehicles of modern transportation, the overwhelming growth of human cities—in short, the infestation of earth and sky with all the artifacts of what humans call modern civilization—that caused the sensitive igneos to shrink back more and more into isolated areas, where the possibility of their contact with the noble-hearted among our own race was extremely limited.

But now, we have finally come upon a practical means of bringing the igneos out of hiding. It is through such publications as this, that a sufficient number of igneos-minded humans can be located and identified; so that, finding human friends once more available to them, the igneos may possibly be enticed to return among us.

I have been told point-blank by other igneos experts that this prospect is a pipe-dream on my part; that the noble-hearted human is as extinct as the igneos themselves have popularly been believed to be. However, I emphatically reject such pessimism; and I offer to rebut it with the reactions of the readers of this monograph. Let me refer you to the fact that, at its conclusion, the manuscript shows Shagoth and Morlet, although they are now separated, maintaining their friendship through an exchange of correspondence once a year:

> ". . . Butte yn ye season whenne ye misteltoe
> And holly hangeth hevye on ye bough,
> Ech wrytes to ech a lettere of gude cheere,
> To telle hys friende whatte hym befel thatte yeare."

I stand on my belief that there are among the readers of this publication many of those noble-hearted individuals with whom our time-stranded igneos friends yearn to have contact. And I call on all of you reading this. How many of you would not be willing, like Morlet, to sit down once a year at this holiday season and pen a "lettere of gude cheere" to an igneos friend?

Confident that the positive response to this question will be an overwhelmingly decisive one, I sit back to await the future in an atmosphere of anticipation and high hope. ■

YE PRENTICE AND YE DRAGON

by Gordon R. Dickson

Illustration by Jack Gaughan.
Copyright © 1974 by The Conde Nast Publications, Inc.

Yn frostye season whenne ye misteltoe
And holly hangeth hevye on ye bough;
A deede bothe brave and kindlie once befel;
The tale of whych yn truthe I canne nowe telle.

Ther wasse a Dragon, SHAGOTH, on a clyffe.
I wiss hee wasse a Dragon fatte and styffe;
For thatte since manye settynges of ye sunne
Hee hadde no ferce battaile, nor helthful ronne.

And as bothe Dragones and alle mankinde hathe,
Hys styffnesse fedeth fulle hys anciente wrathe
By alle of whych I shulde be understoode
To saye of hym, hys temper wasse notte gude.

By cause of thys, hys sore infirmitee,
He sheweth no traveleres ne mercie;
Ande suche grym stories of hym didde resound,
Alle folke of hys clyffe passeth far around.

But at ye tyme of whych I nowe relate
Ther cameth one whose renoun wasse notte grete;
A Prentice onlie, but by stronge oathe bounde,
To ronne alle Dragones, and to keepe them sounde.

And as hys rank, tho gentil, wasse not grete,
Hee had no welth, ne any hy estate;
But that rare charitie to Dragonkinde
Whych Sages praiseth, tyme alle oute of mynde

MORLET, hys name, a brave and kindlie youth.
When thatte hee knew ye mattere wasse ynsoothe
Of a Dragon's deepe neede, yvowed thatte hee
Shulde see ye SHAGOTH ronninge lyssomlee.

Yet perille was ynough, as welle he wotte,
Sobye hee came at nyghttyme as ythought,
Wher slepeth SHAGOTH yn a rockye neste,
Groanynge for aches thatte paineth stronge hys reste.

And cleverlye ye Prentice, alle alone,
Beneathe ye necke of SHAGOTH rolled a stone.
So thatte ye Dragon twyst hys necke yn sleepe,
Ye stone from bruysing of his fleshe to keepe.

So slepeth hee wyth twysted necke tyll dawne,
Woke wyth ye sunne and sterteth up anon
A styffe, and certes, a crookede necke to fynde,
Soe thatte he myghte bye no meanes looke behinde.

Soe payned thys laste condicioun, past beliefe,
Thatte SHAGOTH gan to wepe for verie griefe—
"O sadde a Dragon's lyfe," quod hee, "thatte I
Must suffere soe, and am too fatte to flye!"

But scarcelie hadde he made thys woefulle moan,
When hee did feele a poke at hys tayle-bone.
Furieuse, hee tryde to turn hys head and see,
Who poked atte hym; but hys styffe necke stopped hee.

"Hay done!" hee cryed, "Yn Name of Dragon's Wrathe!"
Yette MORLET kneweth welle hys Prentice' pathe;
Wherefor hee proddeth SHAGOTH yette once more
And SHAGOTH lepeth from hys neste, aroare.

So wroth ye Dragon wasse, ne recketh hee
Of alle hys aches and alle hys miserie.
"I shalle thys Pokkere shak fro off my tayle,"
Swered hee, "then dryve hym erthwerd lyke a nayle!"

Rechinge ye open plaine, hee gan gallope
As onlie Dragons canne, withouten stoppe.
At fersom speede hee thundred o'er ye lande,
Ther wasse no distaunce thatte culde hym withstande.

Meantyme, yonge MORLET, faithfulle to hys vowe,
Clunge to ye Dragon's tayle, gratefulle enowe.
For hys gude belte, withe whych tyght-bounde hadde hee,
Hymself to SHAGOTH, leste hee bee throwne free.

So, ryskinge lyfe and lymbe and mortale dethe,
MORLET revowed hys oathe whyle hee hadde brethe,
"I will succour thys Dragon, or wille die.
Such dutie ys ye leeste fro suche as I!"

Yet, if yonge MORLET wulde notte bende hys wille,
Namor culde SHAGOTH's Dragon's wrathe be stille.
Togethere, they continuede on ther ronne
Through mornynge, noone, and settynge of ye sunne.

Acrosse ye wyde plaine, thro ye furthere hilles,
By fieldes and forestes, swampes and rockye rilles,
Chargeth ye SHAGOTH ynto deepeste nyghte.
Fulle warme wasse hee, ne ached, but felte aryghte.

And as ye yongling dawne gan bleede ye skye,
SHAGOTH unto hymself asked, "Bee thys I?
So lyghtlie leping o'er ech hille and dale;
So acheless, fulle of strengthe, ne lyke to fayle?

"Mayhap thys longe gallope hathe done me gude.
Culdest bee thys Pokkere knewe soe, thatte yt wulde?
Yf soe, mystaken wasse my wrathe anon
I muste admitte to hym thatte I wasse wronge."

Hee turned hys heade—nowe on a supple necke,
To speke to MORLET. But hee fayled to recke
Of (juste aheade) a cliffe-edge, sharpe yndeede
From off of whych hee hurtled atte fulle speede.

A cliffe ytte wasse, famos fro lande to lande,
For halfe a myle sheere, felle ytte to ye strande
Of ye deepe sea, wyth grete stones alle aboute,
To smashe ye lyfe fro man and Dragon oute.

Ye whole world knowes—despyte hys fercer parte,
How ech Dragon wythin hathe noble herte;
And yn thys moment whenne fel dethe wasse nere,
Ytte wasse notte for hymself SHAGOTH felte feare.

"Alas!" cryed hee, "ne looked I onne, eftsoone.
I have repayed kyndnesse wyth ferful doome!
Pokkere, t'was thou helped mee—nowe wee muste dye!"
"Nonsense!" quod MORLET. "Needes butte thatte ye flye."

Grete teares therpon bedewed ye Dragon's cheek.
"Alas," hee wept, "I am too fatte and weake!"
"Thatte once wasse true," sayd MORLET, "but namor.
Thy ronne hathe made thee lean and lyght to soare."

"Canne thys bee true?" sayd SHAGOTH. "I wille trye."
Hee tryed, and lo! Hee founde thatte hee culde flye.
As once hadde hee, when butte a Dragon yonge,
Soarynge above ye erthbounde, everechon.

Ah, grete ye bliss of hygh lordes yn ther towers,
And grete ther laydes bliss wythin ther bowers;
But no bliss toucheth that whych doth obtayn,
A Dragon fatte, who nowe canne flye agayne!

Above ye rockye strande and cruel sea,
SHAGOTH bete upward, lyght as fethers bee;
Swoopynge and makynge Turnes Immeleman,
Ande Loope-ye-Loopes, all suche as Dragons canne.

So triumphantlee returned hee home by aire,
To hys own clyffe. Partynge wyth MORLET there,
He didde ye Prentice thanke moste hertilie,
And waved farewel as far as hym culde see.

And soe they parted. Butte since then, ech dawne,
Earlie, SHAGOTH some lengthie leagues doth ronne;
Ande lyfteth hevie weightes to keepe hym trim,
Soe thatte alle other Dragones envie hym.

Meantyme, yonge MORLET hath becom a Knyghte.
Yn manye landes hath shone yn gallaunt fyghte
Ande won hym grete honors, untyl ye Kyng
Hath made hym Baronne, as ye mynstrelles sing.

Soe goeth ech, uponne hys separate waye,
SHAGOTH doth aide alle travelleres gone astraye.
MORLET doth rule hys Baronnie, and fyghte
Alle eville Knyghtes, and trounceth them arygt.

Butte yn ye season whenne misteltoe
And holly hangeth hevye on ye bough,
Ech wrytes to ech a lettere of gude cheere
To telle hys friende whatte hym befel thatte yeare.

MAKE MINE HOMOGENIZED
by Rick Raphael

Illustration by Kelly Freas.
Copyright © 1960 by Street & Smith Publications, Inc.

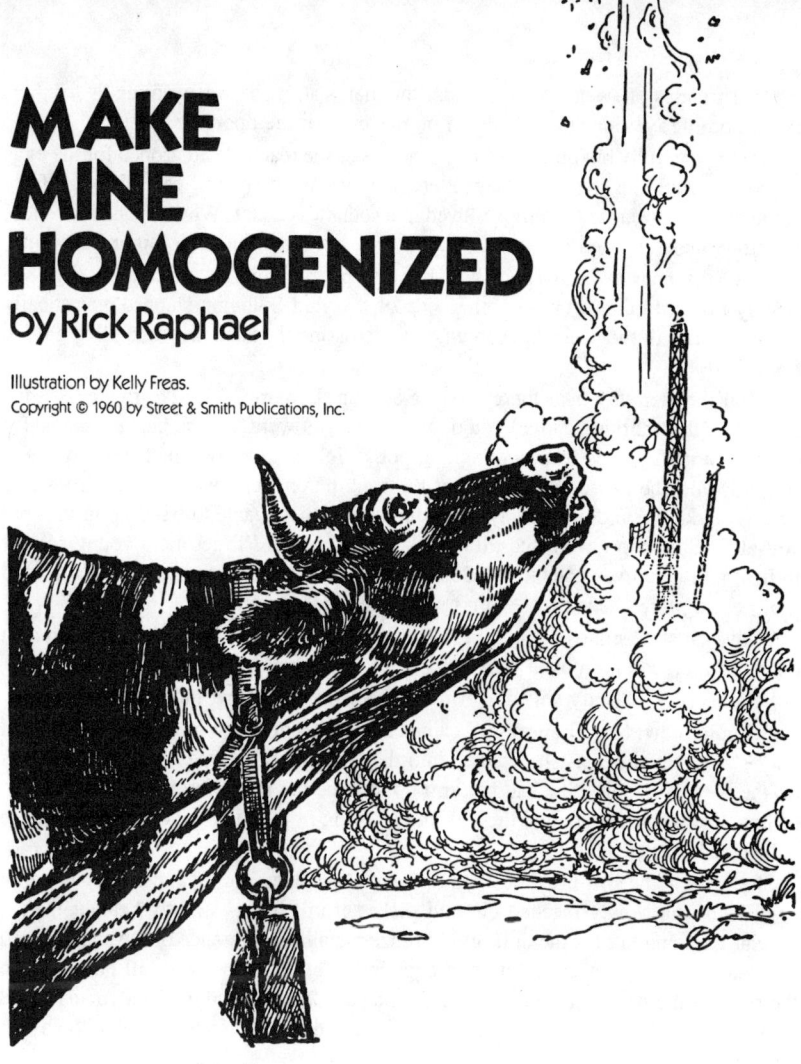

"Shoo," Hetty Thompson cried, waving her battered old felt hat at the clucking cluster of hens eddying around her legs as she plowed through the flock toward the chicken house. "Scat. You, Solomon," she called out, directing her words at the bobbing comb of the big rooster strutting at the edge of the mob. "Don't just stand there like a satisfied cowhand after a night in Reno. Get these noisy females outta my way." She batted at the hens and they scattered with angry squawks of protest.

Hetty paused in the doorway of the chicken house to allow her eyes to become accustomed to the cool gloom after the bright glare of the ranch yard. She could feel the first trickles of sweat forming under the man's shirt she was wearing as the hot, early morning Nevada sun beat down on her back in the doorway.

Moving carefully but quickly through the nests, she reached and groped for the eggs she knew would be found in the scattered straw. As she placed each find carefully in the bucket she carried, her lips moved in a soundless count. When she had finished, she straightened up and left the chicken house, her face reflecting minor irritation.

Again the hens swirled about her, hoping for the handfuls of cracked corn she usually tossed to them. On the other side of the yard Solomon stepped majestically along the edge of the vegetable garden, never crossing the hoed line separating garden from yard.

"You'd better stay over there, you no-account Lothario," Hetty growled. "Five eggs short this morning and all you do is act like you were just the business agent for this bunch of fugitives from a dumpling pot." Solomon cocked his head and stared Hetty down. She paused at the foot of the back porch steps and threw the rooster a final remark. "You don't do any better than this you're liable to wind up in that pot youself." Solomon gave a scornful cluck. "Better still, I'll get me a young rooster in here and take over your job." Solomon let out a squawk and took out at a dead run, herding three hens before him toward the chicken house.

With a satisfied smile of triumph, Hetty climbed the steps and crossed to the kitchen door. She turned and looked back across the yard towards the barn and corrals.

"Barneeeeey," Hetty yelled. "Ain't you finished with that milking yet?"

"Comin' now, Miz Thompson," came the reply from the barn. Hetty let the screen door slam behind her as she walked into the kitchen and placed the bucket of eggs on the big work table. She had her arm up to wipe her moist forehead on the sleeve of her shirt when she spotted the golden egg lying in the middle of the others in the galvanized bucket.

She froze in the arm-lifted position for several seconds, staring at the dully glowing egg. Then she slowly reached out and picked it up. It was slightly heavier than a regular egg, and but for the dull, gold-bronze metallic appearance of the shell looked just like any of the other twenty-odd eggs in the bucket. She was still holding it in the palm of her hand when the kitchen door again slammed and the handyman limped into the room. He carried two pails of milk across the kitchen and set them down near the sink.

"Whatcha lookin' at, Miz Thompson?" Barney Hatfield asked.

Hetty frowned at the egg in her hand without answering. Barney limped around the side of the table for a closer look. Sunlight streaming through the kitchen windows glinted on the shell of the odd egg. Barney's eyes grew round. "Now ain't that something," he whispered in awe.

Hetty started as though someone had snapped his fingers in front of her staring eyes. Her normal look of practical dubiousness returned.

"Huh," she snorted. "Even had me fooled for a second. Something wrong with this egg but it sure as shootin' ain't gold. One of them fool hens must of been pecking in the fertilizer storeroom and got herself an overdose of some of them minerals in that stuff.

"What are you staring at, you old fool," she glared at Barney. "It ain't gold." Hetty laid the egg at one side of the table. She walked to the sink and took a clean, two-gallon milk can from the drainboard and set it in the sink to fill it from the pails of rich, frothy milk Barney had brought in the pails.

"Sally come fresh this morning, Miz Thompson," he said. "Got herself a real fine little bull calf."

Hetty looked at the two pails of milk. "Well, where's the rest of the milk, then?"

"That's Queenie's milk," Barney said. "Sally's is still out on the porch."

"Well bring it in before the sun clabbers it."

"Can't," Barney said.

Hetty swung around and glared at him. "What do you mean, you can't? You suddenly come down with the glanders?"

"No'm, it's just that Sally's milk ain't no good," he replied.

A frown spread over Hetty's face as she hoisted one of the milk pails and began pouring into the can in the sink. "What's wrong with it, Barney? Sally seem sick or something?" she asked.

Barney scratched his head. "I don't rightly know, Miz Thompson. That milk looks all right, or at least, almost all right. It's kinda thin and don't have no foam like you'd expect milk to have. But mostly, it sure don't smell right and it danged well don't taste right.

"Phooey," he made a face at the memory of the taste. "I stuck my finger in it when it looked kinda queer, and took a taste. It shore tasted lousy."

"You probably been currying that mangey old horse of yours before you went to milking," Hetty snorted, "and tasted his cancerous old hide on your fingers. I've told you for the last time to wash your hands before you go to milking them cows. I didn't pay no eighteen hundred dollars for that prize, registered Guernsey just to have you give her bag fever with your dirty hands."

"That ain't so, Miz Thompson," Barney cried indignantly. "I did too, wash my hands. Good, too. I wuzn't near my horse this morning. That milk just weren't no good."

Hetty finished pouring the milk into the cans and, after putting the cans in the refrigerator, wiped her hands on her jeans and went out onto the porch, Barney trailing behind her. She bent over and sniffed at the two milk pails sitting beside the door. *"Whew,"* she exclaimed, "it sure does smell funny. Hand me that dipper, Barney."

Barney reached for a dipper hanging on a nail beside the kitchen door. Hetty dipped out a small quantity of the milk, sipped, straightened up with a jerk and spewed the milk out into the yard. "Yaawwwk," she spluttered, "that tastes worse'n diesel oil."

She stirred distastefully at the swirling, flat-looking liquid in the pails and then turned back to the kitchen. "I never saw the like of it," she exclaimed. "Chickens come out with some kind of sorry-looking egg and now, in the same morning, an eighteen-hundred-dollar registered, fresh Guernsey gives out hogwash instead of milk." She stared thoughtfully across the yard at the distant mountains, now shimmering in the hot, midmorning sun. "Guess we could swill the hogs with that milk, rather'n throw it out, Barney. I never seen anything them Durocs wouldn't eat. When you get ready to put the other swill in the cooker, toss that milk in with it and cook it up for the hogs."

Hetty went back into her kitchen, and Barney turned and limped across the yard to the tractor shed. He pulled the brim of his sweat-stained Stetson over his eyes and squinted south over the heat-dancing sage and sparse grasslands of Circle T range. Dust devils were pirouetting in the hazy distance toward the mountains forming a corridor leading to the ranch. A dirt road let out of the yard and crossed an oiled county road about five miles south of the ranch. The county road was now the only link the Circle T had to the cattle shipping pens at Carson City. The dirt road arrowed south across the range but fifteen miles from the ranch, a six-strand, new, barbed-wire fence cut the road. A white metal sign with raised letters proclaimed "Road Closed. U.S. Government Military Reservation. Restricted Area. Danger—Peligro. Keep Out."

The taut bands of wire stretched east and west of the road for more than twenty-miles in each direction, with duplicates of the metal sign hung on the fence every five hundred yards. Then the wires turned south for nearly a hundred miles, etching in skin-blistering, sun-heated strands, the outlines of the Nevada atomic testing grounds at Frenchman's Flat.

When the wire first went up, Hetty and her ranching neighbors had screamed to high heaven and high congressmen about the loss of the road and range. The fence stayed up. Now they had gotten used to the idea and had even grown blasé about the frequent nuclear blasts that rattled the desert floor sixty miles from ground zero.

Barney built a fire under the big, smoke-blackened cauldron Hetty used for cooking the hog swill. Dale Hamilton, the county agent, had given Hetty a long talk on the dangers of feeding the pigs raw, uncooked, and possibly contaminated, garbage. When Hamilton got graphic about what happened to people who ate pork from such hogs, Hetty turned politely green and had Barney set up the cooking cauldron.

After dumping the kitchen slops into the pot, Barney hiked back across the yard to get the two pails of bad milk.

Hetty was sitting at the kitchen table, putting the eggs into plastic refrigerator dishes, when the hog slop exploded in a whooshing roar, followed a split second later by an even louder blast that rocked the ranch buildings. The eggs flew across the room as the lid of the slop cauldron came whistling through the kitchen window in a blizzard of flying glass and buried itself, edgewise, in the wall over the stove. Hetty slammed backwards head-first into a heap of shattered eggs. A torrent of broken plaster and crockery fragments rained on her stunned figure. Through dazed eyes, she saw a column of purple-reddish fire rising from the yard.

A woman who has been thrown twenty-three times from a pitching bronco and kicked five times in the process doesn't stay dazed long. Pawing dripping egg yolks and plaster from her face, Hetty Thompson struggled to her feet and staggered to the kitchen door.

"Barneeey," she bawled, "you all right?"

The column of weird-colored flame had quickly died and only a few flickering pieces of wood from the cauldron fire burned in scattered spots about the yard. Of the cauldron, there wasn't a sign.

"Barney," she cried anxiously, "where are you?"

"Here I am, Miz Thompson." Barney's blackened face peered around the corner of the tractor shed, "You O.K., Miz Thompson?"

"What in thunderation happened?" Hetty called out. "You try to build a fire with dynamite for kindling?"

Shaken but otherwise unharmed, Barney painfully limped over to the ranch house porch.

"Don't ask me what happened, m'am," he said. "I just poured that milk into the slop pot and then put the lid back on and walked off. I heered this big *whoosh* and turned around in time to see the lid fly off and the kettle begin to tip into the fire and then there was one helluva blast. It knocked me clean under the tractor shed." He fumbled in his pocket for a cigarette and shakily lighted it.

Hetty peered out over the yard and then, looking up, gasped. Perched like a rakish derby hat on the arm of the towering pump windmill was the slop cauldron. "Well I'll be . . ." Hetty Thompson said.

"You sure you didn't pour gas on that fire to make it burn faster, Barney Hatfield?" she barked at the handyman.

"No siree," Barney declaimed loudly, "there weren't no gas anywhere near that fire. Only thing I poured out was that there bad milk." He paused and scratched his head. "Reckon that funny milk coulda done that, Miz Thompson? There ain't no gas made what'll blow up nor burn so funny as that did."

Hetty snorted. "Whoever heard of milk blowing up, you old idiot?" A look of doubt spread. "You put all that milk in there?"

"No'm, just the one bucket." Barney pointed to the other pail beside the kitchen door, now half-empty and standing in a pool of liquid sloshed out by the blast wave. Hetty studied the milk pail for a minute and then resolutely picked it up and walked out into the yard.

"Only one way to find out," she said. "Get me a tin can, Barney."

She poured about two tablespoons of the milk into the bottom of the can while Barney collected a small pile of kindling. Removing the milk pail to a safe distance, Hetty lighted the little pile of kindling, set the tin can stop the burning wood and scooted several yards away to join Barney, who had been watching from afar. In less than a minute a booming *whoosh* sent a miniature column of purple, gaseous flame spouting from the can. "Well whadda you know about that?" Hetty exclaimed wonderingly.

The can had flown off the fire a few feet but didn't explode. Hetty went back to the milk pail and, collecting less than a teaspoonful in the water dipper, walked to

Make Mine Homogenized

the fire. Standing as far back as she could and still reach over the flames, she carefully sprinkled a few drops of the liquid directly into the fire and then jumped back. Miniature balls of purple flame erupted from the fire before she could move. Pieces of flaming kindling flew in all directions and one slammed Barney across the back of the neck and sent a shower of sparks down his back.

The handyman let out a yowl of pain and leaped for the watering trough beside the corral, smoke trailing behind him. Hetty thoughtfully surveyed the scene of her experiment from beneath raised eyebrows. Then she grunted with satisfaction, picked up the remaining milk in the pail, and went back to the ranch house. Barney climbed drippingly from the horse trough.

The kitchen was a mess. Splattered eggs were over everything and broken glass, crockery, and plaster covered the floor, table, and counters. Only one egg remained unbroken. That was the golden egg. Hetty picked it up and shook it. There was a faint sensation of something moving inside the tough, metallic-looking shell. It shook almost as a normal egg might, but not quite. Hetty set the strange object on a shelf and turned to the task of cleaning up.

Johnny Culpepper, the ranch's other full-time hand and Hetty's assistant manager, drove the pickup into the yard just before noon. He parked in the shade of the huge cottonwood tree beside the house and bounced out with an armload of mail and newspapers. Inside the kitchen door, he dumped the mail on the sideboard and started to toss his hat on a wall hook when he noticed the condition of the room. Hetty was dishing out fragrant, warmed-over stew into three lunch dishes on the table. She had cleaned up the worst of the mess and changed into a fresh shirt and jeans. Her iron-gray hair was pulled back in a still-damp knot at the back after a hasty scrubbing to get out the gooey mixture of eggs and plaster.

"Holy smoke, Hetty," Johnny said. "What happened here?" His eyes widened when he saw the lid of the slop cauldron still embedded in the wall over the stove. His gaze tracked back and took in the shattered window.

"Had an accident," Hetty said matter-of-factly, putting the last dishes on the table. "Tell you about it when we eat. Now you go wash up and call Barney. I want you to put some new glass in that window this afternoon and get that danged lid outta the wall."

Curious and puzzled, Johnny washed at the kitchen sink and then walked to the door to shout for Barney. On the other side of the yard, Barney released the pump windmill clutch. While Johnny watched from the porch, the weight of the heavy slop cauldron slowly turned the big windmill and as the arm adorned by the kettle rotated downward, the cast-iron pot slipped off and fell to the hard-packed ground with a booming clang.

"Well, for the luvva Pete?" Johnny said in amazement. "Hey, Barney, time to eat. C'mon in."

Barney trudged across the yard and limped into the kitchen to wash. They sat down to the table. "Now just what have you two been up to?" Johnny demanded as they attacked the food-laden dishes.

Between mouthfuls, the two older people gave him a rundown on the morning's mishaps. The more Johnny heard, the wilder it sounded. Johnny had been a part of the Circle T since he was ten years old. That was the year Hetty jerked him out of the hands of a Carson City policeman who had been in the process of hauling the ragged and dirty youngster to the station house for swiping a box of cookies from a grocery store. Johnny's mother was dead and his father, once the town's best mechanic, had turned into the town's best drunk.

During the times his father slept one off, either in the shack the man and boy occupied at the edge of town or in the local lockup, Johnny ran wild.

Hetty took the boy to the ranch for two reasons. Mainly it was the empty ache in her heart since the death of Big Jim Thompson a year earlier following a ranch tractor accident that had crushed his chest. The other was her well-hidden disappointment that she had been childless. Hetty's bluff, weathered features would never admit to loneliness or heartache. Beneath the surface, all the warmth and love she had went out to the scared but belligerent youngster. But she never let much affection show through until Johnny had become part of her life. Johnny's father died the following winter after pneumonia brought on by a night of lying drunk in the cold shack during a blizzard. It was accepted without legal formality around the county that Johnny automatically became Hetty's boy.

She cuffed and comforted him into a gawky-happy adolescence, pushed him through high school and then, at eighteen, sent him off to the University of California at Davis to learn what the pundits of the United States Department of Agriculture had to say about animal husbandry and ranch management.

When Hetty and Barney had finished their recitation, Johnny wore a look of frank disbelief. "If I didn't know you two better, I'd say you both been belting the bourbon bottle while I was gone. But this I've got to see."

They finished lunch and, after Hetty stacked the dishes in the sink, trooped out to the porch where Johnny went through the same examination of the milk. Again, a little fire was built in the open safety of the yard and a few drops of the liquid used to produce the same technicolored combustive effects.

"Well, what do you know," Johnny exclaimed, "a four-hundred-octane Guernsey cow!"

Johnny kicked out the fire and carried the milk pail to the tractor shed. He parked the milk on a workbench and gathered up an armful of tools to repair the blast-torn kitchen. He started to leave but when the milk bucket caught his eye, he unloaded the tools and fished around under the workbench for an empty five-gallon gasoline can. He poured the remaining milk into the gasoline can and replaced the cap. Then he took his tools and a pane of glass from an overhead rack and headed for the house.

Hetty came into the kitchen as he was prying at the cauldron lid in the wall.

"You're going to make a worse mess before you're through," she said, "so I'll just let you finish and then clean up the whole mess afterwards. I got other things to do, anyway."

She jammed a man's old felt hat on her head and left the house. Barney was unloading the last of the supplies Johnny had brought from Carson in the truck. Hetty shielded her eyes against the metallic glare of the afternoon sun. "Gettin' pretty dry, Barney. Throw some salt blocks in the pickup and I'll run them down to the south pasture and see if the pumps need to be turned on.

"And you might get that wind pump going in case we get a little breeze later this afternoon. But in any case, better run the yard pump for an hour or so and get some water up into the tank. I'll be back as soon as I take a ride through the pasture. I want to see how that Angus yearling is coming that I picked out for house beef."

A few minutes later, Hetty in the pickup disappeared behind a hot swirl of yellow dust. Barney ambled to the cool pump house beneath the towering windmill. An electric motor, powered either from the REA line or from direct current stored in a bank of wet cell batteries, bulked large in the small shed. To the left, a small, gasoline-driven generator supplied standby power if no wind was blowing to turn the arm-driven generator if the lines happened to be down, as was often the case in the winter.

Barney threw the switch to start the pump motor. Nothing happened. He reached for the light switch to test the single bulb hanging from a cord to the ceiling. Same nothing. Muttering darkly to himself, he changed the pump engine leads to DC current and closed the switch to the battery bank. The engine squeaked and whined slowly but when Barney threw in the clutch to drive the pump, it stopped and just hummed faintly. Then he opened the AC fuse box.

Johnny had freed the cauldron lid and was knocking out bits of broken glass from the kitchen window frame before putting in the new glass when Barney limped into the room.

"That pot busted the pump house 'lectric line, Johnny, when it went sailing," he said. "Miz Thompson wants to pump up some water and on top of that, the batteries are down. You got time to fix the line?"

Johnny paused and surveyed the kitchen. "I'm going to be working here for another hour anyway so Hetty can clean up when she gets back. Why don't you fire up the gasoline kicker for now and I'll fix the line when I get through here," he said.

"O.K.," Barney nodded and turned to leave. "Oh, forgot to ask you. Miz Thompson tell you about the egg?"

"What egg?" Johnny asked.

"The gold one."

Johnny grinned. "Sure, and I saw the goose when I came in. And you're Jack and the windmill is your beanstalk. Go climb it, Barney, and cut out the fairy tales."

"Naw, Johnny," Barney protested, "I ain't kidding. Miz Thompson got a gold egg from the hens this morning. At least, it looks kinda like gold but she says it ain't. See, here it is." He reached into the cupboard where Hetty had placed the odd egg. He walked over and handed it to Johnny, who was sitting on the sink drain counter to work on the shattered window.

The younger man turned the egg over in his hand. "It sure feels funny. Wonder what the inside looks like?" He banged the egg gently against the edge of the drain board. When it didn't crack, he slammed it harder, but then realizing that if it did break suddenly, it would squish onto the floor, he put the egg on the counter and tapped it with his hammer.

The shell split and a clear liquid poured out on to the drain board, thin and clear, not glutenous like a normal egg white. A small, reddish ball, obviously the yolk, rolled across the board, fell into the sink and broke into powdery fragments. A faint etherlike odor arose from the mess.

"I guess Miz Thompson was right," Barney said. "She said that hen musta been pecking in the fertilizer chemicals. Never seen no egg like that before."

"Yeh," Johnny said puzzledly. "Well, so much for that." He toosed the golden shell to one side and turned back to his glass work. Barney left for the pumphouse.

Inside the pumphouse, Barney opened the gasoline engine tank and poked a stick down to test the fuel level. The stick came out almost dry. With another string of mutterings, he limped across the yard to the tractor shed for a gas can. Back in the pumphouse, he poured the engine tank full, set the gas can aside and then, after priming the carburetor, yanked on the starter pull rope. The engine caught with a spluttering roar and began racing madly. Barney lunged for the throttle and cut it back to idle, but even then, the engine was running at near full speed. Then Barney noticed the white fluid running down the side of the engine tank and dripping from the spout of the gasoline can. He grinned broadly, put in the pump clutch, and hurriedly limped across the yard to the kitchen.

"Hey, Johnny," he called, "did you put that milk o' Sally's into a gas can?"

Johnny leaned through the open kitchen window. "Yeh, why?"

"Well, I just filled the kicker with it by accident, and man, you orter hear that engine run," Barney exclaimed. "Come see."

Johnny swung his legs through the window and dropped lightly to the yard. The two men were halfway across the yard from the pumphouse when a loud explosion ripped the building. Parts of the pump engine flew through the thin walls like shrapnel. A billowing cloud of purple smoke welled out of the ruptured building as Johnny and Barney flattened themselves against the hot, packed earth. Flames licked up from the pump shed. The men ran for the horse trough and, grabbing pails of water, raced for the pumphouse. The fire had just started into the wooden walls of the building and a few splashes of water doused the flames.

They eyed the ruins of the gasoline engine, "Holy cow," Johnny exclaimed, "that stuff blew the engine right apart." He gazed up at the holes in the pumphouse roof. "Blew the cylinders and head right out the roof. Holy cow!"

Barney was pawing at the pump and electric motor. "Didn't seem to hurt the pump none. Guess we better get that 'lectric line fixed though, now that we ain't got no more gas engine."

The two men went to work on the pump motor. The broken line outside the building was spliced and, twenty minutes later, Johnny threw the AC switch. The big electric motor spun into action and settled into a workmanlike hum. The overhead light dimmed briefly when the pump load was thrown on and then the slip-slap sound of the pump filled the shed. They watched and listened for a couple of minutes. Assured that the pump was working satisfactorily, they left the wrecked pumphouse.

Johnny was carrying the gasoline can of milk. "Good thing you set this off to one side where it didn't get hit and go off," he said. "The way this stuff reacts, we'd be without a pump, engine, or windmill if it had.

"Barney, be a good guy and finish putting in that glass for me, will you? I've got the frame all ready to putty. I've got me some fiddlin' and figurin' to do."

Johnny angled off to the tractor and tool shed and disappeared inside. Barney limped into the kitchen and went to work on the window glass. From the tractor shed came the sounds of an engine spluttering, racing, backfiring, and then, just idling.

When Hetty drove back into the ranch yard an hour or so later, Johnny was rodeoing the farm tractor around the yard like a teen-ager, his face split in a wide grin. She parked the truck under the tree as Johnny drove the tractor alongside and gunned the engine, still grinning.

"What in tarnation is this all about?" Hetty asked as she climbed down from the pickup.

"Know what this tractor's running on?" Johnny shouted over the noise of the engine.

"Of course I do, you young idiot," she exclaimed. "It's gasoline."

"Wrong," Johnny yelled triumphantly. "It's running on Sally's milk!"

The next morning, Johnny had mixed up two hundred gallons of Sally's Fuel and had the pickup, tractor, cattle truck and his 1958 Ford and Hetty's '59 Chevrolet station wagon all purring on the mixture.

Mixing it was a simple process after he experimented and found the right proportions. One quart of pure Sally's milk to one hundred gallons of water. He had used the two remaining quarts in the gasoline can to make the mixture but by morning, Sally had graced the ranch with five more gallons of the pure concentrate. Johnny carefully stored the concentrated milk in a scoured fifty-five-gallon gasoline drum in the tool shed.

"We've hit a gold mine," he told Hetty exultantly. "We're never going to have to buy gasoline again. On top of that, at the rate Sally's turning this stuff out, we can start selling it in a couple of weeks and make a fortune."

That same morning, Hetty collected three more of the golden eggs.

"Set 'em on the shelf," Johnny said, "and when we go into town next time I'll have Dale look at them and maybe tell us what those hens have been into. I'll probably go into town again Saturday for the mail."

But when Saturday came, Johnny was hobbling around the ranch on a wrenched ankle, suffered when his horse stumbled in a gopher hole and tossed him.

"You stay off that leg," Hetty ordered. "I'll go into town for the mail. Them girls can just struggle along without your romancing this week." Johnny made a wry face but obeyed orders.

"Barneeey," Hetty bawled, "bring me a quarter of beef outta the cooler." Barney stuck his head out of the barn and nodded. "I been promising some good beef to Judge Hatcher for a month of Sundays now," Hetty said to Johnny.

"If you're going to stop by the courthouse, how about taking those crazy eggs of yours into the country agent's office and leave them there for analysis," Johnny suggested. He hobbled into the kitchen to get the golden eggs.

Barney arrived with the chilled quarter of beef wrapped in burlap. He tossed it in the bed of the pickup and threw more sacks over it to keep it cool under the broiling, midmorning sun. Johnny came out with the eggs in a light cardboard box stuffed with crumpled newspapers. He wedged the box against the side of beef in the forward corner of the truck bed. "One more thing, Hetty," he said. "I've got a half drum of drain oil in the tractor shed that I've been meaning to trade in for some gearbox lube that Willy Simons said he'd let me have. Can you drop it off at his station and pick up the grease?"

"Throw it on," Hetty said, "while I go change into some town clothes."

Johnny started to hobble down the porch steps when Barney stopped him. "I'll get it boy; you stay off that ankle." Barney climbed into the pickup and drove it around to the tractor shed. He spotted two oil drums in the gloomy shed. He tilted the nearest one and felt liquid slosh near the halfway mark, then rolled it out the door. Barney heaved it into the truck bed, stood it on end against the cab and drove the pickup back to the ranch house door as Hetty came out wearing clean jeans and a bright, flowered blouse. Her gray hair was tucked in a neat bun beneath a blocked Stetson hat.

She climbed into the truck, waved to the two men and drove out of the yard. As she bumped over the cattle guard at the gate, the wooden plug that Johnny had jury-rigged to cork the gasoline drum with its twenty-gallon load of pure Sally's milk bounced out.

A small geyser of white fluid shot out of the drum as she hit another bump and then the pickup went jolting down the ranch road, little splashes of Sally's milk sloshing out with each bump and forming a pool on the bottom of the truck. When Hetty cowboyed onto the county road, the drum tipped dangerously and then bounced back onto its base. This time a fountain of milk geysered out and splashed heavily into the box of golden eggs. Hetty drove on.

But not for long.

With a ranch woman's disregard for watching the road, Hetty constantly scanned the nearby range lands where small bands of her cherished black Angus grazed. She prided herself on the fact that, despite her sixty years, her eyes were still sharp enough to spot a worm-ridden cow at a thousand yards.

Two miles after she turned onto the county road which ran through Circle T range land, her roving gaze took in a cow and calf on a hillside a few hundred yards south of the road. Hetty slowed the pickup to fifty miles an hour and squinted into the sun. She grunted with satisfaction and slammed on the brakes. The truck swerved and skidded to a halt at the left side of the deserted road. Hetty leaped from the truck and began a fast walk up the hillside for a closer look at the cow and calf.

She never heard the dull thump of the milk drum tipping onto the edge of the truck bed. Hetty topped the hill and walked slowly toward the cow and calf that were now edging away from her. As she eased down the far side of the hill out of sight of the pickup, a steady stream of Sally's milk was engulfing the box of golden eggs. A minute later, the reduced contents caused the drum to shift and slip. It fell onto the eggs, cracking a half dozen.

The earth split open and the world around Hetty erupted in a roaring inferno of purple-red fire and ear-shattering sound. The rolling concussion swept Hetty from her feet and tumbled her into a drywash gully at the base of the hill. The gully saved her life as the sky-splitting shock wave rolled over her. Stunned and deafened, she flattened herself under a slight overhang.

The rolling blast rocked ranches and towns for more than one hundred miles and the ground wave triggered the seismographs at the University of California nearly two hundred miles away and at UCLA, four hundred miles distant. Tracking and testing instruments went wild along the entire length of the AEC atomic test grounds, a mere sixty miles south of the smoking, gaping hole that marked the end of the Circle T pickup truck.

In a direct line, the ranch house was about eight miles from the explosion.

Johnny was lounging in Hetty's favorite rocking chair on the wideback verandah lighting a cigarette and Barney was perched on the porch railing, when the sky was blotted out by the dazzling violet light of the blast. They were blinking in amazement when the shock wave smashed into the ranch, flattening the flimsier buildings and buckling the side and roof of the steel-braced barn. Every window on the place blew out in a storm of deadly glass shards. The rolling ground wave in the wake of the shock blast rocked and bounced the solid, timber and adobe main house.

The concussion hit Johnny like a fist, pinwheeling him backwards in the rocker against the wall of the house. It caught Barney like a sack of sodden rags and flung him atop the dazed and semiconscious younger man.

The first frightened screams of the horses in the barns and corrals were mingling with the bawling of the heifers in the calf pens when the sound of the explosion caught up with the devastation of the shock and ground waves.

Like the reverberation of a thousand massed cannon firing at once, the soul-searing sound rumbled out of the desert and boiled with almost tangible density into the shattered ranch yard. It flattened the feebly stirring men on the porch and then thundered on in a tidal wave of noise.

Barney moaned and rolled off the tangle of porch rocker and stunned youth beneath him. Johnny lay dazed another second or two and then began struggling to his feet.

"Hetty," he croaked, pointing wildly to the south where a massive, dirty column of purple smoke and fire rose skyward like the stem of a monstrous and malignant toadstool. "Hetty's out there."

He stumbled from the porch and broke into a staggering run to the pile of broken planks that seconds ago had been the tractor shed. As he crossed the yard, a great gust of wind whipped back from the north, pumping clouds of dry, dusty earth before it. The force of the wind almost knocked the bruised and shaken Johnny from his feet once again as it swept back over the ranch, in the direction of the great pillar of purple smoke.

"Implosion," Johnny's mind registered.

He tore at the stack of loose boards leaning against the station wagon, flinging them fiercely aside in his frantic efforts to free the vehicle. Barney limped up to join him and a minute later they had cleared a way into the wagon. Johnny squeezed into the front seat and drove it back from under more leaning boards. Three of the side windows were smashed but the windshield was intact except for a small, starred crack in the safety glass. Clear of the debris, Barney opened the opposite door and slid in beside Johnny. Dirt spun from beneath the wheels of the car as he slammed his foot to the floor and raced toward the smoke column that now towered more than a mile and a half into the air.

Beneath her protective overhang, Hetty stirred and moaned feebly. Twin rivulets of dark blood trickled from her nostrils. Thick dust was settling on the area, and she coughed and gasped for breath.

On the opposite side of the hill, a vast, torn crater, nearly a hundred feet across and six to ten feet deep, smoked like a stirring volcano and gave off a strange, pungent odor of ether.

Johnny Culpepper's dramatic charge to the rescue was no more dramatic than the reaction in a dozen other places in Nevada and California. Particularly sixty miles south, where a small army of military and scientific men were preparing for an atomic underground shot when the Circle T pickup vanished.

The shock wave rippled across the desert floor, flowed around the mountains, and funneled into Frenchman's Flat, setting off every shock-measuring instrument. Then came the ground wave, rolling through the earth like a gopher through a garden. Ditto for ground-wave measuring devices. Lastly, the sound boomed onto the startled scientists and soldiers like the pounding of great timpani under the vaulted dome of the burning sky.

On mountain top observation posts, technicians turned unbelieving eyes north to the burgeoning pillar of smoke and dust, then yelped and swung optical and electronic instruments to bear on the fantastic column.

In less than fifteen minutes, the test under preparation had been canceled, all equipment secured; and the first assault waves of scientists, soldiers, intelligence, and security men were racing north behind white-suited and sealed radiation detection teams cradling Geiger counters in their arms like submachine guns. Telephone lines were jammed with calls from Atomic Energy Commission field officials reporting the phenomena to Washington and calling for aid from West Coast and New Mexico AEC bases. Jet fighters at Nellis Air Force base near Las Vegas were scrambled and roared north over the ground vehicles to report visual conditions near the purple pillar of power.

The Associated Press office in San Francisco had just received word of the quake recorded by the seismograph at Berkeley when a staffer on the other side of the desk answered a call from the AP stringer in Carson City, reporting the blast and mighty cloud in the desert sky. One fast look at the map showed that the explosion was well north of the AEC testing ground limits. The Carson City stringer was ordered to get out to the scene on the double and hold the fort while reinforcements of staffers and photographers were flown from 'Frisco.

Before any of the official or civil agencies had swung into action, the Circle T station wagon had rocketed off the ranch road and turned onto the oiled, county highway leading both to Carson City—and the now-expanding but less dense column of smoke.

Johnny hunched over the wheel and peered through the thickening pall of smoke and dust, reluctant to ease off his breakneck speed but knowing that they had to find Hetty—if she were alive. Neither man had said a word since the wagon raced from the ranch yard.

There was no valid reason to associate the explosion with Hetty, yet instinctively and naggingly, Johnny knew that somehow Hetty was involved. Barney, still ignorant of his error of the oil drums, just clung to his seat and prayed for the best.

The dust was almost too thick to see, forcing Johnny to slow the station wagon as they penetrated deeper into the base of the smoke column. Hiding under his frantic concern for Hetty was the half-formed thought that the whole thing was an atomic explosion and that he and Barney were heading into sure radiation deaths. His logic nudged at the thought and said, "If it were atomic, you started dying back on the porch, so might as well play the hand out."

A puff of wind swirled the dust up away from the road as the station wagon came up to the smoking crater. Johnny slammed on the brakes and he and Barney jumped from the car to stand, awe-struck, at the edge of the hole.

The dust-deadened air muffled Johnny's sobbing exclamation:

"Dear God!"

They walked slowly around the ragged edges of the crater. Barney bent down and picked a tiny metallic fragment from the pavement. He stared at it and then tapped Johnny on the arm and handed it to him, wordlessly. It was a twisted piece of body steel, bright at its torn edges and coated with the scarlet enamel that had been the color of the Circle T pickup.

Johnny's eyes filled with tears and he shoved the little scrap of metal in his pocket. "Let's see what else we can find, Barney." The two men began working a slow search of the area in ever-widening circles from the crater that led them finally up and over the top of the little hill to the south of the road.

Fifteen minutes later they found Hetty and ten minutes after that, the wiry, resilient ranchwoman was sitting between them on the seat of the station wagon, explaining how she happened to be clear of the pickup when the blast occurred.

The suspicion that had been growing in Johnny's mind, now brought into the open by his relief at finding Hetty alive and virtually unhurt, bloomed into full flower.

"Barney," Johnny asked softly, "which oil drum did you put in the back of the pickup?"

The facts were falling into place like the pieces of a jigsaw puzzle when the Carson City reporter, leading a caravan of cars and emergency vehicles from town by a good ten minutes and beating the AEC and military teams by twenty minutes, found the Circle T trio sitting in the station wagon at the lip of the now faintly smoldering crater.

A half hour later, the AP man in San Francisco picked up the phone.

"I've just come back from that explosion," the Carson City stringer said. The AP man put his hand over the phone and called across the desk. "Get ready for a '95' first lead blast."

"O.K.," the San Francisco desk man said, "let's have it." He tucked the phone between chin and shoulder and poised over his typewriter.

"Well, there's a crater more than one hundred feet across and ten feet deep," the Carson City stringer dutifully recounted. "The scene is on County Road 38 about forty miles east of here, and the blast rocked Carson City and caused extensive breakage for miles around."

"What caused it?" the AP desk man asked as he pounded out a lead.

"A lady at the scene said her milk and eggs blew up," the Carson City stringer said.

Ten miles south, the leading AEC disaster truck stopped behind the six-strand fence blocking the range road. Two men with wire cutters jumped from the truck and snipped the twanging wires. The metal "Keep Out" sign banged to the ground and was kicked aside. The truck rolled through the gap and the men swung aboard. Behind them was a curtain of dust rising sluggishly in the hot sky, marking the long convoy of other official vehicles pressing hard on the trail of the emergency truck.

When the range road cut across the county highway, the driver paused long enough to see that the heaviest smoke concentrations from the unknown blast lay to the west. He swung left onto the oiled road and barreled westward. In less than a mile, he spied the flashing red light of a state trooper's car parked in the center of the road. The scene looked like a combination of the San Francisco quake and the Los Angeles county fair.

Dozens of cars, trucks, two fire engines, and a Good Humor van were scattered around the open range land on both sides of the vast crater still smoldering in the road. A film of purple dust covered the immediate area and still hung in the air, coating cars and people. Scores of men, women, and children lined the rim of the crater, gawking into the smoky pit, while other scores roamed aimlessly around the nearby hill and desert.

A young sheriff's deputy standing beside the state trooper's car raised his hand to halt the AEC disaster van. The truck stopped and the white-suited radiation team leaped from the vehicle, counters in hand, racing for the crater.

"Back," the chief of the squad yelled at the top of his lungs. "Everybody get back. This area is radiation contaminated. Hurry!"

There was a second of stunned comprehension and then a mad, pandemonic scrambling of persons and cars, bumping and jockeying to flee. The radiation team fanned out around the crater, fumbling at the level scales on their counters when the instruments failed to indicate anything more than normal background count.

All of the vehicles had pulled back to safety—all except a slightly battered station wagon still parked a yard or two from the eastern edge of the crater.

The radiation squad leader ran over to the wagon. Three people—two men and a dirty, disheveled and bloody-nosed older woman—sat in the front seat munching Good Humor bars.

"Didn't you hear me?" the AEC man yelled. "Get outta here. This area's hot. Radioactive. Dangerous. GET MOVING!"

The woman leaned out the window and patted the radiation expert soothingly on the shoulder.

"Shucks, sonny, no need to get this excited over a little spilt milk."

"Milk," the AEC man yelped, purpling. "Milk! I said this is a hot area; it's loaded with radiation. Look at this—" He pointed to the meter on his counter, then stopped, gawked at the instrument and shook it. And stared again. The meter flicked placidly along at the barely-above-normal background level count.

"Hey, Jack," one of the other white-suited men on the far side of the crater called, "this hole doesn't register a thing."

The squad chief stared incredulously at his counter and banged it against the side of the station wagon. Still the needle held in the normal zone. He banged it harder and suddenly the needle dropped to zero as Hetty and her ranch hands peered over the AEC man's shoulder at the dial.

"Now ain't that a shame," Barney said sympathetically. "You done broke it."

The rest of the disaster squad, helmets off in the blazing sun and lead-coated suits unfastened, drifted back to the squad leader at the Circle T station wagon. A mile east, the rest of the AEC convoy had arrived and halted in a huge fan of vehicles, parked a safe distance from the crater. A line of more white-suited detection experts moved cautiously forward.

With a stunned look, the first squad leader turned and walked slowly down the road toward the approaching line. He stopped once and looked back at the gaping hole, down at his useless counter, shook his head and continued on to meet the advancing units.

By nightfall, new strands of barbed wire reflected the last rays of the red Nevada sun. Armed military policemen and AEC security police in powder-blue battle jackets patrolled the fences around the county road crater. And around the fence that now enclosed the immediate vicinity of the Circle T ranch buildings. Floodlights bathed the wire and cast an eerie glow over the mass of parked cars and persons jammed outside the fence. A small helicopter sat off to the right of the impromptu parking lot and an NBC newscaster gave the world a verbal description of the scene while he tried to talk above the snorting of the gas-powered generator that was supplying the Associated Press radio-telephone link to San Francisco.

Black AEC vans and dun-colored military vehicles raced to and from the ranch headquarters, pausing to be cleared by the sentries guarding the main gates.

The AP log recorded one hundred eighteen major daily papers using the AP story that afternoon and the following morning:

CARSON CITY, NEV., May 12 (AP)—A kiloton eggnog rocked the scientific world this morning.

"On a Nevada ranch, forty miles east of here, 60-year-old Mehatibel Thompson is milking a cow that gives milk more powerful than an atomic bomb. Her chickens are laying the triggering mechanisms.

"This the world learned today when an earth-shaking explosion rocked . . ."

Inside the Circle T ranch house, Hetty, bathed and cleaned and only slightly the worse for her experiences, was hustling about the kitchen throwing together a hasty meal. Johnny and Barney had swept up a huge pile of broken glass, crockery, and dirt, and Hetty had salvaged what dishes remained unshattered by the blast.

She weaved through a dozen men grouped around the kitchen table, some in military or security police garb, three of them wearing the uniform of the atomic scientist in the field—bright Hawaiian sports shirts, dark glasses, blue denims, and sneakers. Johnny and Barney huddled against the kitchen drainboard out of the main stream of traffic. The final editions of the San Francisco *Call-Bulletin*, Oakland *Tribune*, Los Angeles *Herald-Express*, and the Carson City *Appeal* were spread out on the table. Hetty pushed them aside to put down dishes.

The glaring black headlines stared up at her. "Dairy Detonation Devastates Desert," the alliterative *Chronicle* banner read; "Bossy's Blast Rocks Bay Area," said the *Trib*; "Atomic Butter-And-Egg Blast Jars LA," the somewhat inaccurate *Herald-Ex* proclaimed; "Thompson Ranch Scene of Explosion," the *Appeal* stated, hewing to solid facts.

"Mrs. Thompson," the oldest of the scientists said, "won't you please put down those dishes for a few minutes and give us the straight story. All afternoon long it's been one thing or another with you, and all we've been able to get out of you is this crazy milk-egg routine."

"Time enough to talk after we've all had a bite to eat," Hetty said, juggling a platter of steaks and a huge bowl of mashed potatoes to the table. "Now we've all had a hard day and we can all stand to get on the outside of some solid food. I ain't had a bite to eat since this morning and I guess you boys haven't had much either. And since you seem to have made yourselves to home here, then by golly, you're going to sit down and eat with us.

"Besides," she added over her shoulder as she went back to the stove for vegetables and bread, "me 'n Johnny have already told you what story there is to tell. That's all there is to it."

Make Mine Homogenized

She put more platters on the now-heaping table and then went around the table pouring coffee from the big ranch pot. "All right, you men sit down now and dig in," she ordered.

"Mrs. Thompson," an Army major with a heavy brush mustache said, "we didn't come here to eat. We came for information."

Hetty shoved back a stray wisp of hair and glared at the man.

"Now you listen to me, you young whippersnapper. I didn't invite you, but since you're here, you'll do me the goodness of being a mite more polite," she snapped.

The major winced and glanced at the senior scientist. The older man raised his eyes expressively and shrugged. He moved to the table and sat down. There was a general scuffling of chairs and the rest of the group took places around the big table. Johnny and Barney took their usual flanking positions beside Hetty at the head of the board.

Hetty took her seat and looked around the table with a pleased smile. "Now that's more like it."

She bowed her head and, after a startled glance, the strangers followed suit.

"We thank Thee, dear Lord," Hetty said quietly, "for this food which we are about to eat and for all Your help to us this day. It's been a little rough in spots but I reckon You've got Your reasons for all of it. Seein' as how tomorrow is Your day anyway, we ask that it be just a mite quieter. Amen."

The satisfying clatter of chinaware and silver and polite muttered requests for more potatoes and gravy filled the kitchen for the next quarter of an hour as the hungry men went to work on the prime Circle T yearling beef.

After his second steak, third helping of potatoes and gravy, and fourth cup of coffee, the senior scientist contentedly shoved back from the table. Hetty was polishing the last dabs of gravy from her plate with a scrap of bread. The scientist pulled a pipe and tobacco pouch from his pocket.

"With your permission, ma'am," he asked his hostess. Hetty grinned. "For heaven's sake, fire it up, sonny. Big Jim—that was my husband—used to say that no meal could be said properly finished unless it had been smoked into position for digestion."

Several of the other men at the table followed suit with pipes, cigars, and cigarettes. Hetty smiled benignly around the table and turned to the senior scientist.

"What did you say your name was, sonny?" she asked.

"Dr. Floyd Peterson, Mrs. Thompson," he replied, "and at forty-six years of age, I deeply thank you for that 'sonny.' "

He reached for the stack of newspapers on the floor beside his chair and, pushing back from his place, laid them on the table.

"Now, Mrs. Thompson, let's get down to facts." He rapped the headlines with a knuckle. "You have played hell with our schedule and I've got to have the answers soon before I have the full atomic commission and a congressional investigation breathing down my neck.

"What did you use to make that junior grade earthquake?"

"Why, I've already told you more'n a dozen times, sonny," Hetty replied. "It must of been the combination of them queer eggs and Sally's milk."

The brush-mustached major sipping his coffee, spluttered and choked. Beside him, the head of the AEC security force at Frenchman's Flat leaned forward.

"Mrs. Thompson, I don't know what your motives are but until I find out, I'm deeply thankful that you gave those news hounds this . . . this, butter and egg business," he said.

"Milk and eggs," Hetty corrected him mildly.

"Well, milk and eggs, then. But the times has ended for playing games. We must know what caused that explosion, and you and Mr. Culpepper and Mr. Hatfield," he nodded to Johnny and Barney sitting beside Hetty, "are the only ones who can tell us."

"Already told you," Hetty repeated. Johnny hid a grin.

"Look, Mrs. Thompson," Dr. Peterson said loudly and with ill-concealed exasperation, "you created and set off an explosive force that dwarfed every test we've made at Frenchman's Flat in four years. The force of your explosive was apparently greater than that of a fair-sized atomic device and only our Pacific tests—and those of the Russians—have been any greater. Yet within a half hour or forty-five minutes after the blast there wasn't a trace of radiation at ground level, no aerial radiation, and not one report of upper-atmosphere contamination or fallout within a thousand miles.

"Mrs. Thompson, I appeal to your patriotism. Your friends, your country, the free people of the world, need this invention of yours."

Hetty's eyes grew wide and then her features set in a mold of firm determination. Shoving back her chair and raising to stand stiffly erect and with chin thrust forward, she was every inch the True Pioneer Woman of the West.

"I never thought of that," she said solemnly. "By golly, if my country needs this like that, then by golly, my country's going to have it."

The officials leaned forward in anticipation.

"You can have Sally's Cloverdale Marathon III and I don't want one cent for her, either. And you can take the hens, too."

There was a stunned silence and then the Army major strangled on a mouthful of coffee; the security man turned beet red in the face and Dr. Peterson's jaw bounced off his breastbone. Johnny, unable to hold back an explosion of laughter, dashed for the back porch and collapsed.

The kitchen door slammed and Dr. Peterson stamped out on to the porch, pipe clamped between clenched teeth, his face black with anger and frustration. He ignored Johnny, who was standing beside the rail wiping tears from his eyes. Culpepper recovered himself and walked over to the irate physicist.

"Dr. Peterson, you're a man of science," Johnny said, "and a scientist is supposed to be willing to accept a fact and then possibly determine the causes behind the fact after he recognizes what he sees. Isn't that so?"

"Now, look here," Peterson angrily swung around to face Johnny. "I've taken all I intend to take from you people with your idiotic story. I don't intend to . . ."

Johnny took the older man by the elbow and gently but firmly propelled him from the porch toward the barn. "I don't intend to either insult your intelligence, Dr. Peterson, or attempt to explain what has happened here. But I do intend to show you what we know."

Bright floodlights illuminated the yard and a crew of soldiers were stringing telephone wires from the guarded front gate across the open space to the ranch house. Beyond the new barbed wire fence, there was an excited stir and rush for the wire as a sharp-eyed newsman spotted Johnny and the scientist crossing the yard. The two men ignored the shouted requests for more up-to-the-minute information as they walked into the barn. Johnny switched on the lights.

The lowing of the two prize Guernseys in the stalls at the right of the door changed to loud, plaintive bawling as the lights came on. Both cows were obviously in pain from their swollen and unmilked udders.

"Seeing is believing, Doc?" Johnny asked, pointing to the cows.

"Seeing what?" Peterson snapped.

"I knew we were going to have some tall explaining to do when you fellows took over here," Johnny said, "and, of course, I don't blame you one bit. That was some blast Hetty set off out there."

"You don't know," Dr. Peterson murmured fearfully, "you just don't know."

"So," Johnny continued, "I deliberately didn't milk these cows, so that you could see for yourself that we aren't lying. Now, mind you, I don't have the foggiest idea WHY this is happening, but I'm going to show you at least, WHAT happened."

He picked up a pair of milk buckets from a rack beside the door and walked towards the cow stalls, Peterson trailing. "This," Johnny said, pointing to the larger of the two animals, "is Queenie. Her milk is just about as fine as you can get from a champion milk-producing line. And this," he reached over and patted the flank of the other cow, "is Sally's Cloverdale Marathon III. She's young and up to now has given good but not spectacular quantities or qualities of milk. She's from the same blood line as Queenie. Sally had dried up from her first calf and we bred her again and on Wednesday she came fresh. Only it isn't milk that she's been giving. Watch!"

Kicking a milking stool into position, he placed a bucket under Queenie's distended bag and began squirting the rich, foaming milk into the pail with a steady, fast, and even rhythm. When he had finished, he set the two full buckets with their thick heads of milk foam outside the stall and brought two more clean, empty buckets. He moved to the side of the impatient Sally. As Peterson watched, Johnny filled the buckets with the same flat, oily-looking white fluid that Sally had been producing since Wednesday. The scientist began to show mild interest.

Johnny finished, stripped the cow, and then carried the pails out and set them down beside the first two.

"O.K., now look them over yourself," he told Peterson.

The scientist peered into the buckets. Johnny handed him a ladle.

"Look, Culpepper," Peterson said, "I'm a physicist, not a farmer or an agricultural expert. How do you expect me to know what milk is supposed to do? Until I was fifteen years old, I thought the milk came out of one of those spigots and the cream out of another."

"Stir it," Johnny ordered. The scientist took the ladle angrily and poked at the milk in Queenie's buckets.

"Taste it," Johnny said. Peterson glared at the younger man and then took a careful sip of the milk. Some of the froth clung to his lips and he licked it off. "Tastes like milk to me," he said.

"Smell it," Johnny ordered. Peterson sniffed.

"O.K., now do the same things to the other buckets."

Peterson swished the ladle through the buckets containing Sally's milk. The white liquid swirled sluggishly and oil-like. He bent over and smelled and made a grimace.

"Go on," Johnny demanded, "taste it."

Peterson took a tiny sip, tasted, and then spat.

"All right," he said, "I'm now convinced that there's something different about this milk. I'm not saying anything is wrong with it because I wouldn't know. All I'm admitting is that it is different. So what?"

"Come on." Johnny took the ladle from him. He carried the buckets of Queenie's milk into the cooler room and dumped them in a small pasteurizer.

Then carrying the two pails of Sally's milk, Johnny and the physicist left the barn and went to the shattered remains of the tractor shed.

Fumbling under wrecked and overturned tables and workbenches, Johnny found an old and rusted pie tin.

Placing the tin in the middle of the open spaces of the yard, he turned to Peterson. "Now you take that pail of milk and pour a little into the pan. Not much, now, just about enough to cover the bottom or a little more." He again handed the ladle to Peterson.

The scientist dipped out a small quantity of the white fluid and carefully poured it into the pie plate.

"That's enough," Johnny cautioned. "Now let's set these buckets a good long ways from here." He picked up the buckets and carried them to the back porch. He vanished into the kitchen.

By this time, the strange antics of the two men had attracted the attention of the clamoring newsmen outside the fence and they jammed against the wire, shouting pleas for an interview or information. The network television camera crews trained their own high-powered lights into the yard to add to the brilliance of the military lights and began recording the scene. Dr. Peterson glared angrily at the mob and turned as Johnny rejoined him. "Culpepper, are you trying to make a fool of me?" he hissed.

"Got a match?" Johnny queried, ignoring the question. The pipe-smoking scientist pulled out a handful of kitchen matches. Johnny produced a glass fish-casting rod with a small wad of cloth tied to the weighted hook. Leading Peterson back across the yard about fifty feet, Johnny handed the rag to Peterson.

"Smell it," he said. "I put a little kerosene on it so it would burn when it goes through the air." Peterson nodded.

"You much of a fisherman?" Johnny asked.

"I can drop a fly on a floating chip at fifty yards," the physicist said proudly. Johnny handed him the rod and reel. "O.K., Doc, light up your rag and then let's see you drop it in that pie plate."

While TV cameras hummed and dozens of still photographers pointed telescopic lenses and prayed for enough light, Dr. Peterson ignited the little wad of cloth. He peered behind to check for obstructions and then, with the wrist-flicking motion of the devoted and expert fisherman, made his cast. The tiny torch made a blurred, whipping streak of light and dropped unerringly into the pie plate in the middle of the yard.

The photographers had all the light they needed!

The night turned violet as a violent ball of purple fire reared and boiled into the darkened sky. The flash bathed the entire ranch headquarters and the packed cars and throngs outside the fence in the strange brilliance. The heat struck the dumfounded scientist and young rancher like the suddenly opened door of a blast furnace.

It was over in a second as the fire surged and then winked out. The sudden darkness blinded them despite the unchanged power of the television and military floodlights still focused on the yard. Pandemonium erupted from the ranks of newsmen and photographers who had witnessed the dazzling demonstration.

Peterson stared in awe at the slightly smoking and warped pie tin. "Well, cut out my tongue and call me Oppenheimer," he exclaimed.

"That was just the milk," Johnny said. "You know of a good safe place we could try it out with one of those eggs? I'd be afraid to test 'em anywhere around here after what happened to Hetty this morning."

An hour later, a military helicopter chewed its way into the night, carrying three gallons of Sally's milk from the ranch to Nellis AFB, where a jet stood ready to relay the sealed cannister to the AEC laboratories at Albuquerque.

In the ranch house living room Peterson had set up headquarters, and an Army field telephone switchboard was in operation across the room.

An AEC security man was running the board. Hetty had decided that one earthquake a day was enough and had gone to bed. Barney, bewildered but happily pleased at so much company, sat on the edge of a chair and avidly watched and listened, not understanding a thing he saw or heard. At the back of the room Johnny hunched over Big Jim Thompson's roll-top desk, working up a list of supplies he would need to repair the damages from the week's growing list of explosions.

Peterson and three of his staff members were in lengthy consultation at a big table in the middle of the room. The Army field phone at Peterson's elbow jangled.

Across the room, the switchboard operator swung around and called: "It's the commissioner, Dr. Peterson. I just got through to him." Peterson picked up the phone.

"John," he shouted into the instrument, "Peterson here. Where have you been?" Tinny, audible squawks came from the phone, and Peterson held it away from his ear.

"Yes, I know all about it," he said. "Yes . . . yes . . . yes. I know you've had a time with the papers. Yes, I heard the radio. Yes, John, I know it sounds pretty ridiculous. What? Get up to the ranch and find out. Where do you think I'm calling from?"

The squawking rattled the receiver and Peterson winced.

"Look, commissioner," he broke in, "I can't put a stop to those stories. What? I said I can't put a stop to the stories for one reason. They're true."

The only sound that came from the phone was the steady hum of the line.

"Are you there, John?" Peterson asked. There was an indistinct mumble from Washington. "Now listen carefully, John. What I need out here just as quickly as you can round them up and get them aboard a plane is the best team of biogeneticists in the country.

"What? No, I don't need a team of psychiatrists, commissioner. I am perfectly normal." Peterson paused. "I think!"

He talked with his chief for another fifteen minutes. At two other telephones around the big table his chief deputy and the senior security officer of the task force handled a half-dozen calls during Peterson's lengthy conversation. When Peterson hung up, the machinery was in motion gathering the nation's top biochemists, animal geneticists, agricultural and animal husbandry experts, and a baker's dozen of other assorted -ists, ready to package and ship them by plane and train to the main AEC facility at Frenchman's Flat and to the Circle T.

Peterson sighed gustily as he laid down the phone and reached for his pipe. Across the table, his assistant put a hand over the mouthpiece of his telephone and leaned toward Peterson.

"It's the Associated Press in New York," he whispered. "They're hotter than a pistol about the blackout and threatening to call the president and every congressman in Washington if we don't crack loose with something."

"Why couldn't I have flunked Algebra Two," Peterson moaned. "No, I had to be a genius. Now look at me. A milkmaid." He looked at his watch. "Tell 'em we'll hold a press conference at 8 A.M. outside the ranch gate."

The assistant spoke briefly into the phone and again turned to Peterson. "They say they want to know now whether the milk and egg story is true. They say they haven't had anything but an official runaround and a lot of rumor."

"Tell them we neither deny nor confirm the story. Say we are investigating. We'll give them a formal statement in the morning," Peterson ordered.

He left the table and walked to the desk where Johnny was finishing his list of building supplies.

"What time do you usually get those eggs?" he asked.

Make Mine Homogenized

"Well, as a rule, Hetty gets out and gathers them up about nine each morning. But they've probably been laid a couple of hours earlier."

"That's going to make us awfully late to produce anything for those babbling reporters," the scientist said.

"Come to think of it," Johnny said thoughtfully, "we could rig up a light in the chicken house and make the hens lay earlier. That way you could have some eggs about four or five o'clock in the morning."

Barney had been listening.

"And them eggs make a mighty fine breakfast of a morning," he volunteered cheerfully. Peterson glared at him and Johnny grinned.

"I think the doctor wants the golden kind," he said with a smile.

"Oh, them," Barney said with a snort of disgust. "They wouldn't make an omelet fit for a hog. You don't want to fuss with them, doc."

Under Johnny's direction, a crew of technicians ran a power line into the slightly-wrecked chicken house. There were loud squawks of indignation from the sleeping hens as the men threaded their way through the nests. The line was installed and the power applied. A one-hundred-fifty-watt bulb illuminated the interior of the chicken house to the discordant clucking and cackling of the puzzled birds.

Solomon, the big rooster, was perched on a crossbeam, head tucked under his wing. When the light flooded the shed he jerked awake and fastened a startled and unblinking stare at the strange sun. He scrambled hastily and guiltily to his feet and, throwing out his great chest, crowed a shrieking hymn to Thomas A. Edison. Johnny chuckled as the technicians jumped at the sound. He left the hen house, went back to the house and to bed.

He set his alarm clock for 4 A.M. and dropped immediately into a deep and exhausted sleep.

When he and the sleepy-eyed Peterson went into the chicken house at 4:30, there were eleven of the golden eggs resting on the straw nests.

They turned the remainder of the normal eggs over to Hetty, who whipped up a fast and enormous breakfast. While Peterson and Johnny were eating, a writing team of AEC public information men, who had arrived during the night, were polishing a formal press release to be given to the waiting reporters at eight. The phones had been manned throughout the night. Peterson's bleary-eyed aide came into the kitchen and slumped into a chair at the table.

"Get yourself a cup of coffee, boy," Hetty ordered, "while I fix you something to eat. How you like your eggs?"

"Over easy, Mrs. Thompson, and thanks," he said wearily. "I think I've got everything lined up, doctor. The eggs are all packed ready to go in your car, and the car will be ready in about ten minutes. They're still setting up downrange but they should be all in order by the time you get there.

"The bio men and the others should be assembled in the main briefing room at range headquarters. I've ordered a double guard around the barn, to be maintained until the animal boys have finished their on-the-ground tests. And they're padding a device van to take Sally to the labs when they're ready.

"And . . . oh yeah, I almost forgot . . . the commissioner called about ten minutes ago and said to tell you that the Russians are going to make a formal protest to the U.N. this morning. They say we're trying to wipe out the People's Republic by contaminating their milk."

The sound of scuffling in the yard and loud yells of protest came through the back porch window. The door swung open and a spluttering and irate Barney was thrust into the room, still in the clutches of a pair of armed security policemen.

"Get your hands off'n me," Barney roared as he struggled and squirmed impotently in their grip. "Doc, tell these pistol-packing bellhops to turn me loose."

"We caught him trying to get into the barn, sir," one of the officers told Peterson.

"Of course I was going into the barn," the indignant ranch hand screamed. "Where'd you think I would go to milk a cow?"

Peterson smiled. "It's all right, Fred. It's my fault. I should have told you Mr. Hatfield has free access."

The security men released Barney. He shook himself and glared at them.

"I'm terribly sorry, Barney," Dr. Peterson said. "I forgot that you would be going down to milk the cows and I'm glad you reminded me. Do me a favor and milk Sally first, will you? I want to take that milk, or whatever it is, with us when we leave in a few minutes."

The sun was crawling up the side of the mountains when Johnny and Dr. Peterson swung out of the ranch yard between two armored scout cars for the sixty-mile trip down the range road. Dew glistened in the early rays of light, and the clear, cool morning air held little hint of the heat sure to come by midmorning. There was a rush of photographers toward the gate as the little convoy left the ranch. A battery of cameras grabbed shots of the vehicles heading south.

It was the beginning of a day that changed the entire foreign policy of the United States. It was also the day that started a host of the nation's finest nuclear physicists tottering toward psychiatrists' couches.

In rapid order in the next few days, Peterson's crew, reinforced by hundreds of fellow scientists, technicians, and military men, learned what Johnny Culpepper already knew. They learned that (1) Sally's milk, diluted by as much as four hundred parts of pure water, made a better fuel than gasoline when ignited.

They also learned that (2) in reduced degrees of concentration, it became a substitute for any explosive of known chemical composition; (3) brought in contact with the compound inside one of the golden eggs, it produced an explosive starting at the kiloton level of one egg to two cups of milk and went up the scale but leveled off at a peak as the recipe was increased; (4) could be controlled by mixing jets to produce any desired stream of explosive power; and (5) they didn't have the wildest idea what was causing the reaction.

In that same order it brought (1) Standard Oil stock down to the value of wallpaper;

(2) ditto for DuPont; (3) a new purge in the top level of the Supreme Soviet; (4) delight to rocketeers at Holloman Air Force Research Center, Cape Canaveral, and Vandenburg Air Force Base; and (5) agonizing fits of hair-tearing to every chemist, biologist, and physicist who had a part in the futile attempts to analyze the two ingredients of what the press had labeled "Thompson's Eggnog."

While white-coated veterinarians, agricultural experts, and chemists prodded and poked Sally's Cloverdale Marathon III, others were giving a similar going-over to Hetty's chicken flock. Solomon's outraged screams of anger echoed across the desert as they subjected him to fowl indignities never before endured by a rooster.

Weeks passed and with each one new experiments disclosed new uses for the amazing Eggnog. While Sally placidly chewed her cud and continued to give a steady five gallons of concentrated fury at each milking, Solomon's harem dutifully deposited from five to a dozen golden spheres of packaged power every day. At the same time, rocket research engineers completed their tests on the use of the Eggnog.

In the early hours of June 4th, a single-stage, two-egg, thirty-five-gallon Atlas rocket poised on the launching pad at Cape Canaveral. From the loud-speaker atop the massive blockhouse came the countdown.

"X minus twenty seconds. X minus ten seconds. Nine . . . eight . . . seven . . . six . . . five . . . four . . . three . . . two . . . FIRE!"

The control officer stabbed the firing button, and deep within the Atlas a relay clicked, activating a solenoid that pushed open a valve. A thin stream of Sally's milk shot in from one side of the firing chamber to blend with a fine spray of egg batter coming from a jet in the opposite wall.

Spewing a solid tail of purple fire, the Atlas leaped like a wasp-stung heifer from the launching pad and thundered into space. The fuel orifices continued to expand to maximum pre-set opening. In ten seconds the nose cone turned from cherry-red to white heat and began sloughing its outer ceramic coating. At slightly more than forty-three thousand miles an hour, the great missile cleaved out of atmosphere into the void of space, leaving a shock wave that cracked houses and shattered glass for fifty miles from launching point.

A week later, America's newest rocket vessel, weighing more than thirty tons and christened *The Eggnog,* was launched from the opposite coast at Vanderburg. Hastily modified to take the new fuel, the weight and space originally designed for the common garden variety of rocket fuel was filled with automatic camera and television equipment. In its stern stood a six-egg, one-hundred-gallon engine, while in the nose was a small, one-egg, fourteen-quart braking engine to slow it down for the return trip through the atmosphere.

Its destination—Mars!

A week later, *The Eggnog* braked down through the troposphere, skidded to a piddling two thousand miles an hour through the stratosphere, automatically sprouted gliding wing stubs in the atmosphere and planed down to a spraying halt in the Pacific

Ocean, fifty miles west of Ensenada in Baja California. Aboard were man's first views of the red planet.

The world went mad with jubilation. From the capitals of the free nations congratulations poured into Washington. From Moscow came word of a one-hundred-ton spaceship to be launched in a few days, powered by a mixture of vodka and orange juice discovered by a bartender in Novorosk who was studying chemistry in night school. This announcement was followed twenty-four hours later by a story in *Pravda* proving conclusively that Sally's Cloverdale Marathon III was a direct descendant of Nikito's Mujik Droshky V, a prize Guernsey bull produced in the barns of the Sopolov People's Collective twenty-six years ago.

Late in August, Air Force Major Clifton Wadsworth Quartermain climbed out of the port of the two-hundred-ton, two-dozen-egg, two-hundred-thirty-gallon space rocket *Icarus,* the first man into space and back. He had circled Venus and returned. No longer limited by fuel weight factors, scientists had been able to load enough shielding into the huge *Icarus* to protect a man from the deadly bombardment of the Van Allen radiation belts.

On September 15th, Sally's Cloverdale Marathon III, having been milked harder and faster than any Guernsey in history, went dry.

Less than half of the approximately twelve hundred gallons of fuel she had produced during her hay days remained on hand in the AEC storage vaults.

Three days later, Solomon, sprinting after one of his harem who was playing hard to get, bee-lined into the path of a security police jeep. There was an agonized squawk, a shower of feathers, and mourning. A short time later, the number of golden eggs dropped daily, until one morning there were none. They never reappeared. The United States had stockpiled twenty-six dozen in an underground cave deep in the Rockies.

Man, who had burst like a butterfly into space, crawled back into his cocoon and pondered upon the stars from a worm's-eye point of view.

Banging around in the back end of a common cattle truck, Sally's Cloverdale Marathon III came home to the Circle T in disgrace. In a corner of the truck, the late Solomon's harem cackled and voiced loud cries of misery as they huddled in the rude, slatted shipping coop. The truck turned off the county road and onto the dirt road leading to the main buildings. It rattled across the cattle guard and through the now unprotected and open gate in the barbed wire fence. Life had returned almost to normal at the Circle T.

But not for long.

Five days after Sally's ignominious dismissal from the armed forces, a staff car came racing up to the ranch. It skidded to a halt at the back-porch steps. Dr. Peterson jumped out and dashed up to the kitchen door.

"Well, for heaven's sake," Hetty cried. "Come on in, sonny. I ain't seen you for the longest spell."

Peterson entered and looked around.

"Where's Johnny, Mrs. Thompson?" he asked excitedly. "I've got some wonderful news."

"Now ain't that nice," Hetty exclaimed. "Your wife have a new baby or something? Johnny's down at the barn. I'll call him for you." She moved toward the door.

"Never mind," Peterson said, darting out the door, "I'll go down to the barn." He jumped from the porch and ran across the yard.

He found Johnny in the barn, rigging a new block and tackle for the hayloft. Barney was helping thread the new, manila line from a coil on the straw-littered floor.

"Johnny, we've found it," Peterson shouted jubilantly as he burst into the barn.

"Why, Doc, good to see you again," Johnny said. "Found what?"

"The secret of Sally's milk," Peterson cried. He looked wildly around the barn. "Where is she?"

"Who?"

"Sally, of course," the scientist yelped.

"Oh, she's down in the lower pasture with Queenie," Johnny replied.

"She's all right, isn't she?" Peterson asked anxiously.

"Oh, sure, she's fine, Doc. Why?"

"Listen," Peterson said hurriedly, "our people think they've stumbled on something. Now we still don't know what's in those eggs or in Sally's milk that make them react as they do. All we've been able to find is some strange isotope, but we don't know how to reproduce it or synthesize it.

"But we do think we know what made Sally give that milk and made those hens start laying the gold eggs."

Johnny and Barney laid down their work and motioned the excited scientist to join them on a bench against the horse stalls.

"Do you remember the day Sally came fresh?" Peterson continued.

"Not exactly," Johnny replied, "but I could look it up in my journal. I keep a good record of things like new registered stock births."

"Never mind," Peterson said, "I've already checked. It was May 9th."

He paused and smiled triumphantly.

"I guess that right if you say so," Johnny said. "But what about it?"

"And that was the same day that the hens laid the first golden egg too, wasn't it?" Peterson asked.

"Why it sure was, Doc," Barney chimed in. "I remember, cause Miz Thompson was so mad that the milk was bad and the eggs went wrong both in the same day."

"That's what we know. Now listen to this, Johnny," the scientist continued. "During the night of May 8th, we fired an entirely new kind of test shot on the range. I can't tell you what it was, only to say that it was a special atomic device that even we didn't know too much about. That's why we fired it from a cave in the side of a hill down there.

"Since then, our people have been working on the pretty good assumption that something happened to that cow and those chickens not too long before they started giving the Eggnog ingredients. Someone remembered the experimental test shot, checked the date, and then went out and had a look at the cave. We already had some earlier suspicions that this device produced a new type of beam ray. We took sightings from the cave, found them to be in a direct, unbroken line with the Circle T. We set up the device again, and using a very small model tried it out on some chick embryos. Sure enough, we got a mutation. But not the right kind.

"So we're going to recreate the entire situation right here, only this time we're going to expose not only Sally but a dozen other Guernseys from as close to her blood line as we can get.

"And we already knew that you had a young rooster sired by Solomon."

"But, Doc," Johnny protested. "Sally had a calf early that morning. Isn't that going to make a difference?"

"Of course it is," Peterson exclaimed. "And she's going to have another one the same way. And so are all the other cows. You're the one that told me she had her calf by artificial insemination, didn't you?"

Johnny nodded.

"Well, then she's going to have another calf from the same bull and so will the other cows."

"Pore Sally," Barney said sorrowfully. "They're sure takin' the romance outta motherhood for you."

The next day the guards were back on the gate. By midafternoon twelve fine young Guernseys arrived, together with a corps of veterinarians, biologists, and security police. By nightfall, Sally and her companions were all once again in a "delicate condition."

A mile from the ranch house, a dormitory was built for the veterinarians and biologists, and a barracks thrown up for the security guards. A thirty-five-thousand-dollar, twelve-foot-high chain link fence, topped by barbed wire, was constructed around the pasture, and armored cars patrolled the fence by day and kept guard over the pregnant bovines by night in the barn.

Through the fall, into the long winter, and back to budding spring again, the host of experts and guards watched and cared for the now calf-bloated herd.

The fact that Sally had gone dry had been kept a carefully guarded national secret. To keep up the pretense and show to the world that America still controlled the only proven method of manned space travel, the Joint Chiefs of Staff voted to expend two hundred gallons of the precious, small store of milk on hand for another interplanetary junket, this time to inspect the rings around Saturn.

Piloting a smaller and more sophisticated but equally well protected version of *Icarus,* Major Quartermain abandoned the fleshpots of Earth and the adulation of his coast-to-coast collection of worshiping females to again hurtle into the unknown.

"It was strictly a milk run," Major Quartermain was quoted as saying as he emerged from his ship after an uneventful but propaganda-loaded trip.

By the middle of May, it was the consensus of the veterinarians that Delivery Day would be July 4th. Plans were drafted for the repeat atomic cave shot at 9 P.M., July

3rd. The pregnant herd was to be given labor-inducing shots at midnight, and, if all went well, deliveries would start within a few hours. Just to be sure that nothing would shield the cows from the rays of the explosion, they were put in a corral on the south side of the barn until 9:30 P.M. on the night of the firing.

Solomon's successor and a new bevy of hens were already roosting in the same old chicken house, and egg production was normal.

On the night of July 3rd, at precisely 9 P.M., a sheet of light erupted from the Nevada hillside cave, and the ground shook and rumbled for a few miles. It wasn't a powerful blast, nor had been the original shot. Sixty miles away, thirteen Guernsey cows munched at a rick of fresh hay and chewed contentedly in the moonlight.

At 3:11 A.M. the following morning the first calf arrived, followed in rapid order by a dozen more.

Sally's Cloverdale Marathon III dropped her calf at 4:08 A.M. on Independence Day.

At 7 A.M., she was milked and produced two and a half gallons of absolutely clear, odorless, tasteless and non-ignitable fluid. Eleven other Guernseys gave forth gushing, foaming, creamy rich gallon after gallon of Grade A milk.

The thirteenth cow filled two buckets with something that looked like weak cocoa and smelled like stale tea.

But when a white-smocked University of California poultry specialist entered the chicken house later in the morning, he found nothing but normal, white fresh eggs in the nests. He finally arrived at the conclusion that Solomon's old harem had known for some time; whatever it was that Solomon had been gifted with, this new rooster just didn't have it.

A rush call went out for a dozen of the precious store of golden eggs to be sent to the testing labs down range.

Two hours later Dr. Peterson, surrounded by fellow scientists, stood before a bank of closed-circuit television monitors in the Frenchman's Flat headquarters building. The scene on the screens was the interior of a massive steel-and-concrete test building several miles up range. Resting on the floor of the building was an open, gallon-sized glass beaker filled with the new version of Sally's milk.

Poised directly above the opened beaker was a funnel-shaped vessel containing the contents of one golden egg.

Dr. Peterson reached for a small lever. By remote control, the lever would gradually open the bottom of the funnel. He squeezed gently, slowly applying pressure. An involuntary gasp arose from the spectators as a tiny trickle of egg fluid fell from the funnel toward the open beaker.

Instinctively, everyone in the room clamped their eyes shut in anticipation of a blast. A second later, Peterson peered cautiously at the screen. The beaker of milk had turned a cloudy pale blue. It neither fizzed nor exploded. It just sat.

He levered another drop from the funnel. The stringy, glutenous mass plopped into the beaker and the liquid swirled briefly and turned more opaque, taking on more of a bluish tinge.

A babble of voices broke through the room when it was apparent that no explosion was forthcoming.

Peterson slumped into a nearby chair and stared at the screen.

"Now what?" he moaned.

The "what" developed twelve hectic hours later after time lost initially in shaking, bouncing, and beaming the new substance on the outside chance it might develop a latent tendency towards demolition.

Satisfied that whatever it was in the beaker wasn't explosive, the liquid was quickly poured off into sixteen small half-pint beakers and speeded to as many different laboratories for possible analysis.

"What about the other stuff?" Peterson was asked, referring to the brownish "milk" subsequently identified as coming from a dainty young cow known as Melody Buttercup Greenbrier IV.

"One thing at a time," replied Peterson. "Let's find out what we have here before we got involved in the second problem."

At 9 P.M. that night, Peterson was called to the radiation labs. He was met at the door by a glazed-eyed physicist who led him back to his office.

He motioned Peterson to a seat and then handed him a sheaf of photographic papers and other charts. Each of the photo sheets had a clear, white outline of a test beaker surrounded by a solid field of black. Two of the papers were all white.

"I don't believe it, Floyd," the physicist said, running his hands through his hair. "I've seen it, I've done it, I've tested it, proven it, and I still don't believe it."

Peterson riffled the sheaf of papers and waited expectantly.

"You don't believe what, Fred?" he asked.

The physicist leaned over and tapped the papers in Peterson's hands. "We've subjected that crazy stuff to every source and kind of high and low energy radiation we can produce here, and that means just about everything short of triggering an H-device on it. We fired alphas, gammas, betas, the works, in wide dispersion, concentrated beam and just plain exposure.

"Not so much as one neutron of any of them went beyond the glass surrounding that forsaken slop.

"They curved around it, Floyd. They curved around it."

The physicist leaned his head on the desk. "Nothing should react like that," he sobbed. He struggled for composure as Peterson stared dazedly at the test sheets.

"That's not the whole story," the physicist continued. He walked to Peterson's side and extracted the two all-white sheets.

"This," he said brokenly, "represents a sheet of photographic paper dipped in the crud and then allowed to dry before being bombarded with radiation. And this," he waved the other sheet, "is a piece of photo paper in the center of a panel protected by another sheet of ordinary typing paper coated with that stuff."

Peterson looked up a him. "A radiation-proof liquid," he said in awed tones.

The other man nodded dumbly.

Make Mine Homogenized

"Eight years of university," the physicist whispered to himself. "Six years in summer schools. Four fellowships. Ten years in research.

"All shot to hell," he screamed, "by a stinking, hayburning cow."

Peterson patted him gently on the shoulder. "It's all right, Fred. Don't take it so hard. It could be worse."

"How?" he asked hollowly. "Have this stuff milked from a kangaroo?"

Back in his office, Peterson waved off a dozen calls while he gave orders for fresh quantities of the blue milk to be rushed to the Argonne laboratories for further radiation tests and confirmation of the Nevada results. He ordered a test set up for the brown fluid for the following morning and then took a call from the AEC commissioner.

"Yes, John," he said, "we've got something."

Operation Milkmaid was in full swing!

The following morning observers again clustered about the monitoring room as Peterson prepared to duplicate the tests, using a sample of Melody's brownish milk.

There was the same involuntary remote cringing as the first drop of egg fell towards the beaker, but this time, Peterson forced himself to watch. Again the gentle plop was heard through the amplifiers and nothing more. A similar clouding spread through the already murky fluid and when the entire contents of one egg had been added, the beaker took on a solid, brown, and totally opaque appearance. The scientists watched the glass container for several minutes, anticipating another possible delayed blast.

When nothing occurred, Peterson nodded to an assistant at an adjoining console. The aide worked a series of levers, and a remotely controlled mechanical arm came into view on the screen. The claw of the arm descended over the beaker and clasping it gently, bounced it lightly on the cement bunker floor. The only sound was the muffled thunk of the glass container against the concrete.

The assistant wiggled his controls gently and the beaker jiggled back and forth, a few inches off the floor.

Peterson, who had been watching closely, called out. "Do that again."

The operator jostled the controls. "Look at that," Peterson exclaimed. "That stuff's hardened."

A quick movement confirmed this, and then Peterson ordered the beaker raised five feet from the floor and slowly tipped. Over the container went as the claw rotated in its socket. The glass had turned almost 180° toward the floor when the entire mass of solidified glob slid out.

The watchers caught their breath as it fell to the hard floor. The glob hit the floor, bounced up a couple of inches, fell back, bounced again, and then quivered to a stop. What was soon to be known as Melody's Mighty Material had been born.

The testing started. But there was a difference. By the time the brown chunk had been removed from the bunker it had solidified to the point that nothing would break or cut it. The surface yielded slightly to the heaviest cutting edge of a power saw and then sprang back, unmarked. A diamond drill spun ineffectually.

So the entire block started making the rounds of the various labs. It was with downright jubilation that radiation labs reported no properties of resistance for the stuff. One after the other, the tests proved nothing, until the physical properties unit came up with an idea.

"You can't cut it, break it, or tear it," the technician told Peterson, as he hefted the chunk of lightweight enigma. "You can't burn it, shoot holes in it, or so much as mark the surface with any known acid. This stuff's tougher than steel and about fifty times lighter."

"O.K.," Peterson asked, "so what good is it?"

"You can mold it when you mix it," the technician said significantly.

"Hey, you're right," Peterson jumped up excitedly. "Why, a spacer cast out of this stuff and coated with Sally's paint would be light enough and shielded enough to work on regular missile fuels."

Working under crash priorities, the nation's three leading plastics plants turned out three lightweight, molded, one-man space vehicles from the government-supplied Melody's Mix. A double coating of Sally's Paint then covered the hulls and a single-stage liquid fuel rocket engine was hooked to the less-than-one-ton engineless hull.

Twenty-eight days after the milk first appeared, on a warm August evening, the first vehicle stood on the pads at Cape Canaveral, illuminated by towers of lights. Fuel crews had finished loading the tanks which would be jettisoned along with the engine at burn-out. Inside the rocket, Major Quartermain lounged uncomfortably and cramped in the take-off sling for a short but telling trip through the Van Allen radiation fields and back to Earth.

The take-off sling rested inside an escape capsule, since the use of chemical fuel brought back many of the old uncertainties of launchings. On the return trip Quartermain would eject at sixty thousand feet and pull the capsule's huge parachute for a slow drop to the surface of the Atlantic, where a recovery fleet was standing by. The light rocket hull would pop a separate chute and also drift down for recovery and analysis.

Inside the ship, Quartermain sniffed the air and curled his nose. "Let's get this thing on the road," he spoke into his throat mike. "Some of that Florida air must have seeped in here."

"Four minutes to final countdown," blockhouse control replied. "Turn on your blowers for a second."

Outside the ship, the fuel crews cleared their equipment away from the pad. The same ripe, heavy odor hung in the warm night air.

At 8:02 P.M., twenty-eight days after the new milks made their first appearance, Major Quartermain blasted off in a perfect launching.

At 8:03 P.M., the two other Melody Mix hulls standing on nearby pads began to melt.

At 8:04 P.M., the still-roaring engine fell from the back end of Quartermain's rocket in a flaming arc back toward Earth. Fifteen seconds later, he hurtled his escape capsule out of the collapsing rocket hull. The parachute opened and the daring astronaut drifted toward the sea.

Make Mine Homogenized

Simultaneously, in a dozen labs around the nation, blocks and molds of Melody's Mix made from that first batch of milk collapsed into piles of putrid goo. Every day thereafter, newer blocks of the mix reached the twenty-eight-day limit and similarly broke down into malodorous blobs.

It was a month before the stinking, gooey mess that flowed over the launching pads at the Cape was cleaned up by crews wearing respirators and filter masks. It took considerably longer to get the nation's three top plastics firms back in operation as the fetid flow of unfinished rocket parts wrecked machinery and drove personnel from the area.

The glob that had been Quartermain's vehicle fell slowly back to Earth, disintegrating every minute until it reached the consistency of thin gruel. At this point, it was caught by a jet air stream and carried in a miasmic cloud halfway around the world until it finally floated down to coat the Russian city of Urmsk in a veil of vile odor. The United States disclaimed any knowledge of the cloud.

"LAS VEGAS, NEV., May 8 (AP) The Atomic Energy Commission today announced it has squeezed the last drop from Operation Milkmaid.

"After a year of futile experimentation has failed to get anything more than good, Grade-A milk from the world's two most famous cows, the AEC says it has closed down its field laboratory at the Circle T ranch.

"Dr. Floyd Peterson, who has been in charge of the attempt to again reproduce Sally's Milk, told newsmen that the famed Guernsey and her stablemate, Melody, no longer gave exotic and unidentifiable liquids that sent man zooming briefly to the stars.

" 'For a while, it looked like we had it in the bag,' Peterson said. 'You might say now, though, that the tests have been an udder failure.'

"Meanwhile, in Washington, AEC Commissioner . . ." ■

ALLAMAGOOSA
by Eric Frank Russell

Illustration by Kelly Freas.
Copyright 1955 by Street & Smith Publications, Inc.

It was a long time since the *Bustler* had been so silent. She lay in the Sirian spaceport, her tubes cold, her shell particle-scarred, her air that of a long-distance runner exhausted at the end of a marathon. There was good reason for this: she had returned from a lengthy trip by no means devoid of troubles.

Now, in port, well-deserved rest had been gained if only temporarily. Peace, sweet peace. No more bothers, no more crises, no more major upsets, no more dire predicaments such as crop up in free flight at least twice a day. Just peace.

Hah!

Captain McNaught reposed in his cabin, feet up on desk, and enjoyed the relaxation to the utmost. The engines were dead, their hellish pounding absent for the first time in months. Out there in the big city four hundred of his crew were making whoopee under a brilliant sun. This evening, when First Officer Gregory returned to take charge, he was going to go into the fragrant twilight and make the rounds of neon-lit civilization.

That was the beauty of making landfall at long last. Men could give way to themselves, blow off surplus steam, each according to his fashion. No duties, no worries, no dangers, no responsibilities in spaceport. A haven of safety and comfort for tired rovers.

Again, hah!

Burman, the chief radio officer, entered the cabin. He was one of the half-dozen remaining on duty and bore the expression of a man who can think of twenty better things to do.

"Relayed signal just come in, sir." Handing the paper across, he waited for the other to look at it and perhaps dictate a reply.

Taking the sheet, McNaught removed the feet from his desk, sat erect and read the message aloud.

Terran Headquarters to Bustler. *Remain Siriport pending further orders. Rear Admiral Vane W. Cassidy due there seventeenth. Feldman. Navy Op. Command, Sirisec.*

He looked up, all happiness gone from his leathery features, and groaned.

"Something wrong?" asked Burman, vaguely alarmed.

McNaught pointed at three thin books on his desk. "The middle one. Page twenty."

Leafing through it, Burman found an item that said: *Vane W. Cassidy, R-Ad, Head Inspector Ships and Stores.*

Burman swallowed hard. "Does that mean—?"

"Yes, it does," said McNaught without pleasure. "Back to training-college and all its rigmarole. Paint and soap, spit and polish." He put on an officious expression, adopted a voice to match it. "Captain, you have only seven ninety-nine emergency rations. Your allocation is eight hundred. Nothing in your log book accounts for the missing one. Where is it? What happened to it? How is it that one of the men's kit lacks an officially issued pair of suspenders? Did you report his loss?"

"Why does he pick on us?" asked Burman, appalled. "He's never chivvied us before."

"That's why," informed McNaught, scowling at the wall. "It's our turn to be stretched across the barrel." His gaze found the calendar. "We have three days—and we'll need 'em! Tell Second Officer Pike to come here at once."

Burman departed gloomily. In short time Pike entered. His face reaffirmed the old adage that bad news travels fast.

"Make out an indent," ordered McNaught, "for one hundred gallons of plastic paint, Navy-gray, approved quality. Make out another for thirty gallons of interior white enamel. Take them to spaceport stores right away. Tell them to deliver by six this evening along with our correct issue of brushes and sprayers. Grab up any cleaning material that's going for free."

"The men won't like this," remarked Pike, feebly.

"They're going to love it," McNaught asserted. "A bright and shiny ship, all spic and span, is good for morale. It says so in that book. Get moving and put those indents in. When you come back, find the stores and equipment sheets and bring them here. We've got to check stocks before Cassidy arrives. Once he's here we'll have no chance to make up shortages or smuggle out any extra items we happened to find in our hands."

"Very well, sir." Pike went out wearing the same expression as Burman's.

Lying back in his chair McNaught muttered to himself. There was a feeling in his bones that something was sure to cause a last-minute ruckus. A shortage of any item would be serious enough unless covered by a previous report. A surplus would be bad, very bad. The former implied carelessness or misfortune. The latter suggested barefaced theft of government property in circumstances condoned by the commander.

For instance, there was that recent case of Williams of the heavy cruiser *Swift*. He'd heard of it over the spacevine when out around Bootes. Williams had been found in unwitting command of eleven reels of electric-fence wire when his official issue was ten. It had taken a court-martial to decide that the extra reel—which had formidable barter-value on a certain planet—had not been stolen from space-stores or, in sailor jargon, "teleported aboard." But Williams had been reprimanded. And that did not help promotion.

He was still rumbling discontentedly when Pike returned bearing a folder of foolscap sheets.

"Going to start right away, sir?"

"We'll have to." He heaved himself erect, mentally bidded good-bye to time off and a taste of the bright lights. "It'll take long enough to work right through from bow to tail. I'll leave the men's kit inspection to the last."

Marching out of the cabin, he set forth toward the bow, Pike following with broody reluctance.

As they passed the open main hall, Peaslake observed them, bounded eagerly up the gangway and jogged behind. A pukka member of the crew, he was a large dog whose ancestors had been more enthusiastic than selective. He wore with pride a big collar inscribed: *Peaslake—Property of S. S. Bustler*. His chief duties, ably performed, were to keep alien rodents off the ship and, on rare occasions, smell out dangers invisible to human eyes.

The three paraded forward, McNaught and Pike in the manner of men grimly sacrificing pleasure for the sake of duty, Peaslake with the panting willingness of one ready for any new game no matter what.

Reaching the bow-cabin, McNaught dumped himself in the pilot's seat, took the folder from the other. "You know this stuff better than me—the chart room is where I shine. So I'll read them out while you look them over." He opened the folder, started on the first page. "K1, Beam compass, type D, one of."

"Check," said Pike.

"K2. Distance and direction indicator, electronic, type JJ, one of."

"Check."

"K3. Port and starboard gravitic meters, Casini models, one pair."

"Check."

Peaslake planted his head in McNaught's lap, blinked soulfully, and whined. He was beginning to get the others' viewpoint. This tedious itemizing and checking was a hell of a game. McNaught consolingly lowered a hand and played with Pealake's ears while he ploughed his way down the list.

"K187. Foam rubber cushions, pilot and co-pilot, one pair."

"Check."

By the time First Officer Gregory appeared they had reached the tiny intercom cubby and poked around it in semidarkness. Peaslake had long departed in disgust.

"M24. Spare minispeakers, three each, type T2, one set of six."

"Check."

Looking in, Gregory popped his eyes and said, "What's going on?"

"Major inspection due soon." McNaught glanced at his watch. "Go see if stores has delivered a load and if not why not. Then you'd better give me a hand and let Pike take a few hours off."

"Does this mean land-leave is canceled?"

"You bet it does—until after Hizonner has been and gone." He glanced at Pike. "When you get into the city search around and send back any of the crew you can find. No arguments or excuses. Also no alibis and/or delays. It's an order."

Pike registered unhappiness. Gregory glowered at him, went away, came back and said, "Stores will have the stuff here in twenty minutes' time." With bad grace he watched Pike depart.

"M47. Intercom cable, woven-wire protected, three drums."

"Check," said Gregory, mentally kicking himself for returning at the wrong time.

The task continued until late in the evening, was resumed early next morning. By that time three-quarters of the men were hard at work inside and outside the vessel, doing their jobs as though sentenced to them for crimes contemplated but not yet committed.

Moving around the ship's corridors and catwalks had to be done crab-fashion, with a nervous sidewise edging. Once again it was being demonstrated that the Terran life form suffers from ye fear of wette paynt. The first smearer would have ten years willed off his unfortunate life.

It was in these conditions, in mid-afternoon of the second day, that McNaught's bones proved their feelings had been prophetic. He recited the ninth page while Jean Blanchard confirmed the presence and actual existence of all items enumerated. Two-thirds of the way down they hit the rocks, metaphorically speaking, and commenced to sink fast.

McNaught said boredly, "V1097. Drinking bowl, enamel, one of."

"Is zis," said Blanchard, tapping it.

"V1098. Offog, one."

"*Quoi?*" asked Blanchard, staring.

"V1098. Offog, one," repeated McNaught. "Well, why are you looking thunderstruck? This is the ship's galley. You're the head cook. You know what's supposed to be in the galley, don't you? Where's this offog?"

"Never hear of heem," stated Blanchard, flatly.

"You must have. It's on this equipment-sheet in plain, clear type. Offog, one, it says. It was here when we were fitted-out four years ago. We checked it ourselves and signed for it."

"I signed for nossings called offog," Blanchard denied. "In the cuisine zere is no such sing."

"Look!" McNaught scowled and showed him the sheet.

Blanchard looked and sniffed disdainfully. "I have here zee electronic oven, one of. I have jacketed boilers, graduated capacities, one set. I have bain marie pans, seex of. But no offog. Never heard of heem. I do not know of heem." He spread his hands and shrugged. "No offog."

"There's got to be," McNaught insisted. "What's more, when Cassidy arrives there'll be hell to pay if there isn't."

"You find heem," Blanchard suggested.

"You got a certificate from the International Hotels School of Cookery. You got a certificate from the Cordon Bleu College of Cuisine. You got a certificate with three credits from the Space-Navy Feeding Center," McNaught pointed out. "All that—and you don't know what an offog is."

"*Nom d'un chien!*" ejaculated Blanchard, waving his arms around. "I tell you ten t'ousand time zere is no offog. Zere never was an offog. Escoffier heemself could not find zee offog of vich zere is none. Am I a magician perhaps?"

"It's part of the culinary equipment," McNaught maintained. "It must be because it's on page nine. And page nine means its proper home is in the galley, care of the head cook."

"Like hail it does," Blanchard retorted. He pointed at a metal box on the wall. "Intercom booster. Is zat mine?"

McNaught thought it over, conceded, "No, it's Burman's. His stuff rambles all over the ship."

"Zen ask heem for zis bloody offog," said Blanchard, triumphantly.

"I will. If it's not yours it must be his. Let's finish this checking first. If I'm not systematic and thorough Cassidy will jerk off my insignia." His eyes sought the list. "V1099. Inscribed collar, leather, brass studded, dog, for the use of. No need to look for that. I saw it myself five minutes ago." He ticked the item, continued, "V1100. Sleeping basket, woven reed, one of."

"Is zis," said Blanchard, kicking it into a corner.

"V1101. Cushion, foam rubber, to fit sleeping basket, one of."

"Half of," Blanchard contradicted. "In four years he has chewed away other half."

"Maybe Cassidy will let us indent for a new one. It doesn't matter. We're O.K. so long as we can produce the half we've got." McNaught stood up, closed the folder. "That's the lot for here. I'll go see Burman about this missing item."

The inventory party moved on.

Allamagoosa 259

* * *

Burman switched off a UHF receiver, removed his earplugs and raised a questioning eyebrow.

"In the galley we're short an offog," explained McNaught. "Where is it?"

"Why ask me? The galley is Blanchard's bailiwick."

"Not entirely. A lot of your cables run through it. You've two terminal boxes in there, also an automatic switch and an intercom booster. Where's the offog?"

"Never heard of it," said Burman, baffled.

McNaught shouted, "Don't tell me that! I'm already fed up hearing Blanchard saying it. Four years back we had an offog. It says so here. This is our copy of what we checked and signed for. It says we signed for an offog. Therefore we must have one. It's got to be found before Cassidy gets here."

"Sorry, sir," sympathized Burman. "I can't help you."

"You can think again," advised McNaught. "Up in the bow there's a direction and distance indicator. What do *you* call it?"

"A didin," said Burman, mystified.

"And," McNaught went on, pointing at the pulse transmitter, "what do you call *that?*"

"The opper-popper."

"Baby names, see? Didin and opper-popper. Now rack your brains and remember what you called an offog four years ago."

"Nothing," asserted Burman, "has ever been called an offog to my knowledge."

"Then," demanded McNaught, "why did we sign for one?"

"I didn't sign for anything. You did all the signing."

"While you and others did the checking. Four years ago, presumably in the galley, I said, 'Offog, one,' and either you or Blanchard pointed to it and said, 'Check.' I took somebody's word for it. I have to take other specialists' words for it. I am an expert navigator, familiar with all the latest navigational gadgets but not with other stuff. So I'm compelled to rely on people who know what an offog is—or ought to."

Burman had a bright thought. "All kinds of oddments were dumped in the main lock, the corridors, and the galley when we were fitted-out. We had to sort through a deal of stuff and stash it where it properly belonged, remember? This offog-thing might be any place today. It isn't necessarily my responsibility or Blanchard's."

"I'll see what the other officers say," agreed McNaught, conceding the point. "Gregory, Worth, Sanderson, or one of the others may be coddling the item. Wherever it is, it's got to be found. Or accounted for in full if it's been expended."

He went out. Burman pulled a face, inserted his earplugs, resumed fiddling with his apparatus. An hour later McNaught came back wearing a scowl.

"Positively," he announced with ire, "there is no such thing on the ship. Nobody knows of it. Nobody can so much as guess at it."

"Cross it off and report it lost," Burman suggested.

"What, when we're hard aground? You know as well as I do that loss and damage must be signaled at time of occurrence. If I tell Cassidy the offog went west in space, he'll want to know when, where, how, and why it wasn't signaled. There'll be a real ruckus if the contraption happens to be valued at half a million credits. I can't dismiss it with an airy wave of the hand."

"What's the answer then?" inquired Burman, innocently ambling straight into the trap.

"There's one and only one," McNaught announced. "*You* will manufacture an offog."

"Who? Me?" said Burman, twitching his scalp.

"You and no other. I'm fairly sure the thing is your pigeon, anyway."

"Why?"

"Because it's typical of the baby-names used for your kind of stuff. I'll bet a month's pay that an offog is some sort of scientific allamagoosa. Something to do with fog, perhaps. Maybe a blind-approach gadget."

"The blind-approach transceiver is called 'the fumbly,' " Burman informed.

"There you are!" said McNaught as if that clinched it. "So you will make an offog. It will be completed by six tomorrow evening and ready for my inspection then. It had better be convincing, in fact pleasing, in fact its function will be convincing."

Burman stood up, let his hands dangle, and said in hoarse tones, "How can I make an offog when I don't don't even know what it is?"

"Neither does Cassidy know," McNaught pointed out, leering at him. "He's more of a quantity surveyor than anything else. As such he counts things, looks at things, certifies that they exist, accepts advice on whether they are functionally satisfactory or worn out. All we need do is concoct an imposing allamagoosa and tell him it's the offog."

"Holy Moses!" said Burman, fervently.

"Let us not rely on the dubious assistance of Biblical characters," McNaught reproved. "Let us use the brains that God has given us. Get a grip on your soldering-iron and make a topnotch offog by six tomorrow evening. That's an order!"

He departed, satisfied with this solution. Behind him, Burman gloomed at the wall and licked his lips once, twice.

Rear Admiral Vane W. Cassidy arrived right on time. He was a short, paunchy character with a florid complexion and eyes like those of a long-dead fish. His gait was an important strut.

"Ah, captain, I trust that you have everything shipshape."

"Everything usually is," assured McNaught, glibly. "I see to that." He spoke with conviction.

"Good!" approved Cassidy. "I like a commander who takes his responsibilities seriously. Much as I regret saying so, there are a few who do not." He marched through the main lock, his cod-eyes taking note of the fresh white enamel. "Where do you prefer to start, bow or tail?"

"My equipment-sheets run from bow backward. We may as well deal with them the way they're set."

"Very well." He trotted officiously toward the nose, paused on the way to pat Peaslake and examine his collar. "Well cared for, I see. Has the animal proved useful?"

"He saved five lives on Mardia by barking a warning."

"The details have been entered in your log, I suppose?"

"Yes sir. The log is in the chart room awaiting your inspection."

"We'll get to it in due time." Reaching the bow-cabin, Cassidy took a seat, accepted the folder from McNaught, started off at a businesslike pace. "K1. Beam compass, type D, one of."

"This is it, sir," said McNaught, showing him.

"Still working properly?"

"Yes, sir."

They carried on, reached the intercom-cubby, the computer room, a succession of other places back to the galley. Here, Blanchard posed in freshly laundered white clothes and eyed the newcomer warily.

"V147. Electronic oven, one of."

"Is zis," said Blanchard, pointing with disdain.

"Satisfactory?" inquired Cassidy, giving him the fish-eye.

"Not beeg enough," declared Blanchard. He encompassed the entire galley with an expressive gesture. "Nossing's beeg enough. Place too small. Everysing's too small. I am chef de cuisine an' she is a cuisine like an attic."

"This is a warship, not a luxury liner," Cassidy snapped. He frowned at the equipment-sheet. "V148. Timing device, electronic oven, attachment thereto, one of."

"Is zis," spat Blanchard, ready to sling it through the nearest port if Cassidy would first donate the two pins.

Working his way down the sheet, Cassidy got nearer and nearer while nervous tension built up. Then he reached the critical point and said, "V1098. Offog, one."

"*Morbleau!*" said Blanchard, shooting sparks from his eyes, "I have say before an' I say again, zere never was—"

"The offog is in the radio room, sir," McNaught chipped in hurriedly.

"Indeed?" Cassidy took another look at the sheet. "Then why is it recorded along with galley equipment?"

"It was placed in the galley at time of fitting out, sir. It's one of those portable instruments left to us to fix up where most suitable."

"Hm-m-m! Then it should have been transferred to the radio room list. Why didn't you transfer it?"

"I thought it better to wait for your authority to do so, sir."

The fish-eyes registered gratification. "Yes, that is quite proper of you, Captain. I will transfer it now." He crossed the item from sheet nine, initialed it, entered it on sheet sixteen, initialed that. "V1099. Inscribed collar, leather . . . oh, yes, I've seen that. The dog was wearing it."

He ticked it. An hour later he strutted into the radio room. Burman stood up, squared his shoulders but could not keep his feet or hands from fidgeting. His eyes protruded slightly and kept straying toward McNaught in silent appeal. He was like a man wearing a porcupine in his britches.

"V1098. Offog, one," said Cassidy in his usual tone of brooking no nonsense.

Moving with the jerkiness of a slightly uncoördinated robot, Burman pawed a small box fronted with dials, switches, and colored lights. It looked like a radio ham's idea of a fruit machine. He knocked down a couple of switches. The lights came on, played around in intriguing combinations.

"This is it, sir," he informed with difficulty.

"Ah!" Cassidy left his chair and moved across for a closer look. "I don't recall having seen this item before. But there are so many different models of the same things. Is it still operating efficiently?"

"Yes, sir."

"It's one of the most useful things in the ship," contributed McNaught, for good measure.

"What does it *do?*" inquired Cassidy, inviting Burman to cast a pearl of wisdom before him.

Burman paled.

Hastily, McNaught said, "A full explanation would be rather involved and technical but, to put it as simply as possible, it enables us to strike a balance between opposing gravitational fields. Variations in lights indicate the extent and degree of unbalance at any given time."

"It's a clever idea," added Burman, made suddenly reckless, "based upon Finagle's Constant."

"I see," said Cassidy, not seeing at all. He resumed his seat, ticked the offog and carried on. "Z44. Switchboard, automatic, forty-line intercom, one of."

"Here it is, sir."

Cassidy glanced at it, returned his gaze to the sheet. The others used his momentary distraction to mop perspiration from their foreheads.

Victory had been gained.

All was well.

For the third time, hah!

Rear Admiral Vane W. Cassidy departed pleased and complimentary. Within one hour the crew bolted to town. McNaught took turns with Gregory at enjoying the gay lights. For the next five days all was peace and pleasure.

On the sixth day Burman brought in a signal, dumped it upon McNaught's desk, waited for the reaction. He had an air of gratification, the pleasure of one whose virtue is about to be rewarded.

Terran Headquarters to Bustler. Return here immediately for overhaul and refitting. Improved power plant to be installed. Feldman. Navy Op. Command. Sirisec.

"Back to Terra," commented McNaught, happily. "And an overhaul will mean at least one month's leave." He eyed Burman. "Tell all officers on duty to go to town at once and order the crew aboard. The men will come running when they know why."

"Yes, sir," said Burman, grinning.

Everyone was still grinning two weeks later when the Siriport had receded far behind and Sol had grown to a vague speck in the sparkling mist of the bow starfield. Eleven weeks still to go, but it was worth it. Back to Terra. Hurrah!

In the captain's cabin the grins abruptly vanished one evening when Burman suddenly developed the willies. He marched in, chewed his bottom lip while waiting for McNaught to finish writing in the log.

Finally, McNaught pushed the book away, glanced up, frowned. "What's the matter with you? Got a bellyache or something?"

"No, sir. I've been thinking."

"Does it hurt that much?"

"I've been thinking," persisted Burman in funereal tones. "We're going back for overhaul. You know what that means? We'll walk off the ship and a horde of experts will walk onto it." He stared tragically at the other. "Experts, I said."

"Naturally they'll be experts," McNaught agreed. "Equipment cannot be tested and brought up to scratch by a bunch of dopes."

"It will require more than a mere expert to bring the offog up to scratch," Burman pointed out. "It'll need a genius."

McNaught rocked back, swapped expressions like changing masks. "Jumping Judas! I'd forgotten all about that thing. When we got to Terra we won't blind *those* boys with science."

"No, sir, we won't," endorsed Burman. He did not add "any more" but his face shouted aloud, "You got me into this. You get me out of it." He waited a time while McNaught did some intense thinking, then prompted, "What do you suggest, sir?"

Slowly the satisfied smile returned to McNaught's features as he answered, "Break up the contraption and feed it into the disintegrator."

"That doesn't solve the problem," said Burman. "We'll still be short an offog."

"No we won't. Because I'm going to signal its loss owing to the hazards of spaceservice." He closed one eye in an emphatic wink. "We're in free flight right now." He reached for a message-pad and scribbled on it while Burman stood by vastly relieved.

Bustler to Terran Headquarters. Item V1098, Offog one, came apart under gravitational stress while passing through twin-sun field Hector Major-Minor. Material used as fuel. McNaught, Commander. Bustler.

Burman took it to the radio room and beamed it Earthward. All was peace and progress for another two days. The next time he went to the captain's cabin he went running and worried.

"General call, sir," he announced breathlessly and thrust the message into the other's hands.

Terran Headquarters for relay all sectors. Urgent and Important. All ships grounded forthwith. Vessels in flight under official orders will make for nearest spaceport pending further instructions. Welling. Alarm and Rescue Command. Terra.

"Something's gone bust," commented McNaught, undisturbed. He traipsed to the chart room, Burman following. Consulting the charts, he dialed the intercom phone, got Pike in the bow and ordered, "There's a panic. All ships grounded. We've got to make for Zaxtedport, about three days' run away. Change course at once. Starboard seventeen degrees, declination ten." Then he cut off, griped, "Bang goes that sweet month on Terra. I never did like Zaxted, either. It stinks. The crew will feel murderous about this and I don't blame them."

"What d'you think has happened, sir?" asked Burman. He looked both uneasy and annoyed.

"Heaven alone knows. The last general call was seven years ago when the *Starider* exploded halfway along the Mars run. They grounded every ship in existence while they investigated the cause." He rubbed his chin, pondered, went on, "And the call before that one was when the entire crew of the *Blowgun* went nuts. Whatever it is this time, you can bet it's serious."

"It wouldn't be the start of a space war?"

"Against whom?" McNaught made a gesture of comtempt. "Nobody has the ships with which to oppose us. No, it's something technical. We'll learn of it eventually. They'll tell us before we reach Zaxted or soon afterward."

They did tell him. Within six hours, Burman rushed in whth face full of horror.

"What's eating you now?" demanded McNaught, staring at him.

"The offog," stuttered Burman. He made motions as though brushing off invisible spiders.

"What of it?"

"It's a typographical error. In your copy it should read off, dog."

The commander stared owlishly.

"Off, dog?" echoed McNaught, making it sound like foul language.

"See for yourself." Dumping the signal on the desk, Burman bolted out, left the door swinging. McNaught scowled after him, picked up the message.

Terran Headquarters to Bustler. *Your report V1098, ship's official dog Peaslake. Detail fully circumstances and manner in which animal came apart under gravitational stress. Cross-examine crew and signal all coincidental symptoms experienced by them. Urgent and Important. Welling. Alarm and Rescue Command. Terra.*

In the privacy of his cabin McNaught commenced to eat his nails. Every now and again he went a little cross-eyed as he examined them for nearness to the flesh. ∎

RAVENSHAW OF WBY, INC.

by W. Macfarlane

Illustration by Vincent Di Fate.
Copyright © 1970 by The Conde Nast Publications, Inc.

Ravenshaw sat quietly in a limbo region of the Pentagon and wondered whether his head was stuffed full of shredded polyurethane or large-curd cottage cheese. The medical description was circadian rhythm desynchronization. He had been swept through time zones like an auger through an onion, and while his body was present and accounted for in Washington, D.C., he had a disconcerting mental picture of his spirit, winged like the ka of an Egyptian pharaoh, flapping wearily along behind over the Pacific.

General Craddock lifted his eyes from the 210 file he was studying and peered at Ravenshaw over his glasses. "A British study showed that the only officers who dared to innovate were those with independent fortunes."

"Yes, sir," said Ravenshaw.

He was in the same uniform he had put on eighty miles outside of Saigon. He had drowsed on the jet and borrowed an electric razor from the engineer, and from the reflection he had caught in a glass door, he looked presentable enough. Still, his eyesockets were lined with sand, his skin crawled, and he wanted a bath and a bed much more than a chitty-chat with this mysterious two-star general.

"Have you an independent fortune?"

"Independence, sir. No fortune. Independence is a state of mind, sir."

"Hostages to fortune?"

"Only my good opinion of myself."

Ravenshaw had never bandied shorthand conversation with a general before, because he was a polite man and most generals would understand Choctaw as readily, but then, he had never been an anonymous *cause celebre* or been flown halfway around the world without putting foot to the ground, either.

Craddock leaned back in his chair and said, "Ravenshaw, your career has been studded with unorthodoxies like diamonds in a goat's . . . ear. A lieutenant colonel who hires local witch doctors to plant taboos around his battalion area is a little unusual. The ambush you pulled off by tape recording and playing back camp noises, the trick of spreading fluorescent calcites and the use of filtered shortwave ultra-violet light to spot infiltration, all of these things indicate a latitude of mind, a correlative habit of thought that might be put to better use than—" He interrupted himself. "Where did you get the ice-cream machine?"

"I won an LST from the Navy playing poker, sir. I settled for the machine, one hundred seventy-five pounds of mix, and a small generator."

"Well, your use of it is anathema in Europe. Large indignant headlines. Certain elements in our country don't like it very well, either. How did that Swedish journalist find out?"

"She saw children eating strawberry ice-cream cones in the jungle, sir. She backtracked them to my headquarters and watched them swap land mines and booby traps for ice cream. Every Cong within a ten-kilometer area had a dozen kids watching him. As soon as he'd plant some device the kids would bring it to me. I had a barnful, sir."

The general took off his glasses and bit an earpiece. "Cones, Ravenshaw?"

"The mess sergeant and I figured out how to bake them. We used an old tractor grille for waffle marks, and cut and rolled them just out of the oven. We packed them in air-tight cans with silica gel and they stayed crisp. Sergeant Kisslegoff deserves the credit, sir. He also liberated a couple of cases of wheat germ for more nutrition in the batter."

"You are a Baby Killer, a Child Murderer, a Pied Piper of Doom. I am quoting from the Reuters' dispatch picked off Tidningarnas Telegrambyra, the Swedish wire service. There's a demonstration going on now in front of the Stockholm embassy. How did you manage to keep your name out of it? According to this indignant female, the battalion was commanded by Colonel Olepoop."

"Yes, sir. That fool lieutenant from Public Relations was new—he was driving her around—and he didn't know us. Kisselgoff is smart. He saw the fire in her eyes when she turned down a scoop of strawberry. The troops and I take care of each other, sir."

"The follow-up reporters can't find the battalion," said Craddock, with satisfaction. "Your Swedish friend stepped on a small anti-personnel mine just yesterday. She will be lying on her stomach for a month and she will be able to show her war wounds"—he hesitated—"I trust, only to intimate friends. You never saw her?"

"No, sir. I was checking perimeter defense."

"The incident is coincidental. Your orders to report to this office were cut before it happened."

Ravenshaw relaxed. He was surprised he had been so tense. Pragmatic command sometimes demands you sidestep book answers, and getting the job done is not always an acceptable defense. He stifled a yawn, blinked his eyes, and snapped to attention at the general's next words.

"I have been looking for a man with peculiar qualifications. You were mentioned by Command and General Staff school. The people at War College had your name at the top of their list. How did you wangle your way into War College, Ravenshaw?"

"Well, sir—" It was an involved story, beginning with an ambassador's wife and a schnauzer dog.

"I'll hear it later. Your schedule is already tight. The job I have in mind is experimental, highly discretionary, and will establish its own parameters . . . do you understand that term?"

"Form, but not function. It has no precise meaning outside mathematics, but makes an elegant noise."

"Be that as it may. The job is anomalous, and the man will make it. Are you interested?" Before Ravenshaw could more than nod, the general added. "Ostensibly you would be a civilian. In fact, you would be on detached duty from here. And while the cover requires pro-rata payments from—never mind who—unvouchered funds are involved." He pushed his glasses back on his head. "It will take a year to decide if I'm sucking wind or gin tonic. Ravenshaw, it is now 2:30. You will report as a civilian at 5:30 at my home in New Glatz, Maryland, for a situational estimate of your character. Today is Friday and you will stay the weekend as my guest. An informal house-party situation. Questions?"

"Does the job have a name, sir?"

"Get it and you can name it. Other questions?"

"Yes, sir," said Ravenshaw in a state of mild euphoria, "can you provide a native guide to get me out of here?"

Arleigh Ravenshaw had goods, clothing, gear, and equipment in Vietnam; in Evanston, Illinois, where his brother lived; in St. George, Utah, where he had inherited an old yellow waterstone house from his dead wife; and at the hill ranch near Tassafaranda, California, where he had grown up. He had some tropical sport clothing in his bags at Andrews Air Force Base, but it was more suitable for Hong Kong, or Singapore, than Washington in late September. The pool driver assigned him for the afternoon was familiar only with the main trails of the urban jungle, so Ravenshaw put him in a parking lot and found a bank just before closing time, and a car rental agency and a clothing store by himself. He stopped at a florist and a remarkably good fancy-food store. He had the driver lead him to Andrews, where he picked up his luggage and appropriated a bathroom at a BOQ. He parked his rental behind the guide-dog pool car in front of the general's converted farmhouse in New Glatz at 5:25, dismissed the driver, and walked up the winding brick path to the door.

The general's wife answered his knock, a lean woman with calm black eyes, short gray curls and a deep chuckling laugh. She was pleased with the chrysanthemums and not too surprised by the casaba and the grapes. Ravenshaw tentatively pegged her as a domesticated she-wolf, and his regard for the general went up another notch. It was just as well his taste ran in that direction, because the other guests were very hard types indeed.

There was an unfashionably fluffy woman named Rosely Dool who bubbled at him and asked loaded questions with a giggle. Her husband, Brinton Dool, had long sideburns to compensate for a balding head. He was happily vague, loosely avant-garde, and his conversation tended to shamble off into unfinished sentences. Aird Dowker was given to pedantic statements, a short man with a brushy moustache parted in the middle. His wife Retta was languishing and sexy in a knit dress and tended to rub against Ravenshaw.

The single woman was Nell Rowley. She had palomino hair and wore a horse-blanket suit to match.

"Do you feel like the new boy at school?" she asked.

"It works both ways," said Ravenshaw. "You are the new fellas at my school. Mark down overweening egocentricity."

Her voice was lovely, light and sweet. "I have a feeling you have been here before."

"Deja vu? No-o, it's just that I enjoy tests, especially when I have inside information."

"You do?"

"The unexamined life is dull," he paraphrased, "and there's nothing more fun than explaining yourself to others. Also, there was that first-class book after World War II on situational testing by the OSS. I enjoyed it."

She was carefully neutral. "You have the job sewed up?"

"Oh, no." He was a little dizzy under the direct inspection of her frost-violet eyes. "You know what you're after and I don't. I can only be myself, and you have a job to do. This is all first cabin, high level, very flattering." He wondered if the dizziness was circadian rhythm desynchronization, or one of the body's wonderful warning systems when faced by a formidable woman.

"Suppose you don't meet the requirements?"

"Me get my feelings hurt? Huh-uh. They are your requirements."

She stared into her glass. "Detachment is a rare characteristic," she murmured. "And an unlovely one to most people." He made no comment. "Isn't it?"

"I don't know," he said cheerfully. "May I get you another drink?"

"That should be my line, Colonel. Aren't I supposed to ply you with liquor to loosen your tongue? Yes, I'd like another. Do you have an answer to every question?"

"Yes." Ravenshaw grinned. "I don't know."

"And if you need to know?" she pressed him.

"I am a Rikki-tikki-tavi man. 'Run and Find Out' is the motto tattooed on my heart."

While the general busied himself with a martini for Nell Rowley—he mixed a very proper five-to-one with Gilbey's and Noilly Prat—Ravenshaw poured his own pale scotch and water. Brinton Dool asked him, "Ah-Colonel, you've been in the mysterious East for some time, and I-ah wonder if you have seen much inexplicable phenomena—"

"Yes, I have, Mr. Dool. Chiefly in the area of human muddleheadedness. I sometimes feel that philosophy should teach each man to take out his heart and look it in the face."

"We all observe our own phenomena," said Dool, surprised into decisiveness by the direct challenge. "I-ah was thinking more in terms of flying-ah saucers—" he reverted.

"No saucers," said Ravenshaw, "but noctilucent clouds, if they fit into your category." Dool was puzzled. "There's no good explanation I know for a luminous cloud in the dead of night. They come in neon blue and hot pink and green and other colors. Those I've seen are lenticular. They go away after a while."

"Anything else along that line?" said the general, pronging three olives on a toothpick.

"Spots of light. sir. Not spots in front of my eyes, but pinpoints of intense fire hanging in the air. They usually vanish with a snap."

"Hallucinations-ah?"

"I've seen them four times and twice the 'hallucinations' were seen by others. They fit my book of inexplicable phenomena."

"Other entries?" asked the general.

"Quite a few, sir. Rhabdomancy is one." They were puzzled. "Witching, dowsing, divining."

Dool looked dismayed. "You don't mean to say you believe—"

Ravenshaw shrugged. "I don't say I can find water or gold with a dowsing stick. For all I know there are little green men with wood magnets upside down in a hollow earth. The stick goes down beyond my control. It's impossible to fake it, and the experiment repeats. This is of first importance."

"But to believe in-ah—"

"Belief is a non sequitur, Mr. Dool, in observed evidence. You have surely considered that an atheist is the truest kind of believer. Excuse me." He returned to Nell Rowley and found her talking with Aird Dowker.

" . . . cycle of revolution," Dowker said, stroking his moustache.

"What do you think of Jefferson's comment that there should be a revolution every generation?" asked Nell.

Ravenshaw was stabbed again by the honey and quinine quality of her voice. "Well, if you leave violence out of the difinition, we've been revolving like a bowling ball for a hundred years."

"I was speaking of the real thing," siad Dowker.

"You drive a real automobile and watch real TV."

"Teapot tempests!"

"You have been right, to a degree. Tempests are on the surface. We were locked into the human form, and forty-foot waves on an ocean a thousand feet deep have been stimulating only, no matter how obsessed the participants." He turned to Nell. "Mark down tendency to pontificate."

"What do you mean, I have been right?"

"There are depth bombs in the ocean. Molecular biologists may soon force us to consider mankind in a personal, hitherto inviolable area—what is optimum man? And by whose standards? And can a Model T breed a Thunderbird?"

"You are talking nonsense," said Dowker.

"What is your answer?" asked Nell. "Not that I'm sure I understand the question."

Ravenshaw was suddenly weary. "Heigh-ho, and alas and also lack-a-day." He wondered where his ka was now. Over Kansas? "The more I know the more I am overwhelmed by my own ignorance."

"Supper," announced Mrs. Craddock.

Nell Rowley spilled half a glass of burgundy on him and Retta Dowker developed roving hands under the tablecolth. Ravenshaw passed her the gravy boat high and suggestively. She glanced at the décolleté of her dress and desisted. After dinner Brinton Dool mounted a dove of peace and zoomed around the room, Aird Dowker drank bourbon and ginger ale and accused Ravenshaw of making passes at his wife, and Nell Rowley shrieked and told him to take his hand off her knee.

Ravenshaw laughed helplessly.

Mrs. Craddock regrouped and reorganized the party in a military manner, and the general watched with only an occasional twitch to his lips.

On Saturday Ravenshaw helped the general dig a stump out of the back yard, solemnly observed the four grandchildren who had come visiting, and took the Craddocks to dinner at a French restaurant on Pennsylvania Avenue. There was more yard work on Sunday and that evening the Dools and Dowkers and Craddocks and Nell and Ravenshaw all ate crab and drank beer at Jimmy's. They returned to New Glatz to sit for an hour's idle conversation before the party broke up. The general asked Ravenshaw to join him in a nightcap before the dying fire.

"Ravenshaw, I've got facts up to the ears on a tall giraffe, and Gresham's law was never better illustrated than by computer use for decision making. The cheaper drives out the dearer—silver vanished when the sandwich coins came out—and there's this abysmal inclination to shift command responsibility to a computer. Do you know what I'm talking about?"

"The read-out's no better than the in-put. The book can kill you."

The general nodded. "I want to tap an area of information that has never been properly examined, and I want judicious opinion, not a garbage scow full of facts." A log broke and scattered sparks on the hearth. "I don't suppose the fate of nations hangs on our talk tonight, but I have this nagging hunch we'd better explore the wild blue yonder country. It's an easy job in a way, like walking on an edge-up two-by-four—in the dark, with a flashlight, over the Grand Canyon. My tame psychologists and I agree. You get the job."

"Exactly what is it?"

The general told him, and the fire was ashes and dawn was red before they covered some of the possibilities.

Six months later Ravenshaw opened the door of WBY, Inc., in San Diego, California, at nine o'clock in the morning. Nell Rowley was beating the typewriter at her desk. She was wearing an abominable orange-and-blue plaid dress, which at best was some relief from the corridor outside. It was lined with gray marble, suitable for a necropolis, or an austere kind of hell.

"Good morning, Nell."

"Don't bet on it. You have an old lady in tennis shoes, a bushy-tailed college type, a sneaky-pete, a salesman, and a miner-forty-niner tra-la-la-la Clementine. He phoned." She raised her voice over her drumfire typing. It was another of her disconcerting abilities. "Mail's on your desk and dull as Monday morning."

While he read the mail and indicated answers on the letters for Nell's guidance in his quick engineer's printing, Ravenshaw noted again without prejudice his ability to think the worst of people with no difficulty at all.

Nell Rowley disturbed him. They had flown together around the United States for five weeks, visiting the sixteen companies—Lugard, Rodman-Codman Associates, Havesu Foundry, Rubideaux, Simon Photomultipliers, Lyne Jolley and all the others—and not once had she failed to be anything but the perfect secretary. Her hair was never quite tidy and her taste in clothes was remarkable, but she took notes and kept a business journal, made reservations, never complained, and was always efficient. This bothered Ravenshaw, that a behavioral psychologist of better than fair reputation was quite willing to compromise her professional status to further a project that might never achieve its prime objective.

He was standing at the window, scowling at Broadway and the panorama of San Diego Bay, when Nell tapped at the door and said Mrs. Addison Cutleigh was waiting.

Mrs. Cutleigh wore elegant English walkers, but her stockings were lisle, her dress was cut from a gunnysack, and her hat had colored bangles that tinkled frivolously. Her interest in life was pelagoniums and the reform of the Republican Party, which she regarded as crypto-communist. She wanted assurance that her mothod of ending the war would not fall into the hands of the Bolsheviks.

"This office is a clearing house for ideas," said Ravenshaw. "Wide Blue Yonder, Incorporated is a joint venture of sixteen small patriotic corporations, who believe that the inspiration and invention of the people of the United States is too often latent for lack of an outlet. We do not charge for the service. We channel your idea to the interested sponsor, or to the appropriate governmental agency. If your suggestion is technical in nature, I must ask you to sign a release before you divulge it."

Mrs. Cutleigh nodded bird-bright approval, glanced around the room for lurking Chinese or Russian agents, and hissed, "Poison oak. Upas apples. Cockleburrs. Dodder. Deadly nightshade!"

It took another twenty minutes to get her out of the office, but she left with a good deal of satisfaction after Ravenshaw produced a Bible and swore her to secrecy.

Nell announced that Jay Hardinge was waiting and asked what was on the old lady's mind. He told her it was another scheme to drop noxious weed seed on North Vietnam and to be sure Mrs. Cutleigh got an extremely official letter of commendation. Someday he might need an expert in pelagoniums or crypto-communist Republicans.

Jay Hardinge had done his Master's at UCSD in geography and thought it deserved more attention than would be given by the eight people who read the average thesis. It was a method of three-dimensional cartography, and was an obvious and unexploited technique to the best of Ravenshaw's knowledge. He asked the young man what he expected in return. Hardinge said it would be nice to have some jobs to choose from. Ravenshaw set up an appointment ten days hence, dictated six letters to Nell, and felt so good about Jay Hardinge that he gave some very kind advice to the noon appointment, the man Nell called the sneaky-pete.

His name was John Smith and he wanted to sell an industrial process belonging to his employer. He did not seem to realize that his particular industry was a small world and his education and experience made it necessary for him to live in it. Ravenshaw pointed out he was cutting his throat behind his back, but the man left unconvinced. Ravenshaw called Sam O'Fuoco, who ran the newsstand in the lobby of the building, and Sam obliged by getting John Smith's license number. When Nell came back from lunch, Ravenshaw left her to check the license and see that proper notation was sent to a sensitive file. Smith's employer was not notified. WBY did not police business morality. Returning from lunch, Nell told him the driver's description did not tally with the owner of the plates, but a friend had a friend and identity had been established. The funny thing was that sneaky-pete's name was John Smith.

"You are the apple of my ojo," said Ravenshaw. "You are the flower of my heart."

"Mr. Polkinghorn is here," she said in her bitter honey voice.

Joe Polkinghorn was that rarity, a salesman who knew what he was talking about. Ravenshaw learned about paper traffic flow, ingenious carbons and flimsies and filing methods. Polkinghorn suggested that the best information was only as good as the use to which it was put, and information entombed was as useful as a file of nuts forgotten by a squirrel. Ravenshaw agreed that most solutions were peripheral, like building schools instead of teachers, and sent him out to see if Nell was interested.

His second phone buzzed, the direct outside line. General Craddock was on the wire. "Why do you want the confidential file?"

"She's too perfect. I don't believe it."

"You've got a hunch? What do you want to know?"

"Start with date of birth, parents, brothers and sisters, Sunday School classmates, everything."

"No can do," said Craddock. "You'll get the file by courier this afternoon at your apartment, but the first five or six years of her life are blank. I don't know who her parents are, and neither does she."

Nell said, "Mr. Joruve is here." Ravenshaw held up his hand with the fingers apart and she nodded and closed the door.

"The record starts on April 16, 1947. Total anterograde amnesia. Couldn't talk, couldn't dress herself, total retrogression. Worked on her for a year at Houston. Ward of the state. Nothing ever found out about her. Probably the whole family was wiped out. The figures are imprecise—about five hundred fifty killed."

"You lost me on the first curve."

"The Texas City explosion and fire. They found her crawling along a gutter near the waterfront with most of her hair burned off, mewing like a kitten."

"Be damned."

"So that's that. I talked with Ed Millison yesterday in New York. He's very enthusiastic about the rolamite application you sent Lugard. Have you turned up anything for me?"

"Negative."

The general sighed three thousand miles away. "Don't take any wooden dimes—inflation," he said and hung up.

Nell announced, "Mr. Charles Joruve." He was a small boney man in his early seventies with a walloping beak of a nose. He had a black felt hat in his hand and a shopping bag in the crook of his arm. One bright blue eye was slightly cocked.

"Paper said you were honest and would listen to anything. That right?"

Ravenshaw grinned and said he was only reasonably honest, but he always did what he said he would do. Honesty is intention, but his word was his word.

"Fair enough. Now tell me, how does this place work?"

Ravenshaw explained that WBY was supported by companies whose research and development funds were limited. The office cost was shared pro rata, with a percentage assessment against originated ideas up to twenty-five percent of the base expense. He mentioned the machine that crawled upstairs with a refrigerator—for instance—on its back.

"What do you get out of this?" asked Joruve with bluejay curiosity.

"Wages, a chance to try my judgment, and a very small percentage of successful developments."

"Shrewd. I guess you're my man," said Joruve. "I want to get a jeep out of this thing, but I don't suppose I will. What I don't want to get is tooken. Maybe what I really need is advice." He reached into the paper bag and lifted out a black box. "What do you think?"

A black boxer walked into the office about twice a month. Ravenshaw had come to regard them as a side benefit, an unearned increment, a keep-the-spirit-of-Christmas-in-your-heart sort of lagniappe to his job. One man walked in with a cosmic ray to 110-120AC black box complete with a socket on the side. He wanted ten thousand dollars in small bills laid in his hand for a demonstration. Unlimited free power, he said. Ravenshaw called in Nell and told her to get the money and a three-way plug.

More in sorrow than anger, the man put his box back into the case, locked it, chained it to his wrist and left, shaking his head sadly at scoffers.

A pathetic black boxer had made a money machine from which he cranked a worn five dollar bill. He excused himself to the washroom before he could insert another piece of paper and crank out the same bill. There were others, but Ravenshaw especially liked the one who had worn overalls and a straw hat. He put boll cotton into his black box, pushed a button so lights flashed and gears growled, and dramatically pulled out a pillowcase. With development money, he would make a box large enough to manufacture sheets. To Ravenshaw's vast pleasure, he had a little drawer at the bottom from which he removed the cleaned cotton seed.

Ravenshaw admired the black boxers' ingenuity and beguiling sense of wonder. They reinforced his faith in the innocent, indomitable spirit of man. He was a little surprised by Joruve's black box, because the buildup was far from typical. "Cosmic rays to electricity?" he asked.

"Don't know," said Joruve, "I found it making a molino de dios, but other things sure happen." He set the box on a corner of the desk and twiddled with the side.

Until this moment it had been an ordinary day for Ravenshaw. He had finally phoned Washington about Nell Rowley, he had lunch with Fabio Marquien, a sharpshooter who worked both sides of the border, and his customers had been run-of-the-mill customers. There was nothing unusual about Joruve.

This black box was a different horse. An atavistic shudder raised the hair on the back of his head. The box was wider than it should have been wide. The handle was offset to one end. It was traditionally black—and seamless—but the finish was deep, and concentrated light to a single black-green shimmer at one end of the rounded edge. Ravenshaw stood slowly to change his angle of vision, and where the Jo-block smooth top would normally have reflected a sheen of light from the window, it was concentrated into a crawling green shimmer. The handle rose from a shallow indentation. Ravenshaw gingerly touched it with a finger and it retracted into the hollow, leaving a flat surface.

"Hey, now," said Joruve, "feel this."

There was a surge of arctic air from an opening at the end of the box, as if a window had been left unclosed on top of Greenland's icy mountains. It was not like a man whistling, but a turbulent flow, as if a frost giant was endlessly exhaling.

"How about that," said Joruve.

"Cold," said Ravenshaw. He pushed the handle down.

Joruve fumbled at the side of the box and the orifice instantly blew hot air. "Is that all the hotter?" said Ravenshaw absently.

Joruve stuck out his lower lip and twiddled again. A wind from a blast furnace filled the room. Joruve raised his eyebrows and winked his cocked eye. Ravenshaw lifted his hands waist high and shrugged. He had all the moves of a broken-field used-car salesman. Joruve snorted and turned off the furnace blast. He took a pair of steel-rimmed spectacles from his pocket.

"All right, all right," he said and peered closely at the side. "Now, lessee. I never fooled with this thing before—" He turned the box on the desk, the business end toward Ravenshaw. "Now. Maybe something will happen."

What happened was a solid bar of water. It hit Ravenshaw hip high and spun him like a dervish over the chair and off the files into a corner of the room. The firehose stream smashed against the wall and filled the air with water, fog, mist and gouts of spray. Joruve started toward him, was caught in the water and tumbled like a bug in a mixmaster. Niagara Falls thundered. Suddenly the flow shut off.

"Arleigh Ravenshaw, what are you *doing?*"

Water ran off the desk, dripped from the ceiling and sparkled on the windows. The carpet was sodden and so was Ravenshaw. He squelched as he walked to Nell Rowley and the box. "Crazy thing hasn't moved," he said in the dripping silence. "Takes two firemen to hold a blast like that." He squeegeed his face and head with both hands. "What happened to the opposite and equal reaction?"

Nell said, "I don't know. Never saw it. You had it last." She was thoroughly wet and the plaid dress looked much better clinging to her body.

"Did you turn the thing off?" He patted the box. The handle went flat and a trickle ran down the side. She raised her eyebrows. He dismissed the problem.

"Phone down and hold me a taxi. Call Hardy for a cleanup squad, get a cashier's check from the bank made out to Charles Joruve for five thousand dollars, type a release for his signature, bring both to my apartment. Questions?" This was Colonel Ravenshaw in command. Nell wheeled and went to her desk while he plucked Joruve out of the corner—he was feebly stirring—and marched him like a rubber-legged doll into the waiting room.

"How do I explain all that?" asked Nell.

He leaned Joruve against a wall and returned to his desk. He opened a bottom drawer and pulled out a sample campfire starter a happy pyromaniac had invented and brought to him a month before. He pulled the tab and it blazed a tongue of fire and sparks three feet long. He held it to the sprinkler head in the ceiling. The metal melted and a heavy rain started, twenty gallons a minute.

"Damn carelessness." He wrapped the black box in his coat, set the soggy black hat on Joruve's head, and steered the old man out the door while Nell phoned Building Maintenance to turn off the sprinkler.

Sitting in the desert at four o'clock in the morning, up to his arms in a sleeping bag, Ravenshaw reviewed his assumptions. With a great deal of effort he had got himself to his present position on the side of a rocky hill. Far across the badlands and beyond the dry lake a truck was heading east, its lights brave and lonely in the dark night. The moon had set an hour before. There was a dim halation over Superstition Mountain from the Imperial valley towns.

The black box should be in Washington by now.

The courier who delivered the confidential file on Nell Rowley seemed to be an imperturbable young man, but his eyes narrowed when General Craddock told him on the phone to report to Lindbergh Field within twenty minutes to catch an Air Force interceptor. He hefted the suitcase into which Ravenshaw had packed the black box between two pillows. "Hot as a three-dollar pistol," he estimated, and checked the aluminum-frame .32 he kept in a chamois-lined front pocket and the .38 from a clamshell at his belt.

Craddock said to Ravenshaw, "You better take Nell for liaison. I will have two unflappable men in Borrego by noon tomorrow. Nell can guide them to your stakeout. How is Mr. Joruve?"

"He's sitting in a chair wrapped in a blanket with a tumbler of Cutty Sark in his hand. He says he likes Haig better. When I leased this place, I never figured I'd use the dryer, but everything he owns is tumbling around in it now, except his hat."

"Is he—safe?"

"He was a kid sharpshooter with a star-gauged Springfield in World War I. He was with the Seabees in the Second. He's got a motto tattooed on his heart, 'My Country Right or Wrong, My Mother Drunk or Sober.' "

"Where did he find the thing? Are there more?"

"Sir, I think it's rare as a dollar bill with an eagle egg instead of an eye on top of the pyramid. He says he found it squirting dust in the Santa Rosa foothills, right on top of the ground."

"What was he doing there?"

"I asked that question." Ravenshaw took a deep breath. "He's been a prospector a long time. For a vacation he goes Peg-leg Smithing. Peg-leg was the fellow who brought in gold nuggets covered with black varnish. His real name was Thomas L. Smith of Garard County, Kentucky. Joruve figured that Peg-leg wouldn't go anywhere a horse or mule couldn't go, and—"

"Garbage scow full of facts." Ravenshaw could hear the tapping of eyeglass earpieces on the desk. "I suppose you'll tell me next what his leg was made of."

"Juniper, sir." There was a growling noise that could have been atmospherics. "The gold was covered with sulphur dioxide and there's some speculation it was radioactive." The tapping slowed ominously. "There's a story of an Indian woman from Warner Springs who found similar nuggets at a location where she could see the smoke from an SP locomotive taking on water at Salton, before the tracks and the station were covered by the Salton Sea."

"Gigo! Computer people tell me Garbage In, Garbage Out. Ravenshaw, you rationalize these facts. Good-bye."

A cold, soft wind was beginning to blow, and Ravenshaw was pleased with his foresight in buying the sleeping bags. Nell Rowley say beside him. Charlie Joruve was in a sandy patch behind a large boulder. He was a quiet sleeper. Ravenshaw had heard only a few muted snores before the old man turned and was quiet again.

The rest of yesterday evening was blurred by incident. When Nell arrived, it developed that she had no suitable outdoor clothing. When Joruve was dry outside—though wet within—they went to a shopping center, where Nell bought boots and pants and sweaters and a windbreaker, in colors that made Ravenshaw wince. He bought sleeping bags, some nylon line, bar chocolate and a couple of thermos bottles. Joruve wanted to buy everyone a drink and he did when they met with their purchases at a restaurant. The old man was exhilarated by the lights and the music and the opulent display of goods in the crystal windows as they walked through the arcades to Ravenshaw's car after dinner. He even did a few dance steps with Nell on the swirl-patterned terrazzo walk. She was burning with a hard, gemlike flame and her bitter honey voice was plangent—Ravenshaw thought those terms were suitable only to turn-of-the-century novelists, but they swam to the top of his mind like great gawping carp when he tried to put his finger on her manner that evening.

The traffic diminished as they left the freeway to twist and climb through the rock-boned hills of San Diego County. The roads grew more lonely and there was almost no traffic by the time they wound down and down to Borrego on the eastern slope of the mountains. Ravenshaw had the thermos bottles filled with coffee at a drowsy restaurant about to close for the night. He parked under a Security light at the county airport. He rerolled and tied the sleeping bags with their own cords to horse-collar packs, and transferred the gear to Joruve's old Ford, dusty and battered, but with wide tires and good clearance for rough country travel.

The moon was low and black shadows engulfed them when Joruve turned off the road up a nameless wash, and began to pick a way over the sandy gravel around boulders and through the sparse brush. "Hang on," he said as the car lurched over a section of random cobbles. "Been meaning to ask. What's the hurry?"

"Johnny at the rat hole," said Ravenshaw, bracing Nell as they crawled along a slab of rock with a 30° tilt to the side. "Go where the action is. The first principle in fishing is finding water."

"Simple Simon." Nell pushed her hair back into place. "You are an exponent of the obvious, Mr. Ravenshaw."

"Damn right," said Joruve, unexpectedly. "The obvious is what's tricky. The obvious is what snaps at your um . . . heels when you're not looking. Why, I remember—" he interrupted himself. "Here's what we've been looking for. End of the line, gang. We walk from here." He turned the car into a sidewall, backed around and parked heading down the arroyo.

Ravenshaw nodded. "Exit pursued by a bear," he said and wondered if some ursine alien had lost the black box. Joruve led the way up a fall of rock and along the side of a hill. He warned them against cat's claw and cholla cactus, pointed out a clump of Spanish bayonet, and told them to regard all vegetation as a lovesick porcupine until proven innocent.

Something moved. Nell gasped. Ravenshaw ran to her side and stumbled on a rock. When you find an artifact, like a Folsom or Sandia point, you do not expect the owner to stick his head around a bush. Ravenshaw leaped to his feet in front of Nell and turned on his flashlight. The movement was from a bread wrapper caught against a bush, quiet now that a breath of wind had stopped.

A rock dike ran across the open end of the horseshoe flat. Joruve led them to a clump of beaver-tail cactus by which he had found the black box. They searched the area enclosed by rocky hills and then climbed one of the horseshoe heels and had a cup of coffee before they settled down in their sleeping bags for the rest of the night. Ravenshaw could not sleep. The bread wrapper had set up a noise somewhere in his mind like fingernails running down a slate blackboard.

The black box was not a product of any technology he knew. It was an alien artifact. If saucer men had left it here, were they real men, or were they wearing the skins of men as Aztec priests did? He turned to the more cheerful consideration that the box had been manufactured by extramundane octopi or giant spiders. It was made to be used by something with delicate manual control—hands, feelers, tentacles?

Alien to what? To now, to this time and place. It might be a leftover Lemurian product, or an artifact from Mu or Atlantis washed out of the cobble matrix by winter rains. So why was it raising a dust devil?

Or perhaps a fellow on a bicycle had dropped it—Mr. Wells's time machine bicycle, of course. Ravenshaw tried to imagine a short randy man in a high collar and a Norfolk jacket pedaling over the weary years to this howling wilderness. He shifted his weight on the hard rock and the hank of nylon bit into his hip. He moved again. He assured himself wryly, as he had in the past, something will happen.

According to the Arabs, day separates from night when you can distinguish between a black horse hair and a white laid on the palm of your hand, but Nell Rowley was a palomino and the stars were gone before the light showed the color of her hair. As usual, it was untidy. She said, "I made a list of your appointments and called a Kelly Girl to cancel them. She'll be in the office today to baby-sit the telephone. I left the key with Sam O'Fuoco."

"You are the sun of my days," said Ravenshaw. He wondered fleetingly why he translated compliments to Nell directly from a foreign tongue. "Would you rather go to Borrego now or later? You could grab breakfast and a motel and a nap before noon."

"I'll stay if there's more coffee. Are there snakes?" She warmed her hands on the cup. "It's been bothering me."

"Yes, but it's too cold for them." The sky was bright now, and he could have seen the frost-violet of her eyes over the rim of the plastic cup, but he was wondering if instead of giant spiders, the owners of the black box were—maybe—giant snakes with hands.

Charlie Joruve said he was not interested in a chocolate bar for breafast or any other time, and he and Ravenshaw carried the sleeping bags and empty thermos bottles to the car, leaving Nell on watch. She sat between two boulders in the early sun, still with the curious alertness, the waiting tension Ravenshaw had noted the night before.

Back at the horseshoe flat, with Joruve scheduled to return at about eleven, all Ravenshaw's apprehensions of the past night seemed foolish. Nell was preoccupied as she slowly combed her hair, and he walked the enclosure again and climbed the other heel to inspect a magnificent chartreuse blossom on a cholla cactus. The ocotillo were exclamations of burning orange-red bloom. He was attracted to a desert lily and then noticed a patch of bellyflowers. He was on his stomach behind a creosote bush when he heard a hissing noise like a carbon arc light on a dead-still summer night. He raised his head. It was a serious noise, as the buzz of a rattlesnake is serious, and it stopped short with a pop.

Tilted to a near right angle at Nell's side of the horseshoe was a room without walls. A man was sitting in a chair behind a panel of instruments arranged like the keyboard of a Wurlitzer organ, and to his side stood a child with a black eye holding a tray. They were oriented to the floor on which they stood and showed no surprise to find themselves almost horizontal to the sand below them. There were tall cabinets of alternating orange and plum color at the rear of the room nearest the ground. There were improbably shaped masses as foreign to Ravenshaw's eye as a Volkswagen would have been to Charles Duryea. The child held out the tray to the man. He raised the container to his lips while he studied the instrument console. The whole room was drifting toward Ravenshaw.

The man turned, spat on the floor, and threw the contents of the glass at the child. It was a red liquid that splashed and ran down the invisible wall to the floor. It ran to the south from Ravenshaw's viewpoint and he felt a moment of vertigo. There was no sound as the man opened his mouth and cursed. The child stood stolidly on one foot with the instep of the other pressed against her knee. The man glanced at the ground and touched a control tab on the console. The entire room was less than fifty feet from Ravenshaw when it turned blue-gray and disappeared in a small clap of thunder.

Ravenshaw began to breathe again and looked at a bellyflower in front of his nose. It had four petals shading from purple to pink to white in the center. It was about as large as a sixteen-penny nail head. He had an idea that the shape and colors were indelibly printed on his mind.

What happened to Nell?

She was weeping bitterly between the two rocks, her body shaken by great wracking sobs. He dropped to his knees before her, gulping air. A desk-jockey job is not the best training for the hundred-yard dash through soft sand.

"Did you see them?" she wailed. "The girl and the Drishna. They're gone and they left me here. Why didn't you stop them?" The ice princess had melted in bitter hot tears. She snatched the handkerchief he held out and ripped it in two. "Keep your cool! Keep your cool," she said. "I'll tell you this, detachment is denial and denial is death! Why didn't you stop them?"

"What were those little sparkles of fire on the walls?"

"They're gone and I am desolate—get your hand off my shoulder, you gibbering cucumber! I am lost and wretched—go away!"

"Girl?" The child had been dressed in silk sacking with a loose blouse, tight sleeves, and baggy pants. The material was apricot color with shifting poisonous blue flashes wherever it folded. The man was wearing a smooth dove-gray fabric, a wide, thick fuchsia belt, fuchsia piping from ankles to wrists, and a high, thick, fuchsia collar. "Drishna?"

Nell was not listening. She was taut with some internal argumentation. She did not see him. Ravenshaw sighed and stood up. He walked to the area where the tilted room had appeared. It was warm in the morning sun and the first midges of the year swarmed in the quiet air. He waved his hand in front of his face. Joruve called this the Borrego salute and said that strangers thought it the friendliest place in the world, in season. The Salton Sea was a line of blue under the Chocolate mountains.

Nell came up behind him. "Arleigh, I'm sorry. I don't know what got into me. I am altogether mixed up. I am a pig."

"It makes no never mind."

"My head split when I saw that room. Somewhere and sometime I have been here before—galloping on the back of a nightmare—and the girl and that monster are familiar to me as my face in a mirror—and the loneliness—and the rocks on my knees—"

"It is not to worry, querida," said Ravenshaw softly. He lifted his head.

She went on in her honey voice, "Children—especially orphans—often dream they were kidnapped, and their true and loving parents are the King and his consort of Cockaigne—"

"Back to the rocks!" said Ravenshaw. The buzz had begun again.

The carbon arc noise grew louder as they ran and the absurd "pop" followed more quickly than before. They turned and there was the room on an even keel. The man was in rich red clothing with dull green piping and belt and collar, and the girl wore an acid yellow garment. The man nodded to them. He punched a tab on the Wurlitzer.

The random flashes of gnats intersecting the walls stopped when the room settled to the ground. A rectangular section became even more transparent. The man stepped to the sand. He was a young Roman emperor, sleek and a little corpulent, his dark hair a cap of curls. His eyes were at once lazy and feral, like those of a well-fed lion blinking at a flock of sheep.

"Ullo-ullo-ullo," he said. "You've already stolen the nesial node interphaser. Well enough. It brought you here. Fair exchange is no thievery. Abandon that expression of insolent ignorance. Answer my question. Where is the iodine?"

Ravenshaw gawped. He had opened his mouth to say good morning, and glanced at Nell. She was standing on one leg with the other foot pressed against the inside of her knee.

"Popocatepetl istaccihuatl xochimilco?"

"Duh? Whad you say?" Ravenshaw gulped.

"Albionese. Well enough, churd. I don't care for Nahuatl either. Uto-Aztecans are greedy buggers. Where's the iodine on this rotten shim world? I need two puncheons of it."

"Wha-wha—"

"Save me," said the man, lifting his eyes to heaven. He spoke with exaggerated care, as to a retarded child, "Number 53, churd, orthorhombic crystal structure, violet vapor, extracted from seaweed, brines, and the caliche of that preposterous desert at the end of the southern continent." The amber eyes grew sharper. "Don't try my patience, churd. You're wearing a time mensuration device on your wrist, your clothing is mass produced, your bitch is Mier which passes understanding, you're a contumacious quark, and my patience wears thin. There was no orthoentric alarm, so your contingency's not travelers. Iodine, churd?"

"From Chile," said Ravenshaw jerkily. "In ships to the gulf coast. Chief port of entry across from Galveston. Calcium nitrate. Ships full of it. Caliche." Nell was still standing on one leg with a blank expression on her face.

The man spoke in a language unknown to Ravenshaw, and the girl in the room took her foot from her knee and brought a large flat box to the man. She knelt before him. He tapped it and beckoned to Ravenshaw. It was a relief map with no political designations. Ravenshaw put his finger on Galveston Bay and the man tapped the box again. The scale changed and Ravenshaw indicated the mainland coast to the west. The man waved Ravenshaw back and turned two dials until a spot of light was exactly where Ravenshaw had pointed. The man touched a plate to one side of the map and coordinates appeared. A plate on the other side burned red and then green as he made another adjustment. Elevation? Ravenshaw wondered. The girl carried the box back to the room and locked it into the console.

The man spoke again and she walked to one of the plum-colored cabinets. She glanced furtively over her shoulder at Nell and fumbled with the handle of the device she took from the cabinet. Then she brought it to the man and stood behind him to one side.

"The Mier are intractable, recalcitrant, and rare," observed the man, polishing his nails on his sleeve. "Training them from anarchy to obedience is a burden. Only recently I discovered this girl with her hands in the machinery—and she will not learn easily to properly prepare a drink." He held his fingernails up to admire them. "Yours seems well trained. Perhaps, as with elephants, they work better in pairs." He looked Ravenshaw in the eye. "I'll take your Mier."

Ravenshaw pushed Nell and she toppled like a tree. The Roman emperor watched her fall. Ravenshaw did not. He stooped and hurled a jagged, baseball-size rock. It should have caught the man in the throat. Ravenshaw was sure of this because it slowed and stopped there before it fell to the ground. If the last foot of travel had been made of invisible foam rubber, the result would have been the same.

The man laughed and shot Ravenshaw. Then he shot Nell.

It was a humane weapon, Ravenshaw thought in confusion, like those traps to catch birds or animals harmlessly. As a boy he had known a neighbor who deplored the use of firearms. The fellow was highly moral about it. Shoot innocent creatures? Horrible! Ravenshaw was no less confused when he passed the neighbor's farm one day and found the tender heart, having caught a ground squirrel harmlessly, beating it to death with a baseball bat.

The involuntary muscles were not affected, but he had lost control over his body. He continued breathing and his heart must be going, but he was selectively short-circuited. As his thoughts unmuddled, he found his eyes were open and his ears plugged in. He did not worry about a baseball bat, because he did not think the alien carried one with him. He did worry about elapsed time—enough events for a whole day had been jammed into a few minutes—but when he saw the girl bring a glass of the red liquid to the man and take the weapon from him, Ravenshaw concluded he had been only momentarily unconscious.

"You . . . will . . . speak . . . Albionese," said the man slowly. The girl said nothing. He slapped her face with an open hand. She staggered and stood straight again.

"You . . . will . . . speak . . . nothing . . . else . . . until . . . you . . . learn." With a quick blow he slapped the other side of her face. She fell this time. Ravenshaw tried to speak. He tried to move his fingers. He could wiggle his right toes but not his left—and flex his foot—and knee and thigh. So now he could roll over onto his stomach. What for?

The man turned to Ravenshaw and nudged him in the ribs with a foot. "Desynchronizer, churd, for an overweening aborigine. Considering your gross bulk, a full charge should give you two days in which to meditate on courtesy. You may not die. The little ants will keep you amused as you lie there"—he poured the last of his sweet drink on Ravenshaw's face—"and afterward the buzzards. While I am educating your Mier, your last sight will be of a buzzard's beak. They go for the eyes first, I understand. Then the other soft parts. Next the ants and dehydration. Oh, well, keep hope alive in your heart. You may die, churd." He stepped away and said to the girl, "Drag . . . that . . . Mier . . . by . . . the . . . arm—"

Ravenshaw flexed his knee, pushed himself over onto his stomach and flailed out with his leg. He caught the man in the ankles and ripped his feet out from under him. He did a bellyflop onto the sand. Ravenshaw scrabbled to him. He threw himself across the man's head and seized a wrist, which he pulled up his back between his shoulder blades. The other hand tore at the sand.

The protective device built into the suit was a reverse inertial reel, Ravenshaw speculated, and to check this theory he pounded a fist at the man's head. His body was working very well, but the blow stopped short. He pushed gently and had no trouble forcing the face into the sand. He flipped himself to a kneeling position on the man's back, keeping a steady pressure on the wrist. He was perfectly willing to break the arm, or dislocate the shoulder. He had always admired the implicit promise on the only snake flag he knew about: Don't Tread On Me.

The girl was on her knees beside Nell, brushing sand from her cheek. The child looked puzzled and deeply concerned, the first expression he had seen on her face. The day was growing warmer. Ravenshaw saw a pair of buzzards in the sky and turned his attention back to the man under him. He had stopped thrashing, but he made sandy gobbling noises. Ravenshaw pulled the hank of nylon line from his pocket and began to bite off the plastic wrapper. The man tried to lurch forward and Ravenshaw heard a slight creaking noise when he pushed the wrist higher. The feet drummed. Ravenshaw tried to slug him with the nylon hank and failed. It took a little while to run a simple loop around his neck and secure both hands under the shoulder blades. "If a job is worth doing—" muttered Ravenshaw, and he did not scamp the job. Then he got up and stretched. The girl had brought a cushion from the room and put it under Nell's head. She shaded her face while she waited.

Ravenshaw shoved the man over onto his back and said, "You will speak only Albionese. You will answer my questions." The man rolled his eyes, spat sand, and wept. His tongue was not very sandy, considering how he had been whooping and gulping. Ravenshaw waited until his eyes settled to a feral glare. He took a three-bladed knife from his pocket and opened the longest blade. He picked up a flat rock and began to whet the edge. *Wheet-wheet-wheet.* "The first question is, where do you come from?" *Wheet-wheet-wheet.* The sun caught the edge of the blade nicely.

"Grauok." The loop was cutting into his throat. Ravenshaw put two fingers under the line and pulled. The man arched his back and yelled. Ravenshaw heaved him onto his face again and undid the loop. He pulled the wrists down as far as they would go, ran the line between his legs, over the back of his shoulder and around the neck, and back down again. He tied it off at the wrists and tied the two lines together at the back of the neck. If he lifted his wrists, he would saw himself in two. Or strangle. Ravenshaw was pleased with this arrangement. He turned him over again onto a small barrel cactus. He went back to sharpening his knife while the man yelped and writhed away. "Where do you come from?" said Ravenshaw. *Wheet-wheet-wheet.*

"I will kill you horrid!" choked the man.

Ravenshaw tugged on one of the lines.

"Grauok . . . Ang 3207 Nag 4862 . . . kill me . . . I'll tell you no more—"

Ravenshaw continued to whet his knife. "I will slit your nose first," he said conversationally. "I have other things in mind when that is done." Ravenshaw slowly touched his nose with the blade. A drop of blood formed. He used it to lubricate the stone. "What is a shim world?" *Wheet-wheet-wheet.*

"Any fool knows. One in the infinity of worlds, churd."

"Err," growled Ravenshaw.

The man coughed rackingly. When he stopped, his eyes went to the knife. *Wheet-wheet-wheet.* Ravenshaw tested the edge with his thumb and smiled. He shaved a patch of hair from his arm and shook his head. *Wheet-wheet-wheet.* It was not a loud noise, but it was also a serious noise and a subtle one.

"Uh, citizen—elementary explanation is bird who comes to sharpen beak on mountain every hundred years. When mountain is worn down, it is still as nothing in infinity—" His eyes were hypnotized by the knife.

"Shim worlds?" said Ravenshaw softly.

"In our early technology we used multiple layers of metal—shims—to achieve a fit. Shim worlds—you peel them apart with gravity wave multiphaser—we are the Drishna—we are the travelers—will you please stop that—please?"

"Time travel," said Ravenshaw.

"Stupid churd! Time travel is impossible!"

Ravenshaw began to whistle thoughtfully. He bent his whole attention to the very delicate sharpening of the blade. *Wheeta-wheeta*. He looked down and then quickly away. His eyes met those of the girl bending over Nell.

"Aah-ha, aah-ha," the man sucked in air.

Ravenshaw was suddenly appalled. He saw the girl clearly for the first time. Her short hair was a deep gold color. Her eyes were violet. She and Nell made an extraordinary picture with the high blue sky of the desert behind them. Ravenshaw thought furiously. He waved the knife toward the man's nose and the resistance field stopped his hand. He turned a tiger face to his prisoner.

The man sucked in his breath and his mouth trembled. He spoke placatingly, rapidly, in a soft whining voice. "You are right, muh-master. Philosophic theory of the most advanced thinkers . . . aah . . . pup-postulates the master world on which all others are contingent . . . aah . . . from which all innovation flows . . . aah . . . from that world time travel is certainly possible . . . aah . . . take that knife away!"

"*Errr.*"

"I'll give you anything, master. Nesial node interphaser in perfect condition. Not flawed as the one you . . . aah . . . graciously accepted. It will bring you gold, master, from five hundred blics with a pood wide face . . . I made nuggets . . . take it, master!"

Ravenshaw was silent. Nell moaned softly. "Why didn't you get iodine that way," he asked absently.

"It's 28th common, but even on an untouched shim world it takes time. On some it takes years." With Ravenshaw's abstraction, he spoke with tentative confidence. "I will make you master of your world with weapons. The desynchronizer alone, when properly charged, will . . . that bitch! A partially regenerated cartridge! That little bitch!"

"What year is it?" snapped Ravenshaw with a scowl.

Fear flooded back. "Aah . . . 1947 from the birth of Christ . . . your system is better, I'm sure . . . take the Mier, too . . . they're a nicely matched pair . . . what command system do you use . . . certainly an elegant method . . . Mier are not common . . . very expensive . . . you must be a wealthy man, master . . . I will make you richer—" He was babbling and sputum ran down the corner of his mouth.

Nell spoke. "Arleigh," she said. Her voice was piercing sweet. "Arleigh?" Nell's eyes were tightly shut.

Ravenshaw made his decision. The girl stood. He pantomimed drinking a glass of water. Their eyes met. Nineteen forty-seven, was it? She turned and entered the room with all its treasures. Ravenshaw knelt beside Nell. He unwrapped the nylon line from his fist. He held it loosely in his hand. When it jerked through, he let it go.

The man was running, bent over, to the room. The girl stood in the transparent doorway with an anguished face, and he threw his shoulder into her stomach. She sprawled against an orange cabinet. He flung himself into the chair behind the Wurlitzer console and hit the tab on the map box with his chin.

Sparkles of light appeared as gnats intersected the wall. The man looked up and sneered triumphantly at Ravenshaw. The room turned blue-gray and disappeared with a small clap of thunder. Dust rose into the air and drifted away.

Nell had her eyes open. "You let him take the girl." Her lips curled. "I will never forgive you." Her violet eyes were never colder, her honey voice never more bitter.

Late that afternoon, Ravenshaw slumped in a chair in General Craddock's office and finished his report, " . . . So we went back to San Diego, leaving your two men to keep an eye on the place. But I can guarantee you, nothing more will happen."

"Uh-huh?" The general took off his glasses and slipped them into a case. He took a new pair from his desk and put them on.

"What I know is, the girl was Nell herself. Twenty-two years ago. Her existence was contingent . . . I think . . . on something not yet certain. That's why I let them go. On the best evidence, the girl got out of that room before it drifted into the nitrate ship. In 1947, in Texas City."

"Ravenshaw, for the record now—which I think will be decently buried—is everything you said the truth?"

Ravenshaw grinned wearily. "Except that they extract the iodine before the nitrate leaves Chile. Shim worlds? Scrambled time? Take your own best hold. All the proof there is, is a Mier and a black box. And she may be irrecoverable as yesterday—if that means anything anymore."

"Why did she come to work here?"

"If you're interested in inexplicable phenomena, you go where they collect inexplicable phenomena."

"I'll review the rest of the staff," mused the general. "Did she recover her memory? Does she know what happened?"

"I didn't tell her."

Both men were silent. Ravenshaw was depressed. How fouled up can you get—all that advanced loot lost—Nell sore as a bee-stung goat—and incidentally he had killed a man twenty-two years before and never knew it until today. He shook his head.

"Black box, hah!" said the general. "Higher authority took it out of my hands. Quick work. It drove fourteen scientists right up the wall before they busted it. I don't know how." He smiled with some satisfaction. "Ravenshaw, I think you've done exactly right. Be my guest tonight. It's gin-and-tonic season."

Ravenshaw had landed at Andrews in a late spring snowstorm. He leaned back in his chair. He noticed his ka was sitting on his shoulder, wings furled, smoking a large cigar. "And after that, sir?"

"Well, we got one look at the wild blue and yonder country, didn't we? Carry on, Ravenshaw." ∎